SMALL BUSINESS MANAGEMENT AND ENTREPRENEURSHIP IN HONG KONG

Asia Case
Research Centre
THE UNIVERSITY OF HONG KONG

List of Contributors

HKU Academic Supervisors

Professor Michael J. Enright
Professor Ali Farhoomand
Professor Thomas M. Hout
Professor Simon Lam
Mr. Freddie Lee
Professor Simon Tam
Professor P. S. Tso
Professor Gilbert Wong
Professor Benjamin Yen
Professor Bennett Yim

ACRC Research Team

Mary Ho
Phoebe Ho
Amir Hoosain
Andrew Lee
Vincent Mak
Pauline Ng
Dr. Kavita Sethi
Monica Wong

SMALL BUSINESS MANAGEMENT AND ENTREPRENEURSHIP IN HONG KONG

A Casebook

Edited by Ali Farhoomand

香港大學出版社

HONG KONG UNIVERSITY PRESS

Hong Kong University Press
14/F Hing Wai Centre
7 Tin Wan Praya Road
Aberdeen
Hong Kong

ISBN 962 209 758 8

The research on which this book is based was funded by the HKSAR
Trade and Industry Department SME Development Fund. Any opinions,
conclusions or recommendations expressed in this material
(by members of project team) do not reflect the views of the
Government of the HKSAR, Trade and Industry Department or
the vetting committee for the SME Development Fund.

British Library Cataloguing-in-Publication Data
A catalogue record for this book is available from the British Library.

Secure On-line Ordering
http://www.hkupress.org

Printed and bound by Condor Production Co. Ltd., in Hong Kong, China

Contents

Section II Wholesale and Retail, Import and Export, and Restaurants and Hotels

Section III Services (Financial, Real Estate, Social, Transportation, Communications and Others)

Section IV Industry Cases

Preface

Small and medium companies are the prime engine for economic growth in Hong Kong and to a large extent, in southern China. So-called "SMEs" account for 95 percent of companies in Hong Kong and employ about two-thirds of the workforce. The managers and entrepreneurs behind these companies contribute to all aspects of Hong Kong's development. Yet it is interesting to note that the management of small businesses is significantly different from that of multinational companies. Management experiences vary widely on account of the different skills, resources and environmental pressures that SMEs face. There is no doubt that the various facets of SME management warrant deeper study.

The University of Hong Kong's Asia Case Research Centre, with the backing of the Trade and Industry Department of the Hong Kong Government, has undertaken the development of a series of case studies to showcase the challenges facing small businesses and entrepreneurs in Hong Kong, and some innovative approaches they adopted. The case studies are topically diverse, and span a range of functions and sectors (manufacturing, infrastructure, marketing channels, services, international trade, community services and transport, to name a few).

This casebook is an anthology of 28 cases from the series. Taken as a collection, the cases explore various aspects of small business management and entrepreneurship in Hong Kong, spanning the spectrum from the issues that a founder faces when planning to establish a small business, to the operational functions involved in running an enterprise on a daily basis. They constitute a comprehensive self-contained course of study — yet each case can also be considered in isolation.

In addition to companies engaged in mainstay manufacturing industries, we have covered sectors such as global trade, retail and professional services, to identify and examine prevailing trends in the market. Attention has been paid to both industry-specific and macro-economic contexts that shape the developments in the cases — for example, the slump in Hong Kong's retail industry, the cross-border migration of low-tech manufacturing and the SARS crisis.

We have prepared these cases after extensive company and industry research, both primary and secondary. A unique, concise format was developed for our small business and entrepreneurship case studies where each case traces the development of a Hong Kong- or China-based company or an industry and its external environment. Background coverage includes an overview of the industry, the motives that drive the entrepreneur, the company's major products or services, an organisation's competitive premise, overview of opportunities and threats and geographical coverage.

Where appropriate, the case may zero in on a department or function of the organisation and present the history of that unit or function, recent changes, main responsibilities, relations with other units and major challenges. With the context established, cases focus on the specific issue or decision at hand — this may relate to a marketing campaign, human resource issue, IT initiative, brand positioning, etc. Cases are prepared with key questions incorporated in-text, to orient the reader's focus of analysis. Further analysis and application of theory are offered in a "Lessons Learned" section at the end of each case, to ensure that the reader fully grasps the issues at hand. The reader is aided by figures and exhibits that provide visual examples of business concepts, pertinent statistics, or company-supplied content.

This casebook is intended for practicing SME managers, students wanting to study the critical factors in the development and operations of a small firm, individuals with an interest in regional developments and the practices being adopted by small businesses, and entrepreneurs aiming to develop competitive advantages as they brace themselves for the opening up of China's markets.

The cases are written with a strong management perspective to offer a practical and interesting look at how successful entrepreneur-managers in Hong Kong systematically generate innovations in the shape of successful new products, services, processes and technologies when faced with various organisational and environmental challenges. They leverage the strengths and expertise of the Centre in presenting Asian-context business scenarios, and can assist small businesses and entrepreneurs by offering insights into the experiences and best practices adopted by local and regional counterparts.

This series and casebook are an extension of the knowledge and expertise that the Centre has built over the past seven years, achieving regional and worldwide recognition among educational and training establishments as a preeminent producer of full-fledged research intensive business case studies. We aim to inspire the strategic thinking behind business actions.

Ali Farhoomand
Hong Kong, 2005

Introduction

ALI FARHOOMAND AND KAVITA SETHI

Small and medium-sized enterprises (SMEs) are mainstays of the economy in almost every market in the world. Both academics and business practitioners recognise that SMEs cannot be measured with the same yardstick as used for larger, established organisations. The skills and resources available to small business managers, and the environmental pressures they face, can lead to very different managerial experiences from those of managers at the helm of multinational firms. Conceptually, there is substantial agreement that business organisations, both large and small are inseparable from their respective environments.[1] There is also a well-developed hypothesis, which stipulates that SMEs evolve through different stages of venture development, with characteristics symptomatic for different stages of growth.

Over the years, researchers have put forth a range of multistage models that use a diverse array of characteristics to examine the phenomenon of organisation development.[2] While useful in many respects, these models are limited in their application, as they confine their focus to the firm and do not consider the type of industry or the specific environment in which the SME is operating.[3] Studying an SME in isolation of the environment in which it operates is insufficient. In order to understand the diverse range of issues that confront SMEs today, it is necessary to adopt a more comprehensive view. The influences of location, industry and size have to be taken into account, as do those of the business cycle.[4]

Consequently, the first part of this chapter details the development of a framework to provide a holistic view in understanding the diverse issues facing SMEs today. The framework consists of three study dimensions: *focus*, *life cycle* and *environment*. The focus dimension includes analysis at three levels: the national level, the industry level and the enterprise level. The life cycle dimension encompasses the stages of venture development of an SME from birth to growth and maturity, while the environment dimension examines issues related to cultural, economic, technological and regulatory influences. This integrated framework puts into context various issues that confront SMEs at different levels of analysis, at different stages of venture development and in different socio-economic settings. The framework also helps to identify policy implications and develop recommendations for practice.

The second part of this chapter uses the proposed framework to conceptualise the strategic issues and challenges faced by SMEs in Hong Kong. At the enterprise level, it would help SMEs better understand and prepare for emerging challenges and capitalise on new opportunities that result from dynamic shifts in the environment. The framework, as applied to SMEs in Hong Kong, also provides the foundation for understanding organisational growth and transitions that are critical to the success of the enterprise as it transits from one lifecycle stage to the next. Insights can thus be generated into the development processes of SMEs in Hong Kong, thereby formulating guidelines to cope with the changes that have been prevalent in the recent past.

An Integrated Framework

An analysis of the existing models to study SMEs, coupled with an exhaustive literature review, has led to the identification of three dimensions that are critical to the understanding of SME operations. These are: *the focus of analysis, the stages of venture development through which an SME transits, and the environmental influence on the SME.* When integrated, these dimensions give a comprehensive understanding of the key issues faced by SMEs in their specific context. To substantiate the conceptual development of this framework, a series of case studies have been developed to strengthen the empirical foundation of such framework.[5] This approach is interdisciplinary, combining elements of socio-political reasoning, sociological perspectives and business activities.

To delineate the reference criteria, the proposed framework (see Figure 1) firstly subsumes SMEs at three levels: the national level, the industry level and the firm level. The important difference at these three levels is the focus of analysis. Another important difference is the ultimate objective of the analysis. At the national level, the orientation is towards understanding the influence of a country's governance and policies on SMEs, the central concern being to explain international differences in SME organisation and behaviour. At the industry level, the focus shifts to the type of industry. At this level, it may be possible to study the dynamics of SMEs operating in the same type of industry, across geographic and organisational specificities. The final level of analysis, at the enterprise level, is the grass-roots analysis of an SME. This is the level towards which most previous research has been oriented.

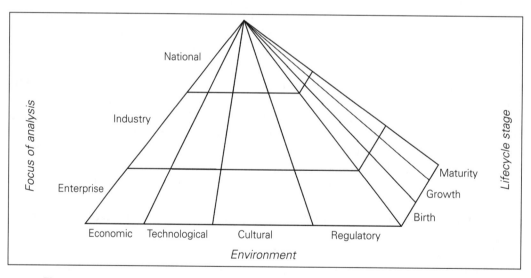

Figure 1   Integrated Framework for Key Issues Facing SMEs and Entrepreneurs

To understand the options facing SMEs at any given point in time, the life cycle stages of an SME form the second dimension of the framework. Life cycle analysis reflects the patterns of changes and problems in the running of small businesses at different growth stages. By determining the developmental stage of an SME, the firm can be proactive and can thus capitalise on changes.[6]

The convergence of the prevalent economic, technological, cultural and regulatory environments under which SMEs operate forms the third dimension of the framework. This dimension includes different aspects of the operating environment of SMEs, lending shape to the relationships between people, events and the strategies adopted at different stages of growth.

Dimension I: Focus of Analysis

Small businesses and entrepreneurs play an unquestionably important role in the economic and social life of a region. They make up the largest number of businesses and generally employ the largest portion of the workforce. Across the globe, highly productive SMEs anchor most economic systems.[7] However, there are no universally acceptable criteria to classify an enterprise as an SME, the interpretation varying across different countries.[8] A commonly accepted view is that it is best to identify small firms through their inherent characteristics.[9] Typical criteria include the non-separation of ownership and control, small market share and quantitative definitions such as the number of employees.[10] Thus an enterprise defined as an SME in one country may not be so defined under the laws of another country. The benefits, schemes and support systems offered by governments to SMEs also differ from one country to another.[11] National policies also influence the operating characteristics of SMEs.[12] In order to study SMEs in light of the classification, constraints and challenges typical to a particular country, it becomes necessary to consider national issues as the first level of analysis.

SMEs exist in nearly every walk of industry, from services to retail to manufacturing. It is evident that each type of industry has unique characteristics and competencies. The government policies, and at times the classification of SMEs also depend on the sector they operate in. This becomes extremely important when viewed in conjunction with the challenges faced by SMEs as they transit through different stages of venture development. Consequently, the second level of analysis is at the sector level, which specifies the industry type.

At the enterprise level, managerial style, organisational structure, extent of formal systems, major strategic goals and the owner's business involvement are the five variables, which change as enterprises transit through different stages of venture development.[13] The proposed framework extends these five dimensions to include operational strategies adopted by the enterprise. This becomes necessary to highlight the different strategic approach adopted by entrepreneurial and non-entrepreneurial firms, even though they both belong to the SME category. As an example, an entrepreneurial organisation engages in innovative activities to develop a distinctive competence; whereas a non-entrepreneurial organisation views innovation as a response to challenges, occurring only when necessary.[14]

Dimension II: Stages of Venture Development

Life cycle stages are one of the most important variables to consider in the strategy formulation of an enterprise.[15] A number of authors, tailoring models for smaller firms, have made seminal contributions to the understanding of the life cycles of small organisations.[16] While the consensus is that changes follow a predictable pattern, characterised by discrete stages of development, the number of stages and the terminology adopted to describe these differ.[17] Empirical research confirms the notion that the criteria for organisational effectiveness, as well as the means for achieving it, shift from stage to stage of the organisational life cycle. Also, as enterprises grow in size and complexity, the role of the owner changes.[18]

To develop the present framework, we use the small business model as shown in Figure 2. This model synthesises the similarities from different life cycle models, presented in literature, and classifies the three critical stages in the growth of a small business as: birth, growth and maturity. The conceptual simplicity of this approach has prompted a number of researchers to adopt similar classifications when referring to the life cycle of SMEs.[19]

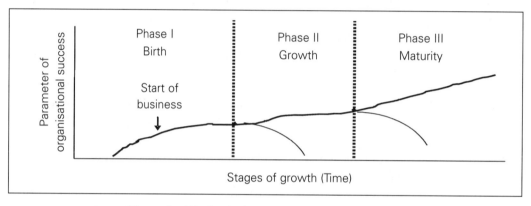

Figure 2   Life Cycle Stages of a Small Business[20]

At the first stage of venture development, birth, the small business owner has no organisational objectives that are distinct from his or her personal objectives. This stage is characterised as being an extension of the psychological being of the small business owner. It is preceded by activities associated with the formulation of the venture. SMEs, more often than not, use simple structures in the first phase of their development. The structure is composed of two parts, the strategic apex and the operating core.[21] The owner-entrepreneur tightly controls such a company. This form of organisational structure enables the owner to make rapid changes of innovation as required for survival, which would prove cumbersome in larger structures that are more bureaucratic. Marketing and financial considerations tend to be paramount during this stage.

The second phase of an enterprise, growth, involves the introduction of new goods and methods of production, the opening up of new markets and new sources of supply, and industrial organisation.[22] This stage is extremely critical for the organisation's survival. It is associated with an influx of expertise, a streamlining of the organisational structure and a transition to a more professional style of management.[23]

The maturity stage of venture development involves various forms of corporate entrepreneurship. According to the literature, these include mergers, acquisitions, diversifications, contracting, licensing and franchising. The structure becomes more elaborate to accommodate techno-structure, support staff and the middle level.[24]

Dimension III: Environmental Variables

The environmental influence on SMEs cannot be understated.[25] SMEs are especially vulnerable to environmental changes, given that they generally lack sufficient resources to buffer themselves from their operating environments.[26] Consequently, the proposed framework considers as the third dimension, various environmental influences, broadly classified into economic, technological, regulatory and cultural issues.

The economic environment includes factors such as level of economic development, population, gross domestic product, per capita income, membership in regional and international economic blocs, monetary and fiscal policies, currency convertibility, inflation and interest rates. The technological environment encompasses factors such as policies that aid or hinder technology transfer and application, infrastructure availability, communication protocols, the adequacy of telecommunications links, Internet capabilities and protection of intellectual property rights. The regulatory environment includes governments' orientation and policies towards SMEs, level of foreign investments, custom levies, taxation system, legal support and infrastructure availability. Finally, the cultural environment includes the influence of the country's historical heritage, prevalent family structure and other socio-ethnic issues.

SMES IN HONG KONG: STRATEGIC ISSUES AND CHALLENGES

SMEs in Hong Kong have gone through turbulent times in the recent past. The economic crisis of 1997 and then the SARS epidemic in 2003 left them faced with unprecedented changes and challenges. The purpose of the integrated framework, proposed previously, is to provide an insight into the developmental processes of SMEs in Hong Kong, thereby conceptualising guidelines to cope with these changes. This will help to identify the concerns of SMEs in terms of the life cycle and the exogenous changes attributable to their dynamic operating environment. The three-dimensional framework, as applied to the context of Hong Kong, raises the following specific issues and challenges relevant for consideration in the SME community.

SMEs in Hong Kong: Focus of Analysis

National Focus

The Government of Hong Kong specifies that manufacturing enterprises with fewer than 100 employees and non-manufacturing enterprises with fewer than 50 employees in Hong Kong come under the category of SMEs. According to this definition, as of June 2004, Hong Kong was home to over 290,000 SMEs, which accounted for about 98 percent of the total establishments in the city. According to the statistics released by the Support and Consultation Centre for SMEs (SUCCESS), these establishments provided job opportunities to about 1.33 million people, about 60 percent of the total employment (excluding civil service).[27]

Since the 1980s, Hong Kong's SMEs have learned to do business against the backdrop of China's rapid development, thus placing the city in a unique position within the region. Given the tough economic conditions in recent years, SMEs in Hong Kong have made painful adjustments for an era of high unemployment, deflation and low consumer confidence. They have done this largely by reducing costs, enhancing efficiency, embracing new technologies and new mediums, and ultimately by going up the value chain to remain competitive. Although half of all Hong Kong SMEs are involved in some aspect of the manufacturing supply chain, the provision of lower-end services has relocated across the border. As Hong Kong further transforms into a service economy, it has shifted its focus to the provision of high-value services such as design, logistics and professional support services. In line with this, the Government of the Hong Kong Special Administrative Region (HKSAR) has institutionalised and stepped up its efforts to assist SMEs to start, build and expand their businesses.

According to the report on support measures for SMEs presented by the Trade and Industry Department, there are two kinds of challenges facing SMEs in Hong Kong: macroeconomic challenges and challenges from the local economy.[28] The macroeconomic challenges include the globalisation of the world's economy, China's accession to the WTO and the new economic order, while the challenges from the local economy focus on the business environment, financing, corporate governance and culture, human resources, technology application and market expansion. Competition and capital funding are the major obstacles faced by SME owner-managers in Hong Kong, as they transit through different stages of venture development.[29] In an address on the opportunities and challenges for SMEs in Hong Kong, Mr. Francis Ho, Director-General of Industry, emphasised the challenges brought about by globalisation and the lessons learnt from the Asian financial crisis. He identified the four key challenges for SMEs in Hong Kong as financing, the risk factor, the impact and adoption of technology and service delivery.[30]

Industry Focus

Although the definition adopted by the Government of Hong Kong only segregates SMEs into the manufacturing and non-manufacturing sectors, the SME sector in Hong Kong is heterogeneous at the industry level. In fact, most of the SMEs in Hong Kong fall under the service category.[31] According to statistics released by SUCCESS, nearly 33 percent of the SMEs in Hong Kong are in the import and export trades (see Figure 3).[32] The next-largest population of SMEs is in the wholesale and retail trades, restaurants and hotels (29 percent). Financing, insurance, real estate and business services follow, making up nearly 18 percent of the SME population. By comparison, the total manufacturing sector accounts for only 6 percent of SMEs in Hong Kong.

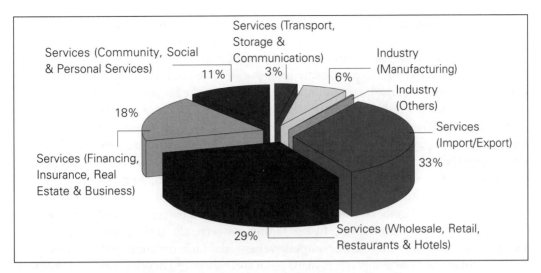

Figure 3   Distribution of SMEs in Hong Kong[33]

The strong performance of Hong Kong's service sector has been accompanied by an apparent decline in its manufacturing sector.[34] This is primarily because, in the recent past, SMEs in Hong Kong have shown a trend to relocate their manufacturing base into mainland China. Hong Kong SMEs however, exhibit a high degree of fluidity in combining light manufacturing with trading activities. Particularly in sectors such as textiles, watches, jewellery and toys, where they are extremely flexible in their responses to market demands. Through organised associations, these SMEs build efficient subcontracting networks. However, one of the challenges that Hong Kong SMEs face is in countering the diminishing trend of the manufacturing sector.[35] In the service sector, Hong Kong is home to several clusters, which have capitalised on the expanding China market to solidify their position. The dramatic rise in the importance of Asia as a source and destination for world trade has also contributed to the shift in the focus from manufacturing to the service sector.

Enterprise Focus

Nearly 90 percent of the SMEs in Hong Kong employ fewer than ten people.[36] The criterion for classification is the number of people employed in Hong Kong, and does not extend to the firm's extensions in mainland China. Hong Kong enterprises have established about 70,000 businesses in the Pearl River Delta, employing a total of five million people in the region.[37] To a large extent, the efforts of Hong Kong's small business managers and entrepreneurs drive market capitalism in Southern China. Research contends that to classify small businesses as a homogeneous group is inappropriate. Predictors of success differ according to the subsets within the greater population, largely influenced by the size of the enterprise.[38] This creates an apparent paradox, as not all SMEs in Hong Kong are large enough to extend their business reach beyond their immediate environment. It therefore becomes essential to take a closer look at the organisation and business culture of SMEs in Hong Kong and their responses to new challenges.

In terms of business organisation, SMEs in Hong Kong are typically family firms.[39] These firms reflect a paternalistic and nepotistic business culture. They usually start on a small scale with a simple structure. In such firms the two social systems — the family and the business organisation — are closely interwoven. The goal of the traditional Chinese corporation is to secure the long-term financial stability of the family.[40] They draw primarily on the family for capital and human resources. Family unity and prosperity, under the direction of the patriarch or matriarch, is the backbone of such enterprises. On the other hand, there also exists another breed of first-generation entrepreneurs, wherein the entrepreneurial founders control the firms. These enterprises have not had time to develop strong traditions, and the proprietors are not the trustees of the family's inheritance in the same way as with the old established family business.

In practice, the family concern and the first-generation entrepreneurial firm are faced with different sets of challenges. In the family concern, the most common challenges include: the lack of commercial competitiveness; the lack of capacity for innovation; problems of managerial competence, managerial succession and development and problems arising from conflicts within the family, which might be at cross-purposes with the business goals. On the other hand, for the first-generation entrepreneurial firms, problems usually arise from rapid growth, autocratic management style and the entrepreneur's inability to make the transition to a professional style of management.

Management succession in SMEs, which involves the transition of decision-making in a firm, is also one of the greatest challenges that confront the owners of a family business in Hong Kong, and may also be one of the causes of its eventual decline.[41] This is not because the owner-entrepreneur does not have a successor, but more often because of the centralised decision-making policy and lack of clear long-term objectives. One of the keys to the success and growth of a small enterprise lies in the ability of the entrepreneur to "lengthen his own shadow", that is to select, recruit and motivate managerial and executive talent who will display the qualities of an entrepreneur. As entrepreneurs are limited by an underlying emotional need to control every minor decision point, far too many of them are insecure about letting their shadow grow beyond the point where they can see, and try to control its every movement.[42] In a family business, an important factor in the succession-planning process is the availability of a child as a potential successor. This process is complicated through interfamily friction and dynamics. In contrast, in a non-family entrepreneurial enterprise, the transition is usually uneventful if the enterprise has matured enough to ensure the successor is at least as competent as his or her predecessor.[43]

SMEs in Hong Kong: Stages of Venture Development

SMEs in Hong Kong are found in all three stages of venture development. In order to comprehend the dynamics of the melting pot of SMEs in Hong Kong, it is necessary to study them with reference to their particular stage of venture development. This will help to establish best practices that can illustrate the typical problems and help other enterprises develop coping strategies to survive and grow.

The life cycle analysis for SMEs in Hong Kong is of particular interest in light of the economic down-turn and the Asian financial crisis. The specific challenges faced by SMEs while they move from one life cycle stage to another call for in-depth investigation. Many SMEs in Hong Kong exist in the first, namely, birth, stage of venture development, where the focus is simply to stay in business. Though these enterprises may have survived the first couple of years of operation, they do not display many of the characteristics which would classify them as having moved into the second, or growth stage. Some of these fall under the category of factories in domestic premises.[44] On the other hand, some of Hong Kong's greatest fortunes have been built by individuals who stated rather humble businesses and built them into large, mature empires.

The problems faced by SMEs in Hong Kong as they shift from one stage of venture development to the next may be classified as either external (customer contact, market knowledge, marketing planning, location, pricing, product considerations, competitors and expansion) or internal (adequate capital, cashflow, facilities/equipment, inventory control, human resources, leadership/direction, organisational structure and accounting systems).[45] These may be core problems or situational problems, the implication being that the core problems are persistent, notwithstanding the level of competition and the stage of the life cycle. As opposed to this, situational problems are more relevant to the transitions between stages of venture development.[46] Finances, human resources and technology application are the main barriers to growth for SMEs in Hong Kong.[47] As enterprises grow, a distinct lack of planning due to scarcity of time, lack of knowledge and lack of expertise and skills may lead to their decline before they have had an opportunity to stabilise.[48]

SMEs in Hong Kong: Environment Variables

Economic Environment

Over the past two decades, Hong Kong's economy has more than doubled in size, with GDP growth averaging an annual rate of 5 percent in real terms.[49] This rate of growth was higher than that experienced by Organisation for Economic Cooperation and Development (OECD) economies. In 2003, HongKong's per capita GDP was US$23,300, surpassing many industrialised economies and coming second only to Japan within Asia.[50]

Hong Kong has often been cited as the best contemporary example of a laissez-faire economy.[51] The territory's institutional strength, simple tax structure, rule of law, communications and transport infrastructure and its strategic location at the gateway to the Mainland have been critical in its development into a leading centre for trade, finance, business and communications. With a population of only 6.9 million (ranking 95th in the world), Hong Kong ranks as the 11th-largest trading entity worldwide; not only does it have the busiest container port in the world but also one of the world's busiest airports (in terms of international passengers and volume of international cargo handled). Perhaps more impressively, Hong Kong was the seventh-largest source of FDI in the world in 2003, according to the United Nations Conference on Trade and Development (UNCTAD), and was until recently the leading foreign investor in China.[52]

Hong Kong's bustling free-market economy and the consequent mushrooming of SMEs were due to the territory's institutional strength and strategic location. However, shortly after the British handover, the Asian financial crisis transformed the economic context of the region and shook the local economy. Property prices began a marked decline and Hong

Kong sank into a six-year economic malaise that hit its nadir with the SARS epidemic of 2003. The net result was that SMEs took a serious hit, with many of them folding under the financial pressure. During this time, regional competitors such as Shanghai, Singapore, Shenzhen and Guangzhou were trying to duplicate Hong Kong's winning formula and worked to bolster their infrastructure and institutions.

The challenging post-handover period was an opportunity for Hong Kong's government and business community to reassess the territory's role within the region. Hong Kong's post-1997 difficulties were, in the view of some, a reflection of the high cost environment that had made the territory uncompetitive.[53] But cost considerations were merely an indication of the need for Hong Kong SMEs to move further up the value chain and compete with other regional centres on the basis of speed, quality and innovation.[54]

The present challenge for Hong Kong SMEs is to compete on the basis of adding value, and in so doing to reinforce Hong Kong's position as a metropolitan centre for a rapidly developing hinterland. The ability of Hong Kong's SMEs to adapt in this regard is already evident in the growth of Hong Kong's services economy, which has averaged an annual growth rate of 17 percent, and which by 2003 accounted for 88 percent of the territory's GDP.[55]

Hong Kong's SMEs have long taken advantage of the low-cost manufacturing base across the border, but recent studies have found that the Mainland market still has immense potential. A 2002 study by the brokerage house CLSA found that 47 percent of its SME sample did not generate any revenue from the Mainland, while 57 percent were earning less than 10 percent of their revenue from the Mainland.[56] As the Chinese mainland continues to liberalise, opportunities will abound for Hong Kong SMEs.

Technological Environment

The success of many SMEs in Hong Kong can be attributed largely to the well-developed physical and technological infrastructure available in the region. Hong Kong's transport and communications networks are among the best in the world and are undergoing constant improvement. Public transport facilities, especially rail, are excellent. The road infrastructure has expanded steadily in recent years. Hong Kong has the busiest container port in the world, with state-of-the-art facilities, although it is coming under competitive pressure from direct shipments from cheaper ports across the border in mainland China. The international airport is one of the best in the world and has spare capacity.

Hong Kong is one of the most connected economies in Asia, in terms of both the use of mobile technology and the Internet. One positive contributor to this is Hong Kong's geographic compactness. Hong Kong's telecommunications policy in recent years has favoured increasing competition in both the fixed-line and mobile markets. These policies have been more successful for mobile operators than for fixed-line operators. Hong Kong was the first major city in the world to have an entirely digital telephone network, and is renowned for its excellent telecommunications infrastructure. In the early 2000s, its broadband networks covered all commercial buildings and over 90 percent of households. In addition, it boasted one of the highest penetration rates of cellular phone services in the world (about 104 percent).[57] Two private companies have de facto regional monopolies on electricity provision. They are regulated by government agreement, and are subject to price controls.

Hong Kong's government and business community had long recognised the importance of establishing a community-wide infrastructure to support electronic business and was among the first in Asia to embrace the use of electronic data interchange (EDI) in the early 1980s, and Internet-based networks in more recent years. For its part, the Government had taken the initiative of setting up a Public Key Infrastructure and had established a framework that granted full legal status to electronic records and digital signatures. In 2004, the Economist Intelligence Unit rated Hong Kong ninth out of 60 countries in its "e-readiness rankings", which were based on a variety of quantitative and qualitative indicators. Intellectual property rights are also legally recognised, but the Government acknowledges that copyright protection is a problem and has been passing new laws and improving enforcement.

Unlike other Asian economies, Hong Kong has not emerged as a large global player in the manufacture of information technology (IT) hardware. The domestic software industry is more significant, although Hong Kong is still a bit-player in the global industry. The IT industry has remained small despite government efforts to encourage development. Among other activities, the Innovation and Technology Commission (ITC) manages funding schemes to help companies develop innovative ideas and technology businesses.

Despite a sophisticated infrastructure and strong backing from the Government, business participation in the networked economy has lagged behind Hong Kong's regional counterparts such as Taiwan, Singapore and South Korea, where high rates of e-commerce adoption are witnessed. The network capabilities of a typical Hong Kong SME have remained fairly rudimentary. One reason Hong Kong's SMEs have not adopted IT solutions at the same rate as in other regional geographies is perhaps the relative scarcity of solutions tailored specifically to the needs of smaller businesses. The widespread acceptance of ATMs, smart cards, mobile telephony and other technologies seems to indicate that there is little resistance to technology in the greater community. Research findings from a number of SME case studies in Hong Kong suggest that the determinants of e-procurement adoption include the value of e-procurement, trust in the supplier, trust in IT and the power of suppliers (in order of significance).[58]

A survey conducted in 2002 reveals that there is a very noticeable gap in IT application between medium enterprises and small enterprises (i.e., those with fewer than ten employees). Medium enterprises are not far behind the large enterprises in IT application. For instance, nearly 80 percent of them have personal computers and over 60 percent have access to the Internet. As for the small enterprises, less than 50 percent of them have personal computers and about 30 percent have access to the Internet. In addition, among those SMEs that do not have computers, less than 5 percent have plans to install them. Among those with no such plans, almost 75 percent consider that installing computers would not be beneficial to their businesses, whereas 16 percent indicate that a lack of computer-literate staff has inhibited them from making good use of IT. Generally, SMEs have certain knowledge about the new technology and equipment applicable to their trade. However, constrained by shortage of capital, SMEs often fail to introduce new technology and equipment, therefore undermining their productivity and efficiency.[59] Certain segments of Hong Kong SMEs have expressed discontent at being branded "uncompetitive" for holding on to long-established manual and physically entrenched processes. Failing to see the direct benefits of investing in technology upgrades, they are willing to deploy IT only if there is a clear benefit. This, according to the analysis by the Trade and Industry Department, may hamper the competitiveness of such SMEs in the age of e-commerce.[60]

Regulatory Environment

In his Policy Address in October 2000, the Chief Executive reaffirmed the importance of small and medium enterprises (SMEs) as an important pillar of Hong Kong's economy, and the Government's commitment to helping SMEs tackle problems encountered at different stages of their development.[61] Hong Kong prides itself on its simple tax system and low rates. With its low tax structure and absence of tariffs and exchange controls, coupled with an excellent infrastructure, Hong Kong offers a low-risk operating environment to SMEs. The evident emphasis of the Hong Kong Government is to maintain a business-friendly environment. Government policies and administrative procedures with an absence of red tape, coupled with a minimum of government intervention, are particularly advantageous to SMEs with limited resources. Within the framework of a free-market economy, the Government, through various departments, provides numerous services designed to help SMEs develop their potential — these include the Trade and Industry Department, the Business and Services Promotion Unit, the Vocational Training Council and the SME Centre of the Hong Kong Productivity Council. In addition, various trade associations collaborate with the Government to provide support to SMEs in Hong Kong. The onus for exploiting the favorable environment and support services, however, rests with the SMEs themselves.[62]

Contractual arrangements are generally secure in Hong Kong, which has a transparent, common-law legal system inherited from the UK. The judiciary has also proven to be independent and impartial. Protection of property and freedom of exchange are enshrined in the Basic Law, Hong Kong's mini-constitution, which is protected by international law. The Basic Law in Hong Kong stipulates that Hong Kong would independently participate in international trade agreements and issue independent certificates of origin after the handover. The transition agreements ensure that Hong Kong retains its border controls with China, its own customs procedures and the right to conduct international trade relations. Hong Kong is a member of the World Trade Organization and the Asia-Pacific Economic Co-operation (APEC) forum. Hong Kong has no general tariff, and excise duties are charged on only four groups of commodities regardless of whether they are imported or made locally. Profits from a Hong Kong trade or business are subject to a profits tax; income from employment or pensions is subject to a salaries tax, and income from property is subject to a property tax. These taxes apply only to income that arises in or derives from Hong Kong. Although, in the recent past, the standard rates of salaries, profits and property taxes have all been raised, the tax burden remains relatively low.[63]

The expansion of the Chinese economy over the last decade, China's accession to the WTO and the second phase of CEPA falling in place have all created an unprecedented opportunity for Hong Kong-based SMEs to increase their revenue base by expanding their operations into the Mainland. The sectors mainly cover transportation, warehousing, wholesale and retail trade, catering, tourism, finance and insurance, real estate, social services, healthcare and sports, social welfare, education, culture and arts, broadcasting, film and television. In addition, CEPA implementation will make Hong Kong goods cheaper in the mainland Chinese market as Chinese import duties will no longer be levied. Although Hong Kong manufacturers, having already relocated to China, are unlikely to move their operations back to Hong Kong, CEPA may encourage SMEs to venture into higher-value-added products requiring high skill levels and high quality standards.

Cultural Environment

SMEs in Hong Kong are deeply rooted in the prevalent cultural environment. A driving force behind the expansion of the SME sector in Hong Kong is the attitude of the Chinese, the majority of the local population, towards business. The Chinese treasure hard work and thrift, and regard business success highly. There is therefore a large resource base available to SMEs.

SMEs in Hong Kong rely on the familial and business networks of individual merchants. The mindscape of the Hong Kong business community is central to Hong Kong's continued economic success. Three features are typically characteristic of Hong Kong SMEs: insecurity, paternalism and trust.[64] The turbulent political and economic history has created a feeling of insecurity, which lends a powerful incentive for self-sufficiency. Paternalism, rooted in Confucian ideology, aids the vertical structure adopted by most SMEs. The owner makes most decisions, which go unquestioned, and benevolent leadership rewards loyalty. SMEs operate in a cultural environment influenced by trust or guanxi, a complex concept meaning contacts, connections or relationships.[65] Widespread guanxi, characterised by trust and informal, reciprocal relationships, constitutes a social capital that is typically Chinese.

When moving through different stages of venture development, SMEs in Hong Kong need to develop the maturity to discriminate between which parts of the traditional system need to be built upon and which need to be discarded. While it may be advantageous to retain the flexibility and speed of response typical to a tightly controlled business, in order to exploit new opportunities, it is also necessary to put into place professional systems and manpower, which would help the enterprises compete on an international level.

ORGANISATION OF THE CASE SERIES

The current literature on SMEs provides seminal contributions, but falls short of establishing an integrated platform to view the strategic issues and challenges faced by SMEs in a holistic manner. This chapter introduces a conceptual framework that can be used to integrate the diverse spectrum of issues faced by SMEs today. The framework consists of three dimensions. The first dimension views SMEs at three levels: the national level, the industry level and the enterprise level. The second dimension is concerned with the stages of venture development from birth to growth and maturity. The third dimension acknowledges the influence of environmental factors on the enterprises, with the representative factors being economic, technological, cultural and regulatory. When applied in the context of SMEs in Hong Kong, the framework serves as a systematic and comprehensive tool to: 1) map out the status of current development of SMEs in Hong

Kong, and 2) expose issues and challenges that are faced by the SMEs in Hong Kong in the three respective dimensions.

SMEs in Hong Kong have faced unprecedented challenges in recent years, enduring the Asian financial crisis, the SARS epidemic and the avian flu scare. In light of their skill and resource limitations, SMEs in Hong Kong have difficulty in adopting best practices to enhance their competitiveness in the world market.[66] A subset to the proposed framework is therefore developed to profile and detail a selected number of best practices adopted by Hong Kong SMEs. Through a series of case studies organized in a Case Matrix in line with the proposed framework (see Appendix 1, pp. xxvi–xxviii), lessons can be drawn to highlight the strategic challenges associated with, as well as the success factors contributing to, the SME development in Hong Kong. The Case Matrix firstly clusters Hong Kong SMEs at the industry level, classifying companies and case studies according to the major industries in Hong Kong. At the enterprise level, case studies are mapped into the stages of venture development to highlight the issues specific to each lifecycle stage of the enterprise. Profiling SMEs in the respective cells of the Case Matrix will communicate best practices adopted by various SME owners to overcome problems in their operating environment in the current setting. The consortium of best practices will then serve two purposes: firstly, parallel lessons can be drawn from each cell for industry-, stage-, and operational-specific issues for the immediate reference of SME practitioners in Hong Kong; secondly, larger issues can be explored to shed light on the success factors and barriers of SME development across all study dimensions for further academic advancement.

1   Anderson, C. R. and Paine, F. T. (1975), "Managerial perceptions of strategic behaviour", *Academy of Management Journal*, Vol. 18, pp. 811–823.

2   Churchill, N. C. and Lewis, V. L. (1983), "The Five Stages of Small Business Growth", *Harvard Business Review*, May-June; Dodge, H. R., Fullerton, S. and Robbins, J. E. (1994), "Stage of the organizational life cycle and competition as mediators of problem perception for small businesses", *Strategic Management Journal*, Vol. 15, pp. 121–134; Flamholtz, E. (1995), Managing Organizational Transitions: Implications for Corporate and Human Resource Management, *European Management Journal*, Vol. 13, No. 1, pp. 39–51; Hill, Nancarrow and Wright.

3   Curran, J. (2000), "Small and medium enterprise development: Borrowing from elsewhere? A research and development agenda — A comment on Allan Gibb's paper", *Journal of Small Business and Enterprise Development*, Vol. 7, No. 3, pp. 212–219.

4   Gray, C, (2002), Entrepreneurship, resistance to change and growth in small firms, *Journal of Small Business and Enterprise Development*, Vol. 9, No. 1, pp. 61–72.

5   The organization of these case studies will be further elaborated at the end of this chapter.

6   Helms, M. M. and Renfrow, T. W. (1994), "Expansionary processes of the small business: A life cycle profile", *Management Decision*, Vol. 32, No. 9.

7   Zimmerer, T. W. and Scarborough, N. M. (1994), *Essentials of Small Business Management*, New York: Macmillan.

8   Smyth, G. F. (1975), "Identifying and developing an entrepreneur", in Gordon Lippet and Bernard Taylor (eds.) *Management Development and Training Handbook*, McGraw-Hill Book Co. (UK) Ltd.

9   McMahon, R., Holmes, S., Hutchinson, P. and Forsaith, D. (1993), *Small Enterprise Financial Management: Theory and Practice*, Sydney: Harcourt Brace Jovanovich.

10 Holmes, S and Zimmer, I. (1994), "The Nature of the Small Firm: Understanding the Motivations of Growth and Non-Growth Oriented Owners", *Australian Journal of Management*, Vol. 19, No. 1 (June), pp. 97–120.

11 Koning, A de and Snijders, J. (1992), "Policy on Small and Medium Sized enterprises in countries of the European Community", *International Business Journal*, Vol. 10, No. 3, pp. 25–39.

12 Storey, D. (2000), "Six steps to Heaven: Evaluating the impact of public policies to support small businesses in developed economies", in D. L. Sexton and H. Landstorm (eds.), *The Blackwell Handbook of Entrepreneurship* Oxford: Blackwell Publishers Ltd.

13 Churchill and Lewis (1983).

14 Miller, D. and Friesem, P. H. (1982)," Innovation in conservative and entrepreneurial firms: Two models of strategic momentum", *Strategic Management Journal*, Vol. 3.

15 Day, D. L. (1987), "A contingency theory of product life cycle, relatedness and resulting synergies", in N. C. Churchill, J. A. Hornaday, J. A. Timmons, and K. H. Vesper, (eds.), *Frontiers of Entrepreneurship Research*, Wellesley, MA: Babson College; Moy J. W. and Luk, V. W. M. (2003).

16 Chandler, A. (1962), *Strategy and Structure*, Cambridge, MA: MIT Press; Churchill and Lewis (1983); Scott, B. R. (1973), "The industrial estate: Old myths and new realities", *Harvard Business Review*, Vol. 51; Steinmetz, L. L. (1969), "Critical stages of Small Business Growth, Business Horizons, 1969", in Clifford M. Baumbach and Joseph R. Mancuso (eds.), *Entrepreneurship and Venture Management*, Englewood Cliffs, NJ: Prentice Hall.

17 Flamholtz (1995); Kuratko, D. F. and Hodgetts, R.M. (1998), *Entrepreneurship: A contemporary approach*, Florida: Harcourt Brace College Publishers; Quinn, R. E. and Cameron, K. (1983), "Organisational lifecycle and shifting criteria for effectiveness: some preliminary evidence", *Management Science*, Vol. 29, No. 1; Scott, M. and Bruce R. (1987), "Five stages of growth in a small business", *Long Range Planning*, Vol. 20, pp. 45–52.

18 Churchill and Lewis (1983); Gartner, W.B. (1988),"'Who is an entrepreneur?' is the wrong question", *American Journal of Small Business*, Vol. 12, No. 1; Kaish, S. & Gilad, B. (1991), "Characteristics of opportunities search of entrepreneurs versus executives: Sources, interests, general alertness", *Journal of Business Venturing*, Vol. 5; Quinn and Cameron (1983).

19 Cooper, A. C. (1989), *Strategic Management: New ventures and Small businesses*, Entrepreneurship: Creating and managing new ventures, Pergamon Press, UK; Jones, G. R. and Butler, J. E. (1992), "Managing internal corporate entrepreneurship: An agency theory perspective", *Journal of Management*, Vol. 18. No. 4; Steinmetz (1969).

20 Adapted from: G.T. Solomon (1983).

21 Gerloff, A. (1985), *Organisation theory and design*, New York: McGraw-Hill Book Company; Galbraith J. R. and Nathanson, D. A. (1978), *Strategy implementation: The role of structure and processes*, St Paul, MN: West Publishing Company; Scott (1973).

22 Vesper, K. H. (1980), *New Venture Strategies*, Englewood Cliffs, NJ: Prentice-Hall; Vesper, K. H. (1980), "New Venture Ideas: Do not overlook the experience factor", *Harvard Business Review*, Vol. 58, No. 1, pp. 164–167; Schumpeter, J. A. (1934), *The Theory of Economic Development*, translated by R. Opic from the German edition, Cambridge: Harvard University Press (1946).

23 Kuratko and Hodgetts (1998).

24 Mintzberg, H. (1981), "Organisation Design: Fashion or Fit", *Harvard Business Review*, Vol. 59.

[25] Carper, W. B. and Snizek, W. E., (1980), "The nature and type of organizational taxonomies: An overview", *Academy of Management Review*, Vol. 5, pp. 65–75.

[26] Carter, N. M. (1990), "Small firm adaptation: Responses of physicians' organizations to regulatory and competitive uncertainty", *Academy of Management Journal*, Vol. 33, pp. 307–333.

[27] Statistics as per the Support and Consultation Centre for SMEs (SUCCESS), http//www.sme.gcn.gov.hk/smeop/English/smehk.cfm/, accessed 18 October 2004.

[28] Report on support measures for Small and Medium Enterprises, Trade and Industry Department, http://www.tid.gov.hk/english/aboutus/publications/, accessed 20 October 2004.

[29] Moy J. W. and Luk, V. W. M. (2003), "The Lifecycle Model as a Framework for Understanding Barriers to SME Growth in Hong Kong", *Asia Pacific Business Review*, Vol. 10, No. 2, pp. 199–220.

[30] Ho, Francis, "The opportunities and challenges for small and medium sized enterprises in Hong Kong", http//: www.info.gov.hk/cpu/english/papers/e-franho.rtf/.

[31] Ho.

[32] Statistics as per the Support and Consultation Centre for SMEs (SUCCESS), http//www.sme.gcn.gov.hk/smeop/English/smehk.cfm/, accessed 18 October 2004.

[33] Source: Adapted from statistics published by the Support and Consultation Centre for SMEs (SUCCESS), http//www.sme.gcn.gov.hk/smeop/English/smehk.cfm/, accessed 18 October 2004.

[34] Enright, M. J., Scott, E. E. and Dodwell, D. (1997), *The Hong Kong Advantage*, Hong Kong: Oxford University Press.

[35] Federation of Hong Kong Industries (1982), "The economy in the 1980s: Can Hong Kong afford not to have a growing manufacturing sector", p. 1.

[36] Report on support measures for Small and Medium Enterprises, Trade and Industry Department.

[37] Rohlen, T. P. (2000), *Hong Kong and the Pearl River Delta: One country two systems in the emerging metropolitan context*, http//www.iis-db.stanford.edu/pubs/11897/Rohlen2000.pdf/, accessed 20 October 2004.

[38] Rutherford, M. W., McMullen, P. and Oswald, S. (2001), "Examining the Issue of Size and the Small Business: A Self Organizing Map Approach", *The Journal of Business and Economic Studies*, Fall.

[39] Loh (2002).

[40] Chow, I., Holbert, N., Kelley, L. and Yu, J. (1997), *Business Strategy, An Asia-Pacific Focus*, Singapore: Simon & Schuster (Asia) Pte. Ltd.

[41] Wong, Y. (2003), "Succession planning in family business — Breaking the Taboo", *Better Management*, Issue 52, August 2003, pp. 36–39.

[42] Dalaba, O. G. (1973), "Lengthening your shadow — The key to small business growth", *Journal of Small Business Management*, July 1973.

[43] Smyth.

[44] According to Sit, V. F. S. (1983), *Made in Hong Kong*, there are three local terms that categorise an SME: "chong", meaning factory, "kung-cheung", meaning workshop, and "shan-tsai", meaning bandit factory or a factory in domestic premises.

[45] Dodge, H. R., Fullerton, S. and Robbins, J. E. (1994), "Stage of the organizational life cycle and competition as mediators of problem perception for small businesses", *Strategic Management Journal*, Vol. 15, pp. 121–134; Helms and Renfrow (1994).

[46] Dodge, Fullerton and Robbins.

[47] Report on support measures for Small and Medium Enterprises, Trade and Industry Department.

[48] Kuratko and Hodgetts (1998).

[49] Hong Kong Government Yearbook 2003.

50 Hong Kong Government Yearbook 2003.

51 In 2004, the Heritage Foundation ranked Hong Kong as the world's freest economy for the tenth year running. Other research bodies consistently rank Hong Kong among the freest economies in the world.

52 UNCTAD World Investment Report 2004 "The Shift Towards Services", http://www.unctad. org/en/docs/wir2004ch1_en.pdf/, accessed 27 October 2004.

53 Report on support measures for Small and Medium Enterprises, Trade and Industry Department.

54 Standard Chartered Bank (2002), "New Themes in Asia: Economic and Market Briefing No. 93", 16 December 2002.

55 CIA World Factbook, http://www.cia.gov/cia/publications/factbook/print/hk.html/, accessed 27 October 2004.

56 As cited by Amar Gill, head of CLSA research, "SME engines of growth poised to take on the world", *HK Trader* (June 2002), http://www.hktrader.net/200206/200101/200101s1.htm/, accessed 27 October 2004.

57 Digital 21 Strategy, Sustainability and Opportunities, Commerce, Industry and Technology Bureau, http:// www.info.gov.hk/citb/ctb/, accessed 28 October 2004.

58 Chan, J. K. Y. and Lee, M. K. O. (2002), "SME E-Procurement Adoption in Hong Kong — The Roles of Power, Trust and Value", *Proceeding of the 36th Hawaii International Conference on System Sciences*. IEEE, Computer Society.

59 Report on support measures for Small and Medium Enterprises, Trade and Industry Department.

60 Report on support measures for Small and Medium Enterprises, Trade and Industry Department.

61 Report on support measures for Small and Medium Enterprises, Trade and Industry Department.

62 SME policies, http://www.actetsme.org/hong/hongpol.htm/, accessed 2 November 2004.

63 Most of this information is extracted from the Executive Briefing: Hong Kong, http://eb.eiu. com/index.asp?layout=oneclick&country_id=1560000156/, accessed 27 October 2004.

64 Loh.

65 Loh.

66 Chung, Pak, and Ng.

Appendix 1: SME Case Matrix

STAGES OF VENTURE DEVELOPMENT			*INDUSTRIES*						
			Manufacturing	Electricity & Gas/ Construction	Import/ Export Trades	Wholesale and Retail Trades/Restaurants & Hotels	Financial, Ins., Real Estate & Business Svcs	Community, Social & Personal Services	Transport, Storage & Communication
BIRTH	Opportunities for Small Businesses	Starting New Business/Buying Existing Business	Sun Toys Motor: How to Put a Startup on Track						
		Identifying Niche Markets				Fenix: Diversified Niche Marketing in the Lifestyle Business		Go2xpert Ltd.: Finding the Right China Strategy	
	Starting Up	Successful Partnership						Proactive Medicare Enterprise (HK) Limited: Providing Healthcare in Mainland China	
		Sources of Capital					Team & Concepts Ltd.: Managing the Growth of a Small Business		
		Location & Facilities	Toyland Rubber Manufacturing: Building a New Factory in Shanghai						
		Legal Form of Organisation						TrademarkLogo. com: Transforming Legal Services on the Internet	

(continued on the next page)

(Appendix 1 *continued*)

INDUSTRIES

	Manufacturing	Electricity & Gas/ Construction	Import/ Export Trades	Wholesale and Retail Trades/Restaurant & Hotels	Financial, Insurance, Real Estate & Business Services	Community, Social & Personal Services	Transport, Storage & Communication
Planning, Organizing, Control Process	Manfield Coatings Co. Ltd.: Quality Management as the Winning Formula					Yu's Tin Sing Enterprises: Proactive Risk and Crisis Management	Eurasia International: Total Quality Management in the Shipping Industry
Human Resources and Staffing (Regulatory Concerns)	Hayco Manufacturing Ltd.: Staff Welfare at the Shenzhen Factory				DispatchPro System: Leveraging Government-initiated IT Infrastructure		
Managing Growth				Fat Angelo's Restaurant: Entrepreneurial Growth			
International Opportunities	Dream International Ltd.: Creating the World's Largest Manufacturer of Plush Toys					LECCOTECH: The "Whole Product" Concept to Export Marketing	
Marketing Research	Nin Jiom: Selling Traditional Chinese Medicine in Modern Hong Kong						
Promotion and Selling Process						OneCard: Building a Savings and Benefits Platform	
Customer Relationship Management		Towngas: Achieving Competitive Advantage through Customer Relationship Management					

Managing Operations / Marketing of Goods and Services

GROWTH

STAGES OF VENTURE DEVELOPMENT

(continued on the next page)

(Appendix 1 continued)

			INDUSTRIES						
STAGES OF VENTURE DEVELOPMENT			Manufacturing	Electricity & Gas/ Construction	Import/Export Trades	Wholesale and Retail Trades/ Rest. & Hotels	Financial, Ins., Real Est. & Business Svcs	Community, Social & Personal Svcs	Transport, Storage & Communication
GROWTH	Marketing of Goods and Services	Brand Building	Old Company, Modern Marketing Strategy: Lessons from Lee Kum Kee			Moiselle: Prêt-à-porter Hong Kong Style			
GROWTH	Finances and Inventory Control	Financial Analysis and Budgeting	SunCorp Technologies: From Bust to Boom						
MATURITY	Strategies	Building Competitive Advantage							PGL: The Entrepreneur in China's Logistics Industry
MATURITY	Strategies	Supply Chain Management				Shun Sang (HK) Co. Ltd.: Streamlining Logistical Flow Small Business			
MATURITY	Strategies	Corporate Strategy	Lung Cheong International: How to Survive in a Changing Business Landscape						Jewellworld. com: Leading Web-based IT Development in the Jewellery Industry
	Industry Cases				Hong Kong's Trading Industry: Challenges from Mainland China	Mainland China's Travel Liberalisation and Hong Kong's SMEs in Late 2003			Hong Kong's Container Truckers: The Mid-stream Fee Dispute

1

Sun Toys Motor
How to Put a Start-up on Track[1]

SIMON TAM AND VINCENT MAK

PART I: BACKGROUND AND ISSUES

Introduction

In 1983, Simon Shi Kai-biu, a 28-year-old Hong Kong entrepreneur, started a toy motor manufacturing firm called Sun Toys Motor Ltd. He had some experience in managing motor factories and small start-ups, and only a little cash. However, he needed to compete with large, well-established motor manufacturers and to establish a customer base. Survival itself was in question. How should Shi make use of his previous business experience and management skills to make his next step? Also, what could he observe from the changes that were taking place in the industry?

The Hong Kong Toy Industry until the Early 1980s

Labour-intensive toy manufacturing existed in Hong Kong as early as the 1940s.[2] After the Second World War, Hong Kong grew to become an internationally competitive centre of toy production, reputed for its low production costs, on-time delivery, respect for intellectual property rights and flexible marketing strategies. Toy manufacturers were eager to attract overseas customers by establishing a good image for quality production. These manufacturers were mostly OEM, i.e., they manufactured products, according to customers' specifications, that were then sold under the customers' brand names. In the early 1980s, Hong Kong became the biggest toy exporter in the world.

By that time, more and more toy products used electric motors, and some Hong Kong companies thrived as manufacturers of such small motors, which were called micromotors. Probably the most successful among them was Johnson Electric, which was founded in 1959 and grew to become a highly-diversified world-class micromotor producer. In the early 1980s, Johnson had already been long reputed for its high-quality motors for high-end model racing cars. Although the company's focus was on high-quality micromotors, it also diversified its product lines, making many kinds of industrial and automotive motors. The company was listed on the Hong Kong Stock Exchange in 1984.

Shi: In the Years before Sun Toys Motor Ltd.

Shi was born in 1955 into a lower-class family and grew up in the urban districts of Kowloon. He did various odd jobs while still at primary and secondary school. His interest in electrical products was kindled at this time as his home in Kowloon district of Sham Shui Po was on Ap Liu Street, famous for second-hand electrical appliances and electronic components. The young Shi was fascinated by the goods and gadgets sold by the hawkers and small shops there.

In 1970, Shi entered the Hong Kong Polytechnic to study for a Diploma in Electrical Engineering, which he obtained in 1973.[3] He then spent two years as a television technician for Radiffusion, a radio and television broadcasting company. His duties consisted of repairing televisions for customers such as hotels, restaurants and wealthy households — at that time only rich people had televisions at home. This was his first long-term, full-time job, and his rank was that of a junior engineer. He started off working industriously. However, the company suffered low staff morale because of poor management. Shi's senior colleagues were lazy, working only two to three hours a day, yet making more money from tips than their basic income. "I was hard-working for one and a half years, but was then influenced by the seniors and became lazy as well," Shi said. He was fired six months later.

Shi's first attempts at starting a business took place shortly before and after his stint at Radiffusion. Those were short-lived, small-scale television repairing start-ups founded by a few people. Shi said that those start-ups did not live long because he was inexperienced and the management authority and obligations were not clearly laid out between the partners.

In his next long-term job, Shi started off as a warehouse assistant for a motor factory in Hong Kong. He was such a hard-working and enthusiastic employee that within five years he had risen quickly up the corporate ladder to become assistant factory manager. By that time, however, the company was plagued by bad business; its factory area had shrunk from four floors to two. Shi's new position, high as it sounded, actually meant that he had to deal with everything from management to sales and purchasing. When he realised that there was little prospect for him to move further up, Shi accepted an invitation to become a 20 percent shareholder and managing director of another motor factory in 1981. However, he soon discovered that he would receive no dividend, even though the company's accounts indicated that the company was making a profit. He also noticed that some other shareholders seemed to have secretly pocketed part of the payments received from customers. In 1983, Shi therefore decided to leave that company and set up his own firm, which he named Sun Toys Motor Ltd.

Sun Toys Motor Ltd.: At the Crossroads

Shi had raised HK$500,000 from friends and customers to form his new company. He himself held 40 percent of the shares. He had also mortgaged his flat to raise capital for the new company, and was determined to devote all his energies to it. His task was daunting: he had to establish a customer base in the face of strong, renowned competitors.

Moreover, his new company had very limited capital, and so he had to keep labour and equipment costs down while trying to get a foothold in the market.

Nevertheless, Shi's previous experience in various toy motor factories had given him insights into the industry and indicated some possible directions. He could see that more and more new toy products were incorporating motors, so toy manufacturers were likely to order more motors in the future. Shi had also come to know many customers from his previous jobs, and felt he could persuade them to switch to his company, provided he was persistent enough and had a good sales pitch. But what should that pitch be? How could Shi attract customers to order from him instead of established firms such as Johnson? These bigger firms could produce motors of exceptional quality, and many of them had the benefit of economies of scale, proven track records and numerous ways to lock in their customers. How could Shi lure those customers away from the big brand names?

Moreover, demand for toy products was inherently fickle, and hugely dependent on the shifting preferences of children. The very question of whether motors would become a permanent fixture in toys was problematic — there was no obvious answer at the time. Should Shi therefore invest his future in toy motors? And even if he were to enter that arena, how could he fight the big players? What should Shi do to ensure that his fledgling enterprise survived its first few years?

PART II: LESSONS LEARNED

The Global Toy Industry in the 1980s — Discontinuities On the Demand Side

From 1978 to 1983, the video game business was booming in the developed world, led by such companies as US-based Atari. The game-makers were hailed as revolutionising the whole industry through electronics, and the change was seen to be as momentous as the introduction of plastic toys after the Second World War. However, boom turned to bust in 1983, and a number of leading video game companies suffered losses. At the same time, there was a return to traditional toys, such as the action-figure line "G. I. Joe" and the fashion doll series "Barbie". The consumer mania caused by the Cabbage Patch Kids, a doll series that was launched in the same year, testified to the temporary demise of video games. But when the Cabbage Patch Kids craze subsided by 1986, video game-makers fought back, led by US and Japanese companies such as Nintendo. By 1988, the electronic revolution had secured its foothold in the toy industry.

Also in the 1980s, there was a fundamental restructuring of toy distribution, beginning in the United States. The mega-sized toy retail chain Toys 'R' Us became hugely successful and expanded rapidly, consolidating the market along the way. The company had branches all over the United States and beyond, overshadowing independent small retailers. It sold toys throughout the year, with relatively few seasonal changes in purchasing compared to department stores, which mostly emphasised the Christmas season. Toys 'R' Us therefore ordered massively from its suppliers all-year-round. Low-cost toy manufacturers in Asia, in particular small and medium-sized Hong Kong toy and toy accessory makers such as Shi, benefited from this new mode of operation. Hong Kong manufacturers had an international reputation for flexibility, on-time delivery and high standards of product quality, so bulk purchasers from the United States were drawn to them.

Hong Kong's Toy Industry in the 1980s — Discontinuities on the Supply Side

A fundamental structural imbalance between manufacturing industries in mainland China and Hong Kong emerged in the 1980s. The subsequent prospering of the toy industry was only one part of a larger transformation.

On Hong Kong's side, the changes arose from the territory's industrial boom in the 1960s and 1970s. The industrial boom was using up land, driving up property prices and rents, and leading to the rise of multi-storey industrial buildings. The boom had also pushed up labour costs, and labour turnover was high: hence, manpower shortage became a critical, chronic problem for manufacturers.

Meanwhile, China carried out economic reforms from the late 1970s onwards, leading to the rise of private companies and the introduction of outside capital. Chinese leader Deng Xiaoping masterminded the reform and was instrumental in the establishment by the Central Government of the Special Economic Zones (SEZs) of Shenzhen, Zhuhai, Shantou and Xiamen in 1979. What followed was that the critical shortage of labour and land in Hong Kong contrasted sharply with the abundant availability of cheap labour and land in the Mainland. For example, costs in the Pearl River Delta region in Guangdong Province at that time were only one-tenth of those in Hong Kong. Such contextual structural differences lay at the heart of the transformation of Hong Kong's manufacturing industry in the early 1980s, allowing entrepreneurs such as Shi to capture exceptional profits as well as market share from dominant players.

However, this transition from one context to another meant that manufacturers first had to overcome a number of hurdles. Moving production lines to the Mainland while trying to maintain the level of quality control (QC) that international customers expected from a Hong Kong manufacturer required no less than a total process innovation. But for Shi, apart from this, there were factors beyond his control. For example, there was the basic question of whether China's economic reforms would be abandoned. Throughout the 1980s, Deng had never quite been capable of silencing the opposition of several highly respected and very conservative political figures, so in 1984 he had to take a tour to southern China to boost reform spirits. Moreover, the SEZs were all located in the southern coastal Chinese provinces of Guangdong and Fujian, far away from the economic and political centres of Shanghai and Beijing. If the reform experiments failed, the bankruptcy of a few southern towns would not have had any dangerously negative impact on the whole country (or on Deng's political status), and China could still have returned to its old ways.

Even if reform went ahead, Shi could have fallen into other traps. One of the most serious potential traps was the lack of a market mentality among government officials. The customs department, for one, could have imposed rather unpalatable rules and procedures on Hong Kong entrepreneurs. Worse, a policy could have been interpreted very differently at different times by different officials. There was also a serious lack of protection for property rights. Beneath all these ran a deep-seated and traditional disrespect of the

Chinese government for merchants, something that went back to the Imperial era.

Furthermore, there might not have been enough supporting industries in the vicinity of a Hong Kong entrepreneur's Mainland factory, and conditions such as the continuous supply of electricity could not be taken for granted.

Lastly, Hong Kong toy company bosses had to be aware that mainland Chinese workers might do their jobs according to different ethical standards. Sometimes trust was necessary, but sometimes Hong Kong bosses needed to watch out for undesirable dealings, or even theft. In addition, an entrepreneur such as Shi could not have expected to find skilled, experienced labour on the Mainland. If he moved his production lines to the Mainland, he would have had to concentrate on manufacturing technologically unsophisticated products that could be sold at cheap prices, possibly cheaper than most Hong Kong-based factories could afford. But even if Shi moved his production lines to the Mainland, his headquarters would still have to stay in Hong Kong, where he and his colleagues would have to perform post-production quality control of products manufactured in the Mainland. Hong Kong was also where Shi's customers were located and industry news spread around quickly.

Hong Kong's Toy Industry in the 1990s and Early 2000s

The structural imbalances of the 1980s were not resolved until the early 1990s, following a second tour by Deng Xiaoping to southern China in 1992, during which he reaffirmed the Central Government's determination to press ahead with economic reform, and Guangdong's important role in it. By then, many Hong Kong enterprises had moved or outsourced their production lines northwards, thereby increasing their productivity by five to 20 times. This production mode was termed "front shop, back factory"; the "front shop" in Hong Kong took care of management, marketing, financial control and some product design, while the "back factory" in Mainland, usually in the Pearl River Delta, was mainly responsible for production.

In the 1990s, Hong Kong's toy industry underwent another transformation towards technology-intensive production, corresponding with the return of electronics to the global toy industry. Higher-grade electronic toys as well as multi-functional, interactive toys became popular. Electronic-component manufacturing, software development and game design became important pillars of the toy industry. However, plastic toys were still the biggest segment within Hong Kong's manufacturing industry, and it was common for Hong Kong plastic toy manufacturers to have their office in Hong Kong and to set up factories in mainland China. Chinese toy exports had increased from US$3.55 billion in 1995 to US$5.35 billion in 1998, and the industry provided two million jobs for mainland Chinese workers; most of those exports were handled via Hong Kong.[4]

Hong Kong was still the world's largest exporter of toys by 2001, if re-exports were included.[5] The territory was responsible for providing 60 percent of the world's toy market. About half of Hong Kong's toy exports went to the United States. The next largest export destination was Japan, followed by the United Kingdom, Germany and Canada. Global recession and the September 11 terrorist attacks on New York in 2001 had decreased demand, but the accession of China to the World Trade Organisation in late 2001 was a counterbalancing factor. There were about 6,000 toy producers in mainland China by 2001, and most of their factories were located near coastal cities. Of those factories, 4,000 were in Guangdong Province, and most of those invested by Hong Kong businessmen. Mainland China remained an attractive region for manufacturers because of its low costs. A survey carried out in 2000 showed that the hourly wage was less than US$1 for manufacturing production workers in mainland China, compared with US$5.53 in Hong Kong, US$19.86 in the United States and US$22 in Japan.[6]

The Growth of Sun Toys Motor Ltd.

When Shi started his company, he had to make an important decision: should he move his production lines into mainland China? At that time, some Hong Kong firms had set up factories in the Mainland, but reform had started a few years earlier and the country was still relatively unexplored by Hong Kong manufacturers. A Hong Kong entrepreneur such as Shi would have to learn new "rules of game" there, as discussed before.

Despite the risks, Shi chose to move his production lines to mainland China. The first six months or so of Sun Toys Motor's existence became a time of challenges and experimentation to test and prove Shi's business concepts. The company's Hong Kong headquarters consisted of no more than a rather empty-looking office in Kwai Chung; the only staff was Shi, his wife and two employees who had been Shi's colleagues in his previous jobs. All the production, which in effect involved no more than a bunch of workers hand-assembling components into motors, was done in a small space in a Mainland factory that Shi rented out from the factory owner. Shi rented this factory space to shelter himself from the larger context, where property rights were unclear and a private business climate was almost non-existent. After the first six months, the company established its first factory near Shenzhen, but it was still a small workshop with no heavy equipment. The workers were mostly poor farmers from the northern part of mainland China who had gone south in the hope of better income. They had little technical training, but after all, assembling motors did not require much skill. Post-production QC was important, however, and it served to link up production in Mainland with the standard of product quality that customers expected from a Hong Kong manufacturer. Sun's QC at that time was carried out in a part of the Hong Kong office. The product batches would be sent there and fully checked before being delivered to customers. At that time, demand conditions and production costs in Mainland were so favourable that Shi could set prices that enabled him to make his business profitable even if one out of every three motors that his workers made was not up to standard and had to be rejected.

Shi sought to create an advantage by lowering his prices while keeping the quality adequately high and the delivery fast enough. As he discovered, decent quality was not difficult to achieve since assembling motors was not complicated at all — it involved simply putting together about 30 or so components. And Shi could achieve fast delivery rates by maintaining high morale among his workforce and offering them incentives to work fast and for long hours.

In addition, Shi asked his sub-contractors to do some primary assemblage, and then his own workers would do only the final assemblage, so the company was able to save time and survive for a while without having to purchase expensive production equipment.

Shi and his team enjoyed such high morale that, if a customer called them up with an order in the morning, they could deliver the goods by 2 a.m. the next morning. Shi was attentive to customer needs and could design "tailor-made" motors for them, i.e., motors that were either stronger or quieter, or that used up batteries more slowly, according to the customers' demands (it turned out that the technology required for this was often rather simple). Shi himself was an excellent salesman, and could keep old customers happy and persuade new customers to order his products. He had started with a healthy list of customers from his previous jobs, but he also sought out new customers very aggressively. He was insistent and would not be deterred by embarrassment or snubs. This not only helped him get new orders but also made him more successful in asking his suppliers to defer payment for their materials.

By 1986, as business grew and many new orders arrived, Sun Toys Motor moved to occupy larger spaces in the industrial district of San Po Kong, renting entire factory floors. In 1987, Hong Kong was hit by a stock market crash. Shi managed to recover from the crisis, and then made more long-term investment for his company, purchasing production equipment and setting up a second factory in mainland China.[7] The company remained very efficient: what some other manufacturers could only finish in 10 days, Shi's workforce could complete in one. In 1989, Sun diversified its product range into more technologically advanced motors — a reflection of what was going on with Hong Kong's toy industry as a whole. Supported by the installation of advanced machinery and technology from the United States, Germany and Japan, the company adopted a vertically integrated manufacturing system. This improved the productivity and quality of every product and even encouraged enhancements in product design. In 1990, the company, now called Sun Motor Technology Group, set up an OEM (original equipment manufacturer) division to manufacture special-purpose motors to order for Japanese customers. Such motors were used in electrical appliances and audio-visual products. By the 1990s, Shi's firm had become an exemplary small- and medium-sized enterprise (SME) in Hong Kong. Shi himself won many accolades and awards in that decade and afterwards. In 1993, for instance, he was named one of Hong Kong's Ten Outstanding Young Persons, and won the Governor's Award for Industry and the Young Industrialist Award for Hong Kong.

By 2000, Sun Motor Technology Group had developed into a well-structured operation with an annual production of 95 million toy motors, and from 1990 to 2000 it was the largest toy motor manufacturer in the world. In 2001, as a world-wide economic recession took place, Sun began to produce motors for automobiles, an industry that could provide longer-term orders and more stable customers for suppliers such as Sun, but which required yet higher-quality motors. At the same time, Sun continuously improved its ability to manufacture tailor-made items for customers.[8] By 2002, Sun Motor Group had five manufacturing plants in mainland China with a total production floor of 80,000 sq. m., a total workforce of over 3,000 employees, and a daily production capacity of 800,000 motors. There were over 100 employees at the Hong Kong head office. The company had 50 employees in its Research and Development (R&D) department, which was equipped with advanced production systems capable of producing high–precision, high-quality motors for overseas customers. Shi had also hired one German and two Japanese engineers to help him on issues such as advanced technology, quality assurance and overseas marketing.

How Was Shi's Company Able to Survive Its First Few Years Despite an Initial Lack of Cash and Customers?

Sun Toys Motor survived and expanded because of Shi's successful entrepreneurial strategy as well as his personality, which engendered high morale amongst his workers.

Shi had a choice between process innovation and technological innovation, and he chose the former. He then moved along with decisions that were in tune with trends that did not became obvious until later. He was a process innovator among Hong Kong entrepreneurs, being one of the first successful manufacturers in Hong Kong to place his production line entirely in the Mainland. This move had come out of necessity: Shi simply did not have the money to rent Hong Kong factory space or workers for production when he started Sun Toys Motor in 1983. He only had a small office in Kwai Chung for his QC work and other administrative work. All the assembling was done in the Mainland, and although the company did not use any large equipment, all Shi could afford were very low-tech equipment and cheap labour, namely farmers from northern China who had gone south in search of a better income. Those workers put components together by hand to produce motors, and the rejection rate was high, but demand was so huge that Shi could set high-margin prices that more than compensated for the high rejection rate. The business model of "front shop, back factory" drastically cut costs and generated an important competitive advantage for Shi, since many of his competitors still had all their production lines in Hong Kong.

The fact that Shi started his business when the high rejection rate could be compensated for by high profit margins points to another trend beneficial to him: there was a high demand for toy motors in the 1980s, and there was room in the market for new entrepreneurs to enter. As the economy of the United States, Europe and Japan prospered in the decades after the Second World War, labour and land also became more expensive in those parts of the world, and technologically less demanding manufacturing procedures gradually shifted to regions such as Southeast Asia. The manufacturing of toy motors was among those procedures.

By the time Shi set up his company, Hong Kong had already had several decades of history in manufacturing small motors. Johnson Electric, an early pioneer in that field, was already a world-renowned micromotor manufacturer in the 1980s, and by that time had long turned to concentrate on high-quality motors, leaving space for new entrants to produce relatively low-end motors. This opportunity enabled Sun Toys Motor to survive its infancy.

In addition, Shi applied his past experience to the management of his company and to his own pursuit of success. He was the archetypal self-made man — he was from a lower-class family and had gradually made his way up the social ladder. His childhood experience among second-hand electronics vendors and his later studies at the Polytechnic were instrumental in shaping his adult career. But it was his later work experience and his early business failures that taught him how to run a business. His stint in Radiffusion taught him that low morale and poor management could harm a company. For himself, Shi learned the importance of having a hard-working, responsible attitude towards work, and also learned that laziness could cost someone his job. From his failed attempts to set up his own business after being fired from Radiffusion, Shi learned about the importance of clear definitions and agreements regarding the relative management authority and obligations of managers and business partners. Shi's subsequent management experience at two motor factories cultivated his knowledge of the small motor business, his management skills, and his understanding of the importance of sound corporate governance. After setting up Sun Toys Motor, Shi's own stamina and persuasiveness as a salesman, and his charisma, inspired his employees and contributed to the success of Sun Toys.

Conclusion

This case illustrates how an entrepreneur can start a business virtually from scratch. It sheds light on how new strategic opportunities can be crucial to a new company's survival, how to make decisions about the location and facilities of a company's production lines, and how to manage a small, fledgling company.

Shi's decision to enter mainland China, before many of his competitors, was certainly important to the survival of Sun Toys Motor Ltd. It proved to be a far-sighted move that was in line with general trends in Hong's Kong manufacturing industry. In addition to his shrewd strategic decisions, Shi also set an inspiring example for his employees to follow: he was a charismatic, dedicated, honest, persuasive and patient worker, and thus engendered high corporate morale.

---

[1] This case is based largely on interviews with Simon Shi Kai-biu and two of his long-time employees, Ms. So Sau-kuen and Ms. Elaine So.

[2] Nyaw, Mee-kau and Yeung, Raymond (2001) "The Prospects of Hong Kong Toy Industry's Operation, Foreign Business Environment and Development" research report, Hong Kong Institute of Business Studies, Lingnan University, August.

[3] The Polytechnic became a university only much later, in 1994.

[4] "China: Toy Sector Outlook Good, Competition to Intensify" (1999), *China Business Information Network*, 6 December. US$1=HK$7.8 approximately.

[5] Hong Kong Trade Development Council (2001), "Profile of Hong Kong's Toy Industry", http:// toys.tdctrade.com/, 7 December.

[6] Levine, Bernard (2002), "The Cutting Edge", *Electronic News*, 3 June.

[7] Shi was cautious with new equipment during those early years — he would install and operate it in the Hong Kong office for a few years before moving it to mainland China.

[8] For example, the company had its own motor axle production facilities that could produce axles of any length specified by the customer.

2

Toyland Rubber Manufacturing
Building a New Factory in Shanghai

ALI FARHOOMAND AND MONICA WONG

PART I: BACKGROUND AND ISSUES

Introduction

Toyland Rubber Manufacturing Factory was founded by To Hon-chung and his wife in the late 1940s. The factory, located in Hong Kong, grew from 4,000 square feet in the 1950s to over 45,000 square feet in the 1990s. Since 1950, Toyland focused on rubber rollers, mostly used in the textile (dyeing and bleaching), packaging (PE/PP[1] film/bag) and printing industries. Patrick To, second son of the Tos, joined the company in 1974 after he graduated from university and completed further studies in rubber technologies. The To family emphasized workmanship and quality control. Millions of dollars were re-invested in machinery and equipment in 1985. The result was a very strong market position, with turnover growing at double digits since then. Toyland's products captured a 70 percent share in the textile dyeing and bleaching factories market. However, the good times started to slip away in the mid-1990s. Toyland was faced with a drop in the number of customers as more and more factories were either shut down or relocated to the Mainland. In 1995, Toyland's business stagnated for the first time. After 1997, it started to go downhill, and never recovered. Patrick To realised that his family business had to change in order to adapt to the new market situation. He was considering moving his roller manufacturing factory closer to where the orders would be abundant — mainland China. By late 2002, after a long period of research and market assessment, he finally decided to open a new factory in Shanghai. He was eager to get his new factory up and running. Unfortunately, he was forced to slow down due to the tedious process of getting approval from many departments in China. Furthermore, the local Shanghai partner did not live up to expectations. Subsequently, everything was forced to a halt by the SARS outbreak in April 2003. Three months later, after the SARS crisis subsided, he re-evaluated his initial plan and drew up a revised project plan. Staring at his long list of tasks to be accomplished in the following few months, he wondered how to go about setting up a factory in Shanghai.

Company Background

In late 1940s, To Hon-chung worked as a foreman managing a toy production plant for Li & Fung (Trading) Limited, which evolved to become one of Hong Kong's most prominent trading firms. After leaving Li & Fung, he joined a manufacturer of rubber toys and worked there for a few months before the factory ran into trouble. With some money and a little knowledge in rubber toys, he bought the machinery and started his own business. A few months later, another opportunity came knocking on his door. For private reasons, a rubber roller manufacturer decided to leave Hong Kong for mainland China. Foreseeing the potential in the business, To Hon-chung switched his focus to rubber rollers. In the 1950s, textile dyeing and bleaching and paper printing factories mushroomed as Hong Kong was becoming industrialised. The machinery used by these two industries provided a huge market for Toyland's products. Suppliers of chemicals, Bayer, in particular, were also very open in sharing technical knowledge, enabling Toyland to improve its quality. Toyland's business experienced a rapid growth period in the 1950s, and this prosperity continued into the 1960s.

Due to political instability in Hong Kong in 1967, Patrick To left Hong Kong as a teenager to study in the UK. Seven years later he returned to Hong Kong with a degree in mathematics and physics. After a year of studying rubber technology and interning at the laboratory of Bayer in Germany, he took up the family business in 1974. It turned out to be an opportune time to take over the rubber roller business.

The Golden Era

In 1975, a procedural change in the textile-dyeing process brought about tremendous growth for Toyland. Instead of sizing and dyeing being done in two separate processes, which often meant two factories doing the jobs, sizing and dyeing were combined into a continuous process. Furthermore, the width of the roller was extended from 60 inches to 65-75 inches. Orders kept rolling in and the factory had to operate overtime regularly. Annual sales increased from HK$1 million in 1975 to HK$4 million in 1976, a four-fold increase within one year. The profit margin was more than 25 percent. During that time, more than 70 percent of Toyland's customers were purchasing rubber rollers for their Hong Kong factories; about 20 percent were involved in parts manufacturing for indirect export, and the rest were involved in occasional direct exports to Asian countries and Africa.

The first challenge came during 1983–1984 after Lady Margaret Thatcher, then British Prime Minister, met with Chinese government officials to discuss the future of Hong Kong and ominously tripped on the stairs. Instead of bargaining to extend the lease for the northern part of Kowloon and the New Territories, the British government decided to return the whole of Hong Kong to China in 1997. The political environment in Hong Kong was unstable, people lost confidence about the future, interest rates were high and people dumped Hong Kong dollars in exchange for US dollars. With great difficulty, Patrick To weathered these storms.

Changing Landscape

From the mid-1980s, rising production costs, inflated by high labour costs and stringent environmental regulations, led to the establishment of offshore production facilities in low-cost countries. The Mainland offered abundant low-cost, skilled labour, so to take advantage of that, textile-dyeing and textile-printing factories started moving their production to the Mainland. The exodus grew even larger as the suppliers of these factories also moved with their customers.

Patrick To did not feel it was the right time to move, for a number of reasons. First and foremost, doing business in the Mainland during the early days was considered very risky. Widespread corporate fraud, overly restrictive company laws, dysfunctional legal and tax systems and a lack of corporate governance were problems in the Mainland. Patrick To reckoned that the chance for success was very slim. Secondly, the newly opened up mainland market favoured small start-up companies that were more flexible and eager to succeed than well established and profitable organisations such as Toyland. Thirdly, the textile and printing factories in the Mainland were not yet sophisticated enough to appreciate the value of the high-quality rubber rollers offered by Toyland. Fourthly, Patrick To found it difficult to identify the right person to whom he could entrust his new business in China. Last but not least, family concerns also came into the picture. With three pre-teen daughters, Patrick To preferred to spend more time in Hong Kong with his family. Therefore, instead of moving north, around 1985, Patrick To upgraded the manufacturing process by adding more sophisticated machinery.

Market Competition

Toyland continued to supply rubber rollers to textile dyeing factories, and continued to capture 70 to 80 percent market share. Another large group of customers, the printing factories, were more dispersed, as each operated as a small enterprise. These printing factories mostly looked for low-to-medium priced products, because they either lacked capital or were willing to sacrifice quality for price. Toyland focused less on this fragmented printer market. The strategy was to maintain a minimal presence, keeping a market share of approximately 30 percent. Consequently, competitors were attracted to fill the gaps in the printing market. Gradually, these competitors grew stronger and Toyland started to lose its advantage.

The competitive advantages of Toyland were attributable to its superior workmanship and level of quality control. After years of knowledge accumulation through two generations of the To family, Toyland developed rubber rollers that were chemical resistant and low in heat build up, enabling high-speed rotation without heat-induced explosions. As Patrick To put it, "I strongly believe that superior quality of products and customer services are the key to long-term success." He would often instruct his workers to re-produce a roller from scratch if he found the minutest defect. Extra services such as urgent delivery, maintenance and repair, and credit exchanges of used roller cores with new ones were offered to the customers.

Turnover during the 10 years from 1985 grew by 200 percent, from HK$8 million to HK$24 million in 1995. However, with more and more textile-dyeing and bleaching and paper printing factories either closing down or being relocated to the Mainland, sales started to go downhill from 1996.

The problems encountered by Toyland were two-fold, driven by the decrease in number of customers and by competition. The closing down and exodus of customers to the Mainland left Toyland with a shrunken market in Hong Kong. In the 1980s, it was quite a common practice in mainland China to import new textile machinery made in Hong Kong and second-hand printing presses refurbished in Hong Kong. This provided steady sales for Toyland. However, since 1990s, the Chinese government imposed stricter regulation on imports and levied a hefty import tax, which made imported products very expensive compared with mainland products. Even those Hong Kong customers with manufacturing facilities in southern China found the paper work and application process too difficult to consider shipping their used rollers back to Toyland in Hong Kong for re-coating. On the rivalry front, Toyland faced competition from the rubber factories that had moved to China in early 1980s and had grown to surpass Toyland. Patrick To believed that it was time to seriously consider moving to the Mainland market.

Taking an MBA at the University of Hong Kong gave Patrick To a new perspective. Instead of adopting traditional Chinese mentality to think that none of his three girls would be interested in maintaining the business, Patrick To learned that a successful businessman should be able to use his management skills to sustain a business beyond his own lifetime and also without his immediate family actually actively managing it if they had other interests. By 2002, Patrick To believed that it was time to execute his new vision. He seriously considered moving north to better serve the Mainland market.

The Mainland Chinese Market

According to the Tenth Five-Year Plan (2001–2005) released by the mainland Chinese government in 2000, "… the textile industry should keep up with the international development trend of new technology and restructure the traditional industry by using the advanced new technology to accelerate the technological improvement and the upgrading of the industry." Development of textile machinery was also mentioned in the Five Year Plan: "to research and develop 40 types of textile machinery in the area of chemical fibres, yarn spinning, weaving, knitting, dyeing and finishing …"[2]

By 2002, China had already become the biggest dye-producing country in the world. The mainland's annual dye output was maintained at 200,000–250,000 tons, making up over one fourth of the world's total output. According to the forecast, the total value of the textile industry would increase from US$800 billion to US$1,100 billion in 2005, exports of textile garments would increase from US$52 billion to US$75 billion, and the rate of technology improvement would be over 60 percent.

Industry insiders believed China's accession to the WTO would bring a lot of opportunities to its textile industry. The quota of China's textile exports would increase by 25 percent on a yearly basis, and by 2005, the quota system set up by the developed nations restricting China's textile exports would be cancelled.

As for the printing industry, according to the Tenth Five-Year Plan (2001–2005), one of the goals was to "improve the level of productivity by applying high and new technology and quickening the pace of informisation, introducing high-tech means to editing, printing, distributing and supplying, and upgrading the quality of products …" According to statistics from the Administration of Press and Publication, by 2000 there were 82,189 printing houses across China, including 8,152 publication printers, 20,409 package printers (accounting for 24.8 percent of the total), and 53,628 miscellaneous printers.[3]

The packaging sector of the printing industry was also experiencing rapid growth. The mainland planned to import more advanced technology and equipment and raise the output value of packaging to US$53 billion by 2010, which meant a doubling of the output value of packaging products and printing industry within 10 years.

With the stress on technology improvement and the growing targets of textile and printing production, Patrick To realised that mainland China was the place to be. The question was, of all the provinces and cities, where would the best place be to build his new manufacturing home? Following the trend of his customers and competitors, it seemed that he had two choices: Dongguan or Shanghai.

Dongguan in 2003

Dongguan was the third-largest exporting city in China after Shenzhen and Shanghai. Foreign-invested enterprises (FIEs), numbering 3,610 in 2002, were the main economic driving force in Dongguan. Cumulative utilised foreign investments in Dongguan (excluding foreign loans) totalled US$11.27 billion as at the end of 2001, with inflow amounting to US$1.28 billion. FIEs accounted for about 80 percent of industrial production (in terms of output value), and even over 90 percent in the production of textiles, garments, fur, down feather products, leather goods, plastics, stationery, sporting goods and hardware. Dongguan was located 90 km north of Hong Kong, and was easily accessible by water and land. Hong Kong was the most important foreign investor in Dongguan. As at 2002, there were some 7,800 Hong Kong companies in Dongguan engaged in export processing and production; investment from Hong Kong exceeded 60 percent of the city's cumulative foreign capital actually utilised.

The Pearl River Delta (PRD), which included nine cities in Guangdong Province: Guangzhou, Shenzhen, Zhuhai, Foshan, Jiangmen, Zhongshan, Dongguan, Huizhou and Zhaoqing, was becoming the world's printing factory. As of 2003, 70 percent of Hong Kong's printing and publishing facilities had already moved to Pearl River Delta. In the year 2002 alone, the number of printing factories in Hong Kong dropped from 4,300 to 3,300, the biggest drop in 20 years. Most of these printing factories moved to the PRD to take advantage of its low costs and its vicinity to Hong Kong. The annual aggregate printing output value of Hong Kong and the PRD amounted to US$9 billion.[4]

Shanghai in 2003

Shanghai, China's largest city, had enjoyed a long and prosperous history as an industrial and financial centre with a large concentration of textile companies. Shanghai was also a major destination for foreign direct investment (FDI). It ranked first in attracting FDI among all mainland cities. In 2002, Shanghai accounted for 9.5 percent or US$5,030 million of China's total realised FDI. The city's cosmopolitan character, sophisticated and affluent consumers, and highly educated and skilled labour force, as well as the municipal government's preferential policies and service-oriented attitude towards foreign investors, made it highly attractive to overseas investors.[5] Shanghai had decades of textile industry experience, earning it a respected and prominent status in the world's textile industry. In June 2003, Shanghai hosted the 10th International Exhibition on the Textile Industry, also known as the ShanghaiTex. It was a renowned and highly regarded industry event, billed as the largest show of its kind. Shanghai offered an optimistic long-term future not only for textile manufacturers but also for textile machine producers such as Toyland. In May 2003, the Shanghai Textile (Group) Corporation, the China National Textile Industry Council and the Jinshan District Municipal Government (Shanghai) signed a co-operation agreement, according to which the three partners would jointly establish the eight-square-kilometre Shanghai Textile Industry Park. The park, the largest of its kind, would consist of three parts: a knitting industry area, a household textile industry park and a printing dyeing industrial park.[6]

Shanghai or Dongguan?

Both Shanghai and Dongguan were markets with great potential. However, initially, Patrick To would only consider setting up one plant in mainland China. He needed to make a choice. Dongguan was closer to Hong Kong geographically and the Pearl River Delta (PRD) region was highlighted to be one of the world's four printing bases, along with the US, Japan and Germany. On the other hand, Shanghai provided a strong textile base and its neighbouring provinces, Jiangsu and Zhejiang Provinces, were also up-and-coming in the textile industry. Statistics showed that in 2001, Zhejiang's textile manufacturers spent more than RMB12.9 billion (US$1.55 billion) on upgrading their production skills and the technical standard of their equipment, 11.53 percent more than during the previous year.[7]

From the perspective of competition, in Dongguan, Toyland would be facing competitors that had already moved to the PRD in the 1980s. Some of them started off as SMEs (small and medium enterprises) in the 1980s, but they had then grown with the printing factories and reached a level of production capability that surpassed Toyland. Thus making it difficult for a newcomer to compete. On the other hand, Shanghai would be offering Toyland room to compete and grow. In Shanghai, Toyland would face competition from foreign companies as well as local privately owned enterprises. Shanghai imported textile machinery and parts from Italy, Germany, Japan and the US because the quality of local products was not up to standard. Toyland's premium quality products were on a par with foreign imports but were cheaper. The technological know-how was a key competitive advantage Toyland had over the local competitors that produced in the vicinity of Shanghai. Moreover, there was also a printing presence in Shanghai, though it was not as large-scale as the one in the PRD.

After much deliberation, Patrick To concluded that Shanghai was the best place for his new factory. He was confident that even though he was moving a bit later than his peers, it was worth waiting for the right time to act. With his unique technology and superior product and service quality he was absolutely positive about his goal of achieving a ten-fold increase in sales over the next 10 years.

What Next?

With the location decided, Patrick To was eager to set the ball rolling. However, as a "foreigner" building a factory in the Mainland, he was faced with a lot of uncertainties. What were the things that he needed to tackle? How should he go about setting up a factory in Shanghai?

PART II: LESSONS LEARNED

Investing in a "Foreign" Location

Although sovereignty over Hong Kong returned to China in 1997, under the constitution of "one country, two systems", Hong Kong manufacturers are not treated the same as mainland Chinese manufacturers. In fact, within the law and regulations on foreign investment in the Mainland, "any foreign or Hong Kong, Taiwan and Macau enterprises" are categorised in the same group. On 29 June 2003, the Government of the Hong Kong Special Administrative Region and the Central People's Government reached an agreement on the main parts of the Mainland and Hong Kong Closer Economic Partnership Agreement (CEPA). The essence of the agreement is the Mainland's zero import tariff granted to Hong Kong exports (as of the signing of CEPA, rubber products are not included in the zero-tariff list) and the liberalisation of market access in selected service sectors. This gives Hong Kong businesses a slightly more preferential status; however, the standing of Hong Kong manufacturers investing in the Mainland remains equivalent to that of a foreigner. As illustrated in Patrick To's case, despite the close ties between Hong Kong and the Mainland, he had to face the same issues and challenges that every other foreign investor did.

Things to Consider Before Moving

Before any foreign investment decision is made, the following questions must be considered: What is the reason for the move? Where is the best location? When would be the appropriate time? What should the mode of entrance be? And who should look after the business: local hires or expatriates from the home country?

The motives for foreign investment

Different enterprises may have different motives for seeking a foreign presence. In general, there are two major reasons for foreign investment: resources and markets. In terms of resources, the availability of skilled and professional labour, local opportunities for reducing costs and simplifying the transportation of outputs are important incentives. In terms of markets, the opportunities to tap into large and growing domestic and adjacent regional markets are also big carrots for investors.

In Toyland's case, as for many other enterprises, both the abundant resources and huge market potential are enticements to move north. Even though rubber-roller-manufacturing factory is not labour-intensive, it needs space for the machinery, and the Mainland offers both cheap labour and cheap land. Some of the raw materials for his production are sourced from the Mainland, so setting up a factory in Shanghai would provide greater flexibility in choosing domestic or foreign suppliers and to establish a closer, or even an integrated, relationship with them to control material costs. As for market potential, the improving manufacturing standards in the Mainland provide a growing market for Toyland's quality products. That market segment has been occupied by imports from industrialised countries. On top of that, some of Toyland's customers from Hong Kong have already moved to the Shanghai area, so it will be much more cost-effective to deliver the products and to service the accounts if Toyland moves closer to the customers.

The choice of location

When evaluating a location, other than the availability of resources and the market potential, infrastructure is also a critical factor. Of the top 500 multinational companies in the world, 254 have chosen Shanghai to launch factories or to establish their representative offices.[8] The numbers speak for themselves. Shanghai is an important industrial city with a well developed transportation and telecommunications infrastructure. With 3,012 foreign direct investment projects worth a total of US$10.5 billion, Shanghai seems to be destined for expansion and growth. With an extensive network of textile and printing industries in Shanghai region, it is both an ideal manufacturing base and a huge potential market for Toyland.

Finding the right time

Patrick To was reluctant to move in the early days because he wanted to avoid the chaos, the corruption and the high risk involved in doing business in the Mainland. Moreover, in the 1980s, poor quality was an issue in the Mainland. There was little market potential for Toyland. Family concerns also came into play, so he opted to stay in Hong Kong. However, during the 1990s, the Mainland saw rapid growth in technology and quality standards. FDI (foreign direct investment) was the strongest driving force behind the continuous improvement in quality standards. The period of 1990 to1995 saw tremendous growth in FDI in Shanghai. With China's accession to the WTO, a new upward trend in FDI started in 1999. WTO membership catalysed a closer scrutiny in the realms of corporate governance and fair dealings. This is particularly true in Shanghai, where a large number of foreign countries have a vested interest. The other implication of WTO membership is the diminishing barriers to entry. Therefore, Toyland needs to move quickly before even more foreign factories set up their base in Shanghai.

Mode of entrance

There are generally four modes of entry to a market. The choice has a long-lasting impact on the future of a business.

	Partially Owned	*Wholly Owned*
Existing Business Operation	Capital Participation	Acquisition
Building New Business	Joint Venture	Greenfield

Each of these four forms has its own advantages, although in general the greenfield and joint-venture modes tend to be superior performers versus acquisitions (because there is a tendency to pay too much and/or to have integration problems with the other two modes).[9]

Initially Patrick To was inclined to set up a joint venture (JV) with a local partner. Besides cash investment, Patrick To's invaluable contribution to the JV would mainly be the technology know-how which did not come with a price tag. The local partner was expected to contribute his management and networking. The advantage of setting up a business with a local partner would be to leverage the partner's knowledge of the ins and outs of the Mainland market and the established people network. Patrick To knew many rubber roller manufacturers in China but ruled out partnering with them in order to avoid being exploited and then deserted. Instead, he identified a prospect, a textile dyeing-and-bleaching mill and a long-time customer. Everything seemed to be set to go in early 2003. However, the SARS outbreak turned out to be an important lesson for Patrick To. SARS hit Hong Kong and the Mainland from March to June 2003. Like everyone else, Patrick To could not travel anywhere in the Mainland. He relied on his Mainland partner to handle everything to do with the factory plan. After SARS subsided, Patrick To was not happy to discover that there was little progress on the new factory plan. Turnover-wise, while the roller business was over 50 percent of Patrick To's business, it was less than 10 percent for the textile dyeing-and-bleaching mill. Due to the different priorities, expectations and efforts from both sides, the partnership did not turn out to be a good match.

Patrick To changed his mind about the best mode of entry, and decided to start a greenfield venture. The advantage of a greenfield is having complete control over the business, thereby reducing the risk of relying on a partner who might have other priorities or whose intention could be to learn proprietary know-how to set up their own company. Intellectual property piracy was a big concern for Patrick To because Toyland's unique and proprietary technology in producing rubber rollers was the fruit of years of research and fine-tuning. Being a sole proprietor also gave Patrick To greater flexibility in the deployment of equipment resources between his Hong Kong factory and the Mainland. These benefits could be one of the contributing reasons behind the increasing number of wholly owned FDI projects compared with joint ventures in mainland China in recent years.

Finding the right people

Shanghai's population reached 16,737,700 in 2002. There was also an increasing proportion of Shanghainese people receiving higher education. According to the 2000 census, 11.4 percent of population obtained a tertiary education or above, a 4.3 percentage point increase compared with 1990. As of 2002, 3.21 million people, or 40.5 percent of the total 7.92 million workers in Shanghai, were engaged in manufacturing.[10] With a pool of experienced and educated workers in Shanghai, Patrick To reconsidered his earlier decision to hire someone from Hong Kong. In fact, there was an upsurge of locally hired middle management staff in Shanghai replacing Hong Kong and Taiwanese expatriates. A local mainlander would have a better understanding of the ins and outs of business dealings in the Mainland, and experienced managers could also bring along a local business network of contacts. This trend is evident in the statistics. The number of FDI contracts increased by 35.5 percent in 2001 and 22.54 percent in 2002, but the number of Hong Kong and Taiwanese workers in Shanghai only increased from zero to five percent. One reason could be that more and more Taiwanese and Hong Kong investors are hiring from the pool of mainlanders.

Conclusion

> You can't solve many of today's problems by linear thinking. It takes leaps of faith to sense the connections that are not necessarily obvious.
>
> – Matina Horner

Toyland's case illustrates some of the issues that companies need to consider when setting up a production base in the Mainland. Many SMEs are considering moving north for a number of reasons, including low labour costs, bigger markets and lower rents. However, along with these benefits come other issues that could make or break a business. Different businesses have different needs, so SMEs need a clear objective for the move. They need to decide where to move, when to move, how to move, who to entrust the business to and how to enter the market. There is no one-size-fits-all answer to these questions. SMEs that are planning to move need to be clear-headed and must avoid following the herd. Moreover, the differences in culture and work ethics should not be ignored. As Hong Kong and the Mainland share the same cultural roots and speak the same language, things are often taken for granted. However the mentality and work culture in the recently opened socialist Mainland and westernised, capitalist Hong Kong can be quite different. Hong Kong businessmen should not be over-reliant on their familiarity with the Mainland; detailed market research and preparation are vital for the success of any new venture.

Shanghai is a booming city that attracts many FDI ventures. The 2010 World Expo will be held in Shanghai, enhancing its image as a prominent world city. On 30 July 2003, the Shanghai municipal government announced that it had scrapped 101 items and simplified 142 others in its list of charges on companies and construction projects that need a government stamp, a move designed to encourage foreign investment.

The Mainland is offering a lot of carrots to lure investors. But for SMEs, the questions remain — how should they go about getting the carrots without hurting themselves along the way? There could be many different answers. There is always a risk factor. The key is to minimise the unknown and to calculate the risks. SMEs should weigh all the issues mentioned in this case to assess whether the move will be a beneficial one. It may be worth taking the time to think things through thoroughly before taking that giant leap of faith.

1   PE stands for polyethylene and PP stands for polypropylene.

2   "The Tenth Five Year Plan of the Textile Industry" (2002), *Invest in China*, www.fdi.gov.cn, 17 November.

3   "The Tenth Five Year Plan of the Printing Industry" (2002), *Invest in China*, www.fdi.gov.cn, 17 November.

4   "Pearl River Delta, the World's Printing Factory" (2003), *Chinese Graphic Arts Net*, www.cgan. net, 2 July.

5   Hong Kong Trade Development Council (2003), "Market Profiles on Chinese Cities and Provinces", www.tdctrade.com, March.

6   "Large Textile Industry Park to be Established in Shanghai" (2003), *Jiefang Daily*, 21 May.

7   "Textile Industry Profile in East China Province", *Xinhua News Agency*, Hangzhou, 20 February 2002.

8   "Investment Environments, Shanghai Foreign Economic Relations and Trade" (2003), www. investment.gov.cn, July.

9   Beamish, P. W., Morrison, A. J., Rosenzweig, P. M. and Inkpen, A. C. (2000), *International Management*, (Fourth Edition), International Edition, McGraw-Hill Companies, p. 5.

10   Shanghai Statistical Yearbook (2003), www.stats-sh.gov.cn, July.

3

Manfield Coatings Co. Ltd.
Quality Management as the Winning Formula[1]

SIMON LAM AND ANDREW LEE

PART I: BACKGROUND AND ISSUES

Introduction

Manfield Coatings Company Limited (Manfield) was a niche player in the paint and coatings industry, producing customised industrial coatings for various industrial products such as toys, mobile phones, TV cabinets, washing machines etc. As a supplier to manufacturers of such products, Manfield had to meet not only stringent safety and quality standards but also customers' requirements for short production lead-times. To meet such demands, Manfield had developed a quality management structure that delivered its core value of "Prompt and Reliable" supply and service. In recognition of its commitment to quality, the company gained ISO 9001 certification in 1997, and was awarded the Certificate of Merit in the Hong Kong Industry Department's Quality Award in 1999, Q-Mark Licences from the Q-Mark Council from 2000 onwards, the Certificate of Merit in the Hong Kong Management Association's Quality Award, the year 2000 version of ISO 9001 and the Encouragement Award of China National Quality Award in 2003. But Yuen Shu-wah, Manfield's founder and managing director, did not rest on his laurels. In 2003, Manfield submitted an application for ISO 14001, and approval is pending.

Manfield Coatings: Stressing Quality from Day One[1]

Yuen was a chemical engineer by training. Before establishing his own company, he worked for a UK paint company, where he learned to become an expert in paint. By the early 1980s, Yuen saw that there was demand in Hong Kong for high-quality paint that could support local production. And at one point, he convinced his employer to build a plant in Hong Kong. However, the UK firm eventually changed its mind. So, in 1982, Yuen quit and started Manfield Industrial Company, the non-limited forerunner of Manfield Coatings Co. Ltd., with just HK$200,000 (US$25,000) and five people (including Yuen himself). The limited company was incorporated in 1986.

Manfield's first customers were in the toy-manufacturing industry. With Yuen's expertise, Manfield was able to meet the customers' colour and quality specifications exactly, as well as the relevant safety standards (customers in the toy industry generally followed the European EN71 or the American ASTM standards regarding the heavy-metal content of its products). Yuen commented, "While we have to be competitive, price-wise, we never really compete on price." Even when its paint was used on inexpensive products, Manfield was adamant about quality. Given such tenacity regarding quality, Manfield soon established a reputation for quality and professional service, and its customer base also expanded to include manufacturers of electronics and kitchenware, which set very high standards.

Under Yuen's leadership, the company continued to expand. However, during the heyday of the Hong Kong economy in the mid-1980s, Yuen experienced great difficulty in hiring staff. As he recalled, "For almost a year we had an ad running in the Hong Kong newspapers, seeking non-experienced labourers to be trained as colour-matchers. Only 10 responded, of whom only four reported for duty. All of those four left within a few days to take other jobs!"[2] In 1986, a factory was opened across the Chinese border in Shenzhen, with only semi-processing capabilities and a limited capacity. It took time to gradually train the workforce, expand the capacity and capability and instil a quality culture in the Shenzhen facility. Nonetheless, when most of Yuen's customers also moved their manufacturing plants in early to mid-1990s, Manfield was well established to serve them. By 1995, the combined workforce of Manfield in Hong Kong and its production arm in Shenzhen reached 480, and its annual turnover was in excess of HK$150 million (US$19.2 million). That year, Yuen was awarded the Hong Kong Young Industrialist Award.

Embarking on the Road to Quality Management

While most of Manfield's customers were in Hong Kong or mainland China, the company's products were sold all over the world. As competition among manufacturers became keener, their demand to their suppliers, in turn, got higher as well. As Yuen recounted, "In the old days, customers would be satisfied with a five-to-seven-day order lead time; soon they started asking for shorter lead-times." By the mid-1990s, Manfield was able to achieve an order-to-delivery lead-time of three days, but customers were demanding even shorter lead-times.

In 1996, Yuen attended the Chiang Foundation Manufacturing Leadership Training Programme held at the University of Southern California in the United States. At the time, Yuen realised that Manfield was having similar problems to those that Chrysler (one of the biggest car manufacturers in the US) once had, e.g., a lack of co-ordination between functional departments and an inability to respond quickly to challenges. Yuen knew that Manfield needed to be "big and efficient". He also learned how United Parcel Services handled 11 million packages, offered a 24-hour worldwide delivery guarantee and provided customers with information about the real-time status of each delivery. He realised that "big and efficient" was achievable, though it required good planning, determination and commitment. Upon his return, Yuen immediately discussed this with his senior management, and the decision was made to embark upon the road to quality management.

The first goal was to become ISO 9001-certified. Soon afterwards, outside consultants were hired to provide training and to set up a quality management system. This, fortunately, was backed by Manfield's continual investment in and use of management information systems. Nevertheless, "unless the mindset improves, we can never make real achievements," said Yuen. Thus, significant emphasis was placed on training. For one thing, managerial staff members were expected to effectively carry out managerial duties such as planning, organisation, human resources allocation, command and control (see Appendix 1 for the complete training programme for managerial staff). For another, training and education for all employees had to be comprehensive, i.e., not only did it have to include job-specific and related training, but also had to communicate Manfield's value system and way of thinking. Later in 1997, Manfield was audited and successfully certified for ISO 9001 (version 1994). The same year, the motto "Prompt and Reliable" was made the centrepiece of Manfield's service strategy.

In real terms, Manfield made significant progress in enhancing productivity. To Manfield, productivity enhancement was achieved by leveraging cost controls very effectively in order to maximise value creation. To its customers, the greatest value was speed. Previously, a one-day order-to-delivery lead-time was nearly unattainable. In the second half of 1997, Manfield successfully fulfilled 222 one-day orders, compared with only three in the first half of the year. For two-day orders, the number fulfilled rose from 79 in March 1997 to 459 in December 1997. The average monthly rate for delayed deliveries fell from 15.15 percent in 1996 to just 1.68 percent in 1997. These achievements did come with some degree of trade-offs in production costs. Such trade-offs, however, were carefully evaluated and were done without compromising the value to customers or employees' salaries and benefits.

Quality Management at Manfield Coatings

In the ensuing years, Yuen continually pitched the company against audits and examinations through award applications. According to Yuen, this achieved two purposes: first, it helped them see areas of weaknesses they did not normally see; second, it created a further drive for all staff to improve their performance and attain their targets. In the process, the quality management system at Manfield took shape.

> By satisfying customised requirements of customers through provision of 'prompt and reliable' products and service in order to optimize profit to take care of the interest of investors, employees, customers and community.
> — Mission Statement of Manfield Coatings Company Ltd.

> To provide in time products and service that satisfy customers' requirements at reasonable price and cost.
> — Quality Statement of Manfield Coatings Company Ltd.

Leadership

Yuen understood well that the drive for quality had to come from the top. He expected and encouraged his managers to be innovative, while carefully assessing the associated risks.[3] To facilitate discussions among managers, a breakfast room was set aside for managers only. However, to foster an open environment, there was only one common lunch room for all levels of staff. Various types of training (management, quality etc.) were also provided to managers in a purpose-built training room.

Human resources

Staff members were an indispensable part of the quality system. To ensure that they understood their roles and responsibilities well, specific job specifications and job descriptions were provided. The progress of individual skills and abilities was monitored by skill tables. Training programmes for employees were mostly customised, and were provided or facilitated by internal staff through lectures, group discussions and presentations. There was also no annual budget for training — if there was a genuine need for a certain type of training, it would be provided. In the Shenzhen factory, there was also a large meeting hall that could accommodate up to 1,000 people, thus enabling a monthly training session for the entire workforce.

Information and analysis

Manfield implemented an information system with over 100 terminals of various functions. As Yuen put it, there was a lot of data to handle, ranging from formulas to inventory, and from unique customer requirements such as test reports, labelling, etc., to automatic prompts and alerts. The company had to have an effective information system to handle and process data efficiently and to minimise human error. In addition, production data were collected on a regular basis to generate key performance indices(including customer satisfaction indices and productivity indices). These indices were reviewed and scrutinised regularly and were tabulated alongside details of the previous 12 months' performance for benchmarking purposes.

Continuous improvement

Continuous improvement was another important part of Manfield's quality management system. Each year, the Annual Company Quality Objectives designated improvement projects for company-wide involvement. At departmental level, significant issues or areas of weakness were identified and targeted as objectives for improvement. Quality Improvement Groups were established to tackle these tasks. Emphasis was also placed on self-initiated improvement schemes, including Quality Circles and an Employee Good Suggestion Box. Quality achievements were reported, recognised and rewarded during special sessions or at Annual Staff Meetings held at the company's meeting hall.

Process management

In order to meet customers' ever-tightening delivery schedules, smaller production lot sizes and quality demands, Manfield made efforts to manage and control the process flow more effectively. This began with clear process description and definition. For instance, design processes were clearly defined with input requirements, sample trials and adjustments, and product confirmation. Similarly, key production and delivery processes were tied to explicit performance requirements and were depicted clearly with flow charts. The key performance indices were then closely monitored and tracked by each responsible department. To help encourage and reinforce this quality-focused mindset, a company-wide bonus scheme tied to the performance targets was also put in place.

A Tripartite Joint Venture

Manfield had been attempting to make more efficient use of its production capabilities in Shenzhen by partnering with overseas partners that had the necessary technology but that did not have a facility in mainland China. During an award presentation ceremony and exhibition in 1999, a fellow awardee introduced its German partner Weilburger Coatings to Manfield. Weilburger, in turn, introduced its Japanese partner Cashew Chemical Company, which was looking for a facility in China. While Manfield was looking for overseas partners that could provide technology, Weilburger and Cashew were looking for a partner in China that had the same commitment to quality. In June 2000, the joint-venture company, named Weilburger Manfield Limited, was established, with all three companies as the joint-venture partners.

A self-registered company in Hong Kong and a separate trading entity under the management of Manfield, Weilburger Manfield Limited was responsible for sales of the joint-venture products manufactured by Manfield under licence from Weilburger and Cashew. The company successfully passed 16 customer quality audits in 2002. This included a stringent two-day audit conducted by Motorola. By achieving a higher audit score than a major competitor, Manfield's paint sales to the mobile phone industry increased sharply and the turnover of the joint-venture company showed remarkable growth.

Manfield Coatings: 2002/03

By 2002, Manfield's turnover was more than double what it had been 10 years previously. From 1998 to 2003, the rate of delayed deliveries fell from 0.5 percent to less than 0.1 percent; the rate of complaints fell from 0.98 percent to less than 0.63 percent, and productivity in the production department rose from 143.27 kg per person per day to 182.37 kg. Manfield's overall wellbeing was encapsulated in the Hong Kong Management Association's Quality Award 2003 summary report.[4]

> [Manfield] enjoyed a dominant paint supplier position in the traditional core business of metal toy stoving enamel and pad printing inks … . Supported by various schemes and training, the participation rate and adoption rate of the good suggestion scheme is very high. This reflects that employees are highly involved in the improvement process leading to continuous improvement of the company. On-time delivery, one of the most important performance [indicators] valued by customers, is better than benchmarked and is highly appreciated by customers. In addition, the company strategy of joint venture and technology

transfer to move rapidly into new market has yielded high business growth and brought new source of profit. These combined factors enable the continuous increase in turnover and profit by the company despite the harsh and difficult business environment world-wide.

PART II: LESSONS LEARNED

How Does Quality Enable Manfield to Be a Niche Player?

Why is quality an important building block of Manfield's niche-player strategy? What benefits does quality management bring to Manfield? What effects do these benefits have on Manfield's development? What calculated cost must be considered as well?

The centrepiece of Manfield's strategy is "prompt and reliable". In Manfield's business, the ability to produce and deliver within a very short period of time is an important competitive advantage. However, simply being prompt is not enough. Manfield's products have to be reliable as well. This means that its products have to meet all the customer and regulatory requirements. In today's highly competitive environment, "prompt and reliable" is a powerful value proposition. This is especially true since Manfield competes on quality rather than price.

The benefits that a good quality management system brings to Manfield are two-fold. First, with continuous improvement initiatives and streamlined processes, Manfield is better able to shorten its production lead-time, which also implies that it can produce more with the same level of manpower and time. Second, the rate of complaints and defects will also fall. This not only improves customer satisfaction but also reduces production costs. A high complaint/ defect rate means that a lot of time, material and resources are wasted. The lower such rates are, the lower the wastage.

From a longer-term perspective, these benefits help Manfield secure its position as a niche player, and strengthen and further expand its customer base. In addition, Manfield's ability to produce quality products made the JV with Weilburger and Cashew possible. Had Manfield been a mediocre manufacturer, Weilburger and Cashew would not have been interested in co-operating with Manfield.

Nonetheless, quality management does come with some cost. The case alludes to the fact that shortened production lead-times will require some degree of resource increase, be it investment in technology or extra human resources, although in the long run the benefits may outweigh the added costs. Furthermore, investment in time and resources is inevitable to plan and provide the continuous training required, and set up and run the various tracking and monitoring systems.

What Makes the Implementation of Manfield's Quality Management System So Successful?

What factors appear to be critical to the success of Manfield's quality management system? Is ISO 9001 certification a guarantee of quality?

The success of Manfield's quality management systems can be attributed to four main factors. First, there is a genuine quest for quality from the top. As with any major initiative in any company, genuine support from the top makes a huge difference. In Manfield's case, the founder and managing director Yuen Shu-wah was the person who brought the idea back to the company, and who still champions it within the company. This top-down drive sends a very strong message to the rest of the company that it means business and that quality issues should not be taken lightly.

Second, quality has always been an important value of Manfield since day one. Although it did not have a quality management system, quality products were Manfield's strengths. A quality management system merely reinforces such a mindset.

Third, a quality management system cannot be complete without the complimenting information systems that process, share and publicise data and information for effective reporting, tracking and monitoring. The fact that Manfield has fairly comprehensive management information systems facilitates the implementation of a quality management system.

Yuen comments, "Unless the mindset improves, we can never make real achievements." Thus, the fourth key factor is human resources. In this regard, Manfield invests a lot in training, both for managerial staff and for the rest of the workforce, with the content ranging from technical and job-related areas to soft skills and value systems for changing mindsets. There is no separate training budget at Manfield; any training, so long as it is deemed beneficial to the company, will be approved. Knowing that staff involvement is essential to the success of any quality management initiatives, Manfield has also put in place various quality circles, suggestion schemes and reward schemes to motivate its staff to become more proactive.

As for Manfield's financial performance over the period covered in this case, its return on equity mostly stayed above 20 percent, its turnover doubled and its profit quadrupled. Even during the economic downturn in 1998, Manfield managed to record a 19.6 percent return on equity and its profit fell only 7.5 percent compared with 1997. These are solid indicators of financial performance, and proof of the value of a good quality management system.

It is perhaps worth noting here that ISO 9001 merely certifies that the company's process or processes conform to the ISO 9001 requirements. It is not a guarantee of product or service quality, as it does not detail specific product or service requirements.

Conclusion

What Manfield has demonstrated is that quality management is not a white elephant. If it is properly implemented, it translates into sources of competitive advantage through improvements such as wastage reduction and efficiency gains, and by adding value that customers treasure through better product quality and shorter production lead-times. Manfield also showcases how to successfully implement a quality management system. From Manfield's experience, we learn that there are four critical success factors: support from the very top, a genuine quest for quality, a complimenting information infrastructure, and human resources management initiatives that help forge a quality mindset and reward proactive involvement.

There are certainly some companies that claim to have quality management systems and promote the fact that they are ISO-certified. But how many can truly produce quality products and/or services, and reap the benefits of quality management? Meanwhile, others may try to cut corners and compete purely on price. But history shows that poorly run companies succumb easily to economic downturns (such as those that went out of business during and in the aftermath of the SARS outbreak in Hong Kong in 2003). Although formal quality management systems such as ISO 9001, ISO 14001 or Six Sigma may not be for everyone, companies that are truly interested in getting results from a quality management system must realise that the commitment needs to be wholehearted and continuous.

---

[1] Hulpke, John F. (1998), Manfield Coatings, *Hong Kong, China: New century, new challenges?* http://home.ust.hk/~mnhulpke/yuen.doc/.

[2] Hulpke.

[3] Hong Kong Management Association (2003), *HKMA Quality Award Report Summary*, http://www.hkma.org.hk/qa/Manfield_Summary_03.pdf/.

[4] Hong Kong Management Association (2003), *HKMA Quality Award Report Summary*.

Appendix 1   Training Programme for Managerial Staff in 1997

1. Quality, 5S, Communication, TQM
2. Management, Encouragement, Time Management, Interpersonal Relations
3. Chain of Command, Crossing Territory, Management of Daily Operations, 36-Hour Management Course
4. How to Be an Outstanding Officer
5. Inter-departmental reliance
6. Establishing the Company Mission statement, Declaration of Company Culture; How to Be a Good Trainer
7. Seven Habits of Highly Effective People

Source: Manfield Coatings Co. Ltd.

4

Hayco Manufacturing Ltd.
Staff Welfare at the Shenzhen Factory

GILBERT WONG AND MONICA WONG

PART I: BACKGROUND AND ISSUES

Introduction

As one of the world's leading manufacturers of houseware products and cleaning products, Hayco produced three million brushes a month in its Shenzhen plant in 2003. When setting up its new factory in Shenzhen in the mid-1990s, Hayco had to decide how to best manage the issue of staff welfare for its growing number of factory workers. Senior management firmly believed that providing for the well-being of the company's staff would be central to ensuring low staff turnover and good workplace morale, and therefore provided a "Hayco Home-away-from-home" for the workers. Having said that, the labour market has generally always been in favour of employers, and in the mid-1990s many factories were providing just the bare minimum of facilities and benefits for workers (in fact in many factories, the working conditions were appalling). In such an environment, why did Hayco invest money and effort in building the "Hayco Home-away-from-home"? What message or management philosophy was conveyed by these benefits?

Company Background

> To manufacture world-class quality products, create innovative solutions and deliver on time to customers at a competitive price.
>
> – Hayco's Mission Statement

Donald Hay, President and CEO of Hayco Manufacturing Ltd., was the third generation of a family with a long history in the brushware business. In 1890, Donald Hay's grandfather set up the SA Brush Company in South Australia. Hay visited China in the early 1900s searching for a more cost-effective supply of hog bristles. Donald Hay's father helped grow the business into SABCO, a household name in cleaning products in Australia, the United Kingdom, Europe, Japan and South Africa. In 1983, Donald Hay, who saw the potential of Asia as the future production centre of the world, decided to set up Hayco in Hong Kong. Hayco started off by designing and marketing brushes and other cleaning products, subcontracting production to factories in the Mainland and Taiwan.

As the Mainland opened up, Hay decided to establish his own manufacturing facilities in China in 1988. Hayco in China started as a cottage industry with a plant area of about 10,000 square feet, but then developed into a technologically advanced corporation with an extended product line ranging from household cleaning products, brushes, outdoor-equipment covers, garden tools and barbeque appliances to electrical equipment such as electric tooth brushes and electric floor cleaners for export to Australia, America and Europe. Leveraging on its core competence in design and manufacturing, Hayco was able to get products to market more quickly than the competition. For example, a new order for a barbeque set would take only three months from product design to delivery. By 2003, Hayco remained a privately held family business, but it had become the world's leading manufacturer of high-quality houseware products and cleaning products. In terms of capacity and market share, it was the biggest household brush-making business in the world.

Target Market

Hayco's core products were brushes and items of cleaning equipment for the consumer market. The products were of high quality, targeting the premium market. Eighty percent of Hayco's products were sold in the US. Hayco did not produce its own branded products; it operated primarily as an ODM (own design manufacturer), designing and producing products for other companies. Hayco was one of the major suppliers of global consumer goods giants such as Procter & Gamble, 3M and Rubbermaid. These heavyweight buyers set very high compliance requirements on suppliers and demanded low-cost, quick-turnaround, high-quality products. Hayco's outstanding performance was evident in its ability to secure exclusive contracts for a number of brand names managed by these renowned companies. Despite the worldwide economic slow-down and a series of disastrous world events, Hayco recorded double-digit growth in sales and profitability in five consecutive years starting from 1998. The next target was to develop the European and Asian markets further and to double sales turnover and output by 2000 or 2001, and to increase the number of employees to 5,000 by the end of 2003.

The Hayco Plant

The Hayco plant in Shenzhen, established in 1995, was the centre of Hayco's cleaning-brush and cleaning-ware manufacturing activities. Hayco also established joint-venture factories in other locations in southern China to produce fabric and hardware products. Senior management, marketing and customer service functions remained in the Hong Kong head office. The Shenzhen location was ideal because it was only two hours' drive from Hong Kong, which made it easier for members of the management team, who resided in Hong Kong, to commute between head office and the plant. Also, people spoke the same language (Cantonese) in Shenzhen and Hong Kong, ensuring closer and better communication between head office and the factory.

Manufacturing capabilities in the Shenzhen factory included:
- Design and prototyping
- Mold manufacturing and qualification
- In-house molding
- In-house manufacturing of brushes and brooms
- Assembly and packaging lines
- Warehousing and shipment

In 2003, the plant had grown to cover a massive one million square feet, housing the latest and most advanced equipment. At maximum capacity, the plant could produce 60 to 70 million cleaning implements or 50 million items of brushware a year. On average, three million brushes were produced in the Hayco Plant every month.

Hayco's People

Getting skilled labour is my biggest problem. We couldn't make products to the Six Sigma quality levels without them.

– Donald Hay, President and CEO of Hayco[1]

Hayco adopted a quality-oriented strategy to reduce defects and lower its manufacturing costs. In order to carry out this strategy, Hayco needed employees that were dedicated, well trained and focused on quality. The production process involved the assembly of multi-component products that required demanding, detailed work.

In September 2003, there were 4,000 employees working at the Shenzhen plant. The organisational structure was flat, with three levels: management (five percent), staff (clerical and technical, 15 percent) and workers (80 percent). Most of the time, workers at the Shenzhen plant worked on two shifts, but during busy months, the factory would operate around the clock, deploying three shifts of workers.

Faced with the continuous pressure to shorten delivery cycles, labour-intensive businesses constantly sought more output from their existing workers. It was not unusual for factories in mainland China to force workers to do illegal overtime to meet demand. Hayco, adhering to the law, forbade workers from working more than 40 hours per week, and made sure that workers had enough leisure time to rest and relax. However, these arrangements were sometimes not appreciated by the workers, whose main objective was to earn more money. These workers had left their families in the villages in search of opportunities to earn money. They planned to work very hard for a few years to accumulate enough money to return home to improve their families' living standards. Many of them would have preferred paid overtime rather than leisure time, which resulted in some workers leaving Hayco for other factories that were willing to cut corners and allow more overtime. Having said that, Hayco's turnover rate of five to seven percent a year was still lower than the industry average of 10 to 12 percent.

Demography

According to labour laws, workers had to be at least 16 years old. Hayco raised the minimum age for its workers to 18 years old in order to minimise the risk of hiring underage workers. The general profile of Hayco's workforce was young, and educated to middle school (junior high) level. In terms of age distribution, the largest age group in the workforce (46.5 percent) was the 18 to 22-year-old age group. Twenty percent of the workforce was aged between 23 and 24 years old. There were more females than males in the factory: women represented 58 percent of the staff. The majority (88 percent) of management staff had attained a university level of education. Sixty percent of clerical and technical staff had a secondary school education, and 57 percent of the workers had graduated from middle school (equivalent to junior high school).

Compensation level

Clerks and technicians were received monthly salaries, whereas workers were paid by the day. By law, the minimum wage for a worker was RMB460[2] (equivalent to US$55.7) per month, but employees working for Hayco were paid above the market level. On average, the cost per employee to Hayco, including all benefits and wages, was approximately RMB1,200 (US$145.30) per month. Although there was no statutory minimum wage in Hong Kong, hiring a worker to do the same job would cost at least US$450 per month in 2003.

Hayco's "Home-away-from-home"

Almost all factory production facilities in China provided accommodation for their workers, who came from all over China. Hayco was one of the few manufacturers that took a step further in looking after the welfare of its employees. Hayco's accommodation facility, also known as the Hayco Home, was designed as a state-of-the-art "home-away-from-home" for the company's workers. Donald Hay's philosophy behind the Hayco Home was conveyed in his remark:

> Realizing that human resources are one of the crucial factors contributing to successful manufacturing, and as China's industrial sophistication increases and its manufacturing environment gets even more competitive, the management of the Hayco Plant is committed to provide its employees at all levels with a clean, well-equipped and safe work place, adhering to equally high standards in accommodation, food and other benefits.

The HK$9 million Hayco Home covered an area of 314,921 square feet (29,295 square metres), and had 100 operational staff. It contained three separate karaoke lounges, a dance room, a reading room and library, a chess room, a medical centre with a qualified doctor and two nurses on duty, a grocery store (at prices 10 to 20 percent lower than the market), a staff club/gym, three basketball courts, and one badminton court, a table tennis and American pool room, a hair dresser, and make-up services for the female workers. The company also provided English classes for its workers. All workers were also provided with three free meals a day in the staff canteen.

Telephone booths were available for use by employees so they could communicate with people outside Hayco Home in privacy. A bulletin was published to aid internal communication, and employees were encouraged to write articles for the publication.

Workers from different levels in all departments formed a welfare committee to monitor the quality of the welfare services that the company provided to employees, and to act as a mediator between management and workers regarding welfare policies. A staff satisfaction survey was conducted once a year to collect feedback from employees, to be considered by the company when planning future improvements.

Hayco's Benefits Policy

> No matter how advanced and highly developed a company's technology is, it is only as effective as the people operating it. Taking the best possible care of our employees is the basis to improve productivity, retain staff, and improve efficiency.
>
> – Donald E. Hay

Hay emphasised time and again the importance of people. Hayco's management team believed that hardware and pieces of machinery were homogenous items that competitors could easily replicate, but that people were unique individuals who had to be treated as assets, i.e., they had to be taken care of and respected. The message that Hay wanted to convey was simple: employees were members of the Hayco family and the management valued them and considered them a factor that differentiated the company from its competitors, and that contributed to the company's competitiveness and success.

How was Hayco's management philosophy reflected in its benefits policy? Were the benefits offered in the Hayco Home intended to give employees a clear message about Hayco's corporate goals and business objectives? What was the likely effect of these benefits? Also, why did Hayco use its benefits programme as a tool to achieve competitiveness?

PART II: LESSONS LEARNED

Why Did Hayco Invest Money and Effort in Building the Hayco Home?

An employer's benefits programme can encompass a wide variety of facilities and services, such as those offered in the Hayco Home. Some benefits are legally required, such as annual leave and injury insurance, while other benefits are provided voluntarily by employers. Most US companies are particularly concerned with regulatory issues such as overtime work, safety standards and child labour. Any manufacturer found to be non-compliant is immediately disqualified as a supplier. Other than these statutorily required benefits, all other welfare services and benefits are offered on a purely voluntary basis by employers. Hayco's employee benefits are offered in a home-like environment, with a full range of training, free meals, recreational facilities, clean and safe living quarters, free medical care, security and other daily conveniences.

These benefits are aimed at cultivating a family atmosphere, which is in line with the history and identity of Hayco, a third-generation family business. The community setting provides a long-term stable environment that helps build a sense of belonging and loyalty. For Hayco's workers who are alone, far away from home, the Hayco Home becomes their home away from home, fulfilling all kinds of personal needs. According to "Maslow's hierarchy of needs", as proposed by the renowned psychologist Abraham Maslow, these needs are: physiological (food and shelter), safety (security measures), sence of belonging (sport teams, interest classes), esteem needs (pride in being a Hayco worker) and self-actualisation (training courses, libraries and reading facilities).

What Is the Effect of Hayco's Employee Benefits Programme?

Management theorists generally agree that appropriate employee benefits contribute positively to a company's overall performance. However, managers often have a problem quantifying the actual "benefit" of employee benefits. That said, the positive outcomes of Hayco's benefits programme are reflected in its below-average staff turnover rate and above-average product turnover, both achieved through building loyalty, stability and a sense of belonging and ownership among workers. All this in turn boosts staff morale and enhances productivity, ultimately, resulting in the timely delivery of low-cost, high-quality products to customers.

Why Use Benefits as a Tool to Achieve Competitiveness?

Hayco's workers come from all over China. Some of them may have initially had the objective of earning as much money as possible, but Hayco's strict adherence to the laws governing overtime work means that its employees' take-home pay is perhaps not as high as that of workers in some other manufacturing establishments. If cash is that important, why doesn't Hayco simply increase the daily wages that it offers, in order to attract quality people? Why does Hayco use benefits as a tool instead? To answer these questions, the fundamental issue of what Hayco actually wants to achieve with its workforce must be addressed first.

Hayco's competitive advantage lies in its ability to get products to market more quickly and cost-effectively, thanks to its experienced and skilled workers. Therefore, the main staff planning objective is to create a stable, reliable and skilled workforce that is familiar with Hayco's production processes. The retention of experienced staff and the recruitment of committed staff are paramount to the long-term success of Hayco. Hayco does not target people who are looking to earn quick money; rather, the company looks for people who are willing to commit for the long term. Offering a larger proportion of total compensation in the form of benefits is likely to attract people who look for stability and a more settled, long-term job or career.

Aligning Work Culture with Benefits

In recent years, the scope of employee benefits has widened, and benefits programmes have become increasingly important. In Hayco's case, employee benefits range from accommodation, an on-site cafeteria, health promotion, an on-site medical clinic, employee assistance, and staff communication initiatives. For managers, the growth in the scope and variety of available benefits has meant that designing benefits programmes has become more and more complex. Not all benefits options are effective with all employee groups or in all organisations. Indeed, some can even clash with the organisation's goals, values and overriding business strategy. Designing a benefits programme that addresses these issues requires an understanding of the full range of benefits that the organisation is considering. But beyond that, it demands an understanding of the organisation, its values, its business goals and strategies, and the changes that it is going through. It also requires an understanding of the work cultures that are in place in the organisation and how they are evolving. The Hay Group proposed a model that classified work cultures into four types: Functional, Process, Time-Based and Network.[3] The four cultural drivers combine to form four cultural themes:

1. Functional — emphasises technology and reliability. All organisations have this focus, including those that are functional and hierarchical in nature, regardless of how flat they are. This is often viewed as the culture of the past, but there are still strengths in this cultural orientation.
2. Process — emphasises reliability and customer; how vs. what. This culture is most often identified as the desired culture for the future. It emphasises total quality management (TQM) type values, including teamwork.
3. Time-based — emphasises technology and flexibility. Creates demand for specialised, value-added services and products. Emphasis is on change, speed and market dominance. The culture is demanding and very result-oriented.
4. Network — emphasises customers and flexibility. Creates value through alliances, networks and value-added relationships of products and services. Organisations have evidence of this culture, but it rarely dominates.[4]

Hayco's is a functional culture because it focuses on the reliable delivery of standardised products and services through the technology it manages. Tasks are broken down into their simplest form to minimise mistakes. The individuals who perform those tasks focus on narrowly defined functions that require an equally narrowly defined — albeit deep — set of skills. These individuals are rewarded for their reliable performance over time, and for improving their skills and increasing their experience in their functional specialty. This increase in skills and experience adds real value to the organisation, ultimately generating greater reliability, efficiency and effectiveness.[5] The formal division of labour — standardisation, formalisation and specialisation — is the key organisational principle of such companies.[6]

The Hayco Home illustrates a typical range of benefits offered by an organisation with a functional culture. According to the Hay Group study, the benefits in a functional culture typically reflect the values of longevity and security that are common to such organisations. Employees in functional organisations tend to be career-focused individuals who stay with the same company for a long time. The free benefits offered in Hayco Home demonstrate the paternalistic nature of most functional organisations. The employer of an organisation with a functional culture tends to fund a major portion of the benefits. This same paternalistic influence and emphasis on security and stability are also seen in healthcare benefits, which tend to provide few options but are highly comprehensive and mostly employer-funded.[7]

Conclusion

Many organisations claim that people are their most valuable assets, but few of them actually "walk the talk". Often, the human resource strategies in these companies do not support the overall business strategy. When Hayco's management decided to invest millions of dollars in building Hayco Home, they demonstrated their genuine intention to be people-focused. Hayco realises that there is a long-term investment value in its people. By providing benefits and looking after the well-being of its employees, Hayco is able to build a loyal workforce that enjoys high morale and is highly productive, a workforce that helps deliver high-quality products on time. So its workforce has become a critical success factor that has helped Hayco to become an industry leader worldwide.

In designing a benefits package that is tailored to its goals, values and work culture, a company must answer the following questions: What are the messages that the organisation is trying to convey? What should the proportion of pay and benefits be in the total compensation package? What is the organisation willing or able to spend?

The example of Hayco also demonstrates the positive results of the alignment of work culture and benefits policy. Whether a company is a large corporation or a small or medium-sized enterprise, the same principle applies. If companies are able to appropriately align all the individual compensation elements with the appropriate work cultures for the organisation, the accomplishment, end result or bottom-line deliverable is, in fact, a reinforcement of and an attainment of business strategies and goals.[8]

---

[1]   "New Broom in China" (2001), *The Australian*, 27 November.

[2]   US$1 = RMB 8.26, September 2003.

[3]   Flannery, T. P., Hofrichter, D. A. and Platten, P. E. (1996), *People, Performance, and Pay: Dynamic Compensation for Changing Organizations*, The Hay Group, The Free Press, pp. 154–155.

[4]   Fay, C. H., Thompson, M. A. and Knight, D. (2001), *The Executive Handbook on Compensation: Linking Strategic Rewards to Business Performance*, The Hay Group, The Free Press, pp. 187–188.

[5]   Flannery, Hofrichter and Platten, pp. 130–131.

[6]   Flannery, Hofrichter and Platten, p. 155.

[7]   Flannery, Hofrichter and Platten, p. 153.

[8]   Fay, Thompson and Knight, p. 330.

5

Dream International Ltd.
The World's Largest Manufacturer of Plush Toys

SIMON TAM AND MONICA WONG

PART I: BACKGROUND AND ISSUES

Introduction

On 8 June 2003, Dream International Ltd. signed a contract with Warner Bros. to manufacture licensed beanbags and plush stuffed toys using famous branded characters such as Looney Tunes and Tom & Jerry. The contract allowed Dream to distribute its character products through Warner appointed distributors worldwide except for the US territories and Canada. For Dream, the contract not only added a new revenue source but also provided a stepping stone to eventually sell character brands and other plush toy products directly to retailers.

Dream was the world's largest manufacturer of plush toys in terms of production capacity. It was headquartered in Hong Kong, and in February 2002 it became the first Korean-owned company to be listed on the Hong Kong Stock Exchange. The proceeds were used for further expansion of its vertically integrated group structure and to broaden its marketing activities in the US, Japan and Europe.

Despite Dream's remarkable growth, chairman and founder Kyoo Yoon Choi, who was in his fifties and based in Seoul, was not satisfied with the size of the operation. In the highly fragmented plush toy market, Dream had less than a two percent share of the global market. Choi's goal was at least five to six percent. What was Dream's strategic plan for achieving this target? Was vertical integration the best way forward? What were the success factors that made Dream into the world's largest manufacturer of plush toys?

The Toy Industry

On a global scale, the toy industry was a US$80 billion-a-year business, with the US being the number one market, followed by Japan.[1] Mattel, which owned the Barbie dolls, Fisher-Price toys, Matchbox cars and other licensed items, was the world's number one toy maker, followed by Hasbro in the US. Their 2002 sales amounted to US$4.9 billion and US$2.8 billion respectively. In Japan, Bandai was among the top players, with turnover of US$2 billion in 2002.

As the world's largest toy exporter, Hong Kong continued to play an important role in the world's toy industry.[2] Twelve percent of global toy sales, valued at US$9,497 million, were exported from Hong Kong in 2002. Hong Kong was famous for producing high-quality toys, and a large share of industry revenues was derived from contract production for overseas manufacturers and licence-holders. Production on the Chinese mainland had enhanced the price competitiveness of Hong Kong exports.[3] More than 175 small and medium enterprises, characterising the industry's fragmentation, were engaged in toy manufacturing. According to Dream, plush stuffed toys accounted for approximately 12 percent of total toy sales in 1999 and 8 percent in 2000. In Greater China, Dream topped the league in sales, which amounted to US$117 million; in the US, Applause and Russ Berrie were two major manufacturers of plush stuffed toys, with annual turnover estimated at roughly US$200 million and US$300 million respectively.

Company Background

Dream was principally engaged in the design, development, manufacturing and sale of a wide range of plush stuffed toys as well as steel and plastic toys on an OEM and ODM basis. When the ninth manufacturing plant commenced operations in March 2003, production capacity increased by 9 million pieces to 76 million pieces a year.

The "plush dream" began 1984, when Choi set up his own toy manufacturing business, C & H, in Korea, after working in the plush toy division of Daewoo for eight years. Due to the increasing labour disputes and wage hikes following the Seoul Olympics in 1988, Choi moved his business to Sri Lanka to take advantage of the lower labour costs there. The operation ran smoothly until the early 1990s, when the unstable political situation in Sri Lanka forced Choi to look for a new home for his business. Attracted by the low taxation system, flexible business regulations and the proximity to manufacturing facilities in the Chinese mainland, C & H moved its base to Hong Kong in 1992 and started to expand into mainland China. Dream was established to own all of C & H's China production units.

In the year 2002, Dream's turnover amounted to US$117 million, a 20 percent increase over 2001. Gross and net profit margins were 23 percent and 12 percent respectively, maintaining the 2001 level. The public listing in February raised approximately US$22.5 million. About US$593,000 was used for the expansion of marketing in the US market through the acquisition of a 36 percent equity interest in an associate that was engaged in the marketing of plush stuffed toys in the US market. Approximately US$1.4 million was used as general working capital of the group. The remaining net proceeds from the new issue and the placing were placed in principal-guaranteed high-yield deposits with financial institutions. By 2003, Dream had developed into an international organisation with nine production facilities in mainland China, and sales offices in the US, Japan and Europe. Half of Dream's sales came from the US market. Japan followed, contributing 33 percent of the turnover. Plush toys accounted for 93 percent of the group's turnover, while the remaining seven percent came from steel and plastic toys.

1992–2000: OEM and Vertical Integration

After years of hard work in setting up the company and developing its compatibility and reputation in the market, Dream received stable and increasing orders from high-profile customers such as Warner Bros., Bandai, Disney, SEGA and Banpresto. Products ranged from character-licensed products and the more traditional varieties. Dream also produced steel and plastic toys, including tricycles and steel trucks, but such products accounted for less than 10 percent of total turnover.

The three major cost components in the plush toy production process were material costs, labour costs and overhead costs. Material had always been the most critical factor of all because the design, features and attributes of the plush toys depended upon the type of material used. Fabric accounted for 65 percent of Dream's total operation cost. New fabrics became available in the market every day. Fabric-makers sold these raw materials at a 15 to 38 percent mark-up.

By the mid-1990s, Dream was already a sizeable player in the market. It had a competitive advantage in terms of managing its material costs because it could afford the investment required. In 1997, C & H Plush (Suzhou) was established to manufacture fabric for plush stuffed toys. Dream became one of the very few vertically integrated toy manufacturers. Dream produced 40 percent of the fabric raw materials it needed. Internally produced fabrics were mainly basic materials that did not require an extensive R & D investment; the remaining 60 percent was bought. According to Dream, savings of 15 to 20 percent on material translated to a 3 to 5 percent difference in selling price compared with competitors. Nonetheless, Dream also maintained the practice of outsourcing production to smaller manufacturers to help reduce costs by cutting down overtime hours during peak seasons.

2001–2003: Ramping up ODM and Licensed Characters Production

The toy manufacturing industry was crowded and highly competitive, OEM particularly so. Dream continued to thrive on its ability to meet tight delivery schedules with short production lead-times, while containing operating costs to stay competitive. To take the company to the next level, Dream made use of the trademarks "CALTOY" to tap into the ODM market.

The ODM was three times the size of the OEM market in terms of value. Through its sales offices in New York, an important window to ODM customers, Dream expanded into the ODM market, targeting mass retailers such as Walmart, Target, Toys 'R' Us and Costco. New York was a strategically important location, hosting toy industry trade fairs twice a year. Many toy manufacturers established a showroom in the so-called "toy district" in New York City. The year 2001 marked a successful breakthrough in ODM business for Dream, with five percent of total turnover that year being contributed by ODM sales. The strong market response to CALTOY became the driving force for further expansion in Dream's ODM business. Successful ODM relied on heavily on product research, development and design. To ramp up its ODM operations, Dream built a 135-employee research and development team, with more than 30 experienced designers in Korea and 13 designers in Shenzhen.

In 2002, Dream's ODM business jumped from five percent to 12.5 percent of total turnover, and for the first half of 2003, ODM business accounted for 13 percent of total turnover compared with only six percent in the corresponding period in 2002.

While Dream enjoyed a considerable advantage in terms of scale as the world's largest producer of plush stuffed toys in terms of capacity, it had a market share of less than two percent. Given new sales orders and the high factory utilisation at 95 percent, Dream was considering expanding its capacity by sub-contracting to other manufacturers, building its own or through acquisitions.

The licence agreements with Warner Bros., signed in June 2003, allowed Dream to utilise Warner Brothers' popular cartoon characters, as licensed products, in the manufacturing of beanbags and plush stuffed products. The contract was expected to generate an additional five percent growth to Dream's sales in 2003. This agreement not only boosted the business and added a new revenue stream, it also enriched the product mix and escalated Dream's worldwide manufacturing business in cartoon characters.

Future Expansion Strategy

Due to the limited growth potential of OEM markets (only two to three percent per year), Dream planned to focus on expanding its ODM operations. Increases in ODM sales were largely driven by increased orders from major retailers in the US, such as Wal-Mart, Target and Toys 'R' Us. With these contracts from market leaders, Dream intended to concentrate on Japan and the US markets for its ODM business expansion. Dream's target was to raise the ODM contribution from 12–13 percent to 30–35 percent of total turnover within three to four years. Dream planned to achieve this target by focusing its efforts on design and product development as well as sales and marketing capacities, through the acquisition of marketing companies in key markets.

The character-licensing agreement with Warner Brothers reinforced Dream's plan to use the ODM market as a tool to expand its overall market share. There were also plans to acquire US marketing firms, to establish a marketing channel in Europe and to form a joint-venture marketing company in Japan.

For the longer-term future, Dream set its eyes on entering the OBM (Own Brand Manufacturing) market in 2003, as the industry's average gross margin for OBM was as high as 60 to 70 percent. The Group envisaged that this stage would come within four to five years, once the five percent market share target was met. By then, Dream would diversify into businesses complementary to brand-building, for instance creating characters through multimedia products such as video/PC games, cartoons and animation movies.

Despite its grand scheme of creating cartoon movies and such, Dream was not set to diversify out of the plush toy industry. The venture into the multimedia entertainment business was ultimately undertaken in order to generate interest and demand in character toys. What Dream did aim at was to broaden its line of plush-toy products. Specifically, Dream's designers had been adding "mechanical" and "electronics" dimensions, utilising technology to develop interactive plush toys that could be used for educational purposes. The R & D department had also been exploring the use of plush materials in other categories of products beyond the traditional plush stuffed toys.

In order to build the plush toy kingdom with its own brand, Dream gradually started shifting its focus away from production to marketing. Many toy industry giants were essentially marketing companies. Some of them were so good at marketing toys that they sold their service to others. For example, Mattel and Bandai formed a strategic alliance to market each other's toys — Bandai in Japan and Mattel in Latin America.[4]

Given Dream's vertically integrated structure from material production to ODM, would the company's transformation into an OBM be a natural and smooth process? Was Dream's corporate structure in 2003 conducive to its move to expand its market share through ODM and eventually become an OBM? Would Dream be better off having a different type of organisational structure? How should Dream create a balance between subcontracting and in-house production in order to pave the way to OBM? The net proceeds from Dream's public offering amounted to approximately HK$175 million, so how should Dream deploy the capital raised in pursuit of its long-term target?

PART II: LESSONS LEARNED

Dream International's Growth Strategy

Igor Ansoff has proposed a useful framework, called a product-market expansion grid, for detecting new intensive growth opportunities. According to Ansoff, a company first considers whether it can gain more market share with its current products in their current markets (market-penetration strategy). Next it considers whether it can find or develop new markets for its current products (market-development strategy). Then it considers whether it can develop new products of potential interest to its current markets (product-development strategy). Later it will also review opportunities to develop new products for new markets (diversification strategy).[5]

	Current Products	New Products
Current Markets	*1. Market-penetration Strategy*	*3. Product-development Strategy*
New Markets	2. Market-development Strategy	4. Diversification Strategy

In its early days, Dream was an OEM producer, and its rapid growth was fuelled by a market-penetration strategy. In what Dream considered as its Phase One development, the company's target was to secure more orders for its OEM products from buyers. Gradually achieving economies of scale, Dream started to acquire upstream businesses. Fabric-manufacturing facilities in mainland China were established. Dream gained more control and reduced costs, which translated into price reductions.

During its Phase Two development, Dream followed the market-development strategy. It moved to the ODM market, primarily in the US and Japan. The ODM products were essentially the same core plush toys. Dream made use of its trademark, "CALTOY", to market plush toys designed by its own in-house designers. The quest for ODM markets was further fuelled by the 2002 listing in Hong Kong, which raised approximately US$22 million. Dream used part of the proceeds to acquire character-licensing businesses and marketing companies in the US, Japan and Europe to expand its ODM business.

According to Dream, Phase Three development will kick in when Dream reaches an overall market share of five to six percent. The expansion strategy in this stage will be a mixture of a product-development strategy and a diversification strategy. While there will be an increasing focus on the OBM markets through the introduction of new branded products, Dream will continue to develop its ODM markets. Dream plans to incorporate more electronics and mechanical elements into its plush toys to develop new interactive and educational toys. Despite the trend of smart toys, computer games and the decreasing population of children, plush stuff toys have a decorative function, and new varieties applying new technologies can be developed.

Dream also has plans to explore and expand the use of plush materials into other categories of products beyond traditional plush stuffed toys. To facilitate the sale of its branded products, Dream will also diversify into multimedia entertainment business with the aim of creating popular characters in cartoons, animation movies or games.

Analysis of Dream International using Porter's Five Forces Model

Substitutes

As the toy industry is highly fragmented, there are many other toy OEM and ODM producers that can act as substitutes. However, as the world's largest manufacturer of plush toys, Dream enjoys competitive advantages in terms of economies of scale and product design.

New entrants

Although there are many smaller players in mainland China, there are no sizeable new entrants in the sector. Moreover, new entrants will lack economies of scale and relationships with large customers such as Wal-Mart and Bandai.

Customers

Dream's main customers include Disney, Sega and Banpresto for OEM products, and Walmart, Target and Costco for ODM products. The top five customers collectively account for 43 percent of total sales. In a fragmented market with limited growth, buyers can accelerate the consolidation of suppliers by selectively nurturing the more efficient operators. Hence the relationships with these key buyers are critical to Dream's annual turnover.

Dream has the ability to foresee the changing trend in the buyers' market. The emergence and rapid growth of mass retailers such as Walmart, Target and Costco signal a shift in demand from OEM production for exclusive and more expensive brand names to ODM production of a wide variety of original designs for the mass market.

Suppliers

The largest cost item for Dream is fabrics, accounting for over 60 percent of total raw material costs. Most items are sourced locally or from Korea or Taiwan. Forty percent of the fabric is produced in-house to reduce the cost of and reliance on this key production input.

Competitive threats

As the world's largest manufacturer of plush toys in terms of capacity, Dream definitely has the competitive advantage of scale. For new entrants and other smaller competitors, it would take many years to build capacity to such a level. Dream has also developed long-term relationships with key toy brands around the world.

Use of proceeds from the listing

The net proceeds from the public offer, after deducting related expenses, were estimated to amount to approximately HK$175 million. Dream intended to apply the net proceeds as follows:

- approximately HK$23.4 million for vertical integration in the area of spinning yarn;
- approximately HK$70.2 million for the expansion of marketing in the US market;
- approximately HK$23.4 million for the acquisition of character-licence businesses;
- approximately HK$23.4 million for the expansion of marketing in Japan and Europe;
- approximately HK$23.4 million for building its research and development capabilities; and
- the balance of approximately HK$11.2 million as general working capital of the group.

The Way Forward

While Dream paves the way to creating its own brand and, strengthening its marketing capabilities, it continues to acquire production facilities. This strategy of both forward and backward integration requires substantial investment. Very few of Dream's competitors would have the access to capital resources because they tend to be small players, whereas Dream is a publicly listed company. Moreover, Dream's economies of scale and its relationship with leading mass retailers and branded character owners set it apart from the league. With these competitive advantages, the vertical integration strategy gives Dream the following benefits:

1. A steady supply of materials for production, resulting in good cost control.
2. Extra, though incremental, revenue from selling fabric to third parties when its own demand is at seasonal lows.
3. It can eliminate intermediaries and eventually sell plush stuffed toy products to the branded customers and consumers directly.
4. In-house production ensures stringent quality control, enhancing the production process and guaranteeing the quality of products. It also allows for the flexible allocation and commitment of resources among various production bases, enabling the mass manufacturing of products, the meeting of tight delivery schedules and shortening of production lead times.

In short, vertical integration will help Dream to "get the basics right" — the basics being the three things every customer looks for: quality, the ability to deliver on time and the right price. These are things that Dream has excelled in, otherwise it would not have survived and succeeded for so many years in the highly fragmented and competitive OEM market. If Dream focuses just on the forward acquisition, the product quality and design innovation, which rely heavily on fabric material and the production process, might not live up to the standard the brand stands for; on the other hand, if Dream focuses just on backward integration, it will not be able to develop its own brand successfully and transform itself into an OBM producer.

In conclusion, Dream's strategy of vertical integration might not fit-in well with all industries, where partnership may be preferred. However, it fits well with the traditional model of toy manufacturing and is set to assist Dream International Ltd. on its road to becoming a plush toy kingdom.

---

[1] Kurtenbach, E. (2003), "Toy industry group says it will inspect factories in China and elsewhere for worker safety", *Associated Press*, Shanghai, China, 9 October.

[2] Taking into consideration export and re-exports.

[3] Hong Kong Trade Development Council, (2003) "Profile of Hong Kong's Toy Industry", http://toys.tdctrade.com/, 15 December.

[4] Bandai Website, www.bandai.com/.

[5] Kotler, P. (2000), *Marketing Management* (Tenth Edition), Prentice-Hall of India Private Limited, pp. 73–74.

6

Nin Jiom

Selling Traditional Chinese Medicine in Modern Hong Kong

BENNETT YIM AND VINCENT MAK

PART I: BACKGROUND AND ISSUES

Introduction

The Hong Kong brand Nin Jiom was popularly known in the territory by its flagship product "Pei Pa Koa Cough Syrup". It was through the profitable mass-selling of such an over-the-counter traditional Chinese medicine (TCM) that Nin Jiom thrived through decades of history. By the early 2000s, the rapidly modernising consumer culture in Hong Kong and the Hong Kong Government's new TCM policies required manufacturers of TCM products to adapt constantly to a changing business environment. Nin Jiom was attentive to this and was earning annual turnover of several hundred million Hong Kong dollars by the early 2000s. The company was moreover able to continue expanding overseas and in mainland China. How did Nin Jiom's products fit in an era when the Hong Kong Government and the people in Hong Kong as well as other Western countries paid more attention to TCM than before? How did the company manage to maintain its success as a TCM brand in modern Hong Kong?

Traditional Chinese Medicine in Modern Hong Kong[1]

TCM had been practised in China for more than 2,000 years. It was an integral part of Chinese culture and had been used for the prevention and treatment of diseases as well as for health maintenance. It had a unique theoretical system characterised by taking an overall observation of the patient's physical condition and diagnosing an illness in accordance with an overall analysis of symptoms and signs as well as the patient's physical well-being. The discipline involved extensive knowledge, including doctrines such as the "four methods of diagnosis", yin and yang, and others.[2]

Hong Kong Government policy

For decades before the return of sovereignty from Britain to China in 1997, both Western medicine and TCM were widely available in Hong Kong. The colonial British government in Hong Kong used to take a non-interventionist approach towards the practice of Chinese medicine in Hong Kong: any adult of Chinese descent could register to practise in any form of Chinese medicine. The numerous TCM practitioners in Hong Kong only needed to acquire a business registration, and there was no assessment of their qualifications or standard of training. They either ran their own clinics or worked as resident medical practitioners at herbal medicine shops; professional standards varied.

Meanwhile, Western medicine and the Western healthcare system thrived under the British government, being the only form of medicine receiving formal government recognition and support. The Hong Kong Medical College was established in the late nineteenth century to provide Western medical training in the territory (it was subsequently incorporated into The University of Hong Kong). By 1999, more than 9,000 Western medicine doctors were registered in Hong Kong. More than 80 percent of primary healthcare in Hong Kong was provided by the 3,000 private general practitioners. Government-run general outpatient clinics and other registered practitioners, including TCM practitioners, provided the other 20 percent of primary care.

In the 1980s, an increased interest in TCM prompted the colonial government to appoint a Working Party on Chinese Medicine in 1989; upon the Working Party's suggestion, a Preparatory Committee on Chinese Medicine was appointed in 1995. This committee submitted a report to the government in early 1997, shortly before the handover. In his 1997 Policy Address, Chief Executive Tung Chee-hwa of the newly formed Hong Kong Special Administrative Region (HKSAR) Government called for the establishment of a sound regulatory system for TCM. He also expressed his belief in the potential of Hong Kong to develop "into an international centre for the manufacture and trading of Chinese medicine, for research, information and training in the use of Chinese medicine, and for the promotion of this approach to medical care". Subsequently, the Hong Kong Baptist University, the Chinese University of Hong Kong, and The University of Hong Kong all developed course programmes as well as research and application efforts relating to TCM.

The Preparatory Committee on Chinese Medicine continued to operate after the handover, and submitted another report to the Government in 1999, giving recommendations concerning regulation, education and research. A Chinese Medicine Ordinance was drafted as a result and was passed by the territory's Legislative Council in July 1999. One of the major consequences of the Ordinance was the setting up of a regulatory system to monitor the professional standards and conduct of Chinese medicine practitioners and their registration so as to safeguard public health and consumers' rights. The Chinese Medicine Council of Hong Kong (www.cmchk.org.hk) was established to implement the regulatory measures. However, in the same year, proposals by the private sector to build a "Chinese medicine port" — an infrastructure project to house facilities for the standardisation, production and marketing of TCM — failed to attract a subsidy from the Government.

The overseas market and safety concerns

From 1994 to 2002, according to the Hong Kong Trade Development Council, the world market for Chinese medicine had doubled to about US$23 billion. China's aging population and rising wealth contributed to that growth, but Europe (especially Germany) was the biggest market, and US consumption of Chinese medicine was also growing by 25 percent a year. However, there were obstacles hindering the rapid commercialisation of TCM products. For example, it was difficult for TCM products to fulfil the kind of stringent requirements for approval issued by Western regulation authorities in relation to pharmaceutical products. Neither the US Food and Drug Administration nor European regulators considered TCM to be proper drugs — Chinese medicine fell instead under categories such as "dietary supplements" or "health foods". One reason for this difficulty in attaining proper pharmaceutical status for TCM products was that their effect — very often a combination of the effects of many different compounds — could not be traced and affirmed using the "reduction method" of Western drug discovery process, which attempted to single out curative compounds.

The Western regulators' concern was quite valid: it had after all been the case in Hong Kong that some manufacturers had purported that their products contained TCM ingredients with healing properties. The number of warning letters issued by the HKSAR Department of Health against manufacturers making false advertising claims had increased from 178 in 1999 to 1,076 in 2001 — a five-fold increase. Some of these complaints had to do with TCM-related claims by manufacturers.

Consumers' perceptions

A focus group survey of 29 Cantonese-speaking Hong Kong patients (Cantonese being the dominant Chinese dialect in Hong Kong) was carried out in 1997 by P. T. Lam, a practising Western medical doctor who was also in the Family Medicine Unit of The University of Hong Kong's Department of Medicine.[3] The survey revealed certain perceptions towards TCM that were believed to be shared by many Hong Kong Chinese people. For example, Chinese patients tended to consider both TCM and Western medicine to have strengths and weaknesses; they chose TCM or Western medicine according to specific types of illness. TCM was used not only for chronic health problems but was also considered to be good for some milder problems such as coughs and colds. It was seen to be better for "clearing" (complete curing of) the disease, and often used as a supplement to Western medication. A patient might consult a Western medicine practitioner first for quick recovery, and would then use TCM (perhaps together with Western medicine) to "clear the root of the disease". The study also showed that Chinese patients might be taking TCM irrespective of social class and age, while, among Western populations, users of "complementary medicine" such as TCM tended to be better educated, richer and in the age range of 35 to 60.

Nin Jiom[4]

Background

The company called Nin Jiom Medicine Manufactory (HK) Ltd. was founded in 1946, but the herbal cough syrup that it produced dated back to imperial China in the mid-1800s. During the reign of the fifth emperor of the Ching Dynasty, the mother of Yang Kan, an official, was suffering from a serious lung condition. Yang consulted many doctors but to no avail — until Ip Tin-see, a famous physician for the Imperial family, offered a recipe of a cough syrup with herbs and honey, which cured Yang's mother. The Yang family later began to distribute the formulation for a small fee.

Hence the beginning of Nin Jiom's flagship product "Nin Jiom Pei Pa Koa Cough Syrup". The medicine's name sometimes also had the words "Kingto" added at the beginning, which meant "capital", that is, Beijing, where it was originally manufactured. "Nin Jiom" meant "in memory of my loving mother". "Pei Pa" was translated from the Chinese name for loquat, a major ingredient of the product, while "Koa" indicated that it was a syrupy medicine. The medicine was made from natural herbs including loquat and fritillaria, which were blended with honey extract (not counted as a medicinal ingredient). The logo of the company, in honour of the founder's filial piety, showed a man in the attire of a Ching Dynasty gentleman bringing the syrup to his mother, who was seated.

The company remained faithful to this logo into the twenty-first century, but its ownership had changed hands. Upon the Japanese invasion of China in the 1930s, which continued into the 1940s as part of the Second World War, the Yang family moved to Canton (now Guangzhou) and then to Hong Kong. After the war, the family decided to emigrate to Brazil, and sold their business in 1946 to a respected local Chinese medicine practitioner, Tse Siu-bong. Tse was still heading the company as its chairman and managing director in 2002.

Tse first produced the cough syrup in his Chinese medicine shop; formal incorporation of his Nin Jiom Company took place later in 1962. Throughout the years, Tse extended the company's range of products from just one to include other curative herbal remedies in flavoured syrups. By 2000, the company produced two flu remedies, one nutrient tonic for the elderly, a product for feminine problems and a full-body tonic. These products were grouped under the category "Scientific Traditional Chinese Medicine" (STCM). They contained extracted herbal essences, and were available as syrups or as spray-dried concentrated granules. There was also a throat-soothing herbal candy. The cough syrup itself was still the company's main product, and its four types of packaging varied from a 300 ml bottle to a convenient 15 g sachet.

By the 2000s, manufacturing of the Nin Jiom products was based primarily in Hong Kong, with about 150 workers on five floors of an industrial building that had been in use since 1984. The bulk of the manufacturing was fairly well automated, but the packing was still manual and rather labour-intensive. The company had also set up manufacturing plants in Taiwan and Singapore. The Taiwan factory was used for general production, while the Singapore plant was used for general production as well as for research and development of Chinese herbal medicine. The company always stressed that all its factories used advanced equipment and complied with internationally recognised Good Manufacturing Practice (GMP) standards.

For Nin Jiom's Hong Kong production lines, medicinal herbs were bought from a wholesaler, with whom the company had been working for decades. "The wholesaler automatically buys on quality, and we carry out quality tests here as well, so the raw materials get two-fold quality control on the way through our systems," said James Tse, production manager of the company, in an interview published in 2000.[5] The herbs for the cough syrup were grown mainly in western China. The company imported HK$17 million worth of fritillaria into Hong Kong annually by the early 2000s. The other herbs were processed in Guangxi Province and then imported into Hong Kong.

Chan Yin, director and general manager of the company, said in an interview published in 2002 that Nin Jiom's sales had been steady since its inception, because "people always get a cough or sore throat regardless of whether the economy is doing well or not".[6] The company's turnover increased from HK$170 million in 1994 to HK$290 million in 1997. It produced sales of almost HK$350 million in 2001. By 2002, Nin Jiom had built up a global sales network spanning 20 regions, including Taiwan (a major market that the company entered in the early 1960s), mainland China, Malaysia, Singapore, Thailand, Vietnam, North America and others. The company was awarded one of Hong Kong's Top Ten Brandnames in 1999 by the Chinese Manufacturers' Association of Hong Kong.

By the early 2000s, the company had been planning to set up a production plant in southern mainland China, probably in Guangdong or Guangxi. Regarding future plans, James Tse emphasised the need to expand the product range and reach out to Western customers, catering to what they wanted in the future.

Marketing strategies by the early 2000s

The company paid a great deal of attention to advertising in the early 2000s, just as it had done in the 1990s (aggressive advertising during the 1990s contributed to a significant increase in revenues). By the early 2000s, Chan could be sure that his company's products were well known among the middle-aged to older generations, but acknowledged that it needed to tap into the youth market. As a result, the company's marketing focus shifted towards presenting itself as an old, trusted product with a young image. It also adopted a marketing slogan of "Nature, Sweet and Soothing". The Herbal Candy was a product that had a better chance of appealing to young consumers. Also important were the fresh and often amusing advertising campaigns that helped the company build its brand in the minds of the public and also enhance its image as a "trendy" product that also appealed to the younger generation. Nin Jiom products were advertised on television (on which 80 percent of the advertising budget was spent, according to Tse), all-year-round radio, the Chinese press and trade discount events.

Up until the late 1990s, the company used to invite local television and film actress Carol "Dodo" Cheng to star in its commercials, in which Cheng would be shown taking the syrup in a sitting room. A notable change in the 2000s was to hire the young pop singer and actress Miriam Yeung — who had already cultivated a media persona of "the girl next door" — as its products' poster girl. Yeung, belonging to a younger generation than Cheng, appeared in a series of television commercials that showed her recommending the cough syrup in different situations such as a bicycle picnic, a flight or listening to music in a sitting room. Yeung's concert in 2000 was called "Nin Jiom Miriam Yeung My Concert 2000", with Nin Jiom as the main sponsor.

Nin Jiom also launched a series of witty advertisements in the meanwhile, such as a television commercial that began with a son sitting in a teashop with his father, who had a caged bird with him. The father then sneezed and blew all the feathers off the bird, which stuck to the son's face. Looking like he was in shock, the son then handed his father a box of Nin Jiom Cold Remedy. Chan said that the commercial attracted very positive feedback from all age groups.

Nin Jiom also had a Hong Kong Website (www.ninjiom.com) and a Canadian Website (www.njherbal.com). The latter looked like a scientific health product Website, with green and white as main colours. The slogan "Nin Jiom — one of the world's most effective cough syrups. And it's completely natural" was featured on the first text page of the site. There were instructions on dosage and introduction to the cough syrup's ingredients, explaining each of them and their properties. The Website featured a game that sought to familiarise the player with the herbs. An FAQ section answered questions such as whether people with diabetes or pregnant women should take the syrup. The Hong Kong site (available in Chinese and English versions) was more like a Website for a long-established consumer brand: there was richer corporate information, the traditional "filial piety" logo appeared consistently on the outer frame, and the main colours were red and yellow. Even the game featured in the site was about matching different stills from the Miriam Yeung commercial. Interestingly, the company advertised in the Hong Kong Website that the cough syrup could serve as a thirst quencher, a substitute for dessert syrup, an ice-cream topping, a soothing remedy for dry throats in cold weather, and even a paste for bread. There were also health tips given from a TCM perspective.

PART II: LESSONS LEARNED

Key Questions

How did Nin Jiom's products fit in an era when the Hong Kong Government and public paid more attention to TCM than before?

Nin Jiom was very well positioned in the new era. It had been a well known brand for many decades, having built up enough consumer trust to distinguish it from other purportedly TCM products with dubious claims. Although awareness of TCM had been on the rise, consumers in modern Hong Kong mostly did not know much about TCM, and there was always a safety issue with TCM products, which were usually not tested as rigorously as their Western counterparts before being launched. Therefore, brand reputation was important, and age-old TCM brands such as Nin Jiom could persuade consumers to trust it simply because of its brand name. In establishing such trust, Nin Jiom was in fact telling consumers that it had been successfully tested by generations of users, if not by stringent clinical trials.

This brand equity was complemented by the fact that Nin Jiom's flagship syrup and lozenges (herbal candy) were for treating coughs, which, according to Lam's survey, were among the illnesses that Hong Kong Chinese patients more frequently used TCM to treat. Lam's survey could in fact be seen as an assertion that Nin Jiom had been successful for so long because its products offered results that many Chinese people believed TCM could deliver effectively (or maybe the success of Nin Jiom over the years had even helped to form this belief). As an over-the-counter, mass-selling product with a word-of-mouth track record of efficacy as well as a clean safety record, Nin Jiom would not have to wait for a regulatory authority's approval before it could garner good sales for its syrup and lozenges. Its STCM products might benefit a great deal from a regulator's approval in the future, but consumer confidence in the syrup and lozenges would benefit them as affiliated products. Meanwhile, increased government regulation could drive away some of Nin Jiom's competitors, which might be advertising their products with exaggerated claims. Regulation also increased consumer confidence in TCM — the medicine was elevated from pure "folk" status to something more established, more "scientific" and better regulated. A long-trusted TCM brand such as Nin Jiom could only become even more trusted as a result.

The trends described in this case also suggest that the consumer base for TCM was expanding. Despite the lack of approval from Western regulatory bodies, the TCM market among US and European consumers was apparently growing. Lam's survey further showed that Hong Kong Chinese patients were taking TCM irrespective of social class and age. Hence younger people as well as older people would take TCM. For Nin Jiom, this meant that exploring the younger age groups in Hong Kong (its core market) was not only a necessary move to guarantee long-term brand success, but also potentially rewarding. Added to the fact that several tertiary education institutions in Hong Kong were promoting TCM education and research, the younger generation could be expected to be more aware of TCM in future years. Nin Jiom's syrup and lozenges certainly could fit in with and benefit from such as scenario.

How did the company manage to maintain its success as a TCM brand in modern Hong Kong?

Kevin Lane Keller (1998) put forward these two questions as central to reinforcing a brand over time:[7]
1. What products does the brand represent; what benefit does it supply; and what needs does it satisfy?
2. How does the brand make those products superior? What strong, favourable and unique brand associations exist in the minds of consumers?

Nin Jiom's marketing efforts attempted to answer these two questions in terms of its own brand equity plus the rising awareness of TCM in Hong Kong and the West. For example, it modernised its production methods according to "Western" standards, and adapted its packaging to modern living. The company sought to make its production facilities GMP-compliant and advertised its excellent quality control and scientific processing. As for packaging, the Nin Jiom cough syrup sachet and herbal candy, as well as the company's advertising messages that such products could be enjoyed like normal food, all represented attempts to modernise and popularise the image of the products. Nin Jiom was therefore trying to make its products satisfy more needs of modern life — not only the need to treat coughs, but also the need for a convenient, safe product for treating coughs anywhere. A combination of age-old TCM wisdom, a strong brand reputation and Western-style processing and packaging then gave the company's products a strong point of differentiation from competitors' products.

Despite much product diversification, Nin Jiom still set aside most of its advertising budget for its flagship products, on which the brand image depended. And it used pop stars to advertise those products. Significantly, Nin Jiom replaced Dodo Cheng with the younger Miriam Yeung as its poster girl in the late 1990s, a move that revealed its strategy of targeting younger age groups. The company capitalised on Yeung's "girl-next-door" image to advertise its cough syrup as a commodity that young people needed to keep by their side. The series of commercials with her were very carefully designed as vignettes in the life of a young person, and showed that the traditional cough syrup could be useful and enjoyable in such a life. Other Nin Jiom commercials were also very sophisticated and wittily tailor-made to appeal to younger audiences. The commercial about the father with a caged bird and his son in particular had the son (the younger generation) recommending Nin Jiom Cold Remedy to the father (the older generation) — with the implicit message that TCM was embraced by the young, maybe even more so than by the old.

On the overseas front, Nin Jiom's Canadian Website was decidedly more "health-food"-like, with a scientific and "green" feel about it, while its Hong Kong Website was more down-to-earth, seeking to appeal to a larger audience. This difference in marketing strategy was consistent with the difference in consumer acceptance in Hong Kong Chinese and Western societies, as described in the last section.

---

[1]   Sources: Lam, T. P. (2001), "Strengths and weaknesses of traditional Chinese medicine and Western medicine in the eyes of some Hong Kong Chinese", *Journal of Epidemiology and Community Health*, Vol. 55, No. 10, October; Chinese Medicine Council of Hong Kong, www.cmchk.org.hk/; "Chinese Medicine Practitioners", Careers Advisory Service, Labour Department, the Government of the Hong Kong Special Administrative Region, www.careers.labour.gov.hk/2000/job/htm/ei_doctor_chinese.htm/; "Modern treatment for Chinese medicine" (2002), *South China Morning Post*, 21 February; Schwartz, Susan (2002), "Consumers told to beware of companies promising to deliver medical miracles; Warnings soar over spurious health ads", *South China Morning Post*, 12 June; "Potions and profits; Traditional Chinese medicine" (2002), *The Economist*, 27 July.

[2]   The "four methods of diagnosis" included observation, auscultation and olfaction, interrogation, and pulse feeling and palpation.

[3]   Lam.

[4]   Major sources: Nin Jiom Website, www.ninjiom.com; Newson, John (2000), "Herbal Remedy", *Food: HK Food 00* Vol. 1, www.tdctrade.com/prodmag/food/fod200001cp.htm/; Hong Kong General Chamber of Commerce, "'Nin Jiom' stands the test of time" (2002), *The Bulletin*, May, www.chamber.org.hk/info/the_bulletin/may2002/ninjiom.asp/.

[5]   Newson.

[6]   Hong Kong General Chamber of Commerce.

[7]   Keller, Kevin Lane (1998), *Strategic Brand Management*, New Jersey, US: Prentice Hall, Chapter 13, pp. 502–503.

7

Towngas
Achieving Competitive Advantage through Customer Relationship Management

BENJAMIN YEN AND MONICA WONG

PART I: BACKGROUND AND ISSUES

Introduction

In April 2003, Hong Kong's Secretary for Economic Development and Labour, Stephen Ip Shu-kwan, ruled out government regulation of Towngas's rate of return or its tariff, saying that Towngas had no exclusive right or franchise over gas supply. The call for government regulation was sparked off by a report that revealed Towngas's dominant position in the piped-gas market and its high return on assets. Towngas captured 70 percent of the piped-gas market, at the expense of centralised LPG (Liquefied Petroleum Gas).[1] In spite of its dominant position in the piped-gas market, Towngas faced competition from Hong Kong Electric, China Light and Power (CLP) and other bottled-gas suppliers.

Government policies certainly helped Towngas to become one of the dominant players in the energy market, however such policies were subject to change. Government regulations were forces external to the company, so Towngas realised that it had to work on strengthening the company from within. In order to get more customers to use town gas as their energy source of choice, Towngas started a series of customer focus initiatives in the early 1990s. Flagship programmes such as the Total Quality Management and the Business Process Re-engineering programmes — known internally and respectively as Superior Quality Service (launched in 1992) and Continuing Transformation (launched in 1996) — had been catalysts for a sea change in quality attitudes and behaviour within Towngas. These programmes turned out to be the cornerstone of Towngas's Customer Relationship Management initiatives. Why did Towngas, an exclusive town gas supplier, choose CRM as a tool to strengthen its business? How did Towngas, primarily a gas production and distribution company, implement successful CRM strategies? What did it do differently to many other companies that had also invested a lot of money in CRM only to find that the system was not generating the expected returns?

Company Background

Incorporated as the Hong Kong and China Gas Company, more commonly known as Towngas, the company was Hong Kong's oldest energy supplier, established during colonial times.[2] It had been listed on the Hong Kong Stock Exchange since 1960. Its business consisted mainly of the production and distribution of gas, and the marketing of gas and appliances. It was the sole supplier of town gas and related services for 1.4 million households and businesses in Hong Kong.

Residential, commercial and industrial markets made up the three major customer groups of Towngas. They contributed 45 percent, 35 percent and three percent respectively of the company's total turnover in 2002, with the remaining 17 percent being contributed by equipment sales and other sources. These customers were looked after by major marketing departments within Towngas — Retail Marketing managed domestic household customers; Commercial & Industrial Marketing serviced restaurants, hotels, supermarkets and industrial markets, and Project Marketing was responsible for residential project bidding and account servicing for real estate development projects.

Faced with increasing competition and rising consumer expectations, Towngas launched a number of new initiatives, starting in the 1990s. Besides expanding business in the Chinese mainland, significant resources were devoted to the marketing and customer relationship-building effort.

Customer Relationship Management (CRM) at Towngas

> CRM is for the survival and success of Towngas. We make sure that our employees at all levels have the same understanding and aspiration to the core customer value. We are glad that Towngas gets recognition in the utility industry both locally and internationally for the years of hard work we put in. CRM is definitely one of the reasons contributing to Towngas's success.
>
> – Catherine Wong, Customer Relationship Manager, Towngas

CRM strategy

Every year, twelve million contacts (including telephone calls handled by the call centre) were made between the staff and customers of Towngas. They interacted for a variety of reasons — 24-hour emergency service, appliance and piping installation, meter reading, regular maintenance and safety checks, bill payments and other servicing. The call centre handled an average of more than 6,500 enquiries per day, seven days a week. The customer information database contained detailed information about the 1.4 million customers and more than two million items of equipment installed throughout Hong Kong. General user profiles, gas consumption rates, types of equipment purchased, the condition of equipment, bill-related information such as payment patterns, banking information and other data were updated every time there was an interaction between Towngas and its customers. This tremendous database formed the pillar of Towngas's CRM strategies, which in turn transformed customer service, sales and marketing strategies at Towngas. Leveraging the value contained in the customer database, the ultimate corporate goal was to achieve competitive advantages through CRM.

Customer service

In the past, Towngas's customers had to deal with multiple contact points for different service requirements. For example, there would be one number to call to open an account, and another number to arrange equipment installation. The process was streamlined in 1994 with the launch of a 24-hour Customer Service Hotline. Like every other hotline, it served as a one-stop-shop, but what differentiated this one from the competition was the five-language human answering feature. The multi-language answering was an added benefit to many Towngas customers, who relied upon their Filipino or Indonesian domestic helpers to handle household chores. Human answering was not only preferable to pre-recorded messages, it also gave Towngas an opportunity to actively collect immediate feedback from customers while they were on the telephone line.

Customer contact did not end with the call; in fact, it was just the beginning. According to the customer's need, relevant departments would follow up with appropriate action. For services that required on-site procedures, field servers would visit the households. After each field visit, more detailed information regarding gas consumption patterns, equipment type and conditions would be collected. More comprehensive feedback was usually collected on these occasions. In 1993, Towngas also launched the Customer Focus Team (CFT) Programme. The CFTs were formed by senior representatives of various departments. The teams visited residential estates and obtained direct and first-hand information and feedback from customers. Other channels of customer interaction included the customer centres and the Internet. For commercial and industrial customers, an account manager would usually be the first point of contact, except in the case of emergencies.

The driving reason behind these customer service initiatives was to increase customer satisfaction. Customers were expected to derive some sense of value, satisfaction and loyalty through each and every interaction point, therefore Towngas stressed a consistent quality of service delivery across all contact points. The only way to achieve this consistency was to ensure that the whole company shared the same goal.

In order to benchmark performance against the common goal, Towngas conducted a monthly telephone survey to gauge the level of customer satisfaction. A more comprehensive survey was done yearly to measure customers' overall perceptions of value in relation to Towngas's service.

Sales and marketing strategies

The CRM strategy at Towngas had an influential role in the formulation of sales and marketing strategies, which revolved around having satisfied customers in order to generate more business. With up-to-date customer information, detailed market analyses were carried out to refine products and services to better suit the needs of different market segments.

One example of a marketing strategy stemming from CRM was a new concept store that targeted a more sophisticated segment of customers. Towngas Avenue, which was opened in 2001 in Tsim Sha Tsui, presented a lifestyle concept store selling contemporary gas appliances and other kitchen and bathroom accessories. There was also a cafém equipped with LCD panels showing live action from the kitchen, a recipe-on-request service and a library of cookbooks on display. Towngas Avenue was designed to tap into the segment of high-income customers who were possibly not frequent users of gas at home because of their hectic lifestyle, but who were in constant pursuit of a quality lifestyle. Towngas Avenue was very different from the traditional customer centre, which was nothing more than a showroom with a bill-payment counter. The first store was a huge success, giving Towngas the opportunity to cross-sell and encourage the use of town gas. A second store was opened in Causeway Bay the following year. Other lifestyle-related products included the Towngas/Bank of East Asia joint credit card, and the www.iCare.com.hk portal providing Internet services and selling household merchandise. Towngas's marketing strategy was summed up in a quote in the 2002 Annual Report:

> Promoting gas as a lifestyle choice and versatile energy source is enhancing the company's bottom line.

Internal Alignment

> An innovative mix of marketing and policy strategies impacted bottom line profits last year, and continued to help position gas as an energy source of choice rather than just a commodity of necessity.
>
> – Towngas Corporate Information Booklet, 2002

Despite the proven success with lifestyle marketing, the core business of Towngas remained the production and distribution of gas. Eighty-three percent of its total turnover came from gas sales and 40 percent of its costs were attributable to fuel costs.[3] The company dealt with pipelines and gas, and had previously been very much engineering-focused. When Towngas shifted its focus from an engineering focus to a customer and market focus, it required a corporate-wide culture change. How did the management lead the company through this transition?

Corporate culture change

Mindsets and behaviours could not be changed overnight. The Customer Relationship Management at Towngas could be traced back to the introduction of the Total Quality Management (TQM) concept in 1992. A Superior Quality Service (SQS) group was formed. Small teams of Quality Service Committees were set up in almost every department, each consisting of seven or eight full-time seconded staff. The teams were chartered to identify opportunities for constant improvement. The initiatives engaged employees at all levels to fine-tune processes and procedures in order to enhance the new corporate direction. SQS evolved into the more top-down initiative of Continuous Transformation (CT) in 1996. CT was a continuous improvement group responsible for corporate-wide re-engineering and re-structuring to further the customer-oriented culture of the company. The CT unit was an independent unit with a direct reporting line to the Managing Director. SQS continued to function within CT and the corporate strategies and policies formulated would then be communicated through the "strategy ambassadors" to different departments within the organisation.

The Executive Committee (ECM)[4] was established to put in place an effective management system within Towngas. ECM mapped out the key management focus (KMF) on various aspects and customer value was one of those key focuses. The ECM initiatives culminated in a major organisational restructuring in 1998. Under the ECM, 22 department managers were in charge of different functions and the formulation of functional objectives and tactics, while the section managers were responsible for the implementation of the action plans. Furthermore, Towngas's organisational structure was flattened, reducing the former seven-layer hierarchy to four layers in order to facilitate more direct and effective communication between front-line staff and department managers. Customers were able to talk to the right person and get their problems resolved more efficiently. With empowerment as a common practice, front-line staff could make sensible decisions to take the extra step in delighting customers.

The Towngas Shared Values model

Driven by the goal of delivering customer value, Towngas's quality programmes were designed to fulfil the Towngas Shared Values, a concept that addressed the needs of the company's main stakeholders, namely customers, shareholders and employees, and ensured that their interests were well balanced. The aim was to achieve sustainable business growth through leadership at all levels, maintaining a strong central focus on customers, and offering products and services that delivered high customer value.

The customer value formula

A customer value formula was set for all employees to follow, and the corporate-wide target was to maximise this value through improving quality and/or service and reducing cost and/or lead-times. The formula was simple and easy to understand, and represented ways to achieve a clear and measurable goal. Customer value would be achieved through improving quality in ways such as providing a wider choice of products and services, increasing first-time completion of tasks and maximising the success rate. At the same time, employees had to strive to reduce lead-times and costs to customers by improving productivity.

$$\text{customer value} = \frac{\text{quality} \times \text{service}}{\text{lead time} \times \text{cost}}$$

To infuse all employees with the concept of customer value, a series of training programmes in the areas of customer service concepts and practice was carried out and widely promoted at all levels. The result was the alignment of corporate culture and value, shifting from a traditional utility company mindset to a market and customer focus, and thus a more competitive organisation.

Towngas invested all these resources in changing the corporate value because the management believed that for the customer relationship management to be successful, the corporate culture needed to be customer-centric. In short, customer relationship management (CRM) started with every employee's ingrained concept of customer service.

Outcomes of the Investment in CRM

> The proactive initiatives, backed by our hallmark reputation for reliability and service, were powerful consumer acquisition and retention.
>
> – Towngas Annual Report, 2002

Towngas's investment in CRM continued to pay off. Despite a slow-down in property developments and the Government's decision to stop selling Home Ownership Scheme flats, the number of Towngas's residential customers grew by 4.5 percent during 2002. With weak industrial and commercial sectors, the growth was 0.3 percent. The overall turnover, gas sales and profitability showed a steady upward trend despite the economic downturn and fierce competition.

At the same time, Towngas's published service commitments and targets were being met or exceeded. According to Towngas, 1,334 complimentary letters were received in 2002, five times more than the 286 letters received in 1999. During the same period, the number of complaint letters dropped from 48 to 34. Towngas's CRM effort was also recognised by the Hong Kong Retail Management Association, which selected Towngas as the winner for the 2002 Customer Service Award. The Customer Satisfaction ratings had surged since 1999, and surging together with it was employee productivity.

The Next Step

Towngas was planning to upgrade the customer information system (CIS) into part of a larger operational system that could support the whole company. The planned roll-out date was May 2004. Looking back at the first initiatives of TQM introduced in 1992 and the subsequent re-restructuring and business process re-engineering in 1998, Towngas had waited several years before implementing a comprehensive system that encompassed CRM. So why didn't Towngas install the system earlier? What were the implications for companies that were planning to implement CRM?

PART II: LESSONS LEARNED

What Is CRM?

CRM is about the relationship between companies and their customers, with each contributing to and receiving something from the relationship. From the customer perspective, CRM is about good (i.e., affordable, reliable, personable, trustworthy and responsive) customer service. The challenge from the corporate perspective is to provide customers with value that meets their expectations, and to gain revenue from the relationship. The goals are to keep the customer's business and to dissuade the customer from participating in exchanges that are unprofitable to the company.[5] In a nutshell, CRM from the corporate perspective is primarily about pro-actively creating a positive experience for profitable customers so that they keep coming back.

Why Is It Important to Manage Customer Relationships?

As illustrated in the Towngas example, happy customers have a direct impact on a company's bottom line. Firstly, a happy and satisfied customer is much more likely to make repeat purchases, thereby increasing sales. Secondly, more tailored sales and marketing strategies are possible if the company has a better understanding of its customers. Thirdly, customer satisfaction is the key to customer retention. A highly satisfied customer stays loyal for longer, buys more as the company introduces new products, talks favourably about the company and its products, pays less attention to competing brands and advertising, is less sensitive to price, offers product or service ideas to the company and costs less to serve than new customers because transactions are made routine.

More and more companies are recognising the importance of satisfying and retaining current customers, because it has been shown that:

- Acquiring new customers can cost five times more than satisfying and retaining current customers. It requires a great deal of effort to induce satisfied customers to switch away from their current suppliers.
- The average company loses 10 percent of its customers each year.
- A five percent reduction in the customer defection rate can increase profits by 25 percent to 85 percent, depending on the industry.
- The customer profit rate is inclined to increase over the life of the retained customer.[6]

Finally, in a service company, there seems to be a correlation between happy customers and happy employees. As observed in the Towngas example, employees' productivity surged together with customer satisfaction ratings.

In summary, for Towngas, managing customer relationships well had a direct impact on the profitability of the company.

The CRM System

The CRM strategy discussed in the case was only part of what made up a complete CRM system. Many CRM textbooks feature a graphic showing a web of stakeholders related to CRM, like the one shown in Figure 1:[7]

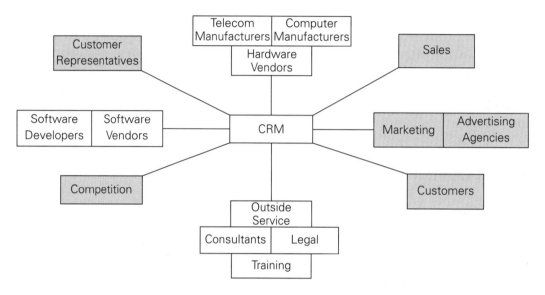

Figure 1   CRM Stakeholders

The shaded areas represent the issues that were discussed in this case, the non-shaded areas represent "plug-in" parts of CRM that are usually acquired from vendors. All of these elements are equally important for the success of a CRM system, however the most important issue of all, the one element that can make or break the CRM, is "Internal Alignment". This is also the most time-consuming one to build. CRM failures are mostly due to a lack of organisational support. Therefore, it is no coincidence that Towngas thrived on Customer Relationship Management. In fact, even before its comprehensive CRM system is due to be installed (in 2004), Towngas has already been reaping the benefits of the "people" part of its CRM system.

The Success Factors of Towngas's CRM System

A common mistake committed by many companies when they launch their CRM effort is the excessive emphasis and attention paid to the CRM software — the system that allows companies to plan and analyse marketing campaigns, to identify sales leads and to manage their customer contacts and call centres. This is no doubt a pillar of CRM, but it is not the whole story. A failure to establish clear business goals before launching a CRM effort is the most common and important source of problems. Misaligned incentives undermine the CRM initiatives. People do things only if they believe that that course of action serves their best interests. If incentives are not in place, as is the case in some companies, front-line users will bypass the CRM system altogether. Incentives for shared goals, such as an increase in customer satisfaction or spending, are therefore essential. Another important diagnostic question is whether senior executives are backing the initiative.

The key to success is to step back and do what all the best practitioners do long before installing CRM: articulate goals; narrow the focus to meet them and then provide the necessary organisational and technological support. Only then can a company expect to see a return on its investment in CRM.[8]

Towngas provided an example of how to put these theories into practice. The senior management was fully in support of CRM and the company did not attribute the success of CRM solely to the sophisticated information system. It put a lot of emphasis on creating a corporate culture of customer value. Measurable goals were set for employees at all levels. The performance of employees was tied-in with their remuneration and was benchmarked against the goal. New and higher targets were constantly established for achieved goals to ensure continuous improvement.

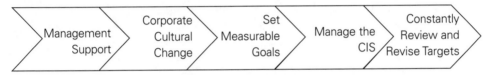

Figure 2   The Success Factors of Towngas's CRM System

Conclusion

Despite its dominant position, Towngas invested a lot of resources in developing a CRM system, in order to ensure its long-term competitiveness. Good CRM software can influence how much customers spend and how loyal they remain. Some companies using CRM programmes have reported double-digit gains in revenues, customer satisfaction and employee productivity, as illustrated in the case of Towngas. Some companies have also achieved dramatic savings in customer acquisition costs. Notwithstanding the success stories, CRM has also proved a disappointment to many. The differing results stem from the "people" side of the CRM system. As illustrated in the Towngas example, the success of a CRM strategy depends on the corporate-wide value alignment and the commitment of employees, especially front-line staff within an organisation. It took Towngas almost a decade to change its corporate culture from an "engineering" focus to a "customer-oriented" focus. SMEs are in an advantageous position as they are smaller, more flexible and therefore more conducive to corporate culture alignment.

We have examined the benefits of CRM for a company, and how potentially costly the failure of CRM can be. Successful CRM enhances a company's competitive advantage, which is why many companies have been interested in CRM. Unfortunately, many people mistake the CRM software system for the CRM strategy. The software system is just a tool, but if the culture and practices of a company do not support its stated goals then the remedy must be: align internal aspirations, scale back the scope of CRM during take-off and build it on the foundation of corporate-wide shared values. This takes time but the investment pays off in the long term.

1   Towngas supplies piped naphtha gas.

2   Towngas was founded in England in 1862 and started supplying town gas to Hong Kong in 1864.

3   The remaining 17 percent of total turnover came from equipment sales and other sources.

4   The ECM consisted of the Managing Director and heads of Finance and Administration, Marketing and Customer Service, Production, Network, Information Technology, Quality and Human Resources.

5   Wiley, J. (2002). *Essentials of CRM: A Guide to Customer Relationship Management*. New York: John Wiley & Sons, p. 157.

6   Kotler, P. (1999), *Marketing Management, The Millennium Edition*, p. 46–49.

7   Adapted from Wiley, J. (2002), *Essentials of CRM: A Guide to Customer Relationship Management*, New York: John Wiley & Sons, p. 157.

8   Ebner, M., Hu, A., Levitt, D., McCrory, J. (2002), "How to rescue CRM", *McKinsey Quarterly*, 2002, Number 4, Technology.

8

Lee Kum Kee
Old Company, Modern Marketing Strategy[1]

BENNETT YIM AND VINCENT MAK

PART I: BACKGROUND AND ISSUES

Introduction

We are a very old company, but we recognise that our customers are changing, so we continually develop new products to reflect this.
— David Lee, managing director, Lee Kum Kee Company[2]

The problem with a lot of family-controlled local brands that have a long history behind them is that it's very easy to become old and run out of steam.
— Antony Chow, vice-president for Greater China, RSCG (an advertising agency)[3]

The sauce company Lee Kum Kee, one of the best known Hong Kong brands, certainly did not have the problem mentioned above, although it did have a long history that began in 1888, and was run by the same family through four generations. The company was founded by Lee Kam Sheung as a small oyster-sauce manufacturer in Guangdong Province, China. It relocated to Macau in the early 1900s, moved once more to Hong Kong after the Second World War, and was based there in the decades afterwards. Lee Kum Kee was already expanding beyond the Guangdong — Macau — Hong Kong distribution network in the 1920s to North America, when it was also making shrimp paste. In the 1970s and 1980s, after the torch passed to third-generation leader Lee Man-tat, there was a diversification of geographical markets as well as products at a very quick pace. Lee Man-tat's sons, who were educated in the West, inherited the leadership from their father in the 1990s, and the pace of modernisation and diversification continued while the company's marketing strategy remained as vigorous and adaptable as ever. The company also overcame a consumer-confidence crisis — called 3-MCPD crisis — in the late 1990s and early 2000s, and continued to thrive. By early 2003, Lee Kum Kee had already developed more than 200 sauces. Its distribution network covered 60 countries in five continents, and its products were available in more than 80 countries. What lessons about strategic brand management can we learn from the way Lee Kum Kee developed, maintained and expanded the reach of its products over a whole century? What lessons about crisis management does the company's handling of the 3-MCPD crisis offer?

Early History[4]

Lee Kam-sheung was born in 1868 in Qibao, a village in Xinhui, Guangdong Province, China. Threat from local gangsters forced him to leave his farming life and move to a small island called Nam Shui in the same province, where oysters were abundant. Lee opened a small restaurant there, often using oysters as stock for soups. One day, while cooking oysters, he absent-mindedly walked away for a long time, so that when he remembered the oysters and looked at the soup, it had already become a thick, strongly aromatic liquid, which he found delicious. Hence the birth of Lee's oyster sauce, which he began producing under the brand name of Lee Kum Kee in 1888 ("Kee" meaning "company" in local Cantonese). In 1902, a fire destroyed Lee Kam-sheung's manufacturing plant, and he moved to nearby Macau, where oysters were also abundant. He began to sell shrimp paste as well as oyster sauce, and his business soon covered Guangdong, Macau and Hong Kong.

Of Lee Kam-sheung's three sons and two daughters, the eldest son died young, and the family business passed to his two remaining sons, Lee Shiu-tang and Lee Shiu-nan. The former was responsible for marketing while the latter took up product quality and improvements to production procedures. The company's products were already selling successfully among the Chinese immigrant population in North American cities at that time.

The company opened a Hong Kong branch in 1932 while expanding to meet the increasing demands of overseas markets. In 1946, after the Second World War, the two brothers moved their headquarters to Hong Kong, where the prospering economic climate was more conducive to businesses.

The 1970s and 1980s[5]

Lee Man-tat, son of Lee Shiu-tang, took over as company chairman in 1972, taking the company to new heights. His era was marked by agile and flexible marketing; production enhancements through the automation and modernisation of production techniques; further expansion of geographical markets and sales networks, and large-scale diversification of sauce products. One of Lee Man-tat's important early moves was to launch a new brand called Panda Oyster Sauce, capturing the hype caused by the Chinese government's gift of a pair of pandas to US President Richard Nixon during his visit to China in 1971. The Panda brand was created as a result of slow growth in the company's traditional product, premium oyster sauce, which was too expensive for many families. Panda Oyster Sauce was reasonably priced and was expected to have stronger market penetration power. The brand, however, did not secure a good foothold at once, but after some effective marketing efforts it became a hit and outperformed the old labels.

Lee Man-tat learned from the success of the Panda brand that he needed to cater to different market segments. He soon launched a string of new products and brands at different prices and for different tastes, such as chilli sauce, sweet and sour sauce, chicken marinade and curry sauce. These products did well particularly in North American Chinese restaurants.

In 1980, the company, which was still quite small, with only 25 staff, began exploring the Mainland Chinese market. It was extremely difficult for them at the start, as they knew little about the market. Everything they exported to the Mainland was wrong, from the products themselves to the packaging and prices, according to Lee Man-tat's son Eddy Lee Wai-man, who joined the company in 1980.[6] The company then reduced the number of products for the Mainland market from 50 to 15, in order to focus its promotional efforts. The products gradually became well-received in the Mainland, although delayed payment from retailers emerged as a problem.

In the 1980s, Lee Man-tat's four sons — Eddy, David, Charlie and Sammy — returned with different US degrees to Hong Kong within a couple of years of each other and joined the company as interns.[7] They all started their stints with low-level duties but as their managerial involvement increased, they began to introduce more and more new concepts from the West. When Lee Kum Kee celebrated its first 100 years in 1988, the company changed its logo to symbolise its vision of "building a cultural bridge between East and West with our sauce products".[8]

Major Events and Developments in the 1990s and Early 2000s

The company underwent still greater changes after the 1980s. As Eddy Lee took on more and more leadership responsibility, becoming managing director and then chairman of the group, he and his brothers introduced new initiatives that combined the flexible strategic approach of their father with Western business thinking. Quality and modernised branding were emphasised, as was an up-to-date information technology system.

New products, brand building and market expansion

In 1992, the company launched a super premium gourmet sauce called XO sauce, which was made from dried scallop, ham and dried shrimp, and had a variety of applications in noodles, porridge, dim sum, sushi, stir fry dishes and other dishes. The sauce's popularity was a great triumph for the company. The sauce was later diversified into additional variants such as XO Seafood Sauce and Premium XO Sauce with Abalone.

In 1994, the company started selling soy sauce, a generic product for which there were established competitors. As a result, sales were slow at the beginning.[9] The company then observed that, in most homes, the amount of soy sauce used for dipping was fairly low, both in frequency and in volume. For the Hong Kong market, however, steamed fish was popular among the Chinese, and housewives wanted to make their home-cooked steamed fish taste like those in the restaurants. Lee Kum Kee saw that it could develop a soy sauce that was sweeter than normal soy sauce, specifically for seafood. The strategy led to success, and the company went on to develop variants including chilli soy sauce, sweet soy sauce, salt-reduced soy sauce, mushroom-flavoured dark/light soy sauces, etc.

Lee Kum Kee did not invest significantly in its brand until the early 1990s.[10] In 1994, it scrapped its old product labels — as David Lee himself said, the old product labels were boring to him.[11] The arch of the company logo became a "Golden Plaque" that implied a guarantee of product quality, while a detail of the traditional Chinese window frame at the border of the plaque reflected the company's Hong Kong heritage.

By the late 1990s, the company aimed to use its name and history in Asia and the many Chinese communities around the world to penetrate the general US and European household market.[12] On the industry side, the company capitalised on its status as a premier Asian food brand to expand its network of retailers, restaurateurs and other manufacturers in the West. Most importantly, to make its products even more consumer-friendly and to appeal to young families that did not wish to spend too much time on cooking, the company continuously widened its product line. Examples included single-use sauce packets with instructions on how to prepare specific dishes, and a larger variety of ready-made sauces that could be used with a range of ingredients. Even its oyster sauce products came in variants such as Premium, Panda Brand, Choy Sun, Vegetarian and others with added dried scallops and mushrooms.

In 1998, the company launched its first five varieties of sauce packets; in the following year, it added 11 more to include dishes such as sweet-and-sour fish, black-bean chicken and spicy tofu. These lines of products became popular in Asia and were then introduced to the West. Throughout the process of geographical diversification, for new as well as old products, the company observed the different needs of different regional markets. As David Lee said:[13]

> We have different packaging and tastes to suit different markets, so a chilli product in Japan will come in smaller bottles and be sweeter and less thick, for instance, than it would be in Hong Kong.

Development in China[14]

Lee Kum Kee built its first factory in China in 1990; the plant was located in the southern province of Guangdong. Its sales expansion also started with the Guangdong Province but gradually moved north; in 1998, the company began to sell its products in Beijing. In 2002, the company's sales in Beijing had already increased more than 10-fold since it entered the market there, while its sales in Guangdong were also growing at a double-digit annual rate. The company had three factories in the Guangdong Province and was considering setting up new ones in northern China.

Lee Kum Kee was turning its market development focus back from overseas to the Mainland in the early 2000s. The potential for the development of this obviously huge market could also be seen in the fact that, of the 200-odd products of Lee Kum Kee, only about 60 were sold in the Mainland. As with other markets, Lee Kum Kee was sensitive about different customers' tastes, so that a Lee Kum Kee sauce in Beijing might taste a little different from a similarly named sauce in Shanghai. By 2002, the company had more than 500 distribution networks in the Mainland, and was ranked fourth in total sales in the sauce market, but it had not yet expanded fully into secondary cities in provinces such as Szechuan and Guangxi. In an interview in 2002, Eddy Lee said it would be great if Lee Kum Kee could secure one percent of the Mainland market, which was very fragmented.

IT development

Lee Kum Kee was also active in implementing information technology strategies such as Enterprise Resource Planning and other gradual improvements in productivity, supply chain management and customer relations management.[15] The company first launched a Website in 1996. The site was gradually improved so that, when it was relaunched in early 2001, it featured recipes and a communication platform between registered members and the company, allowing members to share food tips or culinary ideas with each other and with the company. The company aimed for convenience, communication and customer needs instead of simple hard-selling of products in this design. In addition, the Website was available in English, traditional Chinese, simplified Chinese, Japanese and Korean, and there were specialised versions for New Zealand/Australia and Taiwan.

Setback in the property market

By 1994, when the company scored a major success with the XO sauce, it also expanded into new businesses, such as a packaging concern, a trucking fleet, health products and even property. But the company's property investments were disappointing as the Hong Kong property market crumbled in 1998, and David Lee himself admitted that there was "so much more potential in the things we do well".[16]

The 3-MCPD crisis[17]

In the late 1990s and early 2000s, the company was beset by the 3-MCPD crisis. In 1999, the United Kingdom's Food Standards Agency (FSA) issued a report with a directive that contaminants used in soy sauce should be reduced. The FSA found in late 1999 that Lee Kum Kee was one of several producers whose sauces had levels of two chemicals — 3-MCPD (3-monochloropropane) and a derivative, 1,3-DCP (1,3-dichloropropanol) — in excess of planned European Commission (EC) standards, which were among the most stringent in the world. The standards were due to be enforced in April 2002. The danger of these chemicals to humans had not been conclusively proven, but choloropropane had been linked to cancer in rats, and the agency said they occurred as contaminants in some brands of soy and other sauces in sufficient quantities to harm long-term users. The report and findings had such a negative media effect as to lead London's major tabloid The Sun to publish a headline that read "Chinese food can kill you", and related Hong Kong producers found themselves in trouble.

Eddy Lee said that his company responded by spending between US$130,000 and US$260,000 to upgrade its manufacturing processes, so that the chemicals were reduced to non-detectable levels. However, when the FSA conducted another survey in 2001, it discovered that 22 brands, including five owned by Lee Kum Kee, still exceeded the limit. In June 2001, it issued another warning against those products, sparking a crisis in consumer confidence that spread to regions such as Australia, Singapore, Egypt and South America. Eddy Lee then claimed that the FSA had used as samples old Lee Kum Kee products made before the company had changed its manufacturing processes. He also argued that a recall of the old goods was not necessary because what happened was not a typical food crisis, in which a producer had to remove a batch of bad products from the shelves.

A month after the release of the second FSA findings, the agency issued another statement clearing Lee Kum Kee's name, after the company produced laboratory certificates showing that its new products no longer contained the contaminants. At the same time, the company started a crisis-control campaign. It hired a public relations consultancy, placed advertisements in the media, set up hotlines for consumers, and contacted government food authorities around the world. As Eddy Lee commented: "This type of issue is like a bushfire: if you do not put it out, it might come back again." Even the company Website greeted visitors with a pop-up window detailing international food authorities that "recognised" its products. According to Eddy Lee, the crisis caused the company's sales to plunge for a short time, immediately after the agency issued its (presumably second) warning. The crisis had a longer-term negative effect on Lee Kum Kee's corporate image, and more than a year later, the press was still asking the company questions about product safety.

Achievements and accolades

Lee Kum Kee's worldwide revenue, which increased some 15-fold from the early 80s to the mid-90s, was more than US$100 million by 1994, and was doubling every three years by the late 1990s, according to David Lee.[18] The company's turnover was expected to reach several hundred million US dollars by the early 2000s.[19] The biggest portion of revenues by 1996 came predictably from Asia, and Southeast Asia, China, Taiwan and North Asia, especially Japan, which showed the biggest growth.[20] In Japan, after years of effort, the company had by 2002 conquered 80 percent of the middle to upper end of the Chinese restaurant market; sales of Lee Kum Kee sauces as a whole were ranked second in the Japanese retail market, with a market share of some 27 percent.[21] By early 2003, the company had already developed more than 200 sauces. Its distribution network covered 60 countries in five continents, and its products were available in more than 80 countries.[22] The biggest market at that time had become the United States, followed by China.[23] That did not mean that the company's prestige had waned in its old base. By 2002, according to ACNielsen's market research, Lee Kum Kee's premium brand oyster sauce had an 80 percent market penetration rate among similar products in Hong Kong — almost every family had one bottle.[24] Lee Kum Kee's market share in the North American oyster sauce market was also more than 85 percent during the same period.[25]

Among the many awards and high rankings that Lee Kum Kee gained in the decade, one was the acknowledgement of Lee Man-tat as one of Hong Kong's 100 most influential people by the territory's Next Magazine in 1997 (in fact, his presence was still felt by 2002 as the patriarch and consultant of the company). The brand-management consultancy Interbrand named his company the fourth-best non-Japanese Asian brand in 1999.[26] Lee Kum Kee was recognised as among the top 20 Hong Kong companies in 2001.[27]

PART II: LESSONS LEARNED

There is a great deal about marketing, managing operations, maintaining success and overcoming difficulties that SMEs can learn from the many episodes in the long history of Lee Kum Kee. Here the discussion follows two veins: strategic brand management and crisis management.

Strategic Brand Management

What lessons about strategic brand management can we learn from the way Lee Kum Kee developed, maintained and expanded the reach of its products over a whole century?

a.   Consistent core values that responded to customers' needs
The Lee Kum Kee brand had always represented sauces, although the number and type of sauces that it represented increased throughout its history. From the time when Lee Kum Kee's founder discovered the savoury oyster sauce that was to start his business, the company had remained mainly a sauce producer and focused on that, with only relatively minor distractions in the 1990s. Before the 1970s, the brand represented only oyster sauce and shrimp paste. Afterwards, its product range diversified, but the brand remained the provider of pre-blended sauces that speeded up and improved cooking — the core benefit that the brand supplied. This core value had not changed but was only reinforced by the development of many products that were customised in terms of pricing, taste and packaging. These included oyster sauce in affordable price (the Panda brand), special flavour soy sauce and single-use sauce packets — which reflected the needs of young families that did not have much time for cooking. The triumph of the versatile XO sauce was another significant example. Marketing support to the products had always been strong, from emphasis on the right brand logos to sophisticated Websites with recipes and interactivity. It can therefore be seen that, despite the myriad products and marketing schemes that Lee Kum Kee employed in the 1990s and early 2000s, the company kept close to maintaining benefits that it had supplied to customers for decades.

If a product is beneficial to customers, it must have satisfied some of their needs. Lee Kum Kee's sauces, in terms of speed and flavour, generally met the needs of domestic households that did not have the time, resources or expertise to cook gourmet food using primary ingredients. In addition, early leaders of the company found success partly from their discovery of the needs of overseas Chinese markets. Chinese restaurants and households in the West often found it difficult to buy the right ingredients to cook Chinese food. Therefore, very early on, Lee Kum Kee had branded itself as a provider of sauces that had all the right ingredients in the right proportions, and that were easily available (the company had always paid attention to distribution) in clean, neat packaging. This was why the company did so well overseas. It became such an expert in accommodating the needs of overseas markets that even the packaging and sizes of the bottles differed according to geographical market segments. Its first attempt at entering the Mainland market, when it pushed forward too many products with too little understanding of consumer needs, led to failure; it was only after the company reduced the number of products and focused promotional efforts on them that it achieved success in sales.

It can therefore be seen that Lee Kum Kee had always responded to customers' need for sauces; the manifestation of that need had changed and diversified over space and time, and the company adapted its products and their particular benefits accordingly. Although the company underwent many modernising changes over the decades, the changes served only to maintain, sharpen and refine its strategic direction and brand message, so that the representation of both of them was kept up to date.

b. Successful segmentation strategy

Much of the successful brand management of Lee Kum Kee was attributable to the company's success in product segmentation — the development of different types of products from the initial oyster sauce. The rationale behind such a process was that any single product might not fulfil the needs of every customer, so a diversification of products was needed in order to reach more customers. However, it was important not to abuse such segmentation by introducing new products that were inconsistent or remote from the company's brand image, or that were too similar to the core products of other brands. The first condition meant that brand image could have been "diluted", leading to an overall deterioration of brand perception among customers.

The dilemma between growing business through developing new brands or building on existing ones is a long-standing issue for many companies. One example is the US-based Hershey Foods Corp., which was best known for its chocolate snacks, and which dominated the US chocolate candy business by 2003. However, despite attempts over the years of diversification, Hershey remained a dominating player only in candy products. One observer's comment about Richard H. Lenny, Hershey's CEO, in 2003, illustrated the problem:

> Rather than launching new brands, which are expensive and destined to fail ... Lenny is focusing more time, people, and money on power brands and smartly extending them.
> – Gary M. Stibel, founder, New England Consulting Group[28]

As described previously, the story of Lee Kum Kee illustrated the benefits of segmentation with many examples. The company, throughout its long history, had been treading more or less safely but progressively along the tightrope of segmentation. Lee Kum Kee had diversified enormously from just one oyster sauce, but it also made sure that it stuck almost exclusively to cooking-related sauce products (apart from individual exceptions such as dabbling in property), so it had strayed hardly at all from its core brand. There were occasional setbacks, though, such as the launching of a soy sauce, which was the core product of some other established brands. Lee Kum Kee initially failed in the exercise and only gained success after developing a special soy sauce for steamed fish — because the product filled a niche market that was not filled by its competitors.

c. Strong and unique brand association

Lee Kum Kee's products could be divided into two types that established their special appeal to consumers in opposite ways. The first type included the oyster sauces and the XO sauces, which were marketed as useful for cooking many different dishes. The company had managed to make these products stand out from competing products in terms of either taste (XO sauces and premium oyster sauce) or price (Panda oyster sauce). The second type was the tailor-made sauces for cooking particular dishes, such as a sauce packet for sweet-and-sour fish. Lee Kum Kee had made these products very unique, and with their convenience and flavour they were welcomed by customers. The types of products could overlap, such as an oyster sauce with special flavours. An important example of Lee Kum

Kee's attention to product differentiation was the development of its soy sauce in the mid-1990s: when the company's general-purpose soy sauce could not gain a foothold in the market, it revised the product into a specific-purpose one for steamed fish. The company thus achieved product differentiation for its soya sauce in relation to its competitors' more general-purpose products.

Therefore, in the early 2000s, customers knew Lee Kum Kee as a producer of an age-old, trusted brand of oyster sauce and a versatile range of other sauces, many of which were unique in the market or noted for attentively addressing consumers' needs. This image was more prominent in overseas markets, where Chinese cooking ingredients were not so conveniently available, so immigrant Chinese or Chinese restaurants would often turn to Lee Kum Kee for its reliable sauces.

From the early 1990s, Lee Kum Kee had also been working hard on quality guarantees in order to strengthen the superiority of its products. Even the company logo was modified to reflect the emphasis on quality, which was another factor that created a superior brand image.

After the 3-MCPD crisis, the company was at pains to show the world the quality of its products and its accredited manufacturing processes. This was one aspect of the corporate brand image to which Lee Kum Kee had paid relatively little attention throughout its long history, but the company was quick to make amends for its mistakes.

Crisis Management

What lessons does the company's handling of the 3-MCPD crisis offer?

The crisis was a severe trial on consumer confidence in the company. Being mentioned in relation to press reports that blared out "Chinese food can kill you" was no trivial matter, and the crisis did lead to plunging sales in the short term. In the longer term, the press was still asking the company questions about product safety, even a year after the crisis.

The company responded promptly and very seriously in order to control the crisis. As Eddy Lee said: "This type of issue is like a bushfire: if you do not put it out, it might come back again." His comments were far-sighted: there were cases when failure or negligence in relation to crisis management had severely damaged a brand, while successful crisis management had enabled a brand to bounce back quickly from a serious crisis (see Appendix 1).

Kevin Lane Keller (1998) gave this advice about crisis management:[29]

> Marketing managers must assume that at some point in time, some kind of brand crisis will arise. In general, the more that brand equity and a strong corporate image has been established — especially with respect to corporate credibility and trustworthiness — the more likely it is that the firm can weather the storm. Careful preparation and a well-managed crisis management program, however, [are] also critical. The two keys to effectively managing a crisis [are] that the response by the firm is seen by consumers as both swift and sincere.

Keller went on to point out that, concerning swiftness, the longer it takes a firm to respond to a marketing crisis, the more likely it is that consumers will form negative impressions through media coverage or word-of-mouth. Consumers may even permanently switch to alternative brands if the brand in question does not react swiftly enough. Keller also states the importance of sincerity: the more sincere the response by the firm, the less likely it is that consumers will form negative perceptions of the firm's behaviour. The firm must be ready to acknowledge publicly the severity of the impact on consumers and to display a willingness to take whatever steps are necessary and feasible to resolve the crisis.

At the time of the 3-MCPD crisis, Lee Kum Kee already had a good deal of consumer loyalty, though that was largely limited to Chinese circles. The company had also existed for more than 100 years, and had a good track record. So the company started off at the beginning of the crisis with good brand equity. But it was not smug because of that. When the first FSA report came out in 1999, Lee Kum Kee did not act arrogantly or defensively (for instance by declaring that 3-MCPD had not been proven to be harmful to humans, and by refusing to carry out any follow-up action). Instead, the company spent huge sums to upgrade its manufacturing facilities in order to reduce the 3-MCPD content of its products to non-detectable levels.

The real crisis came after the 2001 FSA warning, which stated that some Lee Kum Kee products were still found to contain 3-MCPD. The consumer confidence crisis concerned not only the quality of the products but also Lee Kum Kee's honesty to consumers and its sincerity in implementing FSA advice. The company claimed that the FSA had used old products made before the manufacturing processes were changed, but such a claim by itself was not enough. Lee Kum Kee also executed a string of other actions swiftly and with apparent sincerity, as Keller would have recommended. The company lost no time in gathering approvals and certifications from public food authorities over the world — most importantly including the FSA, which cleared the company's name a month later — that its products were safe. The approvals were then used to back up the widely broadcast message that Lee Kum Kee's products posed no safety problems. The company used media channels and various public relations strategies to present this message to the public. Its approach in doing this was perceived to be quick, open, clear, honest and forthright. Thanks to such concerted efforts, the company managed to re-establish consumer confidence — although the impact on corporate image was still felt a year later as the press still asked questions about product safety.

---

[1]   This case is based entirely on public sources, including the Lee Kum Kee Website, http://home.lkk.com.

[2]   Gopalan, Nisha (1996), "LKK reveals recipe for success", *South China Morning Post*, 1 October.

[3]   Slater, Joanna (1996), "Spreading the sauce", *Far Eastern Economic Review*, 20 May.

[4]   Major sources: company Website; "The making of an oyster sauce empire", *Malay Mail*, 17 November 2001; Gowri, R. (2001), "The 'Kee' the Lees built", New Straits Times, 29 December.

[5]   Major sources: company Website; *Malay Mail*, 17 November 2001; Li, Sandy (2003), "Lee family still flavours veteran sauce maker" (Interview with Eddy Lee Wai-man), *South China Morning Post*, 18 March; *Yangtse Evening News*, http://www.yangtse.com/gb/content/2002-11/14/content_560328.html/; *People* Website, http://www.people.com.cn/GB/jinji/33/174/20020826/808327.html/, 26 August 2002.

6   Li.
7   Eddy studied food science and technology; David and Sammy studied business; Charlie studied engineering (Owens, James [2002], "Culinary Ambassador", *Marshall Magazine*, Summer).
8   Company Website.
9   Lee-Young, Joanne (1997), "Seasoning adds winning flavour", *South China Morning Post*, 30 October.
10 Slater.
11 Slater.
12 Slater.
13 Gopalan.
14 Major sources: *Economic Digest*, 10 August 2002, quoted in Hong Kong Trade Development Council Website, http://www.tdctrade.com/sme/chinese/manage89.htm/; *People* Website, http://www.people.com.cn/GB/jinji/33/174/20020826/808327.html, 26 August 2002.
15 *Tradelink-eBiz*: e-Post (2002), "Lee Kum Kee — From Bottles to Bytes", http://www.tradelink-ebiz.com/english/331n08or3m9a51l/newscast/ss_0204.html/, December.
16 Slater.
17 Major sources: Leahy, Joe and Wadhwani, Chitra (2002), "Hot issue needs solving", *FT.com*, 26 April; Lee, David (2001), "Clearing the air on 3-MCPD", *Malay Mail*, 17 November.
18 McGurn, William (1994), "The world is their oyster: Lee Kum Kee's saucy challenge", *Far Eastern Economic Review*, 22 September; Gopalan.
19 Lee Kum Kee had neither shown any intention to go public nor disclosed its financial figures in detail. The turnover figures quoted here were just industry estimates or approximates released by senior executives of the company that could be found in, for example, McGurn; *Malay Mail*, 17 November 2001; and Li.
20 Gopalan.
21 *Economic Digest*, 10 August 2002, quoted in the Hong Kong Trade Development Council Website.
22 Company Website and Tradelink-eBiz: e-Post, December 2002.
23 Li.
24 *Economic Digest*, 10 August 2002.
25 *People* Website, 26 August 2002.
26 Slater.
27 *Malay Mail*, 17 November 2001.
28 Barrett, Amy (2003), "Hershey: Candy is Dandy, But ...", *Business Week*, 29 September.
29 From Keller, Kevin Lane (1998), *Strategic Brand Management*, New Jersey, US: Prentice Hall, Chapter 13, pp. 500-549.

Appendix 1   Several Cases of Crisis Management

1.   Exxon's Oil-spill Crisis

In March 1989, the *Exxon Valdez* tanker hit a reef in Alaskan waters, resulting in some 11 million gallons of oil spilling into the sea and creating nothing less than an ecological catastrophe in previously unspoiled waters. Top officials of the oil giant Exxon declined to comment publicly for almost a week after the incident. The public statements that were eventually made often appeared to contradict information from other sources (for instance with regards to the severity of the spill), or assigned blame for the slow cleanup to other parties. Exxon received very bad press and many consumers lost confidence in the company.

2.   Perrier's Benzene Crisis

The bottled water producer Perrier was forced to halt production worldwide and recall all of its existing bottles in February 1994 when traces of benzene, a carcinogenic chemical, were found in excessive quantities in some of its products. Several explanations were offered in the ensuing weeks as to how the contamination occurred, creating confusion and doubt. Perrier water, meanwhile, was off the shelves until May 1994, and consumers found satisfactory alternatives in the interim. Despite an expensive relaunch campaign, the company could not regain lost market share, and a year later sales of Perrier water were less than half of pre-crisis level. The point was that Perrier ads had previously focused on the product's "purity", and once that image had been tarnished by the crisis, the brand lost its means of brand differentiation.

3.   Johnson & Johnson's Tylenol Crisis

The pharmaceutical giant Johnson & Johnson (J&J) bought the company that made Tylenol, a substitute for aspirin when allergic reactions occurred, in 1959. Tylenol's sales then grew steadily and contributed an important portion of J&J's revenues and profits by 1982. However, in early October 1982, seven people died in the Chicago area of the United States after taking Extra-Strength Tylenol capsules that turned out to contain cyanide poison. Although it soon became apparent that the incidents were restricted to that area and were quite certainly the work of some deranged person, consumer confidence was severely shaken. Even market experts expressed pessimism as to the possibility of J&J recovering the sales of Tylenol.

But J&J did not lose heart. Within the first week of the crisis, the company issued a worldwide alert to the medical community, set up a 24-hour toll-free telephone number, recalled and analysed sample batches of the product, briefed the US Food and Drug Administration, and offered a hefty reward for the apprehension of the culprit in the tampering incident. It also withdrew the brand voluntarily, repurchasing 31 million bottles of Tylenol with a retail value of US$100 million. All advertising was stopped, and all communications with the public were in the form of press releases. J&J also started keeping track of consumer sentiment by conducting weekly surveys; the company spent US$1.5 million on market research in the last three months of 1982. Then, in mid-October, J&J offered a capsule exchange offer, promoted in half-page press announcements in 150 markets across the United States, inviting consumers to mail in a bottle of capsules to receive tablets in exchange. The offer met with poor response, however.

All these actions started within the first three weeks of October. In late October, J&J resumed television advertising with the aim of restoring consumer confidence, and of encouraging the use of the safer tablet form of the product (safer than capsules) before more tamper-resistant packaging became available. In the TV commercial, the company's medical doctor spoke with a sincere and reassuring tone to persuade consumers that J&J had been highly trusted in the past and would work hard to keep that trust. The company made sure that the commercial was broadcast frequently. In November, J&J launched a new Tylenol product with highly tamper-resistant packaging, and promoted it through a gigantic coupon campaign. When J&J returned to regularly advertising Tylenol at the beginning of 1983, testimonies from loyal Tylenol users were used to regain consumer confidence. By February 1983, sales of Tylenol had almost returned to pre-crisis levels.

Source: Kevin Lane Keller (1998), *Strategic Brand Management*, New Jersey, US: Prentice Hall, Chapter 2, pp. 57–60, Chapter 13, pp. 543–544.

9

Suncorp Technologies
From Bust to Boom

P. S. TSO AND MONICA WONG

PART I: BACKGROUND AND ISSUES

Introduction

H. B. International, a manufacturer of home telephone equipment, started off as H. B. Electronics Limited in Hong Kong in 1982.[1] The company grew from a 10-person factory into an organisation with 10,000 employees by the late 1990s. A decade of continuous growth and expansion culminated in the May 1994 public listing on the Hong Kong Stock Exchange. In the subsequent three years, it made profits and declared dividends. Then came the 1997 Asian financial crisis — instead of declaring dividends, H. B. International was on the verge of declaring bankruptcy. Luckily, a group of investors came to its rescue. Upon completion of debt restructuring in 1999, the new management team renamed the company SunCorp Technologies Ltd. They quickly implemented various measures to restore the business. Within three years, the new leadership had turned the company around from losing HK$635 million in 1997 to making a profit of HK$33 million in 2002. How did the new team make this happen? What went wrong with HBI? Why were the investors interested in buying HBI in the first place?

Company Background

At the time of public listing, H. B. International was one of the largest manufacturers of telecommunications products in Asia Pacific. It designed, developed and manufactured cordless telephones, digital telephone-answering devices and corded telephones with advanced features. By 1994, HBI had two production facilities in mainland China (in Liantang and Longgang) with a total of 23 production lines and 6,500 staff.

HBI was an ODM (original design manufacturing) operation, meaning that all products were sold under the brand names of its customers. HBI's expertise in producing quality telephone equipment earned it a big contract from British Telecom (BT). With a strong foothold in the market, HBI was also granted approval in the UK for its super-long-range (up to three kilometres) cordless telephone, the first product of its type authorised for use in Europe. In 1991, the UK and Europe markets contributed 77 percent of HBI's total US$192,389 sales for the year. However, the US market grew rapidly, from 4 percent of the company's total sales in 1991 to 51 percent in 1994, surpassing the UK and Europe market by 10 percentage points, whereas Asia Pacific countries contributed 10–20 percent.

HBI invested heavily in research and development. New products were introduced to the market every year. One of the most anticipated products that had been in incubation for almost a decade since the early 1990s was the DECT (Digitally Enhanced Cordless Telephone). It was introduced to the market in 2000 and was an instant hit. In 2002, DECT accounted for 49 percent of total sales — the rest being shared by other cordless phones (40 percent), corded phones (8 percent) and telecom components and accessories (3 percent).

A Ticking Bomb

HBI experienced significant growth in both turnover and profit in 1994, the year the company went public. Within one year, sales had leapfrogged 100 percent, from HK$520 million to HK$1,044 million in 1994. Profits soared 300 percent, to HK$6,600 million compared with the 1993 figure of HK$22 million. New models were purchased by large customers such as BT in the UK and BellSouth in the US. Major changes in the business included the increased proportion of cordless phones sales and the significant shift to the North American market, making it the largest market in HBI's portfolio. Thanks to the rosy reports in sales and profits, the board of directors declared dividends of HK 3.0 cents per share, amounting to a total dividend payout of HK$13.5 million in 1994.

As luck would have it, in 1995, the US Federal Communications Commission made a decision to increase the number of frequencies or "channels" allowed for using cordless telephones from a total of 10 to 25. This regulatory change came as a big blow to HBI. Consequently, HBI increased its stock level. As explained in the 1995 annual report,

> Stock levels rose compared with last year due in part to the changeover from 10 to 25-channel cordless telephone specification in the USA market in April 1995. Components for the new 25-channel products needed to be held in stock until such time as the products were developed and could be shipped to the USA market.

The piling of stock tightened the cashflow situation within HBI because cash had been paid out to the suppliers but the inventory was sitting in the warehouse instead of generating income for the company. HBI had two choices to ease the cashflow situation: to borrow money or to raise money from investors. HBI chose the former, and total bank borrowings reached HK$460 million in 1995, a 76 percent increase over 1994.

In 1996, sales continued to grow by about 10 percent, but net profits had dropped 21 percent to HK$53.5 million. HBI's bank borrowings continued to increase, to HK$684 million. The consequences were predictable: the increasing interest payments further eroded the company's cash position to a deficit of HK$421 million. More difficult to comprehend was the company's decision to declare a dividend of HK$13.4 million, despite that deficit.

Apart from paying out dividends, HB also continued its aggressive expansion plan through investing in fixed assets. HB had continued to increase its purchase of fixed assets since 1994, and in 1995 it invested HK$44.8 million in associated company, Henan Huawei Electronics Company Limited.

The Asian currency crisis in 1997 was a severe blow to the financial sectors in Asia, and Hong Kong was no exception. By then, HBI had already been bleeding cash for more than four years and bank borrowings had snowballed to almost HK$700 million. Short-term bank loans amounted to a sizeable HK$421 million — HBI was in for a rude awakening. Unable to fulfil its repayment obligations, HBI was in breach of its loan agreements. This bad news spread quickly within banking circles, and the 15 banks that had offered credit facilities to HBI immediately called for the repayment of the loans. As an old Chinese saying goes: "Good luck seldom comes in pairs but bad things never walk alone." Apart from the banks' demands for loan repayment, there were other mishaps in 1997. Firstly, the gross margin on products sold to the US dropped substantially. Secondly, there was a significant provision of approximately HK$307.4 million against the interest in and trade receivables from HBI's joint-venture company, Henan Huawei Electronics Co., Ltd. Thirdly, there was a write-off of obsolete stock valued at HK$108.4 million. Fourthly, there was a provision for properties held for sale of approximately HK$10 million. Finally, there was a write-off of trade receivables of approximately HK$96.8 million. The final result for the year 1997 was a loss of HK$635 million. In short, the books were all in the red.

Looking for a White Knight

The story could have ended with HBI being liquidated. However, armed with a robust research and development facility, a trend-setting design team and products that were selling well in overseas markets, HBI set off to search for a new investor. Meanwhile, it also initiated talks with creditors to work out ways to handle its debts. In the end, SunCorp emerged as a "White Knight", injecting new cash into HBI. Suncorp was an investment holding company formed by the Axia Group (holding an approximately 59 percent shareholding). The principal business of the Axia Group was investment and investment advisory services in relation to acquisitions and restructuring in Asia. SunCorp did not dissolve the company to resell it in parts, but took over the whole business and continued the operation. None of the investors had any experience in the telephone equipment manufacturing business, but they believed the industry had a bright future. The best-selling DECT had a very high growth potential in HBI's existing markets, and would help SunCorp to break into new markets. The investors were further reassured when HBI's biggest client, BT, expressed its confidence in the new management and the incumbent production and design teams. SunCorp was confident it could take over the organisation to turn it around. After extensive negotiations, Suncorp, HBI and HBI's 15 bankers reached a restructuring agreement that was considered by all parties as the best rescue plan offered to HBI to resolve its liquidity problems.

Debt Restructuring

According to the restructuring agreement, the banks collectively accepted in full and final settlement of the amount of indebtedness due from HBI (approximately HK$364 million as at 13 February 1998), in consideration of the allotment and issue bank shares and the convertible notes and the cash settlement in an amount of HK$24,712,970. In summary, the agreement involved settlement of HBI's bank indebtedness as shown in Table 1:

Table 1 SunCorp's Debt Restructuring in 1998

	HK$ million	%
Cash	24.7	6.8
Convertible Notes	39.6	10.9
Bank Shares	49.0	13.4
Waived by the Group Banks	250.7	68.9
Total:	364.0	100.0

Turning Around from Bust to Boom

A new page began in 1999, when HBI was officially renamed SunCorp. Doing business wasn't easy during the early days after restructuring. The new management had to assuage creditors' scepticism. HBI's financial problems had dragged down a few suppliers, forcing them into liquidation. Hence, it was no surprise that this second time around, suppliers imposed harsh transaction terms, requiring cash on delivery (COD). Under such circumstances, SunCorp needed to rely on internal funding. The need to cut costs was obvious, forcing the management to make tough decisions quickly. Asset management was closely monitored. Effective sales and marketing strategies needed to be put in place. Management needed to decide which market to go after so as to rationalise the customer base and focus on a few stable and profitable markets. The US market imposed more stringent credit terms than Europe, and it was a relatively new market. In Europe, by contrast, HBI had had a subsidiary in London for more than 10 years that provided first-hand customer feedback and market knowledge to the headquarters in Hong Kong. A customer service hotline was in place to serve BT's customers. This set up was a competitive advantage of SunCorp over other OEM and ODM manufacturers selling to Europe. Naturally, the management chose the European markets and gave up the American market. Inevitably sales volume dropped as a result of the decision, however with the strong foothold in the UK and a presence in other European countries, more and more new customers in Europe were coming onboard, giving SunCorp a chance to rebound and gradually reduce its concentration on only one market.

In order to reduce costs, the new management streamlined processes and laid off excess staff. They also reduced inventory levels and rationalised suppliers in order to improve the cashflow situation. HBI's fiasco was, to a large extent, due to the smokescreen of profit that had disguised the real financial situation. Thus, the new management team made it a high priority to build a proper management information system to facilitate closer monitoring of corporate health and to tighten financial discipline.

On the sales front, SunCorp leveraged HBI's core competencies in product design, customer services and research and development to gradually re-establish a leadership position in the marketplace. SunCorp focused on the DECT, which was of superior digital quality and was capable of new functionality add-ons such as SMS and MMS.

Financial Improvement

The year ended 31 July 1999 was a period during which SunCorp was still encountering significant financial difficulties, and the year ended before the corporate restructuring was fully implemented. Nevertheless, the results for the period confirmed the resilience of SunCorp's core business. The profit attributable to shareholders for the year was approximately HK$2 million, compared with a loss of approximately HK$326 million in 1998.

The year 2000 represented a major turning point. With the introduction of DECT, sales had increased for the first time since 1996. Administrative expenses continued to drop and the profit attributable to shareholders was at HK$202 million (17 months after bank borrowings were waived). The year 2001 continued to have strong sales growth, resulting in a profit of HK$12 million, and administrative expenses dropped by 31 percent compared with the previous years. The liquidity situation had also improved significantly, with a current ratio at 0.8997 as compared with 0.2923 the year before.

After three years' continuous efforts in cost reduction and the realignment of the business and customer focus, 2002 was a year of turning around from bust to boom. For the year 2002, SunCorp made a profit, generated positive cash flow, completed its loan repayments and settled the convertible note six months ahead of schedule. For the first time since 1997, the company declared dividends for its shareholders, at HK0.5 cents per share.

Looking Ahead

As corporate health had been restored, SunCorp's management set their eyes on a longer-term future. SunCorp's five-year plan was aiming for a profitable result by concentrating on what the company had been doing best — ODM of cordless telephone equipment. Despite the lucrative margins of OBM (own brand manufacturing) — as much as 25–30 percent on top of ODM, the management realised that SunCorp's strengths lay in designing and producing telephones, but that brand building and marketing were not the company's areas of expertise.

With a clear corporate direction as an ODM, SunCorp continued to invest in R & D, because innovation was the key to stimulating new demand, which in turn was vital for a sustainable growth. In 2002, SunCorp introduced the mini-DECT and would gradually phase out non-DECT products. SunCorp products could be found in Australia, Hong Kong, India, France, Germany, Belgium, Portugal and Italy. In Europe, SunCorp ranked number three in terms of the cordless telephone market share (10 percent), very closely beaten by Philips (10.7 percent), and the top seller in Europe was Siemens, grasping about 32 percent of the market. With such a remarkable position in the market, SunCorp targeted to expand in Europe through a more diversified customer base. As for the US, SunCorp did not plan to re-enter the market.

Alex Mak, the Executive Director responsible for SunCorp's overall finance and administrative functions, was very pleased with the progress of debt repayment; in fact it was ahead of schedule. At the special general meeting held on 6 June 2003, the declaration of special dividends to shareholders was approved, and Alex realised that the damage control stage was over and that it was time to instigate long-term financial control mechanisms in the company.

PART II: LESSONS LEARNED

What Went Wrong with HBI?

The inability to manage a company's cash needs is often the primary cause of the demise of many seemingly profitable enterprises. Many companies that measure their success by their net income alone have a rude awakening when confronted with cash shortages and angry creditors. Investors may be deceived if they look only at the income statement when seeking a measure of a company's health. On the surface, HBI did not look so bad — it recorded profits and declared dividends for a number of years. But even a cursory glance of the cash flow statement showed that it recorded a negative cash flow for all those years.

In a healthy company, operating activities generate cash to be used in part to pay interest and tax; to purchase machinery or to invest in other assets, or to be retained as reserves. A portion will also be paid out as dividends to shareholders. But with HBI, the operating cash flow was in the red in 1993, 1995 and 1997. The net cash flow of HBI had been negative every year before the restructuring. In short, HBI had a cash deficit and did not have enough working capital to stay operating.

There were two aspects of HBI's cashflow problems: operational and non-operational.

Operational problems

The working capital

Working capital is the short-term, operating assets and liabilities of the company: cash, accounts receivable, inventory and accounts payable. It is often dubbed "the life blood" of the business. Most business is conducted on credit, and most companies maintain inventories of materials or merchandise. These elements of working capital are dealt with on a daily basis as merchandise is bought and sold on credit, receivables are collected from customers, and bills are paid to suppliers. Analysis of working capital is an important tool for day-to-day financial management. Working capital can be defined as:

Working Capital = Cash + Accounts Receivable + Inventory – Accounts Payable

Cash is the central element of working capital. For the other items, the question is: How long will they remain in their present form before they produce (or require) cash? Time-based ratios are thus an important element of analysis.

When calculating working capital in terms of number of days, the "cash gap" represents the number of days (the "gap") from the time the inventory is bought and paid for until it is sold and the company collects the amount due from its customers. This measure is also referred to as the cash conversion cycle.

The cash gap

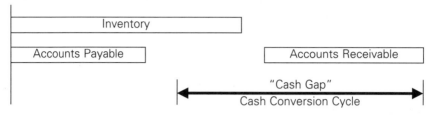

Figure 1   The Cash Gap

Fig. 1 assumes that the inventory is not immediately paid off. The cash gap began when the supplier is paid and extends until cash is collected from the customer. The remaining holding period of the inventory plus the time that the accounts receivable from the customer are outstanding determines the length of the cash gap.

Calculating the cash gap:
1.   Days of inventory turnover = Stock/COGS x 365 days
2.   Days of accounts receivable turnover = Accounts receivable/Sales x 365 days
3.   Days of accounts payable turnover = Accounts payable/Sales x 365 days
Cash Gap = (1) + (2) − (3)

In HBI/SunCorp's case, the cash gap trend is as follows:

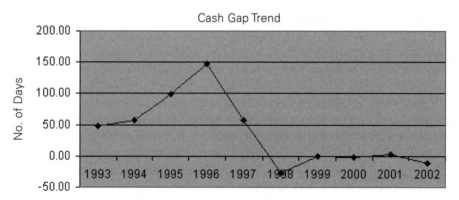

Figure 2   HBI/SunCorp Cash Gap Trend

The inventory level and the time needed for the inventory to generate income rose steadily from 1993 to 1996 — the number of days required to collect money from debtors increased from 74 days in 1993 to 93 days in 1996. This collection slowdown widened the cash gap. The longer the cash gap, the more additional cash would be needed to keep the day-to-day operations afloat. If HBI's source of cash were internal investor funds, it would probably have been able to survive a long cash gap. However, HBI had been relying on debt financing, which dragged it deeper into an abyss. With insufficient cash, HBI borrowed more, but the more it borrowed the more interest it had to pay and the worse cash position it was in — thereby creating a vicious circle. Finally in 1997, HBI was unable to repay the increasing amount of short-term loans, and this triggered the whole group of 15 bankers to demand loan repayment immediately. Only a magic wand could have helped HBI to repay all its debts.

Non-operational Problems

Company expansion

From 1994 to 1997, HBI invested heavily in research and development on new products, including DECT (digitally enhanced cordless telephone). Further expansion for the US market also attributed to a substantial amount of net capital spending.

Financial cash outflow

The large amount of capital spending was funded largely by loans, which created a burden on servicing these bank loans. This put HBI in a difficult situation: on the one hand, it had to meet a substantial amount of cash outflow for debt financing and capital spending; while on the other hand, it continued to pay dividends.

The problem of HBI was two-fold: the operational cash flow problems were primary, and they were compounded by the non-operational cash flow problems – both caused by mismanagement of cash flow and working capital. The management did not address the issue of negative cash flow and kept on paying out dividends, and at the same time the company continued to borrow from banks. There could only be one outcome: bankruptcy.

What Did SunCorp Do to Strengthen its Position?

Financial data are very important for the diagnosis of a company's health. Therefore SunCorp's top priority was to tidy up its financial data by ensuring accurate book-keeping, constantly reviewing its accounting statements and closely monitoring key financial ratios and indicators. The first step was to identify data that would be useful for analysis; the next step was to build an information system to capture those useful data. Based on the information drawn from this central system, performance could then be monitored closely. The management also acted swiftly to stop cash bleeding by cutting excess staff and tightening inventory control, reducing stock levels.

What Can We Learn from This Case?

Cash is critical for operations, and most importantly, to keep a company out of bankruptcy. The cash flow statement is a very important tool for the diagnosis of corporate health, providing information about the sources of cash and the uses to which it is put.

Without cash a business cannot function. The cash flow statement is a management tool to help avoid liquidity problems. Both the income statement and the balance sheet are used to form the cash flow picture of a company. Management should ask the following questions: What is the relationship between cash flow and earnings? How long is the cash conversion cycle? How are dividends financed? How are debts paid off? How is the cash generated by operations used? By using a cash flow statement, managers can plan and manage a company's cash sources and needs. Whatever the sources and uses of cash, the cash flow statement tells us a great deal about the health of a business. To many financial analysts, it is the most important statement of all.

SMEs may fall into the trap of just going after profit, overlooking the situations of cash flow and working capital. This case provides an example of the consequences of cost overruns being disguised under a seemingly profitable result. SunCorp quickly identified the core problem and corrected it with swift cost-cutting measures and the implementation of strict financial discipline.

Looking at the reasons that pulled down HBI, SMEs will learn the importance of monitoring financial health by gathering useful information. This relies on a sound information management system. SME's do not necessarily need a sophisticated IT system, which most of them cannot afford. In fact, SunCorp did not have any money to invest in MIS (management information system) tools when it took over HBI. SMEs could develop a basic MIS just by installing a system to track the appropriate data for processing into useful information for performance measurement, forecasting and decision-making. At the end of the day, the financial database is only a tool; it is ultimately up to managers to use the data in such a way that will ensure corporate financial health.

---

[1]   H. B. Electronics Limited (HBE) was subsequently merged with Sound Wealth and Tak San and the UK-based group of companies, comprising H. B. Europe and its subsidiaries, to become HBBG (H. B. Browns Group Limited) in 1991. HBBG was a wholly owned subsidiary of H. B. International Holdings Limited at the time of HBI's listing.

10
Lung Cheong International
How to Survive in a Changing Business Landscape

BENNETT YIM AND VINCENT MAK

PART I: BACKGROUND AND ISSUES

Introduction

Lung Cheong International Holding Limited was founded in 1979 as an original equipment manufacturer (OEM) of toys in Hong Kong. As the mainland Chinese economy took off in the 1980s and 1990s, China became a great hinterland of cheap land and labour for low-tech manufacturing and also a huge and growing consumer market. Lung Cheong continuously felt the challenges of the changing business landscape. Should it move its production lines to the Mainland or somewhere at similarly low cost-levels? How should it deal with its major Western and Japanese customers in order to maintain good relationships? Should it enter the huge mainland Chinese sales market? If so, how could it compete with Mainland-based manufacturers that enjoyed lower production costs and could sell products very cheaply? How could it deal with rampant copyright piracy problems in the Mainland market? Or should it focus instead on the West, in particular the US market?

The Hong Kong Toy Industry

There was labour-intensive toy manufacturing in Hong Kong as early as in the 1940s.[1] After the Second World War, Hong Kong grew to become an internationally competitive centre of toy production, reputed for its low production costs, on-time delivery, respect for intellectual property rights and flexible marketing strategies. Toy manufacturers were eager to attract overseas clients by establishing a good image for quality production. They were mostly OEMs, i.e., they manufactured, according to customers' specifications, toy products that were then sold under the customers' brand names. In the early 1980s, Hong Kong became the biggest toy exporter in the world. Meanwhile, economic reform in mainland China opened up opportunities for cheap land and labour — costs in the Pearl River Delta at that time was only one-tenth that of Hong Kong levels. Hong Kong enterprises began to move or outsource production lines northwards, thereby increasing their productivity by 5 to 20 times.

In the 1990s, higher-grade electronic toys as well as multi-functional, interactive toys became popular. Hong Kong's toy industry underwent another transformation; there was a trend towards technology-intensive production. Electronic component manufacturing, software development and game design became important pillars of the toy industry. However, plastic toys were still the biggest segment within Hong Kong's manufacturing industry, and it was common for Hong Kong's plastic toy manufacturers to have their head office in Hong Kong but to set up factories in mainland China. Chinese toy exports had increased from US$3.55 billion in 1995 to US$5.35 billion in 1998, and the industry provided two million jobs for mainland Chinese; most of those exports were shipped via Hong Kong.[2]

Hong Kong was still the world's largest exporter of toys by 2001, if re-exports were included.[3] The territory was responsible for providing 60 percent of the world's toy market. About half of Hong Kong's toy exports went to the United States. The next largest export destination was Japan, followed by the United Kingdom, Germany and Canada. Global recession and the September 11 terrorist attack on New York in 2001 had dimmed demand, but the accession of China to the World Trade Organisation in late 2001 was a counterbalancing factor. There were about 6,000 toy producers in mainland China by 2001, and most of their factories were located near coastal cities. Among those factories, 4,000 were in Guangdong Province, most of which owned by Hong Kong businessmen.

The toy market had long been characterised by rapidly changing fashion and taste. When a product suddenly became very fashionable, its manufacturers could earn huge revenues. The meteoric blaze of popularity that the virtual pet Tamagochi ignited in the late 1990s was one example. The demand was so huge that the original manufacturer could not cope with it, enabling many small knock-off manufacturers to make a timely fortune. But once the craze was over, manufacturers that did not pull out in time suffered. On the other hand, the toy industry was not as affected by macro-economic downturns as some other industries, since adults were willing to buy toys for children even in tough times.

Lung Cheong International Holdings Limited

Leung Lun entered the toy manufacturing industry in 1964 as a teenage worker. He founded Lung Cheong as a toy OEM in November 1979; the company's business soon became dominated by OEM of radio controlled cars.

In the early 1980s, many Hong Kong manufacturers were lured by the cheap land and labour in mainland China and moved their production lines northwards. But Leung, cautiously bided his time, and chose to move only some of the parts-processing lines into mainland China. The regulations and rules of game in the Mainland were not the same as in Hong Kong, and he saw that many manufacturers moved back to Hong Kong a few years after trying their hand at setting up Mainland production lines. It was not until 1985 that Lung Cheong transferred production completely to the Mainland, by setting up production lines in Dongguan in the Pearl River Delta region of Guangdong Province. The June 4 Incident in Beijing in 1989 prompted Leung to consider setting up production lines in more than one country to diversify risk. The result was a factory in Indonesia that began operation in 1993, but by the early 2000s it accounted for very little of Lung Cheong's revenue.

By 2002, Lung Cheong was principally engaged in the manufacture and sale of electronic toys, interactive products and moulds to well-known international toy and gaming companies.[4] Its customers by that time included well-known Western and Japanese toy brands such as Taiyo Kogyo, Tomy, Mattel, Little Tikes and Bandai. In addition to owning and operating production facilities in China and Indonesia, the group distributed licensed toys in more than 400 outlets throughout mainland China. The group had further diversified its business into the gift market and expanded its distribution market in the US through the acquisition of toy company Kid Galaxy Inc. Lung Cheong also invested in StatCard Entertainment Inc. in the US, obtaining the production and exclusive distribution rights for its smart trading cards and online gaming accessories. But overall, most revenue still came from OEM of radio controlled and electronic toys.

By March 2002, the company had 5,180 staff, of whom 67 were based in Hong Kong, 4,858 in the Dongguan factories, 240 in the Indonesian factory and 15 in the new US office. Total turnover for fiscal year 2001/02 was more than HK$657 million, and profit attributable to shareholders was more than HK$31 million. Leung remained the chairman, while his younger brother Leung Chung-ming, who had worked in Lung Cheong since its inception, was the managing director. The company had been listed on the Stock Exchange of Hong Kong since 1997.

Challenges, Advantages and New Directions

Lung Cheong's many challenges in the 1990s and early 2000s stemmed mainly from one phenomenon: the rise of mainland China as a low-cost, low-tech manufacturing and a growing consumer market for toys. Moving production lines to China became inevitable for Hong Kong toy manufacturers as it was more or less the only way to maintain competitive production costs, although Leung Lun only completed that by 1985, after learning from other companies' mistakes. Once he had set up factory in the Mainland, unlike some other Hong Kong manufacturers, Leung did not find managing Mainland staff difficult; as he said, he treated them with respect, such as requiring Hong Kong and Mainland staff to wear the same uniform and to eat at the same canteen. He even provided those Mainland factory workers who came to Dongguan from rural villages with instructions about how to live in a city, down to such basics as what traffic lights meant.

The biggest challenge to Lung Cheong came rather from Mainland-based private enterprises that could easily beat Hong Kong-based companies on pricing. Such Mainland-based enterprises did not have to run a Hong Kong headquarters, and they had a better understanding of how to use resources in the Mainland in the cheapest possible way; moreover, their social network in the Mainland could be wider and deeper than that of many Hong Kong-based manufacturers. Along with these advantages, some Mainland-based manufacturers could be quite unscrupulous. First of all, they were not very conscious of product quality — or, perhaps, safety — and, in the name of minimising costs, they could be quite offhand with quality control. Secondly, they could be very cavalier with copyright, and produce poor imitations of new, marketable toy designs owned by someone else, thereby hurting the sales of the original products. Lung Cheong had certainly found poor imitations of its products being sold in the Mainland market. Leung said that once they released a certain new toy in the Mainland sales market, poor-quality imitations would appear very quickly, taking away market share from and putting pricing pressure on Lung Cheong's products.

To combat these problems, Lung Cheong did not at first concentrate heavily on the Mainland sales market. It was definitely a huge market, and Lung Cheong did enter it in 1996. However, Mainland market sales comprised to less than 10 percent of Lung Cheong's sales by 2002, predominantly in the form of licensed toy products of characters from Japanese television cartoons or comic books that were broadcast or published in China at the same time. In fact, Lung Cheong would proactively supply the cartoons — already dubbed in Chinese — to the television stations (which often lacked good cartoon programmes), so that it could market related toy products ahead of competitors and with the most optimal timing to achieve high returns. For this business, Leung would only choose cartoons that were several years old in Japan, so that his company could purchase the cartoons and licences at depreciated prices and sell the cartoon toys at lower levels in China. By 2002, although Mainland toy consumers were generous in buying what their children asked for, they were not too discerning when it came to product quality or safety. However, they could be very price-conscious, so poor, cheap pirated copies were saleable in the Mainland market. Leung therefore preferred to limit his involvement in such a market, despite its high potential.

With Western and Japanese OEM customers and the Western sales markets, Leung had much more confidence, experience and competitive advantage. He understood that those customers put great emphasis on quality, and he was able to meet such requirements by maintaining a high standard of quality control in his factories. One method for quality assurance was vertical integration, by which most of the manufacturing and assembly of components — down to screws and springs — were done in Lung Cheong factories. This also made flexibility in production methods and just-in-time delivery more feasible. To improve Lung Cheong's competitiveness further, the company actively suggested product design improvements to its OEM customers. Leung was moreover able to build up long-term relationships with its customers, some of whom had world-famous brand names. In fact, some OEM customers had been ordering from him for decades, and he had learned to deal with customers from different business cultures. For example, Japanese OEM customers treasured human relationships. Leung said that sometimes he might feel that a Japanese customer's pricing requirements were too harsh and unfair, but he still had to compromise in order to preserve the relationship. US customers were more forthright and objective. They were clear about what they wanted, and would openly work out all the details when negotiating the price of a new order. They were willing to listen to counter-arguments over pricing, but if both sides could not come to an agreement in the end, friendly relationships would not mean much.

Leung saw that Lung Cheong had to move to higher-margin areas, since Mainland-based manufacturers would probably take over more and more OEM businesses. Therefore, the company poured more resources into ODM (original design manufacturing), meaning that Lung Cheong designed and manufactured products that were then sold under its customers' brand names. Lung Cheong also tried to establish a brand presence in Western sales markets. The acquisition in early 2002 of US-based Kid Galaxy — which had its own research and development team in the United States, the "Bendos" brand of plastic toy figurines and an established US network of 2,500 outlets — was a significant attempt at brand-building.

It was apparent that Lung Cheong had not sat still in a changing world. But were any of its strategic shifts in the wrong direction? In the long run, would those changes turn out to be in vain or even drag down the competitiveness of the company?

PART II: LESSONS LEARNED

This case offers a brief overview of the progress of a toy manufacturing SME from the 1980s to early 2000s, with emphasis on how it coped with various challenges in the early 2000s. The case can therefore serve as a best-practice demonstration of how an SME manages its operations in a changing business landscape.

Key Questions

What are the strategic shifts that Lung Cheong made in order to deal with competition from Mainland-based toy manufacturers?

To reduce manufacturing costs and diversify geo-political risks, the company set up factories in Dongguan and also in Indonesia. It consolidated its relationships with long-time customers by offering services that were tailor-made to different customers' ways of doing business, making sure that its products were of the highest quality. To avoid competing head-on with Mainland-based manufacturers of poor-quality but cheap copies of Lung Cheong's products for the Mainland sales market, Lung Cheong placed higher emphasis on the more quality-conscious Western market. The company also went in search of higher-margin business, which Mainland-based competitors were not able to do. For example, it kept boosting its ODM business by 2002, and was also trying to establish its own-brand toys and diversify into other areas. In a major attempt at brand-building, and to facilitate further moves into the US market, Lung Cheong bought the US toy company Kid Galaxy in February 2002.

Has Lung Cheong been right in its many strategic shifts? What general lessons can we draw from its story in the context of SME operation?

The story of Lung Cheong shows — rightly — that, if an SME finds that its old "cheap knock-off maker" image no longer works, it must ensure that every new business move is potentially high-value-added, in terms of business development and marketing. In its many moves in adapting itself to the changing business landscape, Lung Cheong does indeed provide a good example of managing growth for SMEs.

Lung Cheong's gradual transformation in business lines is common to many manufacturers in developing regions that later grew to approach developed regions. These regions, such as Taiwan and Hong Kong in the 1970s, at first appeared to be ideal OEM centres. As they prospered, land and labour became expensive, and manufacturers in those regions had to find alternatives. This problem became more urgent as a new "generation" of low-cost production centres arose, such as mainland China. The rising production costs in Hong Kong did in fact force Lung Cheong to move its production lines to the Mainland, but Leung also realised that Mainland-based competitors would eventually take over more and more OEM deals. The move to Indonesia, understandable due to the feeling of uncertainty towards China immediately after the June 4 incident in 1989, proved to be not very fruitful. Hence, Leung began to explore high-margin and technically or creatively more demanding strategies, such as ODM and brand-building. This has happened to other SMEs as well in similarly evolving economies, and is apparently a natural, inevitable move in many cases.

Lung Cheong also carried out a typical move with its OEM business that other SMEs could adopt to deal with pricing pressure from developing-world competitors. The main point is that it stressed quality assurance (partly through vertical integration), just-in-time delivery, its trustworthy reputation and good customer service, all tailor-made to the customers' business culture. It also began to suggest production design improvements to its OEM customers in order to build up competitiveness (this can also function as an exercise for more substantial ODM projects). Lung Cheong attempted to aggregate all such virtues into a price premium for customers from regions where consumer requirements were more sophisticated. This tactic had succeeded with Lung Cheong's major customers from the West and Japan. Similarly, Lung Cheong pursued brand establishment in the United States first, rather than in mainland China, because the latter sales market was not so brand- or quality-conscious, and intellectual property rights were much better protected in the United States.

Lastly, Lung Cheong was target-specific in devising new strategies. For example, it entered the mainland Chinese sales market through licensed products of characters from television cartoons or comic books that were broadcast or published at the time — it even supplied the television stations with those cartoons. Since China was a huge market and Lung Cheong could not be familiar with every bit of it, linking up with mass-media programmes was likely to be a good bet and would save marketing resources. In addition, the cartoons chosen by Lung Cheong were already several years old in Japan, so the company could purchase the cartoons and licences at depreciated prices and sell related toys in China at lower prices. As for the US sales market, Lung Cheong entered it by acquiring an established toy company — again saving the costs and time associated with building up a presence as an entirely new entrant. This attempt at brand-building in a sophisticated retail market has not always proved to be successful for Asian firms, e.g., Taiwan-based Acer Computer's brand-building in the United States during the 1990s was not successful. However, given the rise of mainland China OEMs, Leung had to start doing it. And after all, he had wisely chosen to do it through acquiring Kid Galaxy, an established US company, thus saving much of the cost related to setting up totally anew in a foreign country.

1   Unless otherwise stated, information in this section is based on Nyaw, Mee-kau and Yeung, Raymond (2001), "The Prospects of Hong Kong Toy Industry's Operation, Foreign Business Environment and Development" research report, Hong Kong Institute of Business Studies, Lingnan University, August.

2   "China: Toy Sector Outlook Good, Competition to Intensify" (1999), *China Business Information Network*, 6 December. US$1 = HK$7.8 approximately.

3   Hong Kong Trade Development Council (2001), "Profile of Hong Kong's Toy Industry", http://toys.tdctrade.com/, 7 December.

4   This paragraph from clients page, Strategic Financial Relations Limited Website, http://www.strategic.com.hk/clients/client_item.asp?client_id=82/, and the company Website.

11

Fenix
Diversified Niche Marketing in the Lifestyle Business

BENNETT YIM AND MONICA WONG

PART I: BACKGROUND AND ISSUES

Introduction

In 2002, the Fenix Group celebrated its 30th anniversary. The commemorative booklet "Gracing Life with Style", featuring a cover decorated with velvet and pages adorned with scented, colourful dried flowers, was the embodiment of the Fenix Group's business — it was about lifestyle, of the classy kind.

Anthony Keung, Managing Director of the Fenix Group, looked back on the company's history and reflected upon the building of Italian fashion brand Anteprima and the establishment of the lifestyle megastore City'super. Both were bold decisions supported by his belief in niche marketing. The two ventures proved to be successful and reinforced the group's "quality lifestyle" market positioning.

Looking out from his top-floor office, as he reminisced about the group's challenges and achievements, Keung pondered what the future would bring and where the next niche market would be.

Company Background

Knitwear manufacturing and marketing

In 1972, Anthony Keung and Masaaki Ogino founded Fenix Hong Kong Limited. The two were former colleagues of a Japanese yarn supplier in Hong Kong. Sharing the same vision, they decided to start their own company. Initially they exported garments made of Japanese materials to the US and European markets, but later noticed that the demand for knitwear in Japan itself was under-served. They went on to set up their own factory. Within a short time, they had successfully established a foothold in Japan — a market considered to be very difficult to penetrate. Their strengths in grasping market trends and in packaging and promoting products were officially recognised when Hong Kong Trade Development Council conferred them the Export Marketing Award in 1998.

Fashion retailing

Building on their knowledge in the apparel business and their ability to identify market trends, Keung and Ogino took on fashion retailing in the 1980s. They started off by introducing Japanese and American brands to Hong Kong, opening boutiques in a popular department store. However, the brands were not well known in Hong Kong and were not supported by adequate promotions. The two retail outlets did not do well and were eventually closed down. The entrepreneurs were down, but not out. Undeterred by the failure, they decided to tap into the market for designer-label goods by obtaining distribution rights of several European brands. This time they found the right formula. The associated value of superior quality, designer labels and fashion from Europe fuelled the rocketing sales. Demand grew rapidly and what started off as niche markets soon became the mainstream. Encouraged by the success, Fenix started to build its own brand name in 1994.

The birth of Anteprima

The upscale lifestyle positioning took shape during the 1980s, when Fenix started handling the then little-known brand — Prada. The Prada brand included fashion, shoes, handbags and accessories. Its funky, minimalist yet intelligent designs using alternative materials appealed to the avant-garde niche market. They spread the trend and within a few years Prada became a leader in the luxury market. The most popular product line was the black nylon bag, which could fetch a few hundred US dollars apiece. Prada successfully banked on people's need to make a statement about their lifestyle through what they carried and wore.[1]

Fenix gained insider know-how that was critical to building a successful high-end designer label and benefited from the superior margins that characterised value-based niche marketing. The Prada experience opened the door to the designer-label world. In 1996, Fenix built its own brand, Anteprima, in Milan and successfully broke into the exclusive, close-knit Milan fashion circle. Ogino's wife, who was in charge of Prada's Japan business, headed up Anteprima as creative director.

Anteprima's unique blend of Italian and Japanese creativity in fashion, knitwear, shoes and handbags appealed to the niche market of consumers who identified with its style of "simple sophistication and seduction".[2] It was a great success in Japan, within a few years 14 Anteprima shops were opened. They were also springing up in Europe, Hong Kong, Taiwan, mainland China and Singapore. By 2002, Anteprima became the flagship label of Fenix, representing more than 50 percent of all its fashion-retailing business.

Transforming grocery shopping: City'super

With the addition of Anteprima to its portfolio, Fenix Group became a truly multinational network of knitwear manufacturing and fashion retailing. The natural next step would be to pursue other areas within the apparel business. However, Keung and Ogino had something else in mind; they had a broader vision.

As they were building Anteprima, they noticed that the quest for high-end fashion was just one aspect of people's pursuit of a stylish and modern lifestyle. The demand for classy premium products extended from fashion to other things in daily life. Keung and Ogino believed that a high-end goods and general merchandise store would fill this gap in the market. At around the same time, a group of retail professionals who had previously managed Seibu, a posh Japanese-styled department store, proposed to partner with Fenix. Sharing the same vision, the two parties came to an agreement on the concept of a new store — City'super.

City'super was a new concept in Hong Kong. The emphasis was on providing exciting, high-quality products. City'super transformed what people used to call "grocery shopping" into an exciting and enjoyable experience. The target customers were advocates of a cosmopolitan lifestyle. City'super offered trendy, alternative and stylish merchandise from around the world, including food items, fashion accessories, gadgets, stationery, interior goods and kitchenware, and skincare and healthcare items. Instead of buying out of necessity, Fenix wanted to create a buying-at-leisure experience. Unlike supermarkets, which used bright lights and a clinically white démcor, City'super was decorated in warm earth tones using wooden floors and shelves. Dimmer and softer lighting was used in the store to create a friendly and welcoming shopping environment. Products were new and exotic imports, choices that could not be found in local supermarkets. Innovative products and services such as the personalised wine (bottles of wine with customised labels) and gourmet-on-demand (fresh food and produce imported to order) were introduced into the store. To match the "e-lifestyle" of its clientele, City'Super offered a Super e-card, a membership and stored-value card that could be used as cash for in-store or online shopping. Value-added services such as valet parking and home delivery were also available in selected locations.

Fenix leveraged its retail experience and knowledge in fashion trends to manage City'super. The first store opened in December 1996. It proved to be a successful venture, so the second store opened in 1998. Contrary to the general view that food and merchandise retailing was an odd choice for an apparel veteran, City'super struck the same chord with Fenix's existing businesses. The diversification and investment in City'super reinforced the group's strategy to focus on high-value-adding niche markets in lifestyle consumer products.

The Fenix Group in 2002

By 2002, Fenix had already created its own environment of satellite companies within a diversified framework that encompassed 19 regional companies, 14 production lines and 80 retail stores worldwide with a workforce of more than 5,000 staff. The subsidiaries were launched in partnership with entrepreneurial employees who were committed and shared the same management philosophy. Annual turnover amounted to US$230 million, of which US$80 million came from manufacturing. Fashion retailing and City'super contributed US$50 million and US$90 million respectively.

Multi-Niche Marketing in the Lifestyle Business

> It is important to identify your competitive advantage in order to find the niche markets in which you can add value.
>
> – Anthony Keung, Managing Director of the Fenix Group

Over its 30-year history, Fenix evolved from a yarn material trader and knitwear manufacturer in the 1970s to a fashion retailer in the 1980s. In the 1990s, the group branched out to become a general merchandise retailer. The common thread that ran through these diverse business units was the strategy of "multi-niche marketing in the lifestyle business".

What Next?

Over the years Fenix had nurtured a mix of brand names in Hong Kong and catered for different niche markets, from trendy teens to independent modern women. Together they accounted for 74 boutiques in seven countries. On the manufacturing side, Fenix had also become one of the largest knitwear suppliers in the Japanese market, producing more than nine million pieces annually.

When asked about his management philosophy, Keung enthused about his "persistence on quality and focus on business closely tied with trendy lifestyle". Behind his pledge that "Fenix will continue to build fruitful partnerships and fill niche markets with innovative and creative products and services," Keung wondered what the next bold step Fenix should take to charter the course of the future, carrying Fenix to new heights.

PART II: LESSONS LEARNED

What Are the Critical Success Factors of Fenix's Multi-niche Marketing Strategy?

According to Philip Kotler, a niche is a narrowly defined group, typically a small market whose needs are not well served.[3] And according to Keung, "the key was to identify a gap in the market and seek to fill it". That sounds rather simple and straightforward. So why don't we see more successful niche marketer around? The missing elements in this apparently simple formula are the critical success factors that differentiate marketers like Fenix from the rest of the field.

Identify "qualified" niche markets

The success of Fenix's multi-niche strategy was partly due to its ability to identify under-served market needs, but that alone is not enough. An attractive niche should have size, profit and growth potential.[4] For a niche market to be "qualified", target customers must buy enough products or services to make it worth the effort. They must be willing to buy from Fenix what it wants to sell. All of the niche markets that Fenix entered into met the above criteria. From the original business of knitwear manufacturing and marketing for the Japanese markets to fashion retailing to lifestyle merchandising, Fenix only approached "qualified" niche markets. Every new niche was identified and filled out of the experience and knowledge gained from the previous venture.

Leverage on competitive advantages

Whereas market segments usually attract several competitors, niches normally attract only one or two.[5] Firstly because the market size is usually too small to accommodate more than a few players, secondly, niche marketing requires a set of competitive advantages that are not easily copied by competitors. Knitwear requires special skills in knitting and embroidery. These skills were not available in Japan but were abundantly available in Hong Kong and China. Coupled with the unique advantage of Ogino's knowledge of the Japanese market, Fenix quickly established a leadership position. In the designer-label market, Fenix leveraged its competitive advantages of knowing the ins and outs of managing high-end fashion gained from working with Prada. The diversion into City'super was an offshoot of Fenix's understanding of quality-seeking, up-market consumers and its sensitivity in trendy lifestyle consumer products cultivated from the creation and development of Anteprima.

Seek out niche markets that are in line with the management philosophy

There is a difference between serving a mature niche and a niche with opportunities for significant growth. Keung and Ogino understood that for Fenix to expand, it had to look for new niches constantly. The selections may seem incongruent, from fashion to groceries, but in reality, all of them reinforced the overall philosophy. This strategy ensured synergy within the diversified network of companies and enabled useful knowledge, e.g., high-end lifestyle marketing, to accumulate within the group.

Add value to the niche market

The key to successful niche marketing is to understand your target customers' needs and do everything possible to satisfy them. In City'super's case, personalised products were offered to match the customers' need for uniqueness. Gourmet-on-demand provided customised service for those who looked for premium quality products and services. A common characteristic of up-market customers is their busy schedule. In response to that, City'Super offered online shopping, home delivery and valet parking. Finally, to appeal to its technology-savvy customers, stored value e-cards were used instead of cash to capitalise on the trend of cashless transactions. These products and services were the result of a comprehensive marketing strategy that successful created a positive perceived "City'super value" in the customers' minds.

Decentralised organisational structure

Niche marketing requires more decentralisation.[6] There are many business units operating independently within the Fenix Group, each of them looking after a niche market. This organisational structure brought about a higher degree of flexibility, enabling the group to react to each distinctive niche market.

What Can We Learn from Fenix's Experience?

Fenix gained its first success by targeting a niche market. This illustrates that even a small company can be a player in niche markets, and that their growth potential should not be underestimated. In fact, small and medium enterprises (SMEs) are in a better position to go after niche markets, because large companies are usually not interested in relatively small niche markets. Also, just like Fenix's subsidiaries, operating in the form of smaller business set-ups, SMEs can fine-tune product or service offerings and adjust prices appropriately for the narrower target customers.

Due to the economies of scale factor, it is usually unprofitable for more than a few companies to co-exist in a market, hence it is very difficult for SMEs to break into and establish a foothold in mainstream markets successfully. The need to spend extra money for name recognition and market reputation in an established market also acts as a deterrent to market entry for new companies.[7] Therefore, SMEs can target niche markets with unfulfilled needs and avoid competing head-on with large companies.

Conclusion

> Fashion, food and the things we fill our homes with stimulate all our senses: sight, hearing, smell, taste and touch. It is these experiences that Fenix Group seeks to enhance with its innovative products and the creative shopping environments it has developed. This attitude of enriching customers' lives by bringing them the best from around the world is at the heart of the group's achievements.
>
> – Fenix's 30th Anniversary Commemorative Booklet

The Fenix story is a lesson in how a company can take advantage of its strengths in understanding overseas and local market trends, creativity, flexibility and quality to tap into high-value-adding niche markets. Keung and Ogino created a successful network of businesses by their dedication and focus on adding value to niche markets that were in line with their management philosophy. For SMEs and potential entrepreneurs, the recipe for successful niche marketing is applicable to companies of all sizes and types.

---

1   The 12-year collaboration with Prada ended in 1999 when Prada Headquarters decided to handle worldwide distribution themselves.

2   According to Anteprima's official Website: www.anteprima.com/.

3   Kotler, P., (2000), *Marketing Management*, The Millennium Edition, Prentice Hall, p. 257.

4   Kotler.

5   Kotler.

6   Kotler.

7   Pindyck R. S. and Rubinfeld D. L., (2001), *Microeconomics*, fifth edition, Prentice Hall, p. 429.

12

Fat Angelo's
Entrepreneurial Growth

SIMON TAM AND MONICA WONG

PART I: BACKGROUND AND ISSUES

Introduction

Since the first meal was served in June 1998, Fat Angelo's had been a great sensation in Hong Kong's culinary scene. The management team of Fat Angelo's introduced a brand new dining concept to Hong Kong — Italian-American home-styled cooking served in large portions at a reasonable price. Sixteen months after the first restaurant opened its doors in Wanchai, Hong Kong Island, the management was ready to open a second branch, this time on Kowloon side. The new location was in Ashley Road, Tsim Sha Tsui. Although it was a backstreet location, it was only three blocks away from Nathan Road, one of the busiest roads in Hong Kong, perpetually packed with locals and tourists alike. The other shops on Ashley Road were mainly restaurants offering different styles of cuisine and varying levels of sophistication — from black-tie steak house to little mom-and-pop wonton noodle shops. The variety of restaurant choices drew a considerable number of hungry stomachs. The debut of the second Fat Angelo's was on 23 September 1999. Like the first one that had opened on the other side of the harbour, it became an instant hit. Two months later, a third branch was added on Elgin Street, Central. The neighbourhood was nicknamed "Soho" (south of Hollywood Road) and was dotted with exotic boutique restaurants.

Behind the bustling scenes, there was an issue occupying the minds of the managing partners. Next to the Ashley Road branch there was an additional room of approximately 2,500 square feet, adjacent to the main restaurant area. The room had its own separate street-front entrance, but due to fire department requirements the two separate rooms were treated as one unit and were included in the same lease agreement. Buying time to work out a long-term plan for the extra space, Andy Chworowsky, Dale Willet and Chris Gallaga, the founders and managing partners of Fat Angelo's, decided to use the space as a temporary store-room and office.

This temporary arrangement lasted for almost a year. In 2001, with the three shops fully up and running, the entrepreneurs thought it was time to take the business further by expanding into a new restaurant concept. After several rounds of meetings, they came down to three proposals to make use of the extra room for a new business: a pizza takeaway shop, a coffee shop or a seafood restaurant. Each option seemed to have its own pros and cons, so which one should they pick? Were there any other choices and possibilities?

Company Background

We were committed to contriving an un-contrived concept.

– Fat Angelo's Business Plan

Fat Angelo's was the brainchild of three entrepreneurs who were ex-colleagues in a successful chain of American-style restaurants in Hong Kong. The idea was actually an offshoot of Chworowsky's research efforts as business development manager at an American restaurant. When he put together his proposal for the board, he was absolutely positive about the idea of opening an Italian-American restaurant — but the board was not convinced.

Chworowsky moved with his missionary parents to Hong Kong in 1973, at the age of ten. Among other things, he had been an actor, a bartender and a ranch hand,and had dubbed kung fu movies into English.[1] Chworowsky received his high-school education in Hong Kong and was also a graduate of Cornell's School of Hotel Management. He went on to work for Dan Ryan's Chicago Grill; in fact, he was the American steak house's first employee in Hong Kong.

Confident that the Italian-American restaurant would be a winning business, Chworowsky decided to leave the company to start his own restaurant chain with two ex-colleagues in 1997. Drawing on the talents of each partner, the roles and responsibilities were defined immediately. Dale Willetts, a Canadian Chartered Accountant with more than 10 years of restaurant experience, would be in charge of finance and general administration. Christopher Gallaga, an Italian and an experienced executive chef with over 16 years in the business, would be in charge of food and kitchen operations.[2]

The Asian financial crisis was a nightmare for many, and the restaurant trade was one of the hardest-hit industries. During 1997, one in every five restaurants in Hong Kong folded after excessive cash bleeding caused by rising rents and escalating labour costs, followed by the outbreaks of bird flu and cholera. However, Chworowsky and his partners seized the opportunity to turn the economic adversity to their advantage. The bursting of the economic bubble pushed the real estate market downward, and many desirable sites suddenly became available at affordable prices. The entrepreneurs also targeted value-conscious customers in Hong Kong, both local Chinese and expatriates, with the formula that fitted perfectly with the prevalent economic climate. As Chworowsky recalled:

> Ours is a "red-ink" business — you always make money selling red ink during a bad economy because people need it. During the 1997 crisis, there were many restaurants, the majority were very expensive. A mid-scale restaurant would easily cost more than HK$300 per head. We aimed at serving inexpensive but decent food in a cheerful setting, targeting an average of HK$150 per person. Hong Kong people were famous for being very value-conscious and they were drawn by the high value we offered. We first opened our doors in early July 1997 and immediately we drew an awful lot of press. We became the talk of the town and were really full every night.

The three managing partners did not plan to do any marketing for the first two months, but tables were filled up by the second week. The successful launch continued to build into a steady operation that yielded a 10 percent net profit margin and a turnover of more than HK$1 million per month per shop.

Financing the Restaurant

> Under-capitalisation is the most common reason for restaurant failure. We did pessimistic, realistic and optimistic columns in our business plan and make sure we have enough capital under all circumstances.
>
> – Dale Willetts, Managing Partner

When the Asian economic crisis was at its worst, the entrepreneurs were about half-way through raising capital. Despite the economic turmoil, they decided to continue lobbying for their business. They had the full support of those investors who had already committed money. Finding additional investors proved to be easier than expected. The "red-ink" business seemed to appeal to the investors' appetites.

The managing partners incorporated the business under the name Gotham City Concepts Limited, and sought to raise HK$3.6 million through the placement of 1.2 million ordinary shares and HK$2.4 million in shareholder loans (debentures), as shown in Table 1 below:

Table 1   Initial Capital Structure

	Shares	Value HK$	Debentures	Value HK$	Total Value HK$
Managing Partners	1,400,000	$1,400,000	0	0	$1,400,000
Investment Partners	1,200,000	$1,200,000	2,400,000	$2,400,000	$3,600,00
Total	2,600,000	$2,600,000	2,400,000	$2,400,000	$5,000,000

The managing partners' capital contribution consisted entirely of share capital, while other shareholders contributed HK$2 of shareholder loan for each HK$1 of share capital. The share structure was designed to provide an incentive for the managing partners to maximise the long-term value of the company. It was also agreed that profits would be used first to pay interest and principal on the shareholder loan. No dividends on shares would be paid until the shareholder loans had been fully repaid.

The Dining Concept

> My partners and I see ourselves very much in the entertainment business rather than just a restaurant. We recreated the communal dining, cozy atmosphere. The philosophy is one of no-nonsense food, served abundantly, in an atmosphere that echoes a raucous countryside cantina.
>
> – Fat Angelo's Business Plan

Fat Angelo's cleverly blended the Chinese tradition of sharing dishes and the Western flair for a fun and entertaining dinning experience. The resemblance of Chinese noodles to spaghetti had gained Italian food a great deal of acceptance by the local palate (spaghetti was dubbed "Italian Noodles" in Chinese). At the same time, most expatriates identified closely with the family-run atmosphere. Instead of spending money on "gimmicks" or creating a high-brow dining environment, Fat Angelo's concentrated on maintaining a low cost base to keep prices at a reasonable level. To reinforce the notion of great value, in addition to the large portions that were served, salad and fresh-baked bread came free of charge with any main dish order.

The Competition

Italian restaurants in Hong Kong fell into two distinct categories. In the high-end segment, the competition for Fat Angelo's included restaurants that placed an emphasis on being "cool", up-to-date, sophisticated and sedate. In these "fine-dining" restaurants (e.g., Grissini and Va Bene), value was perceived in expensive cutlery, fancy china and elegant preparation of dishes. Fat Angelo's most direct competitors were in fact the lower to mid-scale Italian restaurants, most of them fast-food-styled franchised stores (e.g., Pizza Hut and Spaghetti House). Chworowsky and his partners believed that nobody in the Hong Kong restaurant trade understood the tradition of family-style Italian food.

The Menu

The menu at Fat Angelo's was based on the southern Italian food concept, which had a lot of similarities with Cantonese food — substantial, simple but nutritious. The style of food that Fat Angelo's served was also dubbed "immigrant Italian" food, which was typically found in Little Italy in New York City. As Chworowsky explained:

> The early immigrants to the USA from southern Italy had mostly led a rough and tough life back home, the only happy time they looked forward to was meal time when they gathered with their family, sharing the hearty dishes grandmothers prepared. In the New World, these immigrants discovered that rare and expensive foods in Palermo and Naples were relatively cheap. That, added to the bounty of new varieties and new ambitions, meant a credo of *abbondanza*, which remains to this day.

All branches featured the same menu — a simple selection of home-made style dishes. The food was not exotic, gourmet, fusion or some other trendy new taste. It was designed for family-style dining, and each menu item came in a "big" and "not-so-big" size. A "weekly special" featuring non-regular items kept the menu fresh to attract repeat patrons.

The Service

> We plan to break rules. This is not a restaurant to impress snobbish critics!
>
> – Fat Angelo's Business Plan

Compared with the usual dining experience in a Western restaurant, Fat Angelo's service was fast, unfussy and unpretentious. Frontline staff members were given more flexibility in delivering service in order to create a genuine homely and welcoming atmosphere — something Chworowsky referred to as "planned chaos". The philosophy at Fat Angelo's was one of no-nonsense food, served in an atmosphere that echoed a raucous countryside cantina in Italy, rather than a boutique or disco in Manhattan.

The Décor

The décor was also standardised across all Fat Angelo's restaurants. In order to create the ambience of a migration-era city restaurant, Fat Angelo's restaurants featured high ceilings and old-fashioned functional incandescent factory lights. Plain terracotta was used for the floor. Vintage Italian posters and black-and-white Italian family photos adorned the walls. Dark wood tables were large, rugged and covered with coarse green-and-white-checked linen. Chunky crockery, mismatched flatware and plain glass tumblers were used. The Wanchai restaurant was big enough to accommodate about 160 guests (roughly 3,500 square feet). The Tsim Sha Tsui and the Central restaurants had seat capacities of about 200 and 130 respectively. The tables were deliberately put quite close together to enhance the bustling family-run atmosphere and create the intimacy of a Little Italy-style shop-front restaurant.

The Price

> Fat Angelo's will be a place where no one will be afraid of picking up the cheque for a party of eight.
>
> – Fat Angelo's Business Plan

Great value for the money was one of the factors that differentiated Fat Angelo's from its competitors. Prices were set at a level that the management believed customers would find attractive. The targeted average cheque per person was around HK$150 to HK$200. In 1999, this price level was approximately 60 percent above that of the lower-end competitors and 50 percent cheaper than that of the high-end competitors.[3] Raw materials were purchased from local suppliers. Despite the initial difficulties in obtaining credit terms, which was normal for a new business, Fat Angelo's gradually built up a good rapport with its suppliers and was continuously striving to minimise costs. The gross profit margin was maintained at an impressive 75 percent.

The Location

The first Fat Angelo's restaurant was situated on a side street in the area between Wanchai and Causeway Bay. It was easily accessible but not right in the middle of high-rent districts. The locations of the second and third branches were carefully chosen in "shoulder" areas amid A-list locations. This strategy was in line with the management philosophy of maintaining a low cost base. Even though the restaurants were in B-list locations, rental expenses represented up to 30 percent of Fat Angelo's operating costs.

The Tsim Sha Tsui store was a ground-floor site on Ashley Road, between Canton Road and Nathan Road — two of the busiest streets in Hong Kong. The floor area of the main restaurant was approximately 4,000 square feet and the adjacent extra room was approximately 2,500 square feet. The main store was an ideal size for Fat Angelo's to accommodate around 200 customers. Using both stores for Fat Angelo's was not feasible as the total area would be too big to create the cosy and homely atmosphere the owners wanted. Moreover, including a separate area in the restaurant would jeopardise the family feel of the restaurant.

The Options

Having achieved great success in the first three restaurants, the managing partners were keen to grow the business with a new restaurant in the adjacent room. However, competition was intense. Within the 540-feet (180-metre) stretch on Ashley Road, there were 38 restaurants and takeaway stores. Nevertheless, the entrepreneurs were undeterred because they were encouraged by the overwhelming success of the other Fat Angelo's branches. The business was at a level that was 10 percent better than the most optimistic projection in the original business plan. Moreover, the company was cash-rich and had the luxury and flexibility to explore various options. After long late-night coffee sessions, the partners came up with a shortlist of three possible alternatives.

The pizza takeaway

Pizza had gained popularity among young locals as an alternative to Chinese fast food. Tourists staying in nearby hotels or shopping in the area would also be potential customers. Although there were already a few takeaway stores within the same block, none of them specialised in pizzas. Moreover, pizza had always been a menu item at Fat Angelo's, so it would be easy to produce more for the takeaway operation.

The coffee shop

The so-called "coffee culture" had been gaining attention and followers, especially among young locals. There were a few local Chinese-styled caféms and snack shops on Ashley Road, but no Western-style coffee shop. A new coffee shop would fill the void. For people in the area, particularly shoppers, a coffee shop would also provide a place to take a moment to pause for refreshment.

The seafood restaurant

Seafood had always been a basic element in the diet of Hong Kong people. The most popular way to cook seafood was the local Chinese style of steaming or pan-frying. Nonetheless, people also liked Japanese raw fish (sashimi) and other styles of preparing seafood such as baked lobster with cheese. The managing partners were thinking of transferring the winning concept of a fun, unpretentious atmosphere and the value proposition of Fat Angelo's into a new restaurant serving seafood cooked in Western styles.

Each alternative had its own pros and cons. Many blueprints were drafted to help visualise the different options. Thinking of the lines of people waiting to get into Fat Angelo's every night, the managing partners believed that the new restaurant would be able to survive simply by capturing the overflow. As they studied one of the many draft floor plans, some questions remained: Could they apply the Fat Angelo's concept to a seafood restaurant? How about the other two options? Were there any other choices? Which one was the best?

PART II: LESSONS LEARNED

What Were the Critical Success Factors of Fat Angelo's?

In Chworowsky's words, Fat Angelo's was a "red-ink" business. Fat Angelo's market positioning was pitched perfectly to the value-conscious Hong Kong market, right at the time of an economic downturn. The menu price and restaurant ambience filled a niche market between the high-end, elegant Italian dining and the fast-food-styled franchised, localised Italian chain. There were virtually no competitors in Fat Angelo's market, which was a great advantage for a new start-up business — the first mover could have the market all to itself.

The pricing strategy also reinforced the value proposition that Fat Angelo's business was built upon. At 1999 levels, a standard four-course meal with soup, appetiser, main course and dessert would cost HK$300 at Fat Angelo's, compared with HK$580 at Grissini, a top-tier Italian restaurant in a five-star hotel.[4] Although the bill would be 62 percent more than for a similar meal set at Spaghetti House, the portions of dishes presented at Fat Angelo's were substantially larger and the atmosphere a lot more up-market. With a high turnover and a low cost of raw materials, Fat Angelo's enjoyed a gross profit margin of more than 75 percent.

Although the Fat Angelo's dining concept was inspired by the "immigrant Italian" restaurants in New York City, the doors were open for everyone in Hong Kong, Chinese and Westerners alike. Unlike most other Western restaurants in Hong Kong, which relied on expatriates and tourists, Fat Angelo's enjoyed a larger customer base and a greater potential for future growth in different neighbourhoods around Hong Kong.

Cost control was another major strength of Fat Angelo's. Locations were carefully chosen in the "shoulder" areas of high-rent, bustling neighbourhoods. The side-street areas provided the benefit of low rent and at the same time fitted the concept of a family-run, down-to-earth kind of restaurant. In Hong Kong, rental expenses could take up as much as 40 to 50 percent of a restaurant's operating costs, but Fat Angelo's maintained it at below 30 percent. Part of the money saved could then be transferred to the customers through setting reasonable price levels.

Just as any other start-up businesses, the people at the steering wheel had a vital role in the success of the venture. The entrepreneurs' determination, confidence and commitment were evident in the financing arrangement. All profits from the venture, it was agreed, would go straight into the next venture, which demonstrated the long-term commitment of the partners. Moreover, the managing partners also took salary cuts of about 60 percent to 70 percent each to show their determination in making it work. Needless to say, the entrepreneurs invested substantial amounts of "sweat equity" and dropping by the restaurants at odd hours from time to time to make sure everything was going well.

What Happened to the Extra Room?

In the end, the entrepreneurs decided to open a seafood restaurant. Pizza was a core menu item served in Fat Angelo's, a pizza express would cannibalise the restaurant's business. As for the coffee shop, there was simply not enough walk-by traffic to generate the needed turnover.

One hundred and twenty five seats were put into the space and the doors of Buddy's Seafood Restaurant were opened. However, it did not perform as well as expected and lasted only six months.

Evaluation of Buddy's Seafood Restaurant

When asked about his opinion of the short span of Buddy's Seafood Restaurant, Chworowsky said,

> In retrospect, we had over-estimated the acceptance and popularity of Western-styled seafood to the local palates. We were over-optimistic and under-researched. A restaurant is pretty capital-intensive; we just did not have enough turnovers to make the business worthwhile.

Buddy's Seafood Restaurant was designed as a replica of Fat Angelo's winning business formula — simple food at great value, served in a fun and entertaining dining environment. However, with the core product changed from spaghetti and pizza to seafood, the same formula did not yield the same results. Fat Angelo's success was due to the high turnover and the low cost of raw materials, resulting in a lucrative profit margin. Seafood has always been a regular item in a typical local meal, and freshness is the single most important thing people look for when having seafood. Hong Kong people's tastes buds are sharpened from childhood for freshness in seafood. After all, Hong Kong was a fishing village only 150 years ago. However, from a restaurateur's perspective, this means a shorter shelf life for more expensive raw materials, which translates into a higher cost of goods sold and a lower profit margin. It is simply impossible to keep the prices at a low enough level to re-create the Fat Angelo's value proposition and still keep the restaurant profitable.

Managing Entrepreneurial Growth

Most entrepreneurs are well prepared to react to the initial obstacles of launching their business. However, planning for the growth stage often tends to be informal and unsystematic. It is particularly important for an emerging venture that is rapidly expanding, with constantly increasing operations, to formalise its planning, because a great deal of complexity exists.[5] Alfred Chandler has outlined the following stages of a firm's evolution: [6]

1. Initial expansion and accumulation of resources
2. Rationalisation of the use of resources
3. Expansion into new markets to assure the continued use of resources
4. Development of new structures to ensure continuing mobilisation of resources

These four phases in fact correspond to the following stages in a typical venture's lifecycle:

1. New venture development
2. Start-up activities
3. Venture growth
4. Business stabilisation
5. Innovation or decline

The growth stage often causes major changes in entrepreneurial strategy. Competition and other market forces may call for the reformulation of strategies. Some entrepreneurs may want to test their creative ideas in other new ventures. This growth stage may present newer and more dominant problems than those the entrepreneur faced during the start-up stage.[7]

The issue faced by the entrepreneurs in this case seemed to be simply a decision about what to do with the extra space next door to their main restaurant. In fact, the fundamental issue pertained to the strategic planning for the growth stage. Many entrepreneurs are trapped by the usual pitfalls:

1. Once the business is up and running and stabilised, creative entrepreneurs are usually tempted to try out new ideas and will often side-track to other new ventures in search of the satisfaction and excitement they experienced when building the new business.
2. Encouraged by the success achieved in setting up a new business, most entrepreneurs feel invincible. They become overly optimistic and usually rely on their "gut feeling" and intuition rather than objective market research.

Conclusion

> You are only as good as the last meal you served. Our goal is to make sure that more of our guests are leaving a lot happier than when they come in.
>
> – Dale Willetts, Managing Partner

After the Buddy's Seafood Restaurant episode, the extra room was then converted into a Fat Angelo's banquet room for large parties, but the number of party bookings was not substantial enough to make it a profitable operation. Upon lease renewal, this time the managing partners successful re-negotiated with the landlord, who agreed to take back the extra room.

Since then, Gotham City Concepts Limited has continued to prosper. The management learned to be more cautious about branching out into other types of restaurants, and no other new restaurants have been opened, except for a new branch of Fat Angelo's in the residential area of Tseung Kwan O in eastern Kowloon. It was opened at the end of 2002. The management has continued to look for opportunities to open more Fat Angelo's Italian Restaurants. The possibility of introducing Fat Angelo's into food courts is also on the agenda.

The Fat Angelo's case illustrates some of the start-up activities involved in building a new restaurant. SMEs at the development stage could learn from Fat Angelo's experience and take extra care to avoid under-capitalisation. It is easy to under-estimate the cost of fitting out a restaurant. Moreover, it takes both artistic and scientific skills to make a restaurant business successful. Artistic skill is needed to manage issues such as creating the right ambience in the restaurant with suitable music, lighting and decorations, and ensuring the right service style and food presentation. Scientific skill is required to monitor the numbers, build a good information system and track income, inventories and expenses. The managers have to manage the operational flow such as on-time delivery by suppliers and the logistical flow from taking customers' orders to serving the food on the table. Entrepreneurs must also be prepared for difficulties in the early stages, including sceptical suppliers who demand harsh credit terms such as personal guarantees or cash on delivery.

For SMEs that are in the growth stage, it is important to make sure that the concept of the business is still strong and fresh. Innovation is important for the long-term success of a business; however it is equally important to keep strategic focus. The case also provides an example of the importance of knowing when to fold a business. Instead of dragging on the seafood business, Chworowsky and his partners realised that it was not working and wisely made the decision to close down the business and move on. Very often, entrepreneurs have very strong emotional ties with their brainchild and tend to hold on to a failing business longer than necessary.

According to Hong Kong Government statistics, in 2002 there were 7,208 restaurant licences and 2,452 light refreshment restaurant licences in force in Hong Kong. This meant that, on average, there were eight restaurants per square kilometre. Once the rush and excitement of being the new kid on the block is gone, it takes more effort to stay competitive than it does during the initial stages.

---

1 Sharp, J. (2003), "Andy Chworowsky: FCC Member, Restaurateur and ... Elf", *The Correspondent*, Dec 2002-Jan 2003 Issue.

2 Gallaga later left the company in 2001.

3 Tilton, S. (1998), "Fat Angelo's Thrives by Filling a Void", *The Asian Wall Street Journal*, 12 October.

4 Tilton.

5 Kuratko, D. F. and Hodgetts, R. M. (1998), *Entrepreneurship: A Contemporary Approach*, (fourth edition), The Dryden Press, Harcourt Brace College Publishers, p. 465.

6 Chandler, A. (1962), *Strategy and Structure*, Cambridge, MA: MIT Press.

7 Kuratko and Hodgetts, p. 494.

13

Moiselle
Prêt-à-porter Hong Kong Style

BENNETT YIM AND MONICA WONG

It was March 2003. Moiselle had just celebrated the first anniversary of its listing on the Hong Kong Stock Exchange. It was 11 February 2002 when the trading of "Moiselle International" commenced on the main board. The Moiselle Group designed, developed, manufactured, retailed and wholesaled apparel under the brand names "Moiselle", "moi", "imaroon" and "M.kids". The core brand name "Moiselle" was established in 1996 by Boby Chan and his wife, who are chairman and executive director of the company respectively. For the three years prior to the listing, the Moiselle Group achieved enviable gross profit margins averaging 76 percent, as compared to the industry average of 45 percent. In less than 10 years, the entrepreneurial couple had managed to grow their retail business from one lone shop selling generic imports to a network of 72 branded retail stores — 35 in Hong Kong, 32 in mainland China and five in Taiwan. To take advantage of the economic growth in the Mainland and the increasing purchasing power of its residents, they decided to focus the group's future development in the Mainland. How could the Moiselle Group leverage the value of the brand to expand its business in the Mainland? What was the road to success in building the HK$300 million dollar "Moiselle" brand?[1]

PART I: BACKGROUND AND ISSUES

Company Background

From 1982 to 1993: The manufacturing era

In the early 1980s, Hong Kong's average personal income level ranked among the highest in the world, and people pursued improvements in their living standards and were gradually reaching a high level of affluence. People had more disposable income to spend on food, clothes and leisure activities.

Against this favourable social and economic backdrop, the Moiselle Group commenced its business in August 1982. Boby Chan and his wife, together with his wife's brother Chui, established Boo Gie Garment to engage in the trading, manufacturing and wholesale of women's apparel in Hong Kong. Like many other OEMs (original equipment manufacturers) at that time, the operations of the group were conducted in a small-scale factory in Wanchai, Hong Kong, with approximately 24 workers. In 1984, in light of the increasing number of orders, the group relocated to self-owned premises approximately double the size of the Wanchai factory, and the number of workers increased to approximately 70. In 1989, the group started to sub-contract certain production processes to its sub-contractors in order to support the increasing demand for its products.

From 1993 to 1996: Retailing in the early stage

In April 1993, the Chans opened their first store, adding retail to the group's portfolio. They sold only generic imported apparel in the retail store. Gradually, the profit margin was diminishing with the selling of imports, so in 1996 they decided to hire two in-house designers to design and develop a propriety line of women's wear as a new revenue source. At around the same time, a new "yuppie" class of young urban professionals emerged, who enjoyed high salaries and who emphasised quality-of-life issues. They went after famous brand names and good-quality fashion. There was also an increasing number of females joining the white-collar workforce. Given these economic and demographic characteristics, the group decided to position its products in the upper-middle segment, focusing on executive suits for female professionals aged between 25 and 45, who were believed to be underserved. Subsequently, the Moiselle brand expanded to include mix-and-match, eveningwear, casual wear and accessories. In April 1996, the Moiselle brand was officially launched.

From 1997 onwards: Rapid expansion

Soon after the launch of the Moiselle brand name, it received positive feedback from the market and quickly established a group of loyal followers. As the ancient Chinese saying goes, "every crisis brings an opportunity"; the 1997 Asian financial crisis was a disaster for many, but a blessing for the Chans. Landlords slashed rental rates in a falling property market. Shops in prime shopping areas that the group could not afford in the past, became available at low prices. Armed with a healthy cashflow statement, the entrepreneurs started their grandiose expansion plan — nine shops were opened in 1997–98. It was an extraordinary achievement under the economic climate at the time. The Moiselle Group's extensive network of sourcing, manufacturing, retailing and wholesaling started to take shape, and the operation successfully transformed into OBM (own brand manufacturing). Being an OBM means being in the retail business. More Moiselle stores were opened and expansion reached the Chinese mainland and Taiwan. In 2001, diffusion brands were added to broaden the reach within the target market. The store "imaroon" was launched in response to the demand from young working women, offering simple fashion and basic wear with less extravagant decoration. Another store "moi" catered for the "nine-to-five" needs of young female professionals, with clothing offered at more competitive prices, and "M.kids" was the product line for children in Hong Kong. By March 2003, there were 31 Moiselle stores and one imaroon store in 21 cities in the Mainland, five Moiselle stores in Taiwan and 22 Moiselle stores, 12 imaroon stores and one M.kids store in Hong Kong.

The "Moiselle" branded products contributed more than 84 percent of the group's turnover. For the 2001 financial year, the total group turnover was HK$173 million, of which 88 percent came from the retail operation. The gross and net profits after tax were HK$135 million and HK$42 million respectively. Turnover for the years 2002 and 2003 increased by 11 percent and 14 percent, amounting to HK$191 million and HK$218 million respectively.

Hong Kong, being the Moiselle group's major market, accounted for more than 81 percent of the group's total turnover. Notwithstanding this, 20 percent of the sales in Moiselle's Hong Kong stores were to tourists from the Mainland. The proportion of sales coming from retail stores outside of Hong Kong (i.e., from the Mainland and Taiwan) was also increasing.

Building the Moiselle Brand

> If the new brand does not convey its values from the very start, it is quite unlikely that it will manage to become a major brand.
>
> – Jean-Noel Kapferer, Strategic Brand Management

Hong Kong consumers, especially women, were renowned for being brand-conscious and well-versed with top apparel designer names and the latest fashion trends. From the very beginning, the Chans were determined to establish a distinctive brand image to attract customer attention. They realised that a consistent brand image and service across all shops were key factors to sustain further growth. They chose the word "Moiselle" (from the word "Mademoiselle", which means "Miss" in French) to be the brand name and the representation of their feminine-styled products. As the business grew bigger, the building of the Moiselle brand was important not only to maintain a consistent image, but also to create value in the customers' minds and to differentiate Moiselle from its competitors. Therefore, they invested more resources to build the Moiselle brand so that it represented class, style, good quality and high-class values. In order to communicate the set of values, attributes and benefits of Moiselle, the group's decisions on the product offering, price levels, channels of distribution and promotional activities were carefully planned to ensure that the brand value would be enhanced.

Product

When Moiselle was first launched in April 1996, executive suits were the major product line, as Hong Kong consumers tended to prefer casual work wear. The response was not as positive as expected. Therefore, the group introduced mix-and-match collections, eveningwear and complementary accessories. With its own team of Hong Kong designers, the group aimed at achieving the "Moiselle look" — a classic, sleek and feminine style, updated with details to reflect the current fashion trends. A portion of Moiselle merchandise and its "signature" products were hand-made with beads, sequins and embroidery. These products with an emphasis on details appealed to Moiselle's target customers and established a distinctive brand style and value, thereby creating a group of loyal followers.

New stock was added to the stores twice a week and products were reviewed on a weekly basis. Every fashion season, 800 styles were created, which translated into 1,600 styles per year.[2] The rapid turnaround was made possible by the vertically integrated operation structure, which enabled a very short production lead-time, from only one week to one month at most. Each style was produced in relatively small quantities to create a sense of rarity, and this encouraged customers to purchase immediately. This also minimised the need to offer discounts to push leftover items.

Price

The regular price of Moiselle products ranged from HK$599 to HK$12,999, a medium-to-high priced category. When setting the price levels, the disposable income of target customers and the value of the products as perceived by the customers were taken into consideration. Store discounts were intended to be limited to end of season sales. Products were typically sold at the original marked prices at the beginning of the season, through to mid-season. Marked-down items that were not sold at the end of each season were generally moved to the group's clearance centres, which were stores with leases near expiry that the group had no intention to renew or redecorate.

Place

After the successful launch of Moiselle products in 1996, the group expanded its distribution network rapidly by opening new stores. By the end of 2001, the group had 23 Moiselle stores in major shopping malls and central business districts, which were locations frequented by the target group of female customers with middle-plus income. However, attempts to upgrade the brand image by opening new stores in top-tier shopping malls faced obstacles. Local property developers preferred to reserve their prime shopping malls for foreign designer labels and turned away local Hong Kong brands. Gaining a foothold in top-tier locations remained an important strategy for building the image of luxurious feminine fashion.

In addition to choosing the right place, store decoration was equally, if not more, important. An in-house visual merchandising team was established to devise window displays and window dressing that would induce passers-by to enter the stores. Each Moiselle store was decorated to create a spacious, comfortable and upscale store environment with contemporary furnishings and high-visibility glass exteriors.

Promotion

In order to increase brand awareness, the group engaged a young local TV personality as the image model for the Moiselle brand. In 1998, Ada Choi Siu-fan, an up-and-coming television star who was seen as young, gentle and independent, became the house model of Moiselle. She was often portrayed in Hong Kong soap operas as a young professional working woman. Huge posters featuring Ada Choi wearing the latest Moiselle designs were displayed in the stores. Every new season, Ada Choi would pose for the new catalogue to be distributed to customers. Advertisements were placed in popular fashion magazines and newspapers, and on MTR trackside panels and bus panels. Sponsorship of TV game shows and other public relations events were organised. In order to promote an international image for the group's products and to explore overseas markets, fashion shows were held in Beijing and Fukuoka in Japan. As for customer retention, Moiselle also launched a membership scheme offering discounts on merchandise; catalogues and invitations to private sales and fashion shows. In addition, the Moiselle Visa card further strengthened the loyalty programme by adding extra convenience and credit benefits to customers.

The group also won awards from the Hong Kong Trade and Development Council for creativity, marketability and the best use of fabric. This recognition contributed positively to the brand image. Marketing and promotional expenses amounted to approximately HK$1.22 million, HK$2.18 million and HK$3.33 million per year respectively for the three years ending 31 March 2001. In the second quarter of 2001, approximately HK$1.1 million was spent on marketing and promotion.

Industry Competition

In 1999, expenditure on clothing ranked second among all items of expenditure by Hong Kong people, following expenditure on rent, rates, water and housing maintenance charges, which are considered basic necessities. People in Hong Kong dedicated an average of approximately 15.5 percent of their disposable income to clothing (including clothes, shoes and accessories).

The sales value of feminine outerwear increased from approximately HK$2,002 million in 1994 to approximately HK$2,325 million in 1997, representing a compound annual growth rate of approximately 5.1 percent. However, because of the economic downturn after 1998, the per capita sales value of feminine outerwear dropped by approximately 12 percent and approximately 13.2 percent in 1998 and 1999 respectively, compared with their respective previous corresponding years. Faced with Hong Kong's sluggish economy, many fashion retailers turned to places outside of Hong Kong for growth opportunities, and the Mainland was the prime choice for many retailers.

The women's retail apparel industry in Hong Kong was highly competitive. The group competed with numerous domestic and foreign specialty brand retailers, department stores and mass merchandisers engaged in the retail of women's apparel, accessories, footwear and general merchandise in Hong Kong. Moiselle's direct competitors included local brands Jessica and Episode, both targeting the same segment. Moiselle also faced increasing competition from foreign brands such as French Connection (UK), Kookai (France), Agnes B. (France) and Mango (Spain). Indirect competition also came from Veeko and Wanko, which were targeting the mid-range market.

There were more than 200 "home-grown" Hong Kong fashion labels in the market. The majority of them targeted the young female customer group. The table in Exhibit 1 shows a comparison of a few representative Hong Kong brands.

The Mainland Market

Along with the liberalisation of its economy, the Mainland market, in its initial developing stage, experienced rapid growth from the beginning of the 1990s. Amidst the global economic slowdown subsequent to the Asian financial turmoil, the Mainland's economy continued to grow in 1998 and 1999. The per capita GDP grew from approximately RMB 3,923 in 1994 to approximately RMB 7,078 in 2000, representing a compound annual growth rate of approximately 10.3 percent.[3] The general income level in the Mainland also increased steadily during the same period, leading to a gradual improvement in the standard of living.

Population was a major factor contributing to the performance of the retail market. The Mainland had a population of approximately 1.26 billion people in 1999, of whom about 49 percent were female. Clothing ranked as the third-largest among all categories of expenditure in 1999, following food and the second category of recreation/education/cultural services. The total sales value of feminine outerwear grew from approximately RMB170.4 billion in 1994 to approximately RMB228.7 billion in 1999, representing a compound annual growth rate of approximately 6.1 percent.

Moreover, from 1997, visitors from the Mainland replaced Japanese visitors as the top spenders on luxury apparel in Hong Kong. In 2002, Mainland visitors were the highest per capita spenders of all visitors to Hong Kong.

Expansion opportunities

Supported by the rising spending power of Mainland consumers, various Hong Kong products had already established footholds in the Mainland market in the 1990s. In general, Hong Kong brands positioned themselves in the mid-range market segment. Moiselle entered the Mainland retail market in December 2001, through franchise agreements. Seven Moiselle stores were opened in seven major cities: Shenyang, Wenzhou, Foshan, Fuzhou, Chengdu, Kunming and Wuhan. The Moiselle brand name (with its Chinese translation) was a registered trademark and was used in the same way throughout the Mainland.

In the Mainland, there was a big demand for lifestyle products in the middle-to-upper-class segment. According to a survey conducted by the Hong Kong Trade Development Council, Hong Kong brands were ranked number one in the mid-range garment market by respondents in Beijing, Shanghai, Guangzhou, Chengdu and Dalian. Consumers were more brand-conscious than they had previously been and the major factors affecting their buying decisions were style, quality and price. Rapid product cycles and variety in styles were another significant strength of Hong Kong brands. Mainland consumers wanted variety in colour and style, and were willing to pay a premium for higher-quality products.

Moiselle's initial success in the Mainland was attributable to the strong brand image and the wide variety of style in the products. The Moiselle brand represented Hong Kong values and lifestyle, which were highly regarded by Mainland consumers. It symbolised up-to-date style, upper-middle class values and superior quality. Moiselle enjoyed high brand awareness in the Mainland because the house model, Ada Choi, was recognisable to Mainland people who watched Hong Kong television programmes. The large number of Mainland tourists visiting Hong Kong also increased brand awareness, as they saw Moiselle stores in shopping malls.

Moiselle had an advantage over its Mainland competitors in terms of design and store decoration. When compared with European and other imports, its products were priced more reasonably, and it had a better understanding of Mainland customers' tastes and needs than the overseas retailers. All of these added to the equity of the Moiselle brand. Due to the high perceived value of the brand, a premium of 15 to 20 percent higher than the Hong Kong price tag was charged.

As the Mainland market was growing rapidly, with increasing sales potential, the Chans planned to use 35 percent of the HK$56.5 million raised from the new issues of stock in the listing of the group for the development and expansion of the group's operations and stores in the Mainland. They had proved that the brand equity could contribute to the profitability of the group. So how should the group leverage the Moiselle brand equity to expand further in the Mainland and beyond?

PART II: LESSONS LEARNED

Building the Moiselle Brand Equity

Start with the right name

The brand is not the product, but it gives the product meaning and defines its identity in both time and space. [4] It is important that a new brand conveys its values from the very start. The name Moiselle came from the French word *Mademoiselle*, which is a form of polite address for a girl or young woman. The name is associated with France, youth, femininity and a hint of aristocracy, conveying an image of style, quality and elegance. It is a simple word that stands for what the product is — classic, sleek and feminine-styled apparel. Brand building means making a product stand for something, thus creating positive interest that makes target customers buy or support the product and keep supporting it against the efforts of competitors. [5] In that sense, Moiselle took a successful first step in building a new brand, making its product synonymous with feminine style and quality.

Product strategy

The product itself is at the heart of brand equity, as it is the primary influence on what the customer experiences with a brand. Designing and delivery a product that fully satisfies customers' needs is a prerequisite for successful marketing. [6] Moiselle designed and produced hand-made apparel featuring beads and embroidery, creating a distinctive image and a suggestion of value. This style of apparel satisfied, and to a certain extent surpassed, the expectations of Moiselle's target female customers aged between 25 and 45 with middle-plus income, who were looking for high-quality fashion. Moiselle has become a niche player in the underserved market of feminine-styled and elaborately decorated fashion, creating a group of loyal supporters.

Another key feature of Moiselle's product strategy is the variety and rarity of its products. It normally introduces new stock to the stores every Tuesday and Friday. The Company's ability to produce many styles in small quantities is one of its key success factors. "Every shop has two or three pieces, so people know if they want this item, they have to buy it today. Of course, for really popular designs we can do repeat orders, but this way we don't have any pressure to discount," Boby Chan explained. Turning over merchandise more frequently will attract customers to visit the shop more. The variety and rarity also create a sense of uniqueness, thus increasing the perceived value of the brand.

Pricing strategy

Customers may infer the quality of a product on the basis of its price. Furthermore, they may also combine their quality perceptions with their price perceptions to arrive at an assessment of the product's perceived value.[7] For that reason, Moiselle adopts a medium-to-high price policy. Price discounts are minimised through stock planning and production in smaller quantities to avoid out-of-season merchandise. Product clearances take place only in designated clearance centres that are usually locations that it plans to move out of. This pricing policy is consistent with the upper-middle-class brand image and reinforces the brand equity, which in turn means a price premium can be charged. The result is a maximised profit margin, and this explains why Moiselle is able to achieve a profit margin well above the industry average.

Distribution channel strategy

The way a product is sold can have a profound impact on sales success and brand equity. Moiselle distributes its products at its own company stores so as to gain control over the selling process and build stronger relationships with customers. These stores are a means to showcase the brand's distinctive characteristics and all of its different product varieties. For customers, the store decoration and display contribute to the overall consumption experience and increase the perceived value of the product. This is especially true in Hong Kong, where going to shopping malls is one of the most popular pastimes. They serve to enhance the brand equity by offering another channel for differentiation from competitors. The company can also analyse the size, location, demographics, sales and inventory history of each store to determine the quantity of merchandise to be allocated according to each store's customer base, in line with their tastes and needs.

As for the difficulties faced in opening stores in Hong Kong's top-tier shopping malls, Boby Chan's solution was to lease street-front stores next to these top-tier malls so as to capture customers in the high-end segment for a brand upgrade.

Promotional strategy

Moiselle is the first Hong Kong fashion retailer to use a television star as the icon of the brand. The arrangement has turned out to be a win-win strategy — while Ada Choi has gained popularity with increased exposure as a house model, Moiselle has also benefited from her increasing "star power" in Hong Kong, the Mainland and other Asian countries. The matching images of Ada Choi and the Moiselle brand have created a positive reinforcement in customers' minds, enabling Moiselle to stand out from the very crowded market.

Most of the mid-range Hong Kong brands engage generic Western models to feature their products to create an image of foreign imports, which are regarded as superior to local products. Examples are Giordano, G2000 and U.W.N. The common characteristics of these brands are the emphasis on price rather than brand image. Hence they use unknown faces to showcase their products. At the other end of the spectrum, with high-end fashion labels, some successful pioneers in Hong Kong fashion labels such as Vivienne Tam have made it big in New York before returning to the Hong Kong market as "expatriate" labels. They are in a unique category, targeting a very small niche market.

Direct competitors of Moiselle, including Veeko, Wanko, Episode and Jessica, use different promotional strategies. In 2001 and 2002, the Hong Kong brands Wanko and Veeko (both owned by Veeko International Holding Limited), signed up actress Carina Lau Ka-ling and singer-actress Sammi Cheng Sau-man as the respective brand "ambassadors". Following in the footsteps of Moiselle, Veeko International is trying to build a Hong Kong brand image. Wanko is targeted at more mature working women, mainly offering suits, whereas Veeko targets a younger audience, offering mix-and-match casual wear. Both brands aim at the middle-of-the-range segment, hoping that by using two A-list stars as house models, the brand image will be upgraded to the upper-middle segment. However, the prices and products remain in the lower-middle to middle segment, not matching the image of its house models. Therefore, overall, the brand images are less clear.

Episode and Jessica are two brands owned by the Fang Brothers. Since the 1990s, the focus of Fang Brothers' retail business has shifted to Europe, especially the UK. Therefore, no advertisements have been placed in the local Hong Kong market and the number of retail stores has not increased in recent years in Hong Kong. The Fang Brothers want to build the image of Episode and Jessica as international brands.

Leveraging the Moiselle Brand Equity in the Mainland

A strong brand position means the brand has a unique, credible, sustainable and valued place in customers' minds. It revolves around a benefit that helps the product stand apart from the competition.[8] Moiselle applied a consistent market positioning in Hong Kong and the Mainland. Despite the climatic and geographical variations within the Mainland, the culture of Mainland cities and Hong Kong is very similar. Moreover, there is a high level of traffic between the Mainland and Hong Kong, which makes it easier to market the products. If the market positioning varies in different places, the brand image will be diluted or weakened. Given that Hong Kong soap operas are popular in the Mainland, Ada Choi is also a recognised face in the Mainland market, which greatly helps Mainland customers to identify with the characteristics of the Moiselle brand.

It is also important to maintain consistency, as this provides benchmarks and tools to control the quality of service and delivery by the franchisees and authorised stores. Its well known and respected brand name has helped Moiselle to find qualified and experienced franchisees and partners for its authorised stores, greatly reducing the risk exposure and the learning curve for the group.

To capitalise on the strong brand value, Moiselle is able to charge a premium price, usually 30 percent higher than locally made fashion items, and about 15 to 20 percent above the Hong Kong price tag.

Conclusion

As Kapferer said, "Manufacturers make products; consumers buy brands."[9] Moiselle has successfully established its position as a Hong Kong fashion brand in Mainland through marketing strategies in product, price, place and promotion. When customers buy a Moiselle product, they are not buying the clothes, they are also purchasing the Hong Kong lifestyle, the glamour, the self-esteem and the status symbol.

High value, as perceived by customers, makes it possible for the company to charge a premium price and an incremental attraction or loyalty mark-up. Moiselle's success in creating brand value is evident in its superior profit margins compared with other Hong Kong brands.

Companies should realise that a brand is an essential asset. Moiselle is an example of the power of a strong brand. For SMEs, the key to brand building is to define the brand value and culture from the very beginning and to implement a comprehensive marketing strategy to develop the brand. A successful brand not only brings higher profit margins, it also takes a company beyond boundaries and creates great value in the long term.

---

[1] Valuation by Greater China Appraisal Limited dated 31 October 2001, as detailed in the *Prospectus*, Moiselle International Holdings Limited.
[2] Based on two fashion seasons per year: Spring/Summer and Autumn/Winter.
[3] US$1 = RMB 8.27
[4] Kapferer, J.-N. (1997), *Strategic Brand Management*, Second Edition, Kogan Page, p. 17.
[5] Marconi, J. (2000), *The Brand Marketing Book*, NTC and American Marketing Association, p. 9.
[6] Keller, K. L. (1998), *Strategic Brand Management*, Prentice-Hall, p. 176, 183.
[7] Keller, p. 183.
[8] Davis, S. M. (2002), *Brand Asset Management*, Jossey-Bass, p. 109.
[9] Kapferer, p. 132.

Exhibit 1   Hong Kong Brand Comparison

Brands	Target Segment	Product Styles	Approximate Price Range[1]	Promotion and Advertising in 2003	House Model	Store Location	Stores Outside of Hong Kong[2]
Giordano	• Lower-middle segment. • Males and females. • Age 15–35.	• Casual wear, sports wear and jeans, all with very simple designs, for males and females. • Mass-produced garments.	• HK$30–500	• 2003 tagline: "Simply Me". • Mainly in gossip magazines and MTR trackside panels. • Images of models displayed inside the shops.	• No house model. • Use Caucasian or Western-looking models.	• Approx. 40 stores on street level and in major shopping malls.	• The Mainland • Macau • Taiwan • Singapore • Japan
Giordano Ladies	• Lower-middle segment. • Females only. • Age 20–35.	• Suits and basic mix-and-match office wear with very simple design and colour. • Mass-produced garments.	• HK$100–2,000	• Privilege Card loyalty programme. • Images of models displayed inside the shops.	• No house model. Use Caucasian or Western-looking models.	• Approx. 8 stores on street level and in shopping malls.	• The Mainland • Taiwan
G2000[3]	• Lower-middle segment. • Age 20–35.	• Mix and match office wear with simple modern style, for male and female. • Mass produced garments.	• HK$100–1,000	• Minimal advertisements placed. • G2000 Premium Card loyalty programme.	• No house model. Use Caucasian models for catalogues only.	(G2000, and U.W.N. combined) • Approx. 40 stores on street level and in major shopping malls.	(Combined) • The Mainland • Macau • Taiwan • Singapore • Malaysia • Thailand • Indonesia • Korea • The Philippines • The Middle East • Central America
U.W.N. (U2 Women)	• Lower-middle segment • Age 20–35.	• Feminine city-styled casual wear. • Mass produced garments.	• HK$100–300	• Minimal advertisements placed. • U2 Plus loyalty programme.			
Michel Rene[4]	• Middle-of-the-range segment. • Males and females. • Age 20–45.	• Suits and mix-and-match ladies' wear for all occasions.	• HK$200–2,000	• No advertisements placed • Images of models displayed inside the shops. • YGM Membership Card	• Caucasian models used until summer 2003 when two local TV presenters were hired as house models.	• Approx. 20 stores inside department stores and shopping malls.	• The Mainland • Taiwan • Macau • Japan

1 US$1 = HK$7.8
2 Store locations according to information on the Website or annual report of each brand, August 2003.
3 G2000, U2 and U.W.N. are brand names owned by the G2000 Group.
4 Owned by YGM Trading Limited.

Brands	Target Segment	Product Styles	Approximate Price Range	Promotion and Advertising in 2003	House Model	Store Location	Stores Outside of Hong Kong
Veeko[5]	• Middle of the range. • Female Only. • Age 16–29.	• Trendy casual wear. • Many styles, small quantity each.	• HK$100–1,000	• Images of house model displayed at all corners inside the stores. • VIP Loyalty Programme.	• Top Hong Kong movie star, Carina Lau, as house model.	(Veeko and Wanko combined) • Approx. 52 stores on street level and in major shopping malls.	• The Mainland • Taiwan • Macau • Singapore
Wanko	• Middle of the range. • Female Only. • Age 20–36.	• Suits and mix-and-match office wear. • Many styles, small quantity each.	• HK$100–1,000	• Images of house model displayed at all corners inside the stores. • VIP Loyalty Programme.	• Top Hong Kong singer-actress, Sammi Cheng, as house model.		
Episode[6]	• Upper-middle segment. • Female Only. • Age 25–45.	• Elegant "lounge wear" and suits. • Many styles, small quantity each.	• HK$300–20,000	• No advertisements. • Loyalty Programme.	• No house model. • Uses professional Caucasian models.	• 2 stores on street level in the busiest districts.	• UK and Europe
Jessica	• Upper-middle segment. • Female Only. • Age 25–40.	• Young, modern and stylish casual wear. • Many styles, small quantity each.	• HK$100–10,000	• No advertisements. • Loyalty Programme.	• No house model. • Uses professional Caucasian models.	• Approx. 7 stores in major shopping malls and inside street-level Episode stores.	• The Mainland • Taiwan • Macau • Singapore • Philippines • Thailand • The Middle East
Moiselle	• Upper-middle segment. • Female Only. • Age 25–45.	• Suits, mix-and-match items, evening wear and accessories in feminine designs. • Plentiful use of lace, shiny beads, sequins and embroidery. • Many styles, very small quantity each.	• HK$599–12,999	• Images of house model displayed inside the stores. • Loyalty Programme.	• Up-and-coming Hong Kong TV star, Ada Choi, as house model.	• Approx. 22 stores on street level and in major shopping malls.	• The Mainland • Taiwan
Vivienne Tam	• Top-end niche market. • Female Only. • Age 25–35.	• Avant-garde East-meet-West designs, renowned in fashion capitals around the world. (Clients include Madonna and other top-notch Hollywood stars).	• HK$700–20,000	• Designer has written the book "China Chic". • Fashion items collected in New York museums. • Fashion shows on the Great Wall. • International press coverage.	• No house model. • Uses international super-models.	• Approx. 8 stores in Hong Kong.	• Taiwan • Japan • USA

5   Veeko and Wanko are both owned by Veeko International.
6   Episode and Jessica are both owned by Toppy International.

14

Shun Sang (H.K.) Co. Ltd.
Streamlining Logistical Flow

BENJAMIN YEN AND ANDREW LEE

PART I: BACKGROUND AND ISSUES

Introduction

In November 2002, Tsui Kwok-choy, Managing Director of Shun Sang (H.K.) Co. Ltd., reflected upon the IT-enabled measures that his company had been putting into place since 1998 to improve its logistical and operational efficiency. The results were obvious. Not only had there been significant improvements in operational parameters such as order-to-delivery time and average inventory turnover, with near-real-time information and tracking capability at their fingertips, the staff had more time to do their job better, resulting in higher customer satisfaction and better profitability. But Tsui was not content with the status quo. As he looked back at how the company had transformed and what it had achieved, he wondered what other measures the company should embark upon to further improve its competitiveness.

Company Background

When it was founded by Tsui and his wife in 1986, Shun Sang (H.K.) Co. Ltd. had only three employees in a 1,800-square-foot office in Sheung Wan[1] and did not have its own warehouse. It started as a wholesaler of pharmaceuticals and fast-moving consumer goods serving drug stores and retail outlets in Hong Kong. By 1994, Shun Sang had grown into a company of 18 people, serving some 700 accounts. The year also marked a watershed in Shun Sang's development as it was appointed by Proctor and Gamble (P&G) as one of its two distributors in Hong Kong. In December 1997, Shun Sang started to set up its own warehouse and became a full-fledged distributor supporting P&G with sales, merchandising, warehousing and goods-delivery services. The same year, a subsidiary, Shun Sang (Technology) Ltd., was established to provide IT-related solutions to both Shun Sang and third-party companies. In 1998, Shun Sang reached another milestone as it achieved over HK$200 million (US$25.64 million) in sales.[2] In 2000, the two Shun Sang companies were regrouped. Shun Sang Holdings Limited was formed, with Shun Sang (H.K.) Co. Ltd. and Shun Sang (Technology) Ltd. (hereinafter referred to as Shun Sang Technology) as its subsidiaries.

Tsui was always keen to bring in new ideas or management concepts to improve Shun Sang's competitiveness. He was on the board of the Hong Kong Article Numbering Association (HKANA, an organisation that promoted the use and standardisation of bar codes and preached the concepts of supply chain management in Hong Kong) and actively participated in field trips organised by the HKANA in order to keep abreast of the latest developments and best practices around the world. He also put emphasis on developing and rewarding his employees. On average, Shun Sang's training budget was about 10 percent of its total salary expenses. In addition, Shun Sang was one of the few unlisted companies in Hong Kong to offer stock options to its employees. Shun Sang's achievements were publicly recognised in 1998 when it won the Best Managed SME Silver Award of the first Hong Kong Small and Medium Enterprise (SME) Awards in 1998 (a campaign co-organised by the Hong Kong General Chamber of Commerce and the Hong Kong Productivity Council).[3] In 2001, Shun Sang won the Good People Management Award organised by the Labour Department.

In December 2001, Shun Sang moved to a 2,700-square-foot office in San Po Kong, with its own 16,000-square-foot warehouse just across the street.[4] By 2002, Shun Sang had grown to a company of 36 people. Its clientele consisted mainly of some 400 drug stores, and, to a lesser extent, chain stores, department store, supermarkets, cosmetics shops, hotels and movie theatres, with a total of about 1,900 orders and 50,000 cartons of goods sold each month.

Sales and Order Fulfilment: The Early Years

Shun Sang's customers were mainly small to medium-sized drug stores and retail outlets scattered around the territory. To serve them, Shun Sang's salespersons needed to meet them in person and take orders directly. Order forms were then filled out by hand and faxed back to the company at night. The following morning, staff from the invoice-processing department would first verify the orders and then prepare the invoices and packing lists. Packing lists were passed to the warehouse (which was outsourced until December 1997), where the ordered items were issued, packed and cross-checked manually. The delivery service was outsourced to a transportation service provider, which only allocated trucks when it saw the packing lists on the spot.

Tsui reasoned that they faced four major problems with this process. First, the order forms might not be filled out correctly or clearly, and the faxing of the forms could further diminish their readability. Second, sending orders by fax could in itself be problematic — for instance, the line could be busy or the fax machine at the receiving end could be out of paper. Third, staff from invoice-processing were required to spend time verifying each order and the order quantity, and there was still no guarantee that a verified order was error-free. Fourth, as there was little information about the demand for various goods, it was very difficult to control inventory levels.

Since errors could be introduced at various steps of the entire process, when a customer complained that an order was not correctly fulfilled it was nearly impossible to pinpoint what went wrong and when. As Tsui put it, "The customer is always right." The only thing that Shun Sang could do was to apologise to the customer and put things right.

Even when everything went smoothly, the best time that Shun Sang could manage from order placement to goods delivery was 48 hours.

Sales and Order Fulfilment in 1998

> Small and medium enterprises (SMEs) must apply information technology appropriately in order to avoid laying people off.
>
> – Tsui Kwok-choy, Managing Director of Shun Sang (H.K.) Limited

Tsui attended a number of supply chain management seminars organised by the HKANA in early 1997. He was convinced that supply chain management and IT would be the future direction for Shun Sang. To get his middle management to buy his idea, Tsui encouraged them to take courses in supply chain management. After the Asian economic crisis of late-1997, the economy of Hong Kong started its downward spiral. Businesses were hit hard. To survive, some resorted to layoffs to cut costs and improve efficiency. As a small/medium enterprise, Shun Sang was already very lean on its manpower structure. To weather this difficult period, Tsui was more convinced than ever that supply chain management concepts and IT would be the answer to streamlining Shun Sang's operations.

After studying the feasibility, a team from Shun Sang Technology started the development work. The team spent six months developing an intranet ordering system and a Web-based trading system to improve the ordering and invoice processing, and two months on the inventory control system to streamline the inventory operations. In addition, Shun Sang invested over HK$350,000 (US$44,870) on hardware and software for the various systems. Meanwhile, time and resources were also invested to educate and retrain its employees. As Tsui put it, "Most importantly, we have to educate our staff to be open-minded to accept new things and new challenges." Thus, outside consultants were hired to evaluate, advise and provide training to Shun Sang's employees.

In October 1998, the intranet ordering system and the trading system were introduced. Under the new working mode, all salespersons were equipped with a notebook computer. They could download customer information from the company's server any time they wanted. While they still needed to meet their customers and take orders in person, they only needed to log on to the company intranet at night through dial-up access to fill out the online order form. Stock availability was checked instantly and out-of-stock items would be flagged and no order could be placed for such items. Tsui recalled, "We did consider desktop computers, which were obviously cheaper than notebooks. But it would be difficult to bring them back to the office for service. It was timely that the price of notebooks came down to an affordable level. So, we decided to use notebooks."

In November 1998, an inventory control system was also implemented using barcode technology to monitor inventory status. Over 95 percent of Shun Sang's stock-keeping units (SKUs)[5] were barcode-enabled using the same standard (mainly due to the fact that the majority of Shun Sang's SKUs were P&G products and they were all bar-coded when they were delivered to Shun Sang). Through the use of scanners, the in-and-out movements of SKUs were recorded and the inventory records were updated real-time.

All orders uploaded the night before were processed at 8 a.m. the following morning by the trading system. Packing lists and invoices were generated automatically at the warehouse. Equipped with barcode readers, staff at the warehouse scanned and confirmed the issuance of goods. All goods were then packed in accordance with orders, which, along with the packed goods, were verified by another staff member before being picked up by the transportation service provider for delivery.

The results

These new systems delivered a number of obvious benefits. The automated intranet ordering system eliminated many of the error-prone steps in the old system. Although dial-up access could be very slow, and even got cut off totally at times, the system greatly improved order accuracy, and hence customer satisfaction. Similarly, the inventory system enhanced inventory record accuracy and made the warehouse operations more efficient. With accurate and real-time inventory data, Shun Sang was able to better plan its inventory and, as a result, to decrease the average turnover period of fast-moving consumer goods from 12 to 13 days to seven to eight days and the average inventory value, saving 10 percent in inventory interest costs and effectively increasing the warehouse space by 15 percent. Savings were also achieved in the following areas:[6]

	Savings/ Improvements
Invoice processing time	40%
Human Resources	50%
Report Processing Time	75%
Goods Return Rate	70%
Paper Consumption	80%

With these systems in place, Shun Sang successfully launched a 24-hour delivery service, thus reducing its customers' stock replenishment time by 50 percent and increasing the reliability of product supply.

A Failed Attempt

While notebooks were portable by nature, they were still too heavy to be carried around all the time. Thus, in 1999 Shun Sang seriously considered hand-held devices or Personal Data Assistants (PDAs) as an alternative to notebook. As an authorised distributor of P&G, Shun Sang learned about what P&G did with PDAs in mainland China. Encouraged by P&G, Shun Sang went ahead and bought a supply of PDAs, and Shun Sang Technology started developing applications for Shun Sang's own use. However, only later did they realise that the PDA technology at the time was not suitable for Shun Sang's unique requirements, so eventually they had to pull the plug.

Sales and Order Fulfilment in 2002

Although the first attempt to implement a PDA-based system was unsuccessful, Shun Sang was not discouraged. In 2001, when the right PDA technology was available in the market at the right price, the project was promptly revived and development work went full-steam ahead. Once again, system development was led by Shun Sang Technology. After five months of development and trial and an investment of over HK$600,000 (US$76,920) in hardware and software, a new PDA-based ordering system with links to the Web-based trading system was launched in February 2002.

Equipped with a PDA, Shun Sang's salespersons would synchronise the database on their PDAs with the company database at home via their notebooks with broadband Web access so that their PDA had the most updated customer information and details of product availability. Orders could be entered right in front of their customers on the PDA, and any requested items that were out-of-stock would be indicated. Once an order was filled out, it could be transmitted wirelessly via a CDMA phone card back to the company intranet. Alternatively, the salesperson could also upload all the orders all in one go via broadband Web access at the end of the day.

Back in the office, a new Web-based trading system was implemented to integrate sales, administration, warehouse management and reporting functions. All orders were uploaded to the Web-based trading system, where they would be processed. The transportation service provider that was responsible for picking up the ordered goods and delivering them to Shun Sang's customers could log on to Shun Sang's intranet to preview the preliminary delivery order summary for the following day after 11pm, so that it could effectively plan the vehicle deployment well in advance. Because of this promise to provide advance information to the transportation company, salespersons were required to alert their co-workers in invoice-processing if for whatever reason they could not upload the orders in time.

As before, packing lists and invoices were generated automatically at 8am the following morning in the warehouse, where goods were issued by the warehouse staff with the aid of a barcode scanner. As soon as the scanner was placed back in the cradle, the mapping process would be initiated to check whether the goods issued matched with the goods listed in the packing list. If there were any mismatches, an error report would be generated instantly and the error would be corrected before the goods were shipped.

In April 2002, an invoice-tracking system was also put in place after two months of development work and investment of HK$18,000 (US$2,300) in hardware and software. Under this system, the barcodes of the invoice number and the ordered goods were printed on the invoice. The processing times of each invoice for each step in the process (e.g., invoice creation, delivery, delivery confirmation and completion) were recorded in the system. If the customer also employed the barcode technology, they could also use the barcodes on the invoice for goods inspection and for data capturing purposes.

The Results

While PDAs could still not totally replace notebook computers, this new ordering system further simplified the workflow and reduced errors. And on average, each salesperson now spent one less hour per night to complete each day's work. This not only reduced stress but also allowed more time for the salespersons to do their job properly. The integrated Web-based trading system helped by reducing duplicate work and saving about two man-hours per day, and by reducing human errors. The full-blown barcode system in the warehouse delivered many benefits as well. Not only were inventory records updated real time, since the system was a closed loop, the accuracy of the inventory records was also improved. The use of scanner in the cross-checking procedure helped reduce the probability of shipping the wrong goods. The system also made inventory tracking and monitoring, and movement control, possible. Data were available to evaluate the performance of the inventory operations. According to Tsui, the fact that they were confident about their accuracy level made the transportation service provider more cautious, as it knew that if an error occurred, Shun Sang could pinpoint the exact step that caused it. Also, with the invoice-tracking system in place, queries from customers could be answered promptly and accurately, thus increasing customer satisfaction. For the management, the system provided them with online and up-to-date reports. For instance, the sales manager could pull out a salesperson's record and review his/her performance versus targets. When Tsui looked at the quantitative measures, he was very pleased and proud of the achievements of his team.

Goods acceptance and issuance processes	Saved 50% manpower
Logbook updates	Saved 99% manpower
Inventory record accuracy	Approaching 99%
Accuracy of goods movements	Approaching 100%
Follow-up on errors	Saved 99% of time

What Next?

Looking back, we made quite a few things happen in the past few years. And I've been thinking, "What next?"

– Tsui Kwok-choy

Tsui admitted that not too much thought had been put into considering the potential return when Shun Sang first invested money and resources to streamline its operation. This was not to say that the decisions were made without weighing the cost and benefit. In fact, Tsui and his team were very conscious and cautious about the cost. They also knew that they were addressing the right areas to improve the company's competitiveness. But it was not until recently, when he looked back at the financial results, that he realised that the return had been very encouraging. But Shun Sang also learned its lesson. Tsui recalled the first and unsuccessful attempt to adopt PDA technology saying, "We jumped in too quickly." "If we could do it all over again, we would do a small scale trial first," said Tsui. Looking ahead, he wondered about the next big stride his company should take in order to stay competitive.

PART II: LESSONS LEARNED

What Are Shun Sang's Competitive Advantages in 2002?

According to Michael E. Porter, there are two sources of competitive advantage: cost leadership and differentiation.[7] Apparently, Shun Sang's competitive advantage in 2002 derives mainly from its efficient operation, which, by nature, implies that its operating costs are low. Nevertheless, the fact that it can accurately deliver goods within 24 hours and provide good customer service indicates that it is also able to differentiate itself from its competitors.

The efficiencies originate mainly in the areas of order processing and inventory operations, and the fact that the whole system is much less error-prone and provides real-time and accurate information greatly reduces the time required to verify, double-check or rectify errors. Shun Sang shows significant improvements in the following areas.

– The order lead-time has improved from 48 hours to 24 hours as a whole;
– The inventory turnover period has been shortened from 7–8 days to 2–3 days;
– The warehouse is effectively 15 percent larger, and

Invoice Processing Time	Reduced 40%
Human Resources	Saved 50%
Report Processing Time	Reduced 75%
Goods acceptance and issuance processes	Saved 50% manpower
Logbook updates	Saved 99% manpower
Follow-up on errors	Saved 99% of time

Financially, Shun Sang's turnover rose over 25 percent from 1997 to 1998. Its profitability doubled from about one percent profit margin to about two percent from 1998 to 1999 and has stayed around that level since. Profitability, in particular, was improved and subsequently maintained without a significant increase in manpower. In fact, from 1997 to 2001, Shun Sang's workforce only increased from 30 to 34.

What Did Shun Sang Do to Achieve Those Improvements?

Shun Sang implemented new/improved IT systems in 1998 and in 2002 to automate and streamline its processes.

In 1998, the intranet ordering system eliminated error-prone manual processes of taking orders, faxing them, verifying them, and transposing them on packing lists and invoices, while reducing the processing time for all these tasks. The barcode inventory system shortened the time required for processing the in/out movements of goods, and provided real-time and accurate inventory records, which in turn allowed Shun Sang to manage its inventory more effectively and resulted in the 10 percent savings in interest and 15 percent space saving in the warehouse.

In 2002, Shun Sang rolled out a series of upgraded/new IT systems. The PDA ordering system enabled the salespersons to place orders real-time and check stock availability (though not real time), and saved them one hour at night. The Web-based trading system not only integrated internal systems, it also allowed Shun Sang's transportation service provider to preview the following day's order summary and plan the vehicle deployment more efficiently and effectively. The improved inventory system further reduced the probability of shipment errors and contributed to reducing the follow-up time on errors. And the new invoice-tracking system also provided a means to measure and track the performance of Shun Sang and the delivery service.

What Are the Critical Success Factors of Shun Sang's Automation Initiatives?

Technology seems to have played a very important role. "The right technology at the right cost" was essential to Shun Sang's success. In 1998, notebooks became affordable, making the intranet-based ordering system possible. Similarly, in 2002, without the right PDA technology, the PDA-based ordering system would never have materialised. By the same token, the right technology (barcode-based inventory system) enabled Shun Sang to automate its order fulfilment processes and inventory operations in both 1998 and 2002.

Another critical success factor was barcodes, or specifically, standardised barcodes. It is also worth noting that in Shun Sang's case, the streamlined inventory operations generated the most significant portion of the total benefits, and barcodes made it possible, or at least easy, for Shun Sang. It is fortunate for Shun Sang that the majority (some 95%) of its goods are from P&G and they are properly bar-coded. Imagine a distributor or wholesaler that has to deal with many different suppliers from different parts of the world. Not all suppliers put barcodes on their products, and even those that do, may not apply the same standard. In such circumstances, it would be very hard for distributors or wholesalers to implement a system like Shun Sang's.

The human factor also played an implicit but critical role. Shun Sang's employees might have refused to use these systems. They might have fear that the new systems were there to replace them rather than to help them do their job better. While there was nothing in the case that suggested such resistance ever happened, Tsui ensured that his middle-management staff bought his new ideas by encouraging them to take relevant courses. Indeed, not only did Shun Sang proactively retrain/re-educate its employees, it also hired outside consultants to help with managing the change. Above all, Shun Sang promotes a learning culture and encourages life-long learning. The important learning points here are: (1) the human factor should never be ignored, and (2) there are things with respect to the human factor that one can do to make the transition smoother.

Another implicit factor is process. Any good automation initiative should not merely automate the existing process. The process should also be improved, streamlined or simplified as part of the initiative. Shun Sang appears to have understood this very well. On the one hand, the new processes are designed mainly to reduce/eliminate duplication of work, improve accuracy and reduce the probability of introducing error (e.g., the ordering system and the inventory system in general). On the other hand, some duplication is still maintained in order to reduce errors (e.g., checking of packed goods before delivery).

What Can We Learn about Data and Information from Shun Sang's Experience?

Data and information are the key components in any information system. By definition, data is raw data, whereas information is processed or organised data. Shun Sang's success lies in its ability to capture data, process them into useful information, pass such information to the right parties in a timely manner, and feed the information back to support other business activities.

The quality of the data captured is crucial to success. The intranet and PDA ordering systems that Shun Sang implemented in 1998 and 2002 respectively help ensure that the orders are correctly taken and then recorded. Similarly, the barcode inventory system provides real-time and accurate inventory records.

The order data are subsequently transposed into invoices and packing lists. The processes are completely automated, thus the probability of introducing human errors is almost zero (since the system is still developed by humans, and is therefore still prone to "bugs"). In the warehouse, the use of scanners and barcodes also greatly reduces human errors in issuing and packing the goods.

The data are processed to provide Shun Sang's transportation service provider a summary of the following day's orders to assist it in vehicle deployment. Accurate order information and inventory records also help Shun Sang's to forecast demand, reduce its average inventory value and shorten its inventory turn time. Similarly, near real-time inventory record that the salespersons have on their PDAs allows them to provide instant feedback to customers on product availability. All these exemplify how good and relevant information can support related business activities and decisions.

What Can Other SMEs Learn from Shun Sang to Improve Their Competitiveness?

During an economic downturn, SMEs, which tend to have limited resources, tend to lower their price levels to remain competitive and cut costs to stay afloat. The typical ways to reduce cost include reducing manpower, investment or office space. The reduction, in turn, puts pressure and stress on a now reduced workforce to put in more hours and effort to achieve the same results. In the end, SMEs may still not survive the economic downturn.

Shun Sang, however, takes a very different approach. It looks for ways to improve efficiency in its operations (by applying supply chain management concepts) and invests accordingly (e.g., in areas such as human capital, systems development, hardware and software) to upgrade its competitiveness, which it believes will produce greater value to its customers and the company. And Shun Sang has proven that it has done the right thing.

During the interview, Tsui and his management team stressed that it was important to invest in the right area, not to be afraid of making mistakes, and to be bold and just do it. These are really the key points for other SMEs. A famous business maxim says: "You have to spend money to make money." But the money must be spent in areas that create the biggest positive impact on your customers and your company. Since there are only so many cost-benefit analyses that can be done, do not be afraid of making mistakes. Take calculated risks, learn from your mistakes, and improve as you go.

Conclusion

Shun Sang's success is no coincidence. It is in the business of goods distribution, which, essentially, is about turning goods over quickly and accurately. Through its efforts in applying IT-enabled supply chain concepts, Shun Sang has successfully improved its order accuracy, reduced its average inventory value, shortened its inventory turnover period, shortened the delivery lead-time, and improved delivery accuracy. Upon close examination, these achievements are really the results of a combination of factors (right technology, barcodes, the human factor, process, quality data and information). And at the end of the day, all these achievements translate into actual financial gains for Shun Sang. Shun Sang's experience provides a real-life example of how to implement logistics/supply chain management concepts successfully, and allows for a discussion of how a company can improve its competitiveness and profitability.

---

[1] Sheung Wan is located west of Central or the central business district of Hong Kong.

[2] The Hong Kong dollar is pegged to the US dollar at US$1 = HK$7.8.

[3] A quasi-governmental body in Hong Kong whose mission is to promote productivity excellence through the provision of integrated support across the value chain of Hong Kong firms, in order to achieve a more effective utilisation of resources, to enhance the value added content of products and services, and to increase international competitiveness.

[4] San Po Kong is a light industrial district in Hong Kong.

[5] Stock-keeping units or SKUs are the items for which inventory records are kept.

[6] Internal documents of Shun Sang.

[7] Porter, Michael E. (1998), *Competitive Advantage: Creating and Sustaining Superior Performance*, New York: Free Press.

15

Go2xpert Limited
Finding the Right China Strategy[1]

SIMON LAM, VINCENT MAK AND PAULINE NG

PART I: BACKGROUND AND ISSUES

In January 2000, when the Internet boom was sweeping Hong Kong, Nelson Siu and a few friends started a recruitment Website called Go2xpert, with capital of only HK$100,000. Astute marketing skills helped create a market presence for their startup, and Siu himself, as chairman of Go2xpert, became a recruitment trend observer who was often interviewed by the media. After the Internet bubble burst, Siu and his colleagues changed their business strategy. They saw an opportunity in the niche market of helping Hong Kong companies recruit mainland Chinese professionals. Siu soon found himself in a business cul-de-sac doing that type of business, mainly because of complicated immigration procedures and requirements that Mainland professionals needed to fulfil in order to relocate to Hong Kong. However, there was a positive aspect in the exercise: Siu had gained some connections with Mainland recruitment circles in the process. He and his colleagues were aware that they had to change strategy again; their new business would probably still be related to China, and they felt they could make use of their newly acquired social capital. But exactly which direction should they follow next? And how would Siu's own personality and external changes in the business environment help the company move on?

Recruitment Website

Nelson Siu, who was born in 1973, had been a creative artist in the advertising business for more than five years before starting Go2xpert.[2] In January 2000, inspired by the appearance of many Web startups and the promise of a bright Internet economy, and wanting to own a company himself, Siu pooled together HK$100,000 with two partners to start Go2xpert. One partner was a commercial artist like Siu; the other was the founder of the online auction Website Go2HK.com, which had been founded about six months earlier.

Go2xpert.com began as an auction Website for job applicants and vacancies. In 2000, IT professionals were in high demand, and Siu and his partners hoped to provide an auctioning channel for employers in need of IT people and IT people looking for higher-paid jobs. So an employer could post an IT vacancy on the Go2xpert sites and interested professionals could bid for it or a professional who wanted to switch to a new company could post his CV on the Website and employers could bid for him. The Website, in addition, held auctions of IT projects that were contracted out by companies. Revenues came from three streams: commissions from companies auctioning vacancies through the Website; commissions from job seekers, and banner advertisements. Siu and his partners were confident that they did not need a lot of capital or human resources to sustain this business model.

The problem was that the entry barriers to such a business were virtually non-existent — other companies could easily replicate Go2xpert's mode of operation. Competitors sprang up quickly and there was severe pricing pressure. The business did not seem profitable. Meanwhile, the Internet boom seemed to be dying down, with many Websites and Internet-related startups closing up shop. Hong Kong underwent a recession along with the rest of the world, with ever-increasing unemployment rates and deflation. Many companies laid off many employees or cut salaries. Local recruitment as a business was becoming stagnant. Siu needed to find a way out for his company.

But new opportunities arose in the new circumstances. Because of the recession, many Hong Kong companies could no longer afford the high salary levels that local professionals were used to. They started thinking of hiring professionals from mainland China, where salary levels were much lower. Therefore, many employers called for the Hong Kong Special Administration Region Government to relax the immigration requirements for Mainland professionals to come to work in Hong Kong. By early 2001, manpower projection figures indicated that Hong Kong would face a shortage of as many as 120,000 people with high academic qualifications in the coming five years.[3] In response, in March 2001, the HKSAR Government modified the Admission of Mainland Professionals Scheme, which had been set up in 1994, in order to allow more Mainland IT and financial services professionals to be employed in Hong Kong. There seemed to be an opportunity for Siu's business in the recruitment of Mainland professionals to work in Hong Kong.

First Step into China: Job Fair in Guangzhou

At the same time, since the online auctioning of job vacancies and applicants was a new concept, the Go2xpert Website was getting a lot of media exposure, whichwas like free marketing to them. This in particular led to a number of companies approaching Siu to discuss the possibility of co-operation. Quite a few recruitment firms from Shanghai, Beijing, Szechuan and Guangzhou contacted Siu. Among them was a Guangzhou-based company that ran a recruitment Website called jobchina.com; Siu and his partners decided to co-operate with that company. Go2xpert thus began to break into the mainland Chinese market.

In 2000, in mainland China, job fairs were often held in major cities to provide a channel for job-seekers from the provincial towns and villages. However, there had been no job fairs in which Hong Kong companies also participated in recruiting Mainland professionals. Although many Hong Kong manufacturers set up factories in mainland China at that time, it was still a new idea for Hong Kong companies to recruit Mainland professionals to work in Hong Kong. Go2xpert was among the first Hong Kong recruitment companies to spot that potential market. In co-operation with jobchina.com and a Mainland job fair organiser called Sam's Party, it held a job fair for Hong Kong employers in a major Guangzhou hotel for two days in July 2001.[4] Go2xpert's small team of four salespeople, including Siu, worked hard and managed to get 30 Hong Kong companies, including PCCW, Microsoft Hong Kong, Hutchison Telecommunications, Sunday and HSBC, to set up booths in the job fair. Most of these were telecommunications companies looking to recruit 40 to 50 IT professionals from the Mainland. Each company paid a high fee of HK$100,000 per booth to the organiser; the charge also included accommodation and transport for company representatives. Since Go2xpert was aiming at big companies and offered a comprehensive service, the high fee was not particularly a problem for its target clients.

The job fair was successful for Go2xpert in terms of getting Siu's company known among major Hong Kong companies and also among mainland Chinese recruitment circles. For example, Siu came into contact with people from the Guangdong Province and Shenzhen branches of Foreign Enterprise Service Corporation (FESCO). Founded in 1979, the year mainland China started large-scale economic reform, FESCO was a state-owned enterprise and was the first company in China to supply human resources and other services to foreign companies there. In fact, during FESCO's first years, all foreign companies that set up representative offices in mainland China needed to recruit employees through FESCO.[5] The company had diversified by 2002; by then, it was under the Beijing Municipal Foreign Economic Relations and Trade Commission and received policy guidance from the Foreign Affairs Office of the Beijing Municipal Government. A good portion of its revenue came from monthly management fees received from foreign companies in China that employed people referred by FESCO.[6] By 2000, FESCO had provided more than 27,000 employees to foreign companies or institutions in China. Good relationships with FESCO could become very useful to someone interested in establishing business in the Mainland human resources market, such as Siu.

The event also brought Siu some media attention, since cross-border recruitment was a relatively new idea. He was in fact one of the first Hong Kong businessmen to explore the Mainland human resources and cross-border employment market, and hence he became an expert in these areas. Reporters would call him for comments on related issues, and Siu, coming from an advertising background, knew better than many of his competitors how to present his views in the form of media-friendly "soundbites". This same approach was applied to the drafting of Go2xpert's press releases, in which Siu and his colleagues would think from the media's point of view and would highlight what the media would most be attracted to, so as to ensure coverage.

However, the job fair ended up earning very little profit for the organisers. Even more frustrating for Siu was that, out of the more than 100 people recruited by Hong Kong companies in the fair, fewer than 30 managed to get the required work permit from the HKSAR Government's Immigration Department to work in Hong Kong. The reality, as Siu saw it, was that despite the wide publicity for the Admission of Mainland Professionals Scheme, in practice the Immigration Department had no intention of modifying its admission requirements enough so that they would fall in line with the impetus behind the scheme. Frustrated, Siu and his partners began looking for more lucrative business to focus on.

What Next?

Siu was at the crossroads here. It seemed that for him, recruiting Mainland professionals to Hong Kong would not work as a profitable business. He faced a number of choices:

a) Persist in concentrating on recruiting Mainland professionals to Hong Kong, in the hope that the HKSAR Government would relax the related immigration requirements in the near future. But before that happened, Siu's company was bound to waste a great deal of time and money.

b) Revert to a pure recruitment Website business. Siu had tried it and it had not worked; perhaps if he persisted, the market would turn bright again. Moreover, he could try linking up with Mainland recruitment Websites — he had plenty of contacts already.

c) Become a firm dealing with recruitment of Hong Kong professionals for Hong Kong employers, i.e., expand the original Website business plan into a bricks-and-mortar business plan. But Hong Kong's recruitment market was shrinking, the unemployment rate was constantly increasing, and many professionals had lost their jobs. Moreover, Siu's experience and contacts gained from the Guangzhou job fair would be wasted.

d) Help Hong Kong companies recruit Mainland professionals for their Mainland operations. In 2001, Hong Kong employers continued to move low-technology operations such as customer service call centres to the Mainland, because of cheap land and labour there. Moreover, China was on the verge of joining the World Trade Organisation, and it was expected that more and more companies would set up offices in China afterwards. Many of those companies were unfamiliar with Chinese labour laws and other regulations, so the services of a Hong Kong-based (and therefore reliable) recruitment agent for their entry into China would be very welcome. Hence, there seemed to be many similar opportunities and Siu would not have to worry about the HKSAR's immigration procedures in such a business. In addition, the contacts Siu had gained from the Guangzhou job fair would be useful — in fact they would be very much needed — and the whole exercise would not have been futile. In fact, if this became successful, Siu might be able to go even further, turning him and his company into expert consultants to Hong Kong companies, advising them on how to enter the China market.

e) Help mainland Chinese companies recruit Mainland professionals. For Siu, this would mean leaving the Hong Kong market altogether and facing direct competition from the Mainland's own recruitment firms, including FESCO. But Siu could form alliances with one or more of those firms. Siu also would have the advantage of the sophisticated management and marketing skills that he and his colleagues had gained as a result of their experience in the Hong Kong business world. However, his contacts with Hong Kong companies would not be of much use in this scenario.

f) Help Hong Kong professionals find employment in mainland China. By 2001, many Hong Kong professionals were facing the threat of pay cuts or job losses as the recession continued. Many had already lost their jobs. Therefore, the business of introducing Hong Kong professionals to the Mainland market seemed to have great potential, but there were barriers as well. For example, Hong Kong professionals were used to a much higher living standard than in the Mainland. They were also unfamiliar with everything from culture to regulations relating to Mainland business. As for the other side of the equation, many Mainland firms needed the expertise of Hong Kong professionals. China had been a closed state-run economy for 30 years before beginning to re-open itself to foreign companies from 1979, and had much to learn in terms of international business, management skills, marketing and sales expertise, and so on. The demand was huge among mainland Chinese companies for Hong Kong professionals with significant experience of working in a "world city", especially as China wanted to catch up quickly with the economies of the West and become a world power.

PART II: LESSONS LEARNED

What Happened Afterwards?

Nelson Siu first adopted strategy d) — the strategy that arguably made the best use of the resources he already had, and that involved the least change from what he was already doing. Soon, he adopted strategy f) as well. But his company eventually branched out even more and organised training programmes for both Hong Kong and Mainland managers. All of these happened within one-and-a-half years of the Guangzhou job fair. The fate of Siu's company during that period was as follows:

Recruitment for Hong Kong firms' Mainland operations

When it proved difficult to get Mainland professionals to work in Hong Kong, Siu and his partners began doing business the other way round: becoming a Hong Kong representative for FESCO, and helping Hong Kong companies recruit Mainland people for their Mainland operations. After that, up to late 2002, Go2xpert helped several dozen Hong Kong and European companies recruit Mainland employees as they moved parts of their operations from Hong Kong to the Mainland.

China entrance consulting

In late 2001, China was finally admitted to the World Trade Organisation. By 2002, there was growing demand among foreign companies to learn more about how to do business in China. Law firms and accounting firms provided specialised consulting services in legal and accounting matters, but Siu saw an opportunity for Go2xpert to provide a more comprehensive type of consulting for companies that wanted to break into the mainland Chinese market — what Siu called "China entrance consulting services". Go2xpert already had expertise in recruitment, training, human resources management, the nuts and bolts of setting up business in China, and other issues, which it had gained through establishing a wide contact network in the Mainland.

At the same time, a former chief of the Shenzhen branch of FESCO, with whom Siu had been in contact, had retired and started an investment consulting company in Shenzhen. Siu struck a deal with him, and together the two companies held seminars in Hong Kong about entering the Chinese market. They invited authoritative representatives from the Chinese government to give insights about the myriad rules and regulations related to setting up offices and conducting deals in China. Having access to such influential sources attracted very senior managers from major companies. This also meant that Go2xpert could charge a premium price for its one-day seminars.[7] The company set its target at the upper end of the market, aiming to invite senior managers from major companies to participate. The first seminar was held in February 2002, and proved a great success.

The most popular seminars were about how to set up offices in China — from representative office to equity joint venture, co-operative joint venture, and wholly foreign-owned enterprise. Next in popularity were seminars about labour law and how to settle labour disputes in China. The number of participants per seminar was about 30 to 50. Go2xpert advertised its seminars mainly through e-mails, which were effective enough and saved on marketing costs. The seminars not only constituted a good revenue source by themselves, but could also create synergy with Go2xpert's other consulting and recruitment businesses. Companies that participated in the seminars often asked Go2xpert to provide more comprehensive or specific consulting services related to entering the Chinese market, or hired Go2xpert to recruit and train staff for their Mainland operations.

Executive search and training programmes in Mainland China

Connections led to connections, and Siu did not miss any opportunity to make new, useful contacts in the Mainland. At a job fair in Beijing in 2001 — at which Go2xpert was the only Hong Kong-based company to participate — Siu met representatives from the National Human Resources Centre. The centre was set up under the Chinese Ministry of Personnel to provide personnel management and human resource development services to the public across China.[8] Go2xpert later formed a joint venture with the centre, and the joint venture held a licence to conduct recruitment business within the Mainland.

Go2xpert then set up an office in Guangzhou and established long-term affiliate relationships with many local human resources organisations, recruitment firms and career publications in Beijing, Shanghai, Guangzhou and Shenzhen. This allowed them to tap into various local labour markets and brought them in contact with local recruitment business circles without having to bear large set-up and training costs.

Meanwhile, the employment situation in Hong Kong had become so bad by late 2002 that more and more Hong Kong professionals began to consider working in the Mainland. There was also a change of mindset. Hong Kong professionals began to think that, although a Mainland job might not pay as well, they could get a head start in gaining experience that might prove invaluable as the Chinese economy grows. And, as explained before, many Mainland companies were willing to hire them for their expertise. So both supply and demand had become healthily established, and Go2xpert became an executive search firm in the Mainland, recruiting Hong Kong professionals for Mainland firms. Siu and his colleagues also carried on with their highly cost-efficient and media-friendly marketing skills. For example, when publicising a job fair held in Hong Kong in late 2002, Go2xpert did not just send out a run-of-the-mill press release stating what the job fair was about, how many companies participated, etc. Rather, they picked out one very interesting feature — that 60 enterprises from Northwest China offered free cars and flats as gifts to Hong

Kong professionals who were willing to work for them — and put that in the headline. The strategy was successful and the job fair received good coverage.

In addition to the above, Go2xpert had begun recruiting Mainland applicants for the Chinese offices of foreign firms. The company moreover ran training programmes for Mainland and Hong Kong professionals on topics ranging from CV writing and communication skills to government policies and practices, knowledge management, customer relationship management and management skills. It had even arranged US inspection tours for Mainland managers to help them understand first-hand how major companies in the West were run.

Summary of achievements

By late 2002, when the company began to break even, Go2xpert was a recruitment and consulting firm with a recognised brand name among many Hong Kong and Mainland companies. Its business streams included China entrance consulting, recruitment (including cross-border recruitment of professionals, mainland China executive search and related services such as relocation of foreign staff to work in China), and training programmes.[9] These streams created synergy whereby each could feed business to the others. For example, a professional attending one of the training programmes might become interested in Go2xpert's recruitment service as well, and might ask the company to find another employer for him. Or, a company that had participated in one of Go2xpert's China entrance seminars might ask Go2xpert to headhunt and/or train managers for its new office in the Mainland. Siu and Go2xpert's huge network of affiliate companies and contacts in mainland China was also fuelling the company's success through synergy.[10]

Within just three years, Nelson Siu started from nothing to become a Hong Kong pioneer in and expert on Mainland recruitment business, when he had not even reached his thirtieth birthday. Go2xpert changed strategy several times and branched out into different businesses, eventually becoming an executive search company covering the whole of mainland China. Moreover, it successfully established a brand name among many major companies as a trustworthy and authoritative consulting company for doing business in China. Yet, although many business partners and clients thought it was a big company, the Hong Kong and Guangzhou offices of Go2xpert had only about 10 staff each.

In the eyes of the Hong Kong media, Siu had meanwhile become an expert on mainland China-related human resources issues. Journalists would ask him for opinions with respect to, for example, new measures announced by the HKSAR Government that aimed to admit more Mainland residents to work in Hong Kong. Pictures of him could often be seen in newspapers and he often appeared on television. All this was free publicity for Siu and Go2xpert, and helped to build a growing reputation for him: he was later given a column in a major Hong Kong newspaper. Siu would not miss any chance to publicise his company's business whenever he was given media exposure.

Which Aspects of Siu's Personality and Thinking Were Crucial to His Success?

Siu had a very creative personality. His advertising background was proof of that. It was apparent that he was as creative in designing commercials as in spotting new markets and thinking up new business models. Within a span of about three years, he and his colleagues had made several strategic shifts, all of which were about going into business territories that had scarcely been explored by Hong Kong businessmen: talent and job auction Website, recruiting Mainland professionals to work in Hong Kong (recruitment being a traditional business, but here applied to the newly opened China human resources market), China entrance consulting, etc. He was a pioneer in all the cases, and gained first-mover advantage as a result. His and his colleagues' skills in promoting Go2xpert through the media were also ingenious.

Siu's strategic thinking was not that of a text-book-type long-term planner who had visions about what the company was going to do in five years' time. Instead, he aggressively grasped every opportunity that was presented to him and changed his company's strategy accordingly. At a time of quick, dramatic changes — when the Internet bubble was followed by China entering WTO, which sped up the already breathtaking pace of the opening up of China — Siu's adaptability and lack of long-term planning were in fact advantageous. Had he carried out too much planning, he might have lost all his limited capital before he could make his company profitable. There was simply too much uncertainty at any moment to allow for much long-term planning, and adapting swiftly to available opportunities probably actually involved less risk.

How Was the Contemporary Business Environment Favourable to Go2xpert?

Although many things happened to Go2xpert after the Guangzhou job fair, the factors that led to the company's success were all apparent by the time of that event. The main factor was that a niche mainland Chinese human resources market had just appeared for Hong Kong companies around the time the company was founded. What Go2xpert really captured was the chance to be a human resources consultant and recruitment service provider for non-mainland Chinese companies seeking to establish a presence in mainland China. By 2001, there were many of such non-mainland Chinese companies, and their number was growing as China was on its way to becoming a World Trade Organisation member. Another beneficial circumstance for Go2xpert was the fact that mainland Chinese business laws and regulations were still not very well understood by foreign businesses at the time. Go2xpert thus became a guiding light for many of those companies.

Conditions peculiar to Hong Kong had also helped Go2xpert's development. For example, the Hong Kong Government's Admission of Mainland Professionals Scheme sought to allow more Mainland professionals work in Hong Kong. Some employers were thus encouraged to hire Mainland professionals; Go2xpert was also encouraged to explore this line of business. Without the scheme, Go2xpert might not have held a job fair in Guangzhou job at all, or if it had, it might not have managed to persuade so many big Hong Kong companies to participate. Although most of the professionals recruited at the job fair could not work in Hong Kong because of immigration requirements, the event gave Siu his first experience of the Mainland recruitment market. The contacts that Siu made through the exercise were key to Go2xpert's future development.

Conclusion

This case can be used to illustrate how Hong Kong SME entrepreneurs can find the right opportunities offered by the Chinese market. Even more importantly, it sheds light on how SMEs need to change their strategy and manage their operations so as to make the best of a rapidly changing business environment. Siu's and his colleagues' creativity, aggressiveness and maketing skills, as well as Siu's ability to grasp every opportunity, all offer a lesson in how SMEs can market their goods and services very cost-effectively.

Siu's business moves were well timed with respect to the political, social and economic environment in Hong Kong and mainland China. Siu was eager and prescient in building the right contacts and establishing strategically critical partnerships. In addition, he was also a master at using the media for cost-free marketing by presenting himself as an expert interviewee, and also by writing good press releases. Siu's use of e-mail for promoting new seminars was also a simple but effective move. In short, he and his partners ran Go2xpert aggressively and with high profile, which was not how many recruitment firms were run.

---

1   The information in this case is largely based on an interview with Nelson Siu, chairman of Go2xpert.

2   Siu's father was a senior manager in a major mainland Chinese insurance firm, but Siu claimed that his business had never benefited from any connections gained through his father.

3   Chan Felix, (2001), "Growth sectors to gain from extra professionals", *South China Morning Post*, 8 March.

4   The project was conceived and planned from March 2001 onwards, and was going to be the first of its kind. However, when a competitor, also a Hong Kong-based recruitment firm, heard about the project, it started hasty preparations for a job fair that was scheduled to start one day before Go2xpert's. According to Siu, that competitor's job fair turned out to be less well organised, and only a few Hong Kong companies participated.

5   By the late 1990s, four other official labour-service companies had been allowed to compete with FESCO, but FESCO remained a major provider of local staff for the representative offices of foreign companies in China.

6   In fact, the foreign companies did not pay salaries to their local Chinese staff directly, but had to pay FESCO a set fee first, and then FESCO would pay the staff after deducting a management fee.

7   Each participant could be charged as much as HK$4,800 per whole-day seminar, including lunch and a tea break.

8   Source: http://www.zhongquan.org/ZhongQuan/chinese/English1.htm/.

9   Cross-border recruitment means recruiting Hong Kong people to work in Mainland China and recruiting Mainland Chinese people to work in Hong Kong.

10 Go2xpert's Website was still in operation as a channel for job search, self-promotion for professionals, recruitment, business promotion and job-matching requests.

16

Proactive Medicare Enterprise (HK) Limited
Providing Healthcare in Mainland China

GILBERT WONG AND ANDREW LEE

PART I: BACKGROUND AND ISSUES

Introduction

After successfully establishing a VIP floor at Shanghai's International Peace Maternity and Children's Health Hospital, with Johns Hopkins International (JHI) as its US partner, Proactive Medicare Enterprise (HK) Limited, a small and medium enterprise (SME) in Hong Kong, was busy starting up another healthcare venture in Beijing, Guangzhou and Suzhou. The aim was to build a chain of VIP maternity floors in major cities in China.

The Inception of the Idea

YY Wong and Robert Wong were both graduates of the MBA class of 1993 at The University of Hong Kong School of Business, but they certainly did not know each other well then. After working in information technology for 18 years, Robert Wong joined HealthAnswers Asia Pte. Ltd., a comprehensive and integrated health communication company that provides health information and services to patients, as the president overseeing HealthAnswers' Asia-Pacific business. YY Wong, with 15 years of experience in infrastructure projects and China business consultancy, started her own company, Inno-Tech Holdings Limited, aimed at providing state-of-the-art e-property management solutions in the China market.

In late 2000, YY Wong was trying to source some health content for a cyberliving project she was working on. One day she read a name in a newspaper article about the healthcare industry, and she thought it was her former classmate Robert Wong. So, she looked Robert Wong up in the MBA class directory and rang him. It turned out that she was mistaken, but two long-lost classmates were connected again. Eventually they met to discuss the opportunities that faced them. Frustrated with his work at the time, Robert Wong decided to leave HealthAnswers and team up with YY Wong at Inno-Tech in January 2001.

In one of her previous jobs, YY Wong had worked and become acquainted with Mr Chen, a former Secretary General of the Shanghai Committee of the Chinese People's

Political Consultative Conference[1] and the former Assistant Director of the Union Front Department[2] of the Shanghai Committee of the Communist Party of China. Through Mr Chen, YY Wong was introduced to Dr Hu Jin-hua, a medical doctor in mainland China and director of the Shanghai Health Education Institute. YY Wong met with Dr Hu in Shanghai in mid-2000 and made him the Chairman of the Supervisory committee of Inno-Tech, a requirement for Mainland-listed companies but not a requirement for the Hong Kong-registered Inno-Tech. YY Wong was thinking that perhaps she could exploit this connection and do something related to healthcare in China. So she invited Robert Wong to discuss the healthcare industry in China with Dr Hu.

Testing the Water in Shanghai and Beijing

In late 2000 and early 2001, Robert Wong and YY Wong started discussing the idea of a health club providing health check-ups and health information. Around that time, the Shanghai Health Education Institute had just bought a building that it planned to use as an office and conference facility. Coincidentally there were two empty floors in the building that could be converted into a health club. To make the venture more viable, YY Wong asked Dr Herbert Wong, Robert's brother (who had a PhD in Sociology and over 20 years of experience in the US healthcare industry) whether he could help bring in some of the best medical institutes from the US as partners. By August to September 2001, Herbert Wong had linked up with The Cooper Institute, a non-profit research and education centre based in Dallas, Texas that provided training and certification for fitness and health professionals and a health-related fitness assessment programme for children and youth.[3] However, the plan fell through because the Shanghai Health Education Institute decided not to rent the two empty floors to Robert Wong and YY Wong.

In October to November 2001, they took representatives of The Cooper Institute with them to Beijing with the idea of duplicating The Cooper Institute there. A big event was organised at the American Club to introduce the fitness concept to an audience of foreign diplomats and expatriates. However, by December 2001, it was clear to Robert Wong and YY Wong that the health club/health assessment concept was too expensive to realise as they were looking at an initial investment of 12 million yuan (about US$1.3 million) to set up a sizeable facility with modern furnishings and equipment. Another opportunity did come up in Beijing. During his stay in Beijing, Robert Wong was approached by a local Beijing businessman, and they started thrashing out the idea of starting a Sino-overseas joint-venture hospital in Beijing with the assistance of Johns Hopkins University. Later, Robert Wong learned that the Beijing businessman was only interested in getting a contact in Johns Hopkins University and setting up a venture directly with them. Fortunately, due to Herbert Wong's connections with Johns Hopkins, the man's plot to by-pass them fell through, and they never heard from him again.

New Opportunity in Shanghai

No sooner had Mr Chen learned that Robert Wong and YY Wong were discussing plans with someone to set up a Sino-overseas hospital in Beijing than he tried to bring them back to Shanghai. As one of the directors of Shanghai Soong Ching Ling Foundation, the owner of Shanghai's International Peace Maternity and Children's Health Hospital (see Exhibit 1 for a brief description), Mr Chen introduced Robert Wong and YY Wong to the senior administrators of the hospital. Robert Wong discussed with them the idea of a partnership with JHI (see Exhibit 2 for a brief description) to bring in Western-style maternity care to Shanghai. The proposal, if it materialised, would not only put International Peace at the cutting edge of obstetrics and gynaecology, but would also allow it to charge a premium for providing high-quality healthcare.

Convincing the Chiefs

By January 2002, Herbert Wong had gotten JHI interested in the idea of co-operating with a credible hospital in Shanghai. In February 2002, a delegation from JHI visited Shanghai and the International Peace Maternity and Children's Health Hospital. Dr Harold E. Fox, director of the Department of Gynaecology and Obstetrics of Johns Hopkins University's School of Medicine, was convinced that the idea of collaborating with the well known International Peace Maternity and Children's Health Hospital was definitely worthwhile. However the director of the hospital, Dr Cheng, a renowned female obstetrician and gynaecologist in China, who had done research work and had received advanced training at Edinburgh University in Scotland, was not too keen. As Robert Wong explained, "This was probably due to two reasons. First, she had trained in Edinburgh so she was not too keen on co-operating with an American institution. Second, she felt that the hospital was not a profit-making organisation and that there was therefore no point in charging a premium for high-quality healthcare."

To Robert Wong and YY Wong, it was essential to convince Dr Cheng and her senior staff that the idea would work in the context of China as well. To do that, they felt they had to take them to JHI. In the meantime, Robert Wong persistently tried to convince her and offered to take her to have a look at a few US hospitals. Eventually Dr Cheng agreed to send her deputies on the trip and agreed to set aside one bed in the hospital for a trial. As she had a meeting in Geneva during that period, she did not think it was necessary to participate personally in the trip. In the end, understanding the importance of her presence, Mr Chen wielded his political influence with the China Welfare Institute and managed to have Dr Cheng's schedule rearranged to accommodate the trip to the US.

The trip to the US

In April 2002, believing that International Peace had already agreed to work together with JHI, Herbert Wong arranged for the delegation from International Peace to visit hospitals in Denver, Colorado Springs, Austin and Baltimore, i.e., where JHI was located. Robert Wong, on the other hand, did not dare to tell Herbert Wong that he had secured only a very limited number of beds until they arrived in the US.

During the trip, the team was introduced to concepts and technology that were totally new to them. First, they were amazed at the advancements in technology and hospital management in the US, especially at JHI. Second, they learned about the subtle difference between the concepts "non-profit making" and "not-for-profit" from the American hospital administrators. A non-profit making organisation was not allowed to make any profit, but a not-for-profit organisation was allowed to make a profit but had to invest it back into the organisation to improve standards of service and care. Third, they learned about the insurance-based healthcare system in the US.

Towards the end of the trip, Dr Cheng found out that an insurance-based healthcare system would soon be implemented in China as well. Under the new system, each citizen would have a health insurance card and the hospital would receive money from a central insurance scheme in return for providing services to patients. However, there was a cap on the total amount of money that a hospital could receive each year. Robert Wong reckoned that as a top maternity and paediatrics hospital in Shanghai, International Peace would easily reach that cap, and that Dr Cheng would probably see this joint venture as an important revenue source to help finance the hospital's operations and future development. Dr Cheng also understood that hospitals in China were about to face the same challenge as US hospitals had done 20 years earlier, i.e., keen competition and a rat race among hospitals for survival. By the end of the trip, she was convinced that the co-operation with JHI was definitely worthwhile. As Robert Wong recounted, "Although they had to convene a proper meeting back home with all the seniors of the hospital, they were already there in the delegation. Dr Cheng basically told me that they agreed."

Laying the Groundwork

Negotiation with International Peace began in mid-April 2002, and International Peace promptly agreed to set aside one floor with 11 beds for the collaboration. The designated floor, which was to be known as the VIP Sixth Floor, was to become a family-centred maternity unit, including four labour, delivery and recovery rooms and seven postpartum rooms, and an outpatient suite for prenatal care and testing.[4] It would provide US-style, and US-standard delivery and prenatal care to expatriates and locals. The price per delivery was set at a level comparable to that of an upmarket private hospital in Hong Kong. For outpatient care, the price per session was also set at a level comparable to what a renowned specialist in private practice in Hong Kong would charge.

Agreeing on the concept with International Peace was one thing, but overcoming the legal hurdles and settling the commercial terms took some effort. First, the law forbade the establishment of an independent hospital inside another independent hospital. The hospital was considered an asset of the state. Therefore subletting or forgoing control of part of the hospital was illegal. Second, the Provisional Measures for Administration of Chinese-Foreign Joint Equity and Joint Co-operative Medical Institutions that came into effect in 1 July 2000 (see Exhibit 2 for a summary of the conditions) required among other prerequisites an investment of RMB 20 million (or about US$2.5 million). And the approval had to be obtained from both the Ministry of Health and the Ministry of Foreign Trade and Economic Co-operation, which, as YY Wong commented, "could take two or three years and might still be hanging in the air". With Mr Chen's help, they were introduced to the right officials in the appropriate ministries in Shanghai, from whom they learned about the subtleties of the regulations. Eventually, the agreed and legally permissible arrangement between International Peace and Proactive Medicare was that International Peace would remain the sole provider of healthcare services on the designated floor, and that Proactive Medicare with its contractual arrangement with JHI would provide educational and consulting services to International Peace.

Commercially, International Peace wanted a guaranteed annual profit. In the end, the contract stipulated that Proactive Medicare would pay International Peace a fixed amount each year as the guaranteed profit, and there was no mention of International Peace paying Proactive Medicare. As Robert Wong explained, "The spirit of the contract is that we guarantee them a profit level and above that level is what we get. But credible organisations in China, like International Peace, in the past were gullible and got set up by crooks many times. They are afraid of getting burned again. So, we pay them a fixed amount as the guaranteed profit and we get the revenue that they earn from providing the service. Although there is no mention of them paying us in the contract, we have to trust them first in order to earn their trust."

The negotiation with JHI was handled by Herbert Wong. The basic services provided by JHI included "training for staff physicians from International Peace at Johns Hopkins Hospital in Baltimore, as well as ongoing continuing education programmes for physicians provided in Shanghai".[5] Both of these services would be paid for by Proactive Medicare at predetermined rates. JHI also agreed to work with Proactive Medicare in 10 major cities in China, and agreed not to establish another medical institution within a half-an-hour's drive from one where JHI and Proactive Medicare had a pre-existing contract. Furthermore, Proactive Medicare would pay JHI a royalty per baby delivered.

From Renovation to the Delivery of the First Baby

In July 2002, the designated sixth floor was vacated for renovation. On 1 August, renovation work commenced, with a target grand opening date of 15 September. During this period, Proactive Medicare had to pay International Peace a sum equivalent to its loss of income from July to mid-September. In addition, Proactive Medicare bore all the costs of the renovation. The floor was officially opened on 15 September 2002. Shortly after the grand opening and just before the actual start of operations, Robert Wong received a phone call from International Peace. "They were telling me that they did not know how to clean the carpets to germ-free level. It was only when I asked them why they could not steam-clean the carpet that I learned there was actually no carpet steam-cleaning service in Shanghai," Robert Wong said. To rectify the situation, Robert Wong immediately flew from Hong Kong to Shanghai, had the carpet removed and had the floor laid with tiles. The entire floor then needed to be cleaned, aired and sanitised again, and all this was done within four days. On 8 October 2002, the first baby was delivered on the VIP Sixth Floor. The unit was heralded as "the first step in making up for the much-bemoaned lack of international standard healthcare in the city"[6] by the local Shanghai media.

Shanghai and Beyond

By April 2003, the VIP Sixth Floor had delivered 140 babies, with an occupancy rate of over 30 percent, or some 10 percentage points higher than Robert Wong had estimated to be the breakeven occupancy rate. The total number of outpatients served also exceeded Robert Wong's expectations. But Proactive Medicare was not resting on its laurels. Through a remote connection, Proactive Medicare started discussing an opportunity to collaborate with Tsinghua University (one of the top universities in mainland China) in December 2002 in a similar manner as with International Peace. Initially, Tsinghua was looking at establishing a lab with the involvement of JHI, but it had an even grander plan — to build a hospital in Tsinghua's name. Within 30 days, an initial agreement was reached and a Memorandum of Understanding was signed between Proactive Medicare and Tsinghua University to build a hospital in Beijing with JHI's assistance. However, Proactive Medicare's vision was even grander. According to Robert Wong, "Our plan is to build or collaborate with 10 hospitals in mainland China in three years." By May 2003, Robert Wong had raised US$5 million through the issuing of bonds to finance the new venture in other cities in China. Meanwhile, a revised agreement with International Peace was lying on Robert Wong's desk, with all the necessary wording concerning the payments from International Peace to Proactive Medicare.

PART II: LESSONS LEARNED

Key Questions

What was most likely to be on Dr Cheng's mind when she agreed to set aside one bed for a trial? What convinced her that this venture with Proactive Medicare and JHI was worth trying?

At first, Dr Cheng only agreed to let her deputies go, but she herself declined to go. She only went after her schedule had been rearranged to accommodate the US visit. This suggests that, at the time, Dr Cheng was still not interested in the idea. (It must be noted that going on the trip was not equivalent to agreeing to the idea.) Reading between the lines, when Dr Cheng agreed to set aside one bed for trial, she was actually telling Robert Wong to go away.

Dr Cheng would only be convinced that the collaboration was worth trying if it added value to International Peace Maternity and Children's Health Hospital (IPMCHH). The first thing that she would find value-adding to IMPCHH would be the advanced medical technology of JHI. As a renowned obstetrician and gynaecologist in China and the head of a renowned hospital in Shanghai, she probably found the opportunity to have exchanges with the best hospital in the US and one of the top two medical schools in the US too difficult to pass up.

The second turning point was the combination of her understanding of the not-for-profit concept and the fact that a medical insurance scheme was going to be implemented in China very soon. With a cap set on the total amount that a hospital could receive, the medical insurance scheme would put a strain on resources, limit development and cause the quality of healthcare to deteriorate at IPMCHH. However, the not-for-profit concept represented a potential solution to the problem. If the collaboration were profitable, it would become an indispensable source of funding to help finance the operations of rest of the hospital and the further development of the hospital. With IPMCHH's reputation in Shanghai, JHI's reputation around the world and Shanghai's wealthy local and expatriate population, it would probably not be difficult for the collaboration to attract enough people to make it profitable.

What are the characteristics of International Peace Maternity and Children's Health Hospital (IPMCHH) as an organisation? What can we learn about dealing with an organisation such as IPMCHH in China?

IPMCHH can be characterised as follows:
* A renowned and credible organisation that provides quality service;
* It is very proud of its heritage and achievement;
* A quasi-state organisation that is wary of scams;
* It is willing to honour its word. To IPMCHH, the spirit of a contract is worth a lot more than the signed document itself.

Doing business with such an organisation requires patience and perseverance — which Proactive Medicare displayed in trying to convince Dr Cheng. Potential partners also have to be willing to make some sacrifice upfront in order to earn its trust — again, Proactive Medicare was willing to (a) take the risk of not reaching the target profit level and (b) sign an initial agreement without any commitment from IPMCHH to pay it back in return. As it turned out, IPMCHH was willing to revise the agreement later!

What can we learn about setting up a business in China, in terms of working with the people/ organisations, dealing with the legal/administrative system, and the timing of entry?

Undoubtedly, having the right connections is the key in dealing with people and organisations (or at least having the right connection to make the right connection). Without such connections, Robert Wong and YY Wong would not have linked up with IPMCHH in the first place, and Dr Cheng would not have agreed to go on the US trip. Nevertheless, the points mentioned under the previous question are also relevant.

The primary lesson to be learned about dealing with the legal and administrative requirements in China is that it takes an insider who really understands the complexity and the unique interpretations of the legal and administrative requirements to find a legal and viable means to meet them. Proactive Medicare received assistance from Mr Chen to make contact with insiders. Considering the requirements set forth in Exhibit 2, it is a formidable challenge to set up a joint-venture medical institution in China. However, with insiders who understood the subtleties of the relevant laws and regulations as well as the unique business situation, Proactive Medicare found a legal and viable means to bring about this unique venture.

One could argue that the timing of entry is always critical. But the timing of entry is of particular significance in the context of mainland China. Since many different areas in China are undergoing rapid reforms, a particular business or business model might not work today, but might work tomorrow. As exemplified by this case, Dr Cheng might not have been interested in the collaboration without the imminent implementation of the health insurance scheme that made the collaboration valuable to IPMCHH. Thus the timing of entry needs to coincide with the pace of reform.

What role did Herbert Wong and Mr Chen play? Who brought these two totally unrelated persons into this same venture? What role did Robert Wong and YY Wong play? What can we learn about networking from this?

Both Herbert Wong and Mr Chen brought with them indispensable connections that made this venture possible.

Herbert Wong brought with him his connection with the US healthcare industry, especially JHI — one of the top two medical institutions in the US. Without Herbert Wong, it was highly unlikely that a prestigious institution such as JHI would have responded eagerly to just anyone's proposal to collaborate. Similarly, it was Mr Chen, because of his affiliation with IPMCHH, who introduced Robert Wong and YY Wong to IPMCHH. His connection and political influence also ensured that Dr Cheng of IPMCHH visited JHI. In additional, without Mr Chen's connections in the government, it would have been difficult to make the venture legally feasible.

Without Robert Wong and YY Wong, these two disparate networks of Herbert Wong and Mr Chen would never have been linked together. Herbert and Robert Wong were brothers, but their career paths had rarely crossed before. While YY Wong and Mr Chen once worked in the same company, Mr Chen's background was completely different from YY Wong's. Such relationships provided the necessary strong linkages between two people with obvious differences in their background, i.e., between Robert and Herbert Wong (and access to their networks), and between YY Wong and Mr Chen (and access to their networks).

Nevertheless, the linkage between Robert Wong and YY Wong was not strong. They were classmates, but they were not close. They had also worked in very different industries. It was pure serendipity that linked up Robert Wong and YY Wong. And there are problems in linking up people who do not know each other well. On the one hand, such a linkage tends to generate new ideas and makes formerly impossible propositions possible (as they were likely to be of different backgrounds). On the other hand, there is also tension in this linkage. If the people do not know each other well, they may not trust each other. Only when this tension is overcome (when trust is built) can the benefits of this network linkage be realised. In the case of Proactive Medicare, the linkage between Robert Wong and YY Wong also linked the various networks of Herbert Wong and Mr Chen. It was this entire network that made Proactive Medicare's venture possible.

Conclusion

This case is about an SME starting a JV type of business in China with a credible Chinese organisation. By analysing the case along the lines of the above mentioned questions, it should be possible to distil the key success factors in starting a Sino-overseas joint venture in China. First, the JV must add value to the Chinese organisation. The classic question that anyone is likely to ask is "What's in it for me?" Second, investors must be willing to sacrifice short-term gains for long-term benefits. Sometimes, it may be necessary to invest money upfront in order to gain the trust or to allay the concerns of the Chinese partner. Potential investors must balance the risks and the potential gains in doing so, but that is what doing business is all about anyway. Third, legal and administrative requirements are not carved in stone. Sometimes there may be ways to get around them legally. Good connections will definitely help. Fourth, the pace and direction of reform can be pivotal to the success of a JV, so investors must keep their eyes open and stay abreast of the latest developments as well as the direction of development. Fifth, investors should never underestimate the power of networks. Often it is the linkages to people that one does not know well that bring new ideas or creates new opportunities. These critical success factors are by no means the only factors governing the success of a JV in China, but they should provide insights into the uniqueness of doing business in China, and some of them are particularly relevant to SMEs.

---

1   The Committee of the Chinese People's Political Consultative Conference is a quasi-government organisation that serves as the consultation arm of the government, and is very influential in municipal policies.
2   The Union Front Department is responsible for developing business opportunities between the Communist Party and the outside world in political, social and economic aspects.
3   The Cooper Institute Website, http://www.cooperinst.org/1.asp/.
4   Johns Hopkins International, "Health Management Update", http://www.jhintl.net/English/ Institutions/Health_Management_UpdateJanFeb2003.asp/.
5   Johns Hopkins International, "Health Management Update".
6   *Shanghai Daily News* (2002), http://www.cityweekend.com.cn/issues/2002/22/RedTape/, 26 October.
7   Soong was the wife of Dr Sun Yat Sen, the first president and founding father of the Republic of China.
8   The Former Residence of Soong Ching Ling in Shanghai Website, http://www.shsoong-chingling. com/page5.htm/.
9   UNFPA extends assistance to developing countries, countries with economies in transition and other countries, at their request, to help them address reproductive health and population issues, and raises awareness of these issues in all countries, as it has since its inception.
10   Johns Hopkins Medicine brings together the faculty physicians and scientists of Johns Hopkins University's School of Medicine with the organisations, community physicians and professionals of The Johns Hopkins Hospital and Health System to offer a full spectrum of activities in research, teaching and patient care.
11   Johns Hopkins International Website, http://www.jhintl.net/.

Exhibit 1   The Partners in the Shanghai Venture

International Peace Maternity and Children's Health Hospital

In September 1951 Madame Soong Chingling[7] received the 1950 International Stalin Peace Prize of one hundred thousand rubles, and donated it to the China Welfare Institute, of which she was the chairperson, to found the International Peace Maternity and Children's Health Hospital.[8] The hospital actively carried out various programmes, adhering to the policy of "pilot and experimentation" laid down by Madame Soong and the late Premier Zhou En Lai, upholding healthcare-oriented principles by combining healthcare with clinical work.

The hospital actively participated in international medical exchanges and co-operative projects, including collaborative projects with the World Health Organisation (WHO), the United Nations Children's Fund (UNICEF), the United Nations Population Funds (UNFPA)[9] and Edinburgh University. In 1992, the hospital was one of among the first group of hospitals to be named as a "Baby Friendly Hospital" by the Chinese Ministry of Public Health, WHO and UNICEF. In 2001, the International Peace Maternity and Children's Health Hospital was the best obstetrics and gynaecology hospital in Shanghai, with more than 6,000 deliveries a year.

Johns Hopkins International

Johns Hopkins International (JHI), an organisation within Johns Hopkins Medicine[10] in the United States, was charged with advancing the Johns Hopkins mission of teaching, research and patient care internationally.[11] In addition to co-ordinating care for international patients, JHI provides services in healthcare consulting, clinical service development, laboratory management and education programmes for the international medical community. According to the U.S. News & World Report, the School of Medicine of the Johns Hopkins University was one of the top two medical schools in the United States. Johns Hopkins Hospital, affiliated with the School of Medicine of Johns Hopkins University, ranked number one in the U.S. News & World Report's annual Best Hospitals in America survey for 11 years in a row from 1992, and among the 17 specialties surveyed, it also ranked number one in ophthalmology, gynaecology & obstetrics, otolaryngology and urology.

Exhibit 2   Summary of the Provisional Measures for the Administration of Chinese–Foreign Joint-Equity and Joint Co-operative Medical Institutions

Effective date

- From 1 July 2000.

Approval

- Approval must be obtained from both, the Ministry of Health and the Ministry of Foreign Trade and Economic Co-operation.

Conditions for establishing a joint-venture medical institution

- The medical institution must be an independent legal entity;
- The total investment may not be less than RMB 20 million;

- The share of equity or the interest held by the Chinese side in the joint-venture medical institution may not be less than 30 percent;
- The joint-venture term may not exceed 20 years; and
- Other conditions as stipulated by the health departments of the provincial level or higher must be adhered to.

Relaxations

- Appropriate relaxations of the above conditions may be granted:
  - for joint-venture medical institutions to be established in China's central and western regions; or
  - where the scope of medical services falls into the category of "state-encouraged services".

Restrictions

- Wholly foreign-owned medical institutions are strictly prohibited.
- Any Sino-foreign joint-venture medical institution established without proper approval and engaging in medical activities shall be deemed to be practising medicine illegally and will be punishable in accordance with the appropriate laws.

Source: http://www.chinalegalchange.com/Archives/arch0011.html

17

Team and Concepts Limited
Managing the Growth of a Small Business

ALI FARHOOMAND AND MARY HO

PART I: BACKGROUND AND ISSUES

Introduction

Not all small business owners are entrepreneurs. Some small business owners may have limited aspirations for growth and may be satisfied with a steady stream of income from their business. Their business could be a start-up based on a replica of an existing business, or it could be an existing business inherited from the family or acquired from outsiders with nothing novel to offer, compared with other competitors. Technically speaking, these types of small business owners might not be considered entrepreneurs. Although they make management decisions and have equity capital at risk in their business, they fail to develop an innovative process to exploit opportunities and gaps in the market.

Team and Concepts Limited (TnC), an IT company founded by David Lee and his partners in 2003, was not a typical small business. Its owners were innovative, business-savvy entrepreneurs who had audacious goals at heart, and who were working daily towards the goal of growing the business and transforming it from a fledgling set-up to a successful company. The transformation from initial success to long-term growth required comprehensive changes in many aspects of the business. In particular, TnC recognised the need to facilitate this transition by enhancing its managerial, financial, marketing and R&D capacities. In 2004, TnC was facing the challenge of working with new investors and partners, who would likely set conditions for the business and require it to adopt new culture and a new management structure. The company was also exploring the tradeoffs between acquiring outside funds and retaining control in order to make wise decisions about its future strategy.

The Search for an Opportunity Niche

When TnC was set up in February 2003, its owners were still undergraduates at The University of Hong Kong. Although they were relatively young amateurs with little work experience, most of them were fairly talented and had established a good network with IT professionals in the market. Alan Tam, Chief Software Architect of TnC, was a talented technical person. He developed his first computer programme when he was still a primary-school student, and had been running his own sole-proprietorship business sub-contracting IT projects from a listed company for a number of years. Peter Yip was awarded the most outstanding IT Student in 1999. A library application series that he developed had been sold to more than 230 primary and secondary schools. Tony Sung was another award-winning interface designer whose skills were complementary to those of Tam. P. K. Chan was an intelligent young man who was adept at strategic planning. He was involved in the team from its very beginning until September 2002, when the team was on the verge of incorporation, and rejoined TnC as Chief Executive Officer in June 2004. Reggie Chan was a dedicated, diligent and fast-learning analyst programmer. His enthusiasm and optimism served as a strong binding force in the team as well as a catalyst to drive the team forward. David Lee, chairman of the company, was a highly creative and adaptable person with an adventurous spirit. Before setting up the company, David Lee joined the Internet Professionals Association, where he developed a good network with entrepreneurs and professionals. He also participated actively in various e-business plan and web-design competitions held in Hong Kong. In 2001, David Lee formed a team with Tony Sung and some other friends and won an award in the YDC (Young Entrepreneurs Development Council) e-Challenge Competition. They were then selected to represent Hong Kong in a regional business plan competition known as "StartUp@Asia" in Singapore. They lost to the stronger teams from Singapore and only managed to win the best presentation award for their innovative project. After the competition, David Lee paused to acknowledge and reflect honestly on the weaknesses of his team's project. He realised that it was the lack of practicality and concrete implementation details that had caused the failure.

At university, David Lee received both IT and essential business training through the double degree programme of Bachelor of Business Administration (Information Systems) and Bachelor of Engineering (Software Engineering). He realised that all businesses started with a customer, not only with know-how or the "bright idea". After the e-Challenge competition, he actively looked for problems to solve in the market and formed a new team to search for ways of developing a marketable IT product. The initial business plan originated from a marketing project conducted in September 2001, about finding a way to tackle the problem of the barrage of event information at The University of Hong Kong. At that time, event organisers were unable to communicate with university students in an effective way. To market their events, these organisers relied on the simple system of the university's computer centre, which distributed e-mails to all potential interested parties in the university. As a student, David Lee knew that these e-mails often failed to reach their target audiences, whose attention could be easily distracted by junk e-mails. Even if the e-mails eventually caught the attention of the target students, who then responded with favourable replies, the event organisers had to maintain a separate system for event registration or enrolment. The process from event marketing to registration was often time-consuming, and a lot of manual effort was required to monitor and manage progress. From the perspective of the students, the absence of a sophisticated web-based tool for gathering event information and for scheduling study and extra-curricular activities meant that they had to spend additional time on searching for information and scheduling their activities.

David Lee and his partners saw the university's need for a sophisticated system that could help streamline event information management. The team conducted interviews with a number of event organisers at the university and developed an idea to create a customised event information management package for both community members (i.e., the university students) and event organisers. There were no competitors in the market offering similar solutions because the potential for future revenues was probably too small to interest big IT companies. The team, however, was eager to pursue this small but unproven opportunity to serve this niche market. They knew that their initial technology might not be able to compete in the mainstream commercial market, but could probably be sustained in niche markets with small revenue streams. As a small start-up, the team thought they had could mitigate the inflexibility of long-established companies, who might find it difficult to justify investment in an unproven niche market. As a first mover, the team could possibly have the market all to itself. Through continuous testing and improvement in the long run, the team at TnC was confident that their products might complement those from big players, or even reinforce each other in the protracted process of IT innovation.

New Venture Development — Balancing Resources with Realities

David Lee knew very well that good business planning was focused on a vision of the future while recognising current resources and financial realities. To get off to a good start, he persuaded his team members to invest a little money to form a company, work for deferred compensation and make the best use of the limited resources and capital available. With capital amounting to just HK$20,000, they set up TnC in February 2003. In order to secure a reliable source of legal support for the company in the long run, they made a bold decision to pay more than half of the money to an international law firm for formation costs and legal advice. With strong associations with the Department of Computer Science and Information Systems ("CSIS") of The University of Hong Kong, TnC secured a free space at the Student Incubation Centre on the university's campus for its first formal office, and was thus able to save some rental costs. CSIS also provided the necessary IT support, including a server and network access to the team, even before they set up the company. With the server, TnC could implement its business plan and take its products to the market.

TnC developed its first product, "PEM" (Professional Event Management), on a trial-use basis for several customers, including the Hong Kong Policy Research Institute, the Internet Professionals Association, CSIS and a conference organiser. Despite the team's pressing need for money, they decided not to charge these customers for subscription initially, because the subscription model, which could only generate minimal recurrent fees, was not intended to be a long-lasting one. The ultimate goal of TnC was to develop goodwill and trust with the early adopters before launching more complicated, tailor-made systems at a later stage. By not charging these initial customers, the company had more flexibility to test the offering on a trial basis, and obtain early feedback about the real needs of its customers. Based on the clients' response, TnC's critical assumption — about whether the market was really ready for expanded features — was quickly tested and confirmed.

In March 2003, TnC concluded its first deal with the Computer Centre at The University of Hong Kong. Although the deal was far from profitable, it was nonetheless significant as it provided the company with its first stream of operating income. Within a few months, the company had signed three more deals: with the ArtsAll Scheme, the Development and Alumni Affairs Office of the University of Hong Kong and Chevalier (Network Solutions) Limited. At this point, the company could consider how much to pay to the owners. The owners knew that there was no place where self-discipline played a more important role than in setting their own salaries. They had to choose between taking money out to spend on themselves and their interests outside the business, or reinvesting it in the company, where it could power further growth. In any business, the decision to take or reinvest profits is a highly personal one. To prepare the company for long-term growth, TnC decided to take the second option. To show his commitment to sustaining the business, David Lee had even contributed his scholarship funds to the company.

Start Up Activities

PEM, the community event management system developed by TnC, consisted of a package of event management tools based upon the concept of streamlining event information management. This system offered a variety of benefits to users.

Event organisers in the community could enjoy a set of event-management tools that included event posting, a central calendar, and online registration and enrolment. With the e-mail template system, event organisers could easily send customised e-mails to people enrolling in events. This simplified and automated the routine information-dispatching process of event organisers, and helped those who had no professional experience of event organising. Additional support in generating reports and utilities that were customised according to organisers' specific event-management needs (enroller selection, payment, etc) were also incorporated in the system.

Individual community members were provided with an online calendar that was pre-loaded with personalised events such as training sessions, meetings, etc. They could also select their preferred event organisers, and these organisers' events could be auto-imported to the calendar. Personal events could be added with simple click-and-drag. This system was much more user-friendly than conventional web-based calendar systems.

TnC delivered its products with reasonable quality and stability. Its finely designed system efficiently disseminated event information in the form of a user-friendly click-and-drag web interface. It supported enrolment in events with a few clicks by enrollers, after which event organisers could collect the enrollers' information and perform electronic mass-mailing. Event templates could be used in event posting when similar events were being organised repeatedly. No comparable system in the market could offer similar functions to event organisers or community members. Although MSN and Yahoo had developed calendar systems for organising events, their systems were detached from the community. The absence of comparable applications in the market gave TnC more room to set its pricing strategy.

From time to time, TnC built new customised modules into the system. It constantly upgraded the systems with additional functions, including contact management and fax/e-mail channels for monitoring the progress of the promotion tasks for event organisers. The company also explored ways to enhance communication among community users. In July 2003, TnC re-engineered the event-management process for ArtsAll, which was a scheme offered by The University of Hong Kong to undergraduate students who participated in arts events, to support the development of local art and culture. Under the ArtsAll scheme, each student could enjoy a subsidy for attending an ArtsAll approved event. The PEM system that was tailor-made for ArtsAll effectively managed the enrolment and cash reimbursement applications from students, and helped the scheme to save more than HK$100,000. The user interface and support services offered by the company received very good feedback from ArtsAll, which saw a significant increase in leverage of the scheme from 10% to 70%.

Venture Growth

TnC's corporate slogan, "We Innovate, We Drive", concisely captured the company's persistence in innovation and quality in the course of its development. To achieve further growth, TnC was eager to launch its products in the commercial market. However, the company realised that without sufficient technical and financial capacity for market research, it might not be able to pursue further growth opportunities. In early 2004, TnC identified a problem with potential managerial capacity, as some members of the team were about to graduate and were considering whether to stay in the start-up business or start a new career with an established company. The owners knew that the departure of some members of the team was inevitable. In fact, from 2001 to mid-2004 there had been a number of changes in the composition of the team, and this had resulted in the need to redefine responsibilities and to build trust with new members from time to time. TnC foresaw that team members who left the management board but continued to hold shares in the company would possibly place self-imposed limits on the company's growth simply because they were not willing to dedicate additional time and resources to the company. In order to secure management control and reduce the risk of conflicts of interest, David Lee persuaded these non-participating members to transfer part of their stake to members who would stay in the business. This was to ensure that those who left would not hold more than 15% of the shares of the company and affect the board's business decisions.

As the company's business began to expand, David Lee recognised the need to change from a doer and decision-maker to a delegator and direction-setter. Given the limited resources available, he had to work initially not only as the chairman of the company but also as the general manager, the financial controller, the marketing officer and the customer support officer. The customer support hotline was in fact his mobile phone number. David Lee knew that many growth opportunities would be beyond his reach if he could not devote more effort to developing the business and searching for new market, product and service ideas. The faster the company grew, the less time he had to supervise and monitor routine activities. At this point, he and his team decided to hire P. K. Chan as Chief Executive Officer. Chan had sufficient depth of experience to administer the routine functions of the company and to facilitate the profitable execution of new opportunities. By dividing high-level functions between Lee and P. K. Chan, TnC could establish a balance of power and yield better-quality decisions. TnC also decided to recruit trainees who could assist in providing technical support services to their clients. Drawing on the talents of these newcomers, the roles and responsibilities of the team could be redefined for future development of the business.

TnC believed that one way to add marketing and technical capacity quickly was through partnering with other organisations and by co-opting a portion of their managerial, marketing talent and related resources. From September 2003, the company partnered with Chevalier (Network Solutions) Limited ("CNK") to develop an enterprise version of PEM. CNK, a subsidiary of Chevalier iTech Holdings Limited, was one of the leading providers of network and IT service solutions in Hong Kong. It had established an IT system to manage its rich portfolio of customers and support its operation. The company had won a number of large-scale projects in Hong Kong. For instance, it provided a PABX system solution for a six-star hotel at Two International Finance Centre. It also worked for Television Broadcasts Limited to provide fibre network and telephone installation and maintenance solutions to its New TV City in Tseung Kwan O. To cope with the ever-changing business environment, CNK was eager to develop a central and comprehensive CRM infrastructure.

Both CNK and TnC saw significant mutual benefits in the formation of a strategic alliance. From the perspective of CNK, TnC's experience in event information management could help the company to upgrade its CRM infrastructure. From the perspective of TnC, the alliance with CNK could bring a number of benefits that were otherwise beyond its reach. Through the alliance, TnC acquired domain knowledge to explore more fully the complete solution of the event management concept. TnC could also leverage the brand of CNK and gain more knowledge of the requirements and concerns of corporate customers. CNK's marketing expertise could also give TnC enormous leverage in the promotion of new products.

Tapping its social and professional network (for example, through the owners' participation in the Internet Professionals Association and other networks), TnC received invaluable technical advice from IT professionals, lawyers and entrepreneurs. Ringo Lam, who had developed the "WiseNews" product that was used by many academic institutions and large corporations in Hong Kong, provided strategic advice on market trends and business models to David Lee from time to time. William Tang, an experienced consultant and a former director of a listed company, also provided strategic and operating advice to TnC. In order to bring in William Tang as a committed strategic contributor, the team decided to offer him a 3% stake as a financial incentive. Thanks to this assistance from him, in January 2004 the company was able to lease an office in iBay, an incubation centre of ESRI China (Hong Kong) Limited, a global leader of Geographical Information Systems (GIS), located in Cyberport, at a lower-than-market-rate rental. Cyberport was an ultramodern intelligent-office complex in Hong Kong equipped with cutting-edge telecommunications and information facilities to meet the needs of leading multinational and local IT and other related companies. Being part of this cluster of quality companies and professionals specialising in IT content creation and support services would definitely help the company to build its corporate reputation. To further enhance the company's financial and managerial capacity, TnC successfully solicited investments from its first angel investor, Terence Chiu, whom the owners had met at the Internet Professionals Association. Terence Chiu was a lawyer with extensive experience in providing legal advice for venture-capital deals. He was deeply impressed by the team's passion and its persistent efforts to bring its dreams into reality. Chiu acquired a share in TnC and provided the company with a loan, which was personally guaranteed by David Lee himself. The admission of new investors not only strengthened TnC's ability to administer and accommodate its growth but also enabled the founders to spread the risks and share the rewards with the new contributors.

In 2004, the story of the company's success was publicised in the local press, including *Sing Pao, Ta Kung Pao* and *PC Market*. These publications highlighted the proven competence of the young founders and increased public awareness of the company. In August 2004, the technical excellence of TnC was recognised at the 6th IT Excellence Award organised by the Hong Kong Computer Society. PEM was awarded the Bronze Award in the Post Secondary Category.

Transformation

In mid-2004, TnC was ready to move on. The HKSAR Government was offering the Small Entrepreneur Research Assistance Programme (SERAP), a funding scheme of the Innovation and Technology Fund (ITF), aimed at to financing and supporting projects that contributed to innovation and technology upgrading. If TnC's application was successful, the company would receive ITF grants that could be used to meet manpower costs, the cost of the procuring equipment, and other direct R&D costs specifically required for growing the business. The application, however, would require matching funds from a private firm. For this reason, TnC solicited support from its partners and customers as a possible source of the necessary matching funds.

TnC also worked actively on generating a complete product vision. Recognising that the positioning of PEM was an unattractive solution for corporate users, TnC decided to expand its vision to offer a family of Event Information Systems ("EIS") products to serve the needs of different types of event organisers. TnC decided that the EIS product family could rest on three legs, namely:

- EIS Community — This was designed for the community event organisers that TnC had previously served. PEM, TnC's previous flagship product, was realigned under this product line.
- EIS Professional — This was designed for organisers of large-scale and public events.
- EIS Enterprise — This was designed to meet the specific needs of commercial event organisers, who placed higher importance on consumer information management and operational efficiency. Commercial events were, by definition, designed and engineered towards businesses, revenues and profits. Given the nature of these events, managing a comprehensive customer database and identifying the most valuable customers were much more important.

In mid-2004, TnC was actively promoting its Financing Partner Model to finance the development of EIS Professional and EIS Enterprise. Under this model, financing partners would become users of and investors in TnC's products. These users had expertise in the market and required products that could serve their professional needs effectively. TnC's plan was to grant a licence for the use of the finished system to the financing partners while the company kept the ownership of the intellectual property. The financing partners could also enjoy some royalties when the products were resold. As of September 2004, TnC had successfully solicited two renowned public and commercial event organisers to commit as financing partners for EIS Professional and EIS Enterprise respectively.

At this point, TnC was seriously considering the challenges ahead. The company realised that it needed to think through the changes that the new investors, employees, customers and partners would bring to the company. Although the matching funds, the ITF grant and the new investors were expected to bring substantial financial support to the company, there were likely to be tradeoffs as well. David Lee knew that he could not simply consider the pluses while glossing over what they would be trading in exchange for these good things. What effect would the funding have on the core team's control over the company's direction? Were there any downsides to forging more alliances? How could the company build trust with the new members, financing partners and employees and motivate them to prioritise growth? Was the company ready to move forward towards high growth?

TnC's previous experience had been mostly limited to serving academic institutions, ie, the users of EIS Community. The users of EIS Professional and EIS Enterprise would probably use a different set of criteria to evaluate their products. How should the company re-engineer and market its new products to solicit more users? Would the Financing Partner Model work well, and would it help to reduce the risks the company faced?

David Lee thought it was time for the team members to take themselves through an exercise of evaluating the business and thinking about what they wanted it to do. They had to think holistically about the changes required in every area — business strategy, products, innovation and management structure, in order to make the transformation happen.

PART II: LESSONS LEARNED

What Characteristics Are Typical of Entrepreneurs?

How would you differentiate between a small business owner and an entrepreneur? What type of entrepreneurial traits did TnC's owners demonstrate?

The terms "small business owner" and "entrepreneur" are often used interchangeably, but in fact they are not necessarily interchangeable. A "small business owner" is the owner or operator of any small business. The term also has the connotation of a "manager". Compared with owners of large companies, small business owners often face unique problems that originate predominately in owner-manager and size-related characteristics and constraints.

An entrepreneur, according to Gibb, is "an opportunity seeker who combines the factors of production in an innovative manner and who seeks out and exploits opportunities and gaps in the market".[1] Gibb stresses the importance of innovation and opportunity-seeking, and has suggested the addition of other individual characteristics, including independence, coping with uncertainty, risk-taking, creativity, flexibility and various skills, to the definition of an entrepreneur. Watson suggested that the definition of entrepreneur should exclude "any small business owner whose enterprise is a replica of an existing business or who inherit[s] or purchase[s] an existing business and add[s] little or nothing novel to its operation".[2] Hence, the term "entrepreneur" should not be used as a general term that includes all small business managers and owners.

The following summarises some of the entrepreneurial traits that the owners of TnC possessed:

- creativity and innovativeness
- confidence and optimism to pursue a market opportunity that they had identified
- courage and the drive to achieve
- knowledge of product, market and technology
- ability to influence others
- energy and diligence
- perseverance and determination
- ability to take calculated risks
- commitment
- willingness to learn from feedback
- internal locus of control
- vision

The entrepreneurial characteristics of TnC's owners were displayed in the managerial practices they employed in running TnC. Figure 1 shows how the personal attributes of an entrepreneur determine motivations and objectives, which in turn determine the firm's performance. This process is mediated through the markets in which the entrepreneur operates and the managerial practices that he or she employs. The model shows the interdependency between entrepreneurial variables and firm performance. A dynamic element is incorporated by the possibility that business performance may reinforce or change the entrepreneur's motivations and objectives. The possibility of feedback about performance and learning from experience as an important form of entrepreneurial human capital are highlighted in the model.

Figure 1   Model of Small Firm Performance[3]

Based on the above model, the owners of TnC should:
- learn about their business performance
- act upon changes in the business environment
- review their objectives from time to time
- update/reformulate managerial and marketing strategies to transform the company continuously
- understand that new members may have different entrepreneurial characteristics and may therefore bring changes to the firm's objectives and strategies

Life Cycle of Venture Development

The traditional stages of an enterprise's life cycle are shown in Figure 2. These stages are: new-venture development, start-up activities, venture growth, business stabilisation, and innovation or decline.

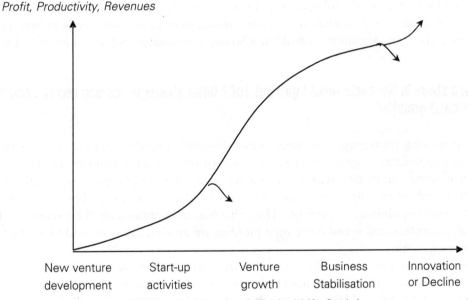

Figure 2   A Venture's Typical Life Cycle[4]

- **Stage 1 – New venture development**
This is a creativity, assessment and networking stage for the initial formulation of entrepreneurial strategy.

- **Stage 2 – Start-up activities**
This stage encompasses the foundation work needed for creating a formal business plan, searching for capital, carrying out marketing activities and developing an effective entrepreneurial team. Such activities typically require the rationalisation of resources.

- **Stage 3 – Growth**

This stage often requires major changes in entrepreneurial strategy. At this stage, the founders need to change from Doers and Decision-makers to Delegators and Direction-setters. New challenges also force the founders into developing a different set of skills while maintaining an entrepreneurial perspective.

- **Stage 4 – Business stabilisation**

During this stage, a number of developments commonly occur. These include increased competition, consumer indifference to the entrepreneur's goods or services and saturation of the market. This stage often precedes the period when the firm either swings into higher profitability or swings towards decline and failure.

While biological systems seem condemned to go through the predictable curve of growth, plateau and decline, Penrose suggested that conscious organisations can determine their own limiting factors. They can consciously think about their internal structure and can understand and react consciously to their changing environments. If they can move beyond their limitations to sustain continuous growth, they may not be pre-destined for the same fate of decline as biological organisms. To overcome the managerial limits and explore new avenues for continuous growth, management of the firm needs to become a Change Catalyst, an Organisation Builder, a Strategic Innovator and the Chief of Culture.

At which stage in the cycle would you put TnC? What strategies do you recommend for its sustained growth?

TnC was moving from Stage 2 to Stage 3 as the owners found limitations on their time and their capabilities to grow the firm. As some of the old team members left the firm, those remaining had to deal with the problems of motivation and managerial capacity, find new members and hire new employees to undertake activities that they did not have the time, skills or abilities to perform. They also had to communicate their vision to the new team members and spend more time building up an effective team and planning for continuous growth.

The ability of TnC to translate opportunities into growth therefore now hinges on the availability of sufficient managerial services. The founders also need to change themselves into Team Builders, Coaches, Planners and Communicators. Participation in day-to-day decision-making procedures must be expanded. Greater emphasis should be placed on the use of formal decision-making techniques. These may involve the selection of new people to supplement or replace indispensable individuals who have performed most of the key operating tasks in the past. Specialists must learn to become functional managers, while functional managers must learn to become general managers.

In managing the growth stage, the owners of TnC should remember two important points: first, TnC should retain certain entrepreneurial characteristics to encourage innovation and creativity; and second, the founders need to translate this spirit of innovation and creativity to their personnel while personally making a transition towards a more managerial style. In other words, they have to strike a balance between an entrepreneurial focus and a managerial focus. In order to facilitate the transformation of their business, successful entrepreneurs must learn how to delegate and outsource the right things at the right time. Many small business owners suffer from an entrepreneurial seizure as they are too busy doing technical work rather than identifying opportunities and thinking outside the box. In order to grow effectively, they must add managerial capacity to the firm to administer and accommodate its growth.

In the book *The Theory of the Growth of the Firm*, Penrose argued that the modern corporate enterprise has to be viewed as an organisation that administers a collection of human and physical resources. The most critical resources reside in humans, because they learn how to make the best use of the firm's productive resources. At any point in time, this learning endows the firm with experience that gives it productive opportunities unavailable to other firms that have not accumulated the same experience, even though they may be in the same industry.

In the Foreword to the 1995 edition of *The Theory of the Growth of the Firm*, Penrose stated:[5]

> [T]he growing experience of management, its knowledge of the other resources of the firm and the potential for using them in different ways, create incentives for further expansion as the firm searches for ways of using the services of its own resources more profitably. The firm's existing human resources provide an inducement to expand and a limit to the rate of expansion. Even growth by acquisition and merger does not escape the constraints imposed by the necessity of using inputs from existing managerial resources to maintain the coherence of the organisation.

The Penrose Model of Firm Growth is shown in Figure 3. Penrose suggested that as members of a management team become better acquainted with the resources of the firm, they begin to identify opportunities beyond their current activities. This allows the firm to grow. However, the introduction of new product and service ideas by the entrepreneurs requires substantial managerial services or managerial capacity to be properly implemented and supervised. A firm cannot simply hire new managers to quickly remedy its shortfall in managerial resources. It takes time for new managers to be socialised, acquire skills and knowledge and establish trusting relationship with other members of the firm. The bottleneck a firm experiences because its managerial resources are insufficient to take advantage of its new product and service opportunities is referred to as the managerial capacity problem.[6]

There are additional challenges related to the managerial capacity problem articulated by Penrose. Sometimes a firm's lack of growth arises from the motivational problem, which results in self-imposed limits on growth.

TnC had to face a managerial capacity and motivational problem as it began to move from the institutional market to the corporate market and transform from a small business to a growth company.

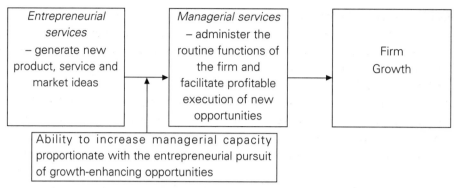

Figure 3   Penrose Model of Firm Growth[7]

What Are the Critical Success Factors of TnC?

The critical success factors of TnC include:

Identifying a niche market

SMEs can often avoid confronting established competitors head-on by finding opportunities in a niche market. TnC, for example, launched its event-management products in a niche market. There were no comparable substitutes in the market because the company was able to find a different twist or a unique way to add value by streamlining the event-management process for the community, comprising both event organisers and community members. The absence of direct competitors gave the company more room to set its pricing strategy.

Implementing an early–adopter programme as a research and marketing strategy

An efficient way for SMEs to conduct research and market their products is to implement an early-adopter programme. Such a programme requires SMEs to get their clients' approval to test offerings on a trial basis for free or at a reduced fee. By testing the product with the early adopters, TnC gained more understanding of the target market and learnt about its clients' real needs. Obtaining early feedback from clients through the beta testing programme helped the company to develop more sophisticated model that would add value to clients. The company's critical assumption — about whether the market was really ready for expanded features — was also quickly tested by the programme.

In a race to define an emerging market, SMEs that learn first can generally capture the first-mover advantage. The learning process must come through trial and error, and generally includes the following steps:
1. Designing an early adopter programme or product for testing;
2. Predicting outcomes and clients' responses;
3. Measuring outcomes and clients' responses;
4. Comparing outcomes with predictions;
5. Drawing conclusions about the future product based on the comparison. If predictions are wrong, future expectations must be adjusted given the new information.

Finding a niche sponsor

SMEs wanting to grow their business have higher odds of success with support from niche sponsors that are experienced in supporting new product development and that can provide a reliable access to a guaranteed market. TnC successfully solicited support from The University of Hong Kong, Chevalier (Network Solutions), ESRI China (Hong Kong) Limited and strategic advisors, and was able to augment its capacity synergistically by co-opting a portion of the sponsors' resources and gaining access to their established marketing network.

Apart from commercial sponsorship, SMEs should also consider applying for government grants to help develop their business.

Building corporate reputation

Most small businesses suffer from "the liability of newness" and are unable to provide clear evidence of their ability to compete against more established firms.[8] This information gap or information asymmetry prevents investors and customers from judging their full capabilities. Consequently, small businesses often find it difficult to attract investment money, customers and competent personnel.

TnC, however, was able to build the intangible asset of corporate reputation systematically. It endeavoured to strengthen its market status by partnering with established IT firms, finding experienced strategic advisors and developing positive opinions from customers. With the assistance of William Tang, TnC moved its office to the luxurious Cyberport complex, where many leading multinational and local IT and other related companies were located. Winning the IT Excellence Award also proved the technical excellence of TnC. The story of the company's success appeared in local newspapers in March, August and September 2004, increasing public awareness of and interest in the company. Its good reputation helped the company to attract investors, encouraged customers to purchase its products, and assisted in the recruitment of skilled manpower.

Research studies suggest that IT enterprises are particularly dependent on a positive reputation, since they lack tangible assets and face the rapid obsolescence of products, more so than enterprises in other sectors.[9] Their performance is often judged while products are still in the development phase, in competition against more established firms. IT enterprises should therefore make an extra effort to develop positive opinions regarding their products and services and to establish strategic relationships with partners. Successful enterprises should be able to use "contacts and connections" in their social milieu to decrease their transaction costs.[10]

What Are the Challenges Ahead?

Managing revenue expectations

Sponsors will have revenue expectations of the company. This means TnC must constantly recalibrate its revenue projections based on accumulated experience and market realities. To assign realistic revenue expectations, TnC must identify and evaluate the impact of different variables (such as the competitive climate, current economic conditions and the market needs) on their business. This will help the company to achieve its goals and avoid the blame game.

Motivating team members and employees to prioritise growth

TnC's full name, "Team and Concepts", implied that the company built its business around a good team and good innovations. New members and employees had to be socialised into the culture of TnC, acquire firm-specific skills and knowledge, and work with other members to establish trusting relationships. However, this takes time, and in future it could create a bottleneck in the ability of the company to pursue attractive market opportunities swiftly and effectively. To facilitate the socialisation process, the company should develop a compelling mission statement that will help experienced members provide clear and unambiguous direction to new members and employees. Incentives could also be provided to new members to encourage them to engage in growth-enhancing activities.

Balancing vision with resource realities

TnC had to allocate resources properly to devote to enhancing existing competencies or toward innovations that could develop future competencies. Given the limited resources available, shareholders might have to sacrifice immediate returns in order to construct a solid base for long-term growth and build a strong organisational infrastructure of skilled manpower. The company's strategy for future orientation, however, might make investors unhappy if profits have to be deferred until a vague later date.

Gauging the risks of strategic alliances

The founders of TnC had to be aware of the downside and risks of forging strategic alliances with established firms, as this could create dependency on their resources. In some cases, a strategic alliance may put a firm at risk of opportunistic actions by stronger and more aggressive partners, who might appropriate technical knowledge and terminate the alliance when they see so further benefit from it. On a personal level, the original founders might also need to consider that alliances could be very risky for themselves. They might eventually be forced out by a stronger partner who prefers more seasoned executives.

Conclusion

Many young people want to control their own destinies by becoming entrepreneurs. The experience of TnC shows that student entrepreneurs have to face a number of challenges when they work to build a successful business. These include:
– Minimising overheads and getting the most out of available resources;
– Learning about the financial side of running a business as it progresses;
– Learning about managing organisational and personnel changes;
– Taking business advice when necessary;

- Managing a good relationship with parents and loved ones and getting their emotional support (because starting up a business means giving up a high-paid job).
- Preparing to take a minimal salary for at least two years
- Accepting failure gracefully, as there are many more failures than successes in the early stages of a business, and
- Soliciting financial, technical and other necessary support from their university, the government and industry.

1. Gibb, A. (1996), "Entrepreneurship and Small Business Management: Can We Afford to Neglect Them in the Twenty-first Century Business School", *British Journal of Management*, Vol. 7, pp. 309–321.
2. Watson, T. (1995), "Entrepreneurship and Professional Management: A Fatal Distinction", *International Small Business Journal*, Vol. 13, No. 2, pp. 34–36.
3. Glancey, K., Greig, M. and Pettigrew, M. (1998), "Entrepreneurial dynamics in small business service firms", *International Journal of Entrepreneurial Behaviour & Research*, Vol. 4, No.3, pp. 249–268.
4. Kuratko, D. and Hodgetts, R., (1992), *Entrepreneurship — A Contemporary Approach*, Fourth Edition, Fort Worth: Dryden Press, p. 493.
5. Penrose, E. (1995), *The Theory of the Growth of the Firm*, Third Edition, Oxford University Press.
6. Barringer, B. R. and Jones, F. F. (2004), "Achieving Rapid Growth: Revisiting the Managerial Capacity Problem", *Journal of Development Entrepreneurship*, Vol. 9, Issue 1 (April), p. 73.
7. Penrose, E. T. (1959) *The Theory of the Growth of the Firm*, New York: John Wiley and Sons.
8. Stinchcombe, A. L. (1965), "Social Structure and Organizations", in *Handbook of Organizations*, ed. J. G. March, Chicago, IL: Rand McNally, p.142–193.
9. Alvesson, M. (1990), "Organization: From Substance to Image?" *Organization Studies*, 11(3), p. 373–394.
10. Gabbay, S. M. (1997), *Social Capital in the Creation of Financial Capital: The Case of Network Marketing*, Champaign, IL: Stipes Publishing.

18

TrademarkLogo.com
Transforming Legal Services on the Internet

ALI FARHOOMAND AND MONICA WONG

PART I: BACKGROUND AND ISSUES

Introduction

In 2000, Robert Wang, senior partner of the Hong Kong law firm Robert W. H. Wang & Co., spearheaded the establishment of TrademarkLogo.com (TML). He believed that legal services, like other businesses, could exploit the opportunities afforded by the Internet. The trademark practice of the Intellectual Property (IP) department was a good candidate for an Internet venture — the process was straightforward and it required few discussions and meetings between the lawyers and the clients. Doing business via the Internet would also greatly reduce the amount of paperwork the firm needed to handle, thereby solving the IP Department's cost over-run problem. However, the bursting of the Internet bubble, coupled with worldwide economic woes, sent the business into a downturn in 2002. The dotcom's appeal seemed to have disappeared along with the Internet hype; traffic on the Website had slowed down, and the number of transactions had tumbled. In 2003, the Government rolled out the new Trade Mark Ordinance and Rules that streamlined and simplified the trademark and service mark registration process. As part of the Government's Electronic Service Delivery (ESD) initiatives, procedural and pricing information became readily available on the Web and anyone could lodge a trademark registration application themselves. The role of an IP service provider was thus being undermined. As the new executive director hired to turn things around, Poorna Mysoor was tasked with reviving the business and identifying opportunities for future growth. As she was preparing her proposal to Robert Wang, she wondered about TML's competitive advantage over its competitors. How could TML make use of the Internet to establish a distinctive strategic positioning? What should TML do to react to the Government's ESD initiative; and how could TML create a strong enough value proposition for its customers and suppliers?

Company Background

Robert W. H. Wang & Co. was a Hong Kong-based full-service law firm, established in 1980. The firm specialised in commercial and corporate law and laws in relation to e-commerce and intellectual property. The firm had six major divisions: the Commercial and Corporate Department, the Company Secretarial Department, the Litigation Department, the Probate Department, the Intellectual Property Department and the Conveyance & Real Estate Department. It was a member of the World Law Group, a network of independent law firms located in more than 40 of the world's major commercial cities. Through the World Law Group, the firm had established a network of correspondents and affiliates to provide worldwide legal services.

The Intellectual Property Department handled cases involving trademarks and service marks, copyright and design protection, design registration and renewal, patent filing and registration, data protection, licensing and technology transfer, unfair competition, and Internet law and litigation.

TrademarkLogo.com (TML) was set up as an independent online entity to handle trademark and service mark services. It shared resources with Robert W. H. Wang & Co. in order to leverage the capital, infrastructure and legal expertise of the parent company.

Trademark or Service Mark Registration

Trademark registration had become common, due to the increasing number of trademark infringement cases. More Hong Kong companies had also come to realise the intangible value of a brand name and they wanted to protect their brand's reputation from goods of inferior quality. Since many Hong Kong companies conducted business worldwide, they needed extensive trademark registration covering multiple overseas countries.

A trademark or a service mark could be a word, brand, label, logo, device, signature, letter, numeral or any combination of these elements. Trademark registration was not mandatory. However, if a company's unregistered trade mark was infringed, the company being infringed upon would need to prove goodwill and reputation in the mark; that there had been a misrepresentation, and that there was damage suffered (or that there was a likelihood of damage). This translated into long, complicated and costly legal proceedings. By the time the case was over, it was usually too late to make up for the loss in sales and the damage done to the image of the company.

If, on the other hand, a company had registered its trademark, it could take infringement action against another party for unethical use of the mark or any similar mark in respect of the same or similar goods or services. The company would simply need to present the trademark certificate and there would be no need to prove anything else. Once registered, a trademark would be valid for 10 years (renewable for every 10 years thereafter). A trademark could be registered before it was used, but once registered, if it was not used within three years it could be cancelled because of this non-use.

The registration procedure in Hong Kong was quite straightforward. Before lodging an application, classification of the product or service and a preliminary search was needed to identify whether someone else had already registered or had applied to register the same or a similar mark. After an applicant submitted the form, together with a scanned image of the logo/mark they wanted to register, the Government's Intellectual Property Department would then check for any deficiencies in the application. After that, a detailed search and examination of the mark based on the criteria laid down in the Trade Mark

Ordinance would be performed. If the examiner objected to the application, the applicant had six months in which to meet the requirements, plus a three-month extension allowance if necessary. If the objection remained, the applicant had three months to satisfy the requirements or call for a hearing.

When all the requirements for registrations were met, the examiner's written confirmation that the mark was acceptable for registration would be published in the *Hong Kong Intellectual Property Journal* at http://www.info.gov.hk/ipd/hkipjournal/. Anyone could view the trademark and lodge an opposition to it within three months of the initial publication. If a third party lodged an objection, a hearing would take place before a hearing officer, who would then make the final decision.

Once the trademark had been accepted for registration, the Registrar of Trade Marks would issue the applicant a certificate of registration. Notice of the trademark registration would also be published in the *Hong Kong Intellectual Property Journal.*

Due to the territorial nature of trademark registration, a company would need to register its trademark in every country where it had a business presence, in order to secure more comprehensive protection.

The Traditional Role of an IP Legal Service Provider

Within the context of trademark registration, a legal service provider such as Robert W. H. Wang & Co. represented its customers throughout the whole application process, offering services such as identifying the relevant class code, conducting preliminary searches, submitting the applications, lodging any objections, defending the applications at hearings, and keeping track of registration renewals. The law firm acted as an intermediary between the Government and the applicants.

As part of the Government's Electronic Service Delivery (ESD) initiatives launched in December 2000, information about trademark registration became accessible to the general public via a simple mouse click.[1] Product and service classification codes, fee schedules and application forms were downloadable from the Government's Website. Anyone could perform a preliminary search on the Web and submit their application to the Government directly. The application process was also streamlined in order to encourage more traders to register their marks — this was in conjunction with the Government's initiatives to raise the public's awareness of intellectual property rights and to fight piracy.

As the Government continued to make its services more easily accessible, its requirements less complicated and its processes more transparent, the role of professional intermediaries became less important. In the realm of trademark registration, the IP departments of law firms not only found themselves competing with other law firms, but also found their role as intermediaries being undermined by the Government's ESD initiatives.

The Business Model of TrademarkLogo.com

From the onset, TML was designed to be a global player. Drawing on its network of international legal professionals who specialised in intellectual property law, TML served companies in Hong Kong that were looking to register their trademarks overseas and vice versa. There would be no need for the lawyers and clients to meet because the whole application process was done entirely through interfacing on the Internet. TML processed the legal paperwork offline, behind the scenes.

During the first six months of operation, TML recorded an average of 4,100 hits per month. Forty percent of its sales came through electronic means, with the rest coming from the traditional channel of telephone calls. In 2003, the average number of hits per month increased to 6,400, with over half of the transactions taking place online. On average, TML received 10 to 15 registration applications per month.

Logo design

TML had established a unique positioning in the trademark registration market — at trade fairs, TML often presented itself among designers rather than among lawyers. TML offered a ready-made and made-to-order logo design service — a service that was completely outside of the scope of legal services. The design service not only made TML stand out in the crowd, creating a one-stop-shop image, it also broadened its target market base.

For a flat rate of US$500, a logo could be designed according to the requirements of the client within seven working days. For clients with urgent needs, the ready-to-use logo gallery posted on the Website offered an instant solution. After the logo design was confirmed, TML would perform a pre-filing search to check whether the design would run into conflict with any existing trademark.

The idea of adding logo design into the service package stemmed from Wang's experience with most of his clients. Customers recognised the importance of trademark registration, but had no idea how to come up with their own logo. Drawing on his personal network of business contacts, Wang was able put together a team of graphic designers to complement his team of experienced trademark lawyers.

Global watch

The one-stop-shop service was completed with the post-registration service, "Global Watch". This was a routine maintenance service that helped companies monitor renewal deadlines. In association with its international network of affiliates, customers who subscribed to Global Watch would also be able to receive reports on any conflicting trademark applications worldwide so that objections could be raised if required.

Pricing

For a basic trademark registration for one class code, the total fee charged by the Government, covering a search of records, preliminary advice on registrability and applying for registration, amounted to US$217. This would be the self-service cost for any individual. Further fees and charges would be incurred if the applicants encountered opposition by the Government or other complications. If an applicant did not want the hassle of handling the application process by themselves, TML offered a package deal costing US$710, which covered service charges and Government fees for a pre-filing search, advice and other necessary services in order to get the mark registered (cases that involved hearings would be charged by quotation).

Value Proposition

Most of TML's clients were traders and retailers of goods. TML targeted small and medium enterprises (SMEs) in Hong Kong because big companies either had their own in-house legal team already or typically preferred to have more face-to-face interactions with lawyers. TML's fundamental operation model was to minimise lawyer-client meetings to keep the bill small, so the service was by nature impersonal. This model suited smaller companies, which also tended to be more flexible and adaptable to new ways of doing business.

The TML Website listed four major services: Logo design, Pre-filing searches, Registration and Global Watch. Detailed descriptions and pricing information on each service were available on the Website. The pricing information was available on the Website in the form of a fee calculator. Customers could select the countries and services they needed and the total charge would be calculated automatically. Customers who wanted any combination of these services simply needed to go to the "Order Now" section and check against the services they required. For example, if a customer needed the Trademark/Logo Design service, the first step would be to fill in a form, providing company information and details of personal preferences on the type of design, the number of colours to be used, the preferred colours (in Pantone colour codes); the countries or territories in which the mark was intended to appear; the class code of the product or service, and personal details about the applicants for billing and correspondence purposes. Similarly for other services, customers simply needed to input relevant information on the order forms.

With the help of technology, TML was able build a close network with IP law firms around the world. Members of the business network worked in partnership to provide a trademark registration service to other member firms in different parts of the world, thereby creating a mutually beneficial mechanism of customer referrals. Standardised formats for graphical representations of a trademark or service mark and information enabled the accurate and speedy transfer of data, reducing inefficiency and costs.

At the front end, interactions between customers and TML took place entirely through the Web, unless complications arose that required hearings or meetings. All correspondence and communications were handled via e-mails and the Website. The digitisation of correspondence reduced paperwork for both the law firm and the clients. This enabled customers to place orders around the clock and standardised the interface between customers and TML, thereby shortening the time and administrative support needed to handle the applications. The ultimate benefit was the saving of time and cost to both TML and its customers.

Competition

A direct competitor, www.Trademark.com.hk, was established shortly after the launch of TML. Although its prices were cheaper than TML's, it only provided a registration service; it did not have worldwide coverage and did not offer any complementary services to the application.

Other "offline" competitors included other law firms and intellectual property agencies in Hong Kong. These were incumbents without the benefit or advantage of an online business. Besides legal firms, trade associations such as the Federation of Hong Kong Industries, a not-for-profit statutory organisation with more than 20 years of experience, also provided a simple trademark registration service in Hong Kong and China.

Beyond Cost Reduction

The five-person TML team included two trademark executives, a marketing officer, a solicitor and an IT professional. In addition, three Singapore-based graphic designers were hired on an agreed piece-rate basis. Resources in the IP Department were freed up for redeployment within the law firm, and it was estimated that time savings of 30 to 40 percent and cost savings of 20 percent were achieved by transforming the business into a Web-based dotcom.

Sales had improved in the first year, but numbers fell in the second year with the bursting of the Internet bubble. Profitability had also been declining since 2001. Despite a slight rebound in 2003, long-term sales performance was precarious as it depended not only on market competition but also on the macro-economic climate, which would in turn affect the number of new businesses or new products/services being launched in the market.

In 2003, TML was looking to add new, complementary businesses into its core trademark registration service. The existing "Global Watch" service was designed for monitoring trademark registration renewal deadlines and reporting applications. TML saw an opportunity to grow the business by adding an active counterfeit surveillance service into the package. With the new service, customers could take a more pro-active and results-oriented approach to protecting their brand assets. A counterfeiting squad comprised of private detectives would provide an effective way to deal with trademark pirates in different parts of the world. TML had contacted anti-counterfeit agents around the world to explore the possibility of co-operation in a model not unlike its association with law firms around the world (essentially a commission-based referral model).

Mysoor's task as the new executive director was to lead TML to a new stage of sustainable growth and development. Would anti-counterfeiting surveillance fit the TML business model?

PART II: LESSONS LEARNED

What Was TML's Competitive Advantage over Its Competitors?

According to Michael Porter, competitive advantage can be achieved by operating at a lower cost, by commanding a premium price, or by doing both. Cost and price advantages can be achieved in two ways:

1. Operational Effectiveness — doing the same things your competitors do but doing them better;
2. Strategic Positioning — doing things differently from competitors in a way that delivers a unique type of value to customers.[2]

By easing and speeding the exchange of real-time information, the Internet has arguably been the most powerful tool available in recent years for enhancing operational effectiveness. However, improving operational effectiveness alone does not provide a competitive advantage. Advantages are gained only if companies are able to achieve and sustain higher levels of operational effectiveness than their competitors.

Rather than relying on operational effectiveness, which could be copied quickly by rivals, TML's competitive advantage was gained through its strategic positioning as a trademark one-stop-shop offering the full scope of services, from before the actual application (logo design) to after the marks had been registered (Global Watch).

How Did Internet Technology Help TML to Establish a Distinctive Strategic Positioning?

As it becomes harder to sustain operational advantages, strategic positioning becomes all the more important. In order to generate higher levels of economic value, a company must gain a cost advantage or price premium by competing in a distinctive way.[3]

Trademark registration alone was an undifferentiated service. TML's ready-to-use trademark gallery and the logo design service were both unique product attributes that differentiated TML from other legal service providers. With the ready-to-use trademark gallery, sample logos could be adapted, thereby simplifying the design process and shortening the turnaround cycle.

TML also made use of the Internet to widen its geographic markets from local to international through partnerships with law firms around the world. As Don Tapscott once said, "In the Internet era, firms can profit enormously from resources that don't belong to them."[4] TML leveraged its network of associated law firms in overseas countries, and was looking into tapping into the resources of anti-counterfeiting agents without investing heavily to build an in-house team.

TML created a "b-web", defined by Tapscott as any system composed of suppliers, distributors, service providers, infrastructure providers and customers who used the Internet for business communications and transactions. By so doing, it created a unique and distinctive positioning among its rivals in the legal service industry as an online trademark service one-stop-shop.

What Was TML's Value Proposition?

Like many other Internet business, cost reductions brought about by efficiency gained through simplified process and shortened turnaround time were the most obvious values created. In TML's case, cost reduction was not the only value created. The Value Drivers of Web Business Models framework (Amit and Zott) can be used to analyse TML's value proposition.[5]

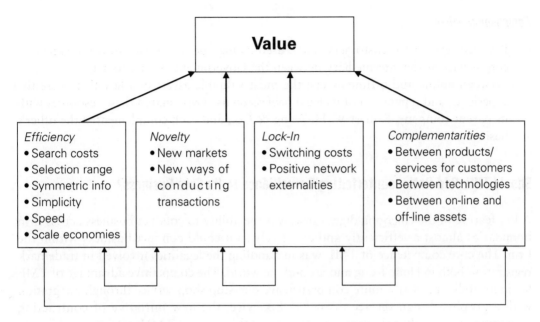

Source: Amit and Zott (2000)

Figure 1   Value Drivers of Web Business Models: A Framework

Efficiency

- Search costs: price and procedural information available on TML's Website, search costs greatly reduced.
- Selection range: a potentially unlimited number of logos could be made available for selection on the Web.
- Symmetric information: detailed process and pricing information available to the public.
- Simplicity and speed: the online application forms simplified the process and reduced turnaround time.

Novelty

- New ways of conducting transactions: the traditional face-to-face client-lawyer meetings were replaced by around-the-clock Internet interfacing.

Lock-in

- Switching cost: TML did not have a well-developed mechanism to increase the cost to customers of switching to another service provider. However, "Global Watch" and the introduction of the anti-counterfeiting surveillance service would help retention and would extend the life-time value of each customer.

Complementarities

– Between services for customers: TML used its logo design service to complement its core service as the intermediary between the Government and customers.
– Between online and offline assets: the most valuable assets in a law firm were the experience and reputation of its legal professionals. TML shared these resources with its parent company, Robert W. H. Wang & Co., and each complemented the other's business.

Should TML Add Anti-counterfeiting Surveillance to Its Core Business?

A key feature of the emerging digital firm was the ability to conduct business across firm boundaries almost as efficiently and effectively as it could conduct business within the firm. The core competence of TML was in handling the legalities involved in trademark registration both in Hong Kong and around the world. The competitive advantage of TML lay in its ability to offer a more comprehensive one-stop-shop service through integration with a graphic design service provider. Likewise, the new initiative of contracting counterfeiting surveillance agents would expand the scope of TML's service capabilities.

For TML, anti-counterfeiting was a new way of serving its customers and capturing value. The new service would increase TML's "share of wallet" from its existing customer base, and would increase the opportunity to get a bigger share of each customer's budget for brand protection.

The benefits of adding an anti-counterfeiting surveillance service included:

- The anti-counterfeiting surveillance agency service would add a new revenue source to the business.
- The anti-counterfeiting surveillance service would help TML to expand into a new market segment of more established companies with valuable brand names.
- Integrating the professional service of designers and anti-counterfeiting agents would help increase the value of the dot-com business, as perceived by customers.
- A continuous service cycle would be created by adding the anti-counterfeiting surveillance programme, which would help to retain customers.
- China remained a world leader in counterfeit consumer products, so overseas companies selling their branded products in China were a huge potential market for TML's anti-counterfeiting surveillance service.

Conclusion

The key question is not whether to deploy Internet technology — companies have no choice if they want to stay competitive — but how to deploy it. Internet technology provides better opportunities for companies to establish distinctive strategic positioning than did previous generations of information technology.

– Michael Porter, *Strategy and the Internet*

The total number of worldwide users of the Internet at the end of 2002 was 600 million plus, and was expected to reach 750 million plus by 2004.[6] As the Internet population continued to grow, it was reasonable to predict the same trend for new business entities on the Internet. However, the Internet was viewed as blessing to some and challenge to others. Companies, especially the well-established ones with long histories, often looked at it as a challenge because in some cases it threatened their survival. Executives were scratching their heads, trying to figure out what e-business meant for their business, what opportunities e-business presented for them, and what threats would it pose to their current business.[7]

TML's story illustrates that dot-coms must first and foremost pursue their own distinctive strategies, rather than copying one another or the positioning of established companies. They must break away from competing solely on price and must instead focus on product selection, product design, service, image and other areas in which they can differentiate themselves.

TML was built upon the notion of innovation and simplification. Its objectives were to provide information, to reduce its overhead costs and to improve its productivity and efficiency. These objectives were met and cost savings were achieved. However, sales and profitability were not easy to come by. TML planned to add a new service component to the existing product in the hope that this would attract new businesses from its existing customer base, and from a new market segment of more well-established companies. By studying the example of TML, SMEs can learn how to take advantage of the Internet's capabilities, how to complement these capabilities with a global network of associates and partners, and then how to turn all this into a competitive advantage. TML demonstrated that transforming a business through the Internet could create new efficiencies and new relationships between an organisation, its customers and suppliers, refining organisation boundaries. Sourcing and prospecting were no longer constrained by geographical limits.

In order for a company to stay competitive and develop sustainable growth, value-adding services are essential, because these are key attributes that customers look for when differentiating between different companies. The business model of TML minimised cost by outsourcing non-core business activities, e.g., logo design and global anti-counterfeiting surveillance, to third parties. This model is particularly applicable to SMEs with limited resources in-house. By integrating service delivery with companies in other professions, "firms can profit enormously from resources that don't belong to them".[8]

---

1   Refer to Farhoomand, A. and McCauley, M. (2002), "Electronic Service Delivery Implementation and Acceptance Strategy", *Centre for Asian Business Cases*, Ref 02/149C, 15 August.
2   Porter, M. E. (2001), "Strategy and the Internet", *Harvard Business Review*, March.
3   Porter.
4   Tapscott, D., "Rethinking Strategy in a Networked World", *Strategy + Business*, Issue 24.
5   Zott, C. and Amit, R. (2000), Strategies for value creation in e-commerce: Best practice in Europe, *European Management Journal*, October, Vol. 18, Issue 5, p. 462.
6   CyberAtlas, http://cyberatlas.internet.com/.
7   Sawhney, M. and Zabin, J. (2001), *The Seven Steps to Nirvana: Strategic Insights into e-Business Transformation*, McGraw-Hill, 2001, pp. 1–2.
8   Tapscott.

19

Yu's Tin Sing Enterprises
Proactive Risk and Crisis Management

FREDDIE LEE, GILBERT WONG AND MARY HO

PART I: BACKGROUND AND ISSUES

On 2 April 2003, Paul Yu, General Manager of Yu's Tin Sing Enterprises Co., Ltd. (YTSE), received an urgent request from a government department in Wanchai to provide general office cleaning services. The request was a bit unusual as the government officer insisted that services had to start the very next day, early in the morning. On an average day, YTSE normally sent its staff to start cleaning in the evening to avoid disturbing the office workers during business hours. At the request of the client, Paul Yu agreed to provide services at the specified time. He then arranged to issue a standard price quotation, which was accepted by the government officer immediately.

The next day began routinely enough until Paul Yu received a call from a supervisor who was assigned to lead the cleaning team at the Wanchai government office. The supervisor and his team were stunned to discover that the government office was completely vacant, even though it was a normal business day. They talked to the security guard of the building, and were advised that a government employee was infected with SARS. As the team members were worrying about the dangers and difficulties of completing the job, Paul Yu ordered the supervisor to stop working and to lead the cleaning team out of the government office. He then sprang into action, left his office in Chai Wan, jumped in his car and headed towards the government building for an emergency meeting with his staff. From Chai Wan to Wanchai, Paul Yu had less than 30 minutes to think about what he could do to protect his staff and to complete the project without breaking his contract with the government.

Company Background

Paul Yu's father, Yu Cheung Ching, founded YTSE in 1958, using the name Tin Sing Maintenance & Cleaning Service Company. In 1979, the business was formally incorporated in Hong Kong. Within 50 years, the small business had grown to become a solid company in its field, with more than 2,000 workers by 2004, and had gained a solid reputation in a market unnoticed by most people. YTSE provided cleaning and pest control services to various government departments, public organisations, schools, residences, commercial buildings and construction sites. Such services included general and deep cleaning, public toilet cleansing, public market cleansing, litter collection and disposal, external wall and skylight cleaning and mosquito control services. YTSE's excellence in providing high-quality services to customers earned the company a great deal of respect in the cleaning industry.

Like many traditional Chinese businesses in Hong Kong, YTSE was a family-run concern. In 2004, the company was largely managed and controlled by Paul Yu and his sisters. As general manager, he was responsible for overseeing the operations of the company, and for managing a number of cleaning teams led by supervisors and managers. For most contracts, each cleaning team normally consisted of one supervisor, one foreman and eight workers.

Risk and Crisis Management Practices

YTSE's success in risk and crisis management could be attributed to a unique and paradoxical blend of leadership, culture and corporate strategy. When Paul Yu joined YTSE after earning his degree in economics, his parents were eager to strengthen his technical and leadership skills that were necessary for the company's continued success. Instead of being assigned to work as a general manager at the beginning of his career, Paul Yu joined one of the cleaning teams as an ordinary worker. He worked with experienced mentors and learned the basic skills of cleaning, disinfection and pest control. Although some people could hardly believe that Paul Yu began his career doing toilet-cleaning assignments, he and his parents thought it was an invaluable exercise for his leadership development. Without such practical experience, it would have been difficult for him to understand the proper cleaning practices. For most people, toilet cleaning appeared to be a simple, low-skill and disgusting job. From the perspective of a cleaning company, however, it was a specialised job that required special training and proper tools.

In his early years of working with different teams, Paul Yu developed not only undisputed expertise in cleaning management but also an understanding of the inherent threats in routine cleaning assignments. By working closely with the workers and the foremen, Paul Yu was able to identify some of the threats, vulnerabilities and malpractices in the industry. For instance, some workers did not use safety belts and helmets when they were doing dangerous assignments. Whenever accidents occurred, the workers plotted together to give managers the false impression that safety tools had been used — the purpose was to claim insurance compensation fraudulently. Paul Yu was also aware that different managers, supervisors and staff had different attitudes towards risk at different times. More experienced staff tended to think of themselves as less likely to be involved in accidents than the average workers, primarily because of their belief that they had substantial experience and above-average skills. Some senior staff even set improper examples for their staff. Although they were often reminded of the importance of risk detection and crisis prevention, they were reluctant to take any proactive steps to prevent crises from happening. To some managers and supervisors, crises could hardly be prevented and therefore they preferred more flexibility in work practices. Even if crises did happen, some managers felt they could derive satisfaction from managing and resolving the crises successfully. Some were even excited about capitalising on crisis opportunities to prove their strength and competence.

Risk Management at YTSE

Risk identification

Paul Yu and his family had travelled a difficult road in growing the family-run business into one of the leading cleaning service providers in Hong Kong. He was fully aware that managing risk was part of the company's business and a key to survival. To ensure the health and safety of its staff and customers, Paul Yu was anxious to develop a proactive risk management system for identifying and assessing the risks in the cleaning business, and for eliminating or reducing those risks to an acceptable level.

There were risks and hazards in every workplace. In the cleaning industry, for example, the level of risks varied with the nature of the cleaning tasks and the way the workers were managed. YTSE had identified some common threats or risks faced by the business:

a. *Staff injury*
    - When cleaning chemicals and equipment were properly used by workers who knew how to use them properly, the risk was low. On the other hand, if such items were misused by untrained or careless staff, the risk of injury was high.
    - When safety belts were not used for manual cleaning tasks that required working at heights or in awkward or dangerous postures, the risk of injury was high. In addition, both the workers and YTSE could suffer financial loss due to failure to obtain insurance compensation for malpractices.
    - The characteristics of the area where the staff carried out their assignments could also affect the level of risks. These elements included floors and other surfaces, noise, lighting, temperature, ventilation, accessibility and housekeeping. Slips, trips and falls could occur when walking on slippery floors after mopping, working in a cluttered space, collecting and disposing of rubbish, carrying equipment on stairs and water blasting.
    - Workers could suffer skin-penetrating injuries, particularly when working at construction sites and in the countryside. Serious infection could enter the body when penetrating wounds broke the protective barrier provided by the skin. Infection could also result from insect bites.

b. *Third-party or customer injury*
    - Third parties or customers who were injured in accidents caused by the negligence of the company's staff could result in claims to recover damages. Such injuries could result from the improper use of cleaning equipment or carelessness by the staff.

c. *Default notice*
    - YTSE had a number of cleaning contracts with the Food & Environmental Hygiene Department (FEHD) of the Hong Kong government. The FEHD's staff monitored YTSE's routine cleaning practices on the streets, in the wet markets and other areas. YTSE's workers were required to perform their work within a specified time limit set by the FEHD. The FEHD could issue default notices and impose penalties on YTSE for non-compliance with the FEHD's requirements. This could affect the company's performance record and result in financial loss.

d. *Labour disputes*
    - Labour disputes could cost YTSE a staggering amount of money, irrespective of whether the company won the case or not. Common labour disputes included unfair dismissal and disputes over wages, hours and terms of employment. In the cleaning

industry, some unethical subcontractors withheld referral fees from the salaries of the workers. Others even ran away with the money after the completion of the projects, leaving the workers unpaid. In some instances, subcontractors or supervisors plotted together with workers to over-state the number of staff working in a site, and thus to demand unreasonable payment from the company. Support from labour unions and enquiries from the government could further complicate such issues.[1]

e. *Complaints from customers*
   * Complaints about the quality and delivery of services were quite common in the cleaning industry. Customers' dissatisfaction could grow if complaints were not handled properly and as quickly as possible. Careful management of job specifications and contract terms with the government was particularly important as this could affect the renewal of short-term cleaning contracts.

f. *Human resources*
   * Because of the short-term duration of the cleaning contracts, it was common for cleaning companies to hire a number of temporary workers to reduce fixed overheads and to increase flexibility to cope with changing market needs. In some instances, hostile competitors in the cleaning industry tried to monopolise the pool of experienced temporary labour due to fierce competition. They discouraged workers from joining YTSE by threatening that their future job applications would not be considered.
   * Traditionally the cleaning industry had a reputation for high staff turnover and low employee loyalty. This was probably due to the work environment and the instability of the employers' contract base.
   * Unscheduled absences and tardiness were quite common among temporary cleaning workers.

Risk Management Strategies

To control the level of risks of the company, YTSE used a number of risk management strategies.

a. *Training*
   * YTSE provided training opportunities to different levels of staff to enhance service quality and reduce the risk of personal injuries. Newly recruited workers were required to attend basic training courses about safe workflow. Taking into account the relatively low educational level of the workers, instructors used a number of pictures to illustrate proper cleaning procedures and practices. This made initial learning easier and faster.
   * Although most of the team leaders were adept at managing cleaning projects, they tended to overlook threats that were inherent in routine work practices. To promote risk awareness among team leaders, supervisors and managers were required to take certified safety courses organised by the Construction Industry Training Authority, government departments and other relevant trade associations. Newspaper clippings about industrial accidents were circulated among team leaders whenever meetings were held at the company's headquarters.

- Workers were required to observe good personal hygiene during and after cleaning assignments. Protective clothing that was contaminated had to be disposed of safely.
- Training records were reviewed by managers regularly to ensure that all workers complied with training requirements.
- One of the major objectives of training was to align every staff with the same risk management objective, such that every staff became a risk manager.

b. *Administration*

- YTSE set regular time limits for its staff to take breaks in order to minimise stress and strain. Reducing exposure time was particularly important for those who had to spend long hours in public toilets or on construction sites.
- Cleaning equipment and tools were checked and maintained regularly to ensure that they were in good condition.
- Supervisors and managers patrolled work areas regularly to ensure that cleaning assignments were completed properly within the time limit. They were also required to maintain good relationship with clients. Through negotiations with the FEHD officers, for example, YTSE was given more flexibility to take remedial action before default notices were issued.
- Workers were required to wear protective clothing, hats, gloves, masks and non-slip shoes where appropriate. Safety belts were available to those who had to work at heights. Supervisors and managers had to ensure that workers adhered to the safety standards, and issued warnings if necessary.
- To monitor the attendance of workers and avoid overpayment of wages to unauthorised staff, daily records were maintained to monitor the number of workers and work progress.

c. *Avoidance / elimination*

- To minimise slip hazards in public areas, cleaning operations were usually carried out when passing pedestrian traffic was minimal.
- To avoid unnecessary complaints from the public and to minimise the risk of third-party injuries, the employees of YTSE avoided the use of brooms or other disruptive cleaning tools or equipment in crowded areas. An agreement had been reached with the FEHD to suspend street-cleaning assignments whenever members of the public were likely to display intense emotions, for instance during mass demonstrations or on festive days. The purpose was to minimise the risk of provoking violence and riots among the public.
- YTSE avoided the use of subcontractors as far as possible to prevent unnecessary labour disputes and corruption.

d. *Separation*

- Warning signs and barricades were used to separate the public from wet cleaning areas when necessary.

e. *Substitution*

- Experienced workers were assigned to more difficult cleaning assignments at construction sites or in the countryside to minimise injuries arising from slips, trips and falls.
- Wireless cleaning equipment was used in wet markets and other public areas where applicable to minimise slip hazards and third-party injuries.

- A pool of stand-by staff were maintained in order to have readily available cover and back-up support in the event of unscheduled absences on site. Back-up support was particularly important when YTSE had to carry out street-cleaning assignments on festive days or during demonstrations.

f. *Redesign of work processes*

YTSE had little control over the work environment because the places where its employees worked were usually private offices, construction sites or other public areas such as wet markets, roads, sidewalks and country parks, etc. However, the company had identified ways to redesign work processes to minimise risks.

- To prevent insect bites when carrying out anti-mosquito assignments in the countryside, workers had to wear long-sleeved shirts and long pants to reduce the amount of exposed skin, and had to use insect repellent. Such practices were strictly enforced following a spate of dengue fever and Japanese encephalitis cases in Hong Kong.[2]

- In the event of hostile actions taken by competitors in an attempt to monopolise the experienced labour pool, YTSE would recruit temporary workers and offer them intensive training. For instance, cleaning on the streets was a complicated assignment that required workers to complete tasks within the specified zones and time limits set by the FEHD. Newcomers were required to rehearse on the streets so that they could acquire the necessary skills and understand the cleaning routes before they started their work. Workers who were not suitable for the job could then be identified and replaced as quickly as possible. Although additional labour costs were incurred for such rehearsals, YTSE believed that it was worth doing so in order to maintain service quality.

g. *Accountability*

- Customers were normally provided with the mobile phone number of the team leader in charge. Any complaints about service quality could be directed to the team leader, who was then required to take remedial action as quickly as possible and to prepare a report about the reason for such complaints and how they were handled. The need to prepare reports made team leaders aware of the importance of taking customer complaints seriously and objectively and of being accountable for their work.

h. *Support from third parties*

- Disputes sometimes occurred between the employees of YTSE and hawkers in the wet markets. For instance, seafood hawkers preferred slippery floors because water symbolised wealth according to Chinese tradition. Their superstition made it difficult for YTSE to carry out floor-cleaning assignments. To avoid unnecessary conflicts, YTSE solicited help from the FEHD officials, who were in a better position to negotiate with the hawkers.

- To deliver the highest possible quality of services, YTSE encouraged its customers to get technical support where necessary for services that were beyond the scope offered by YTSE. For instance, thorough cleaning and disinfection of an office building had to be accompanied by air duct cleaning, however this was beyond the reach of YTSE's workers, who were responsible only for general cleaning. Customers were advised that failure to clean the air duct could erode the benefits of completing other cleaning tasks.

- To control the access of workers to construction sites, YTSE demanded co-operation from construction companies to limit the number of people entering the sites. This was designed to prevent illegal access by unauthorised workers or illegal immigrants, who demanded unreasonable payment from YTSE.
- YTSE negotiated for a change to its contract terms with the government from time to time based on changes in the work environment and the labour market. For instance, YTSE successfully persuaded the government to accept long-sleeved uniforms for its workers undertaking anti-mosquito assignments, in order to prevent them from contracting mosquito-borne diseases.

Managing the SARS Crisis

When the first SARS case in mainland China was uncovered by the media in early 2003, no one imagined that this viral respiratory illness would have a terrifying impact on the Hong Kong economy. SARS first broke out in mainland China in November 2002, but the Hong Kong government was slow to act after being lulled into complacency by the misinformation from the Mainland. As day-to-day life continued as normal, many enterprises in Hong Kong suffered from a "not on my doorstep" syndrome. It was a problem that was considered so distant as to not have any significant, immediate local implications. Such ignorance made the crisis spiral out of control, and SARS began to spread rapidly from mainland China to Hong Kong, and then to more than 20 countries in Asia, North America, South America and Europe.

In early 2003, Yu heard about the SARS virus and its potentially deadly impact on human beings. SARS is different from other infectious diseases and viruses that plagued the world. For example, malaria only occurred in regions with the right climatic conditions, and it is spread by a known agent: the mosquito. Effective vaccinations and treatment could prevent malarial infection. Tuberculosis is rampant in many parts of the world but it had a relatively low death rate among those infected. SARS is, however, quite deadly. The mortality rate was higher than previously thought, more than 50% for older people. The illness usually began with a high fever that was sometimes associated with chills or other influenza-like symptoms. Some people also experienced mild respiratory symptoms at the outset. Diarrhoea was seen in some patients. After two to seven days, SARS patients might develop a dry, non-productive cough that could be accompanied by or progress to hypoxia, a condition in which insufficient oxygen was reaching the blood. Most patients developed pneumonia. The primary way that SARS appeared to spread was by close person-to-person contact. Combined with the lack of treatment or vaccination, the spread of the disease was a frightening prospect. The "unknowns" made SARS such a concern in the community — where did it come from, how was it spread, how could it be quickly identified, how could it be treated, how could people be vaccinated against the virus, and how could infected patients be cured?

At the beginning of the SARS crisis, many cleaning companies in Hong Kong accepted and lived with the risk because of insufficient knowledge about how the virus was spreading. Before undertaking the special cleaning assignment in Wanchai, YTSE did not have any crisis management plans for dealing with SARS. Nevertheless, the company was able to overcome the crisis through unprecedented levels of co-operation and collaboration, as well as the leaders' patience and their understanding of the concerns of the workers.

As soon as Paul Yu arrived at the Wanchai government building that was hit by SARS on 2 April 2003, an emergency meeting was held to advise the staff about the cause of the virus, the incubation period and the change in cleaning procedures. With the support of the FEHD, the company received additional supplies of masks for street-cleaning contracts for distribution to the staff. Paul Yu noticed that his employees had various concerns about the assignments and reacted differently to the crisis. Female workers overreacted to the crisis because of panic and some wanted to stop working immediately. Younger male workers suffered from optimism bias and were excited about undertaking this dangerous assignment. To inspire confidence in all employees, Paul Yu gathered information and communicated important facts to them. These included the health status of the infected person, his last working day in the office and the number of days that had lapsed. Young workers who seemed to be oblivious to the potential dangers were reminded of the safest way to complete the cleaning assignment. Although that cleaning assignment was finally completed safely, YTSE suffered a financial loss because the terms of the original contract did not provide for the additional clothing and chemicals that were necessary to complete the assignment.

During the first and second quarters of 2003, a new wave of terror was unleashed as more SARS cases were reported in Hong Kong. Realising that information and resolute action were the best antidotes against SARS, Paul Yu and the team leaders constantly obtained updated information about buildings that were hit by the virus; checked the latest developments regarding recommended cleaning practices with the Department of Health, and revised their service fee quotations when necessary to account for the additional cost of more risky assignments. The company held special meetings to review cleaning procedures and office layout on a case-by-case basis before undertaking projects in risky buildings. It also implemented new rules for monitoring the health condition of its employees and segregating duties to prevent possible cross-infection. For instance, staff rotation was restricted for risky cleaning assignments such as toilet cleaning and office cleaning in high-risk buildings. Supervisors were advised to pay special attention to whether all staff complied with requirements on the use and disposal of protective clothing. To acknowledge the staff's efforts in completing risky assignments, management showed their gratitude openly and distributed vitamins to the staff. By the time the SARS crisis subsided in July 2003, no employee of YTSE had been infected.

Managing Future Threats and Crises

While many employees were heaving a sigh of relief that the SARS outbreak was finally over, Paul Yu feared that the greatest danger was that employees might let down their guard against future threats or crises. Similar incidents of unprecedented scope and magnitude could happen in the future, and it would be a daunting task to create capacity from scratch in a hurry. Paul Yu decided that he would develop a formal plan for risk and crisis management. This would include redefining the company's operational strategies, the role of risk managers and crisis management teams. He expected that this would

184   Services (Financial, Real Estate, Social, Transportation, Communications and Others)

generate discussion among team leaders in the upcoming management meeting. After all, cleaning was still very much a people industry, and it was important that the front-end staff, who were the backbone of the business, felt valued and protected by the company's risk and crisis management system. Given the instability and the short-term nature of the cleaning contract base, however, Paul Yu had to find a way to justify the planning costs by showing that good crisis planning would benefit the company in the long run.

PART II: LESSONS LEARNED

The Importance of Proactive Risk Management

The convergence of health, industry, regulatory and environmental pressures on organisations have broadened the focus on effective risk management in recent years. In response to both external and internal environmental pressures, some organisations have chosen to improve their risk management systems proactively as a way of preserving organisational value and enhancing stakeholders' confidence in their economic sustainability. However, very few organisations are able to build risk information into their front-end decision-making processes and capitalise on the benefits of risk management as a source of competitive advantage.

To properly understand the concept of risk management, it is essential for organisations to have a clear understanding of what is meant by risk.

The following table sets out the many different definitions of risk.

Table 1   Definitions of Risk

• Risk means uncertainty of loss.
• Risk is the possibility of loss, damage or any other undesirable event.
• Risk is the combination of the probability of an event and its consequences.
• Risk is the probability that future events may be surprisingly different from what is expected.[3]
• Risk is the chance of something happening that will have a negative impact upon the achievement of objectives.[4]
• Risk is an event that could prevent a corporation from meeting its objectives or fulfilling its potential.[5]

A study conducted by English-based consultant Oxford Metrica in 2003 showed that risk management should be viewed as an investment rather than a cost. The study, "Improving Risk Quality to Drive Value", indicated that a strong correlation existed between risk management and the overall financial performance of companies. In the study, risk was determined by the core operational activities of a business, the physical location of the activities, and how the activities were managed and protected. The findings revealed that companies with high-quality risk management had low cashflow volatility, and hence the study concluded that risk management was a strategic issue, a key characteristic of profitable companies and an essential aspect of effective corporate governance procedures.[6]

The Concept and Drivers of Risk

YTSE's concept of risk integrated the meanings of both opportunities and threats. To the company, risk management was a process that involved proactively identifying both the likely impact of risk in its daily operations, and implementation strategies to treat and monitor risk (see Figure 1 and Figure 2). The ultimate goal of the process was to ensure that the company could avoid losses and capitalise on as many opportunities as possible.

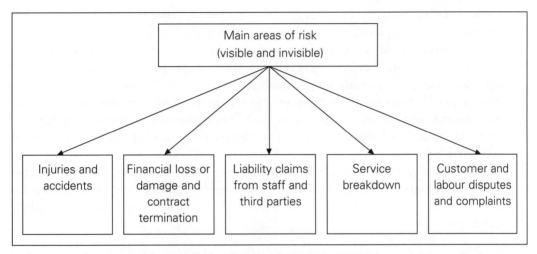

Figure 1   Main Areas of Risk at YTSE

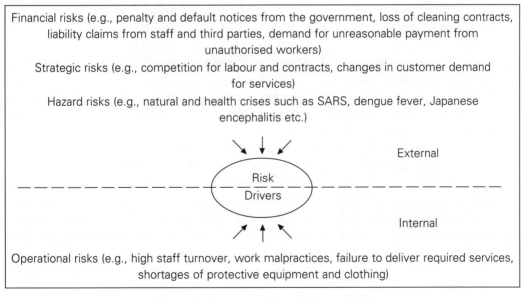

Figure 2   Drivers of Key Risks at YTSE

Objectives and Model of Risk Management

In general, four organisational objectives can be identified for risk management:
1. *Strategic objectives* — These represent high-level goals, aligned with and supporting the mission of an enterprise. At YTSE, for example, strategic objectives could include:
   - securing the renewal of cleaning contracts
   - enhancing the company's image and reputation in the cleaning industry
   - reducing staff turnover to a reasonable level
   - maintaining service quality
2. *Operational objectives* — These relate to the effective and efficient use of an enterprise's resources. At YTSE, workers were provided with sufficient training opportunities to ensure that they could deliver satisfactory services to clients. Additional time was spent on rehearsals so that newcomers could pick up skills as quickly as possible to meet tight deadlines and maintain service quality.
3. *Reporting objectives* — These represent the reliability of an enterprise's reporting to both internal and external stakeholders. At YTSE, customer complaints were handled by team leaders, who were required to report the cause of complaints and be accountable for them.
4. *Compliance objectives* — These represent an enterprise's compliance with applicable laws and regulations. The staff of YTSE, for example, had to comply with work rules set by the relevant government departments and had to adhere to the internal safety standards.

To achieve the four objectives mentioned above, YTSE could develop a formal risk management model featuring the following components:
- *Internal environment* — Management should incorporate the concept of risk management as part of the corporate philosophy. The relationship between risk management, performance and value should be recognised by all staff.
- *Setting of objectives* — The desire to manage risks and capitalise on opportunities inherent in risk events should be integrated with an enterprise's strategic objectives for future planning purposes.
- *Identification of events* — Management should constantly identify potential events that could affect the enterprise's ability to successfully fulfil its objectives, and should determine the level of risk-tolerance.
- *Risk assessment* — Management should assess events from two perspectives, i.e., likelihood and impact, by using a combination of qualitative and quantitative methods. The results should serve as a basis for developing a risk response.
- *Risk response* — Risk options should be identified and assessed in terms of their likelihood and impact, and in relation to risk tolerances and costs versus benefits.
- *Control activities* — Policies and procedures should be developed to ensure that appropriate actions are taken to control risks, given the enterprise's risk tolerance.
- *Information and communication* — Effective communication and information sharing are important to ensure that risk managers and personnel can carry out their responsibilities in a timely and appropriate manner.
- *Monitoring* — Ongoing assessment and monitoring of an enterprise's performance in relation to risk management is important for future learning purposes.

- *Redefining the roles of risk managers* — Traditionally, team leaders and supervisors were expected to have major basic competencies in problem-solving, teamwork and technical skills. They focused mainly on finding solutions to manage pure loss risk only, and were not generally expected to consider gains. The risk management approach would call for an increase in responsibilities and a change in the mindset of risk managers. They should now be empowered to look at the "holistic risk" of an enterprise, and to consider the risks that derived from making wrong decisions regarding gains.

A good risk manager should be able to take the concept of risk management from a purely compliance perspective to a more forward-thinking perspective that focused on capturing business opportunities. In practice, risk managers should have a basic understanding of the interdependencies of an enterprise's products and services and how the risks related to one product or business line affected the risks in another. At YTSE, for example, managers should understand that:

- To secure contract renewal, they should manage the risk of complaints from customers effectively and devote more effort to enhancing service quality.
- To sustain service quality, they should monitor the performance of workers and communicate workers' risk-related training needs to management.
- To prepare for managing new risks, they should identify threats proactively and share information with customers, senior management and staff across different functional lines.
- To make every staff member a risk manager, they should set a good example for staff and be accountable for the management of risk. They should also be alert to the different risk attitudes of staff (e.g., misperception of risks, optimism bias) and identify their training needs.

Factors contributing to risk misperception include:
- *Optimism bias* — This could be due to differences in age, sex, educational background and experience.
- *Availability heuristic* — In thinking about probabilistic events, people frequently use heuristics, or rules of thumb, to arrive at a decision, solve a problem, deduce a conclusion or appraise risk. Heuristics are cognitive processes that require minimal cognitive effort, and they work some but not all of the time. Workers using the availability heuristic to assess risk would search their memory and retrieve many incidents that were risk-free, leading even experienced workers to underestimate their risk exposure.
- *Cumulative risk* — Another potential source of error in risk perception is the failure of workers to understand the effects of cumulative risk. The more frequently a person engages in a risky behaviour, the more likely it becomes that there will be a negative outcome.

Risk Management Strategies

The case of YTSE shows that a number of risk-management strategies can be used for daily operations:

- *Avoidance or elimination* is a mitigation strategy that eliminates the threat of a specific risk, usually by eliminating its potential cause.
- *Substitution is a risk-management strategy* that involves the replacement of staff, tools, equipment or processes to reduce exposure.
- *Transfer of risk by contract or insurance or solicitation of support from third parties* (e.g., purchasing insurance against work accidents; demanding contract premiums for high-risk projects).
- *Reduction of risk by technical or administrative means* (e.g., training, redesign of work processes, purchasing protective clothing and equipment, compliance monitoring).

Crisis Management

Crisis can be defined as "a low-probability, high-impact event that threatens the viability of the organisation and is characterised by ambiguity of cause, effect, and means of resolution, as well as by a belief that decisions must be made swiftly."[7] It often results in disruptions in the primary business or support operations of an organisation and threatens the survival of an organisation. Crises usually arrive as a barrage of urgent, unanticipated and painful events, allowing an organisation little time to organise and plan an appropriate response.

The term "crisis" is often used interchangeably with the notion of threat. By equating the term "crisis" with the notion of threat, however, the dual potential of a crisis is ignored. This common underlying attitude towards crises must be rethought, however, because crises have the potential for both threat and opportunity. When a crisis is perceived as a threat, an organisation usually makes a choice between several possible responses. These include rigidity, magnification, denial and scapegoating.[8]

However, crises also hold opportunities for gains. When a crisis happens, an organisation's limitations may become glaringly apparent. When the SARS crisis occurred, Yu noticed that YTSE did not have a system for identifying risky projects and demanding contract premiums from customers. Staff members were not educated about the dangers of SARS and the proper cleaning procedures before the emergency meeting. After the crisis, YTSE had a chance to look into the limitations in its existing management practices, systems, procedures, structures and processes, and to find ways to tackle those limitations.

The post-crisis period is a critical period for learning. The experience of a crisis often propels people in an organisation to reconsider what needs to be done, or done differently, in the future. Figure 3 shows how a crisis has opportunities for gains.

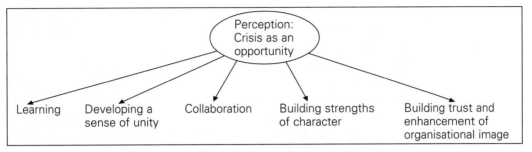

Figure 3   Crisis as an Opportunity

Effective crisis management depends upon planning and people. A solid crisis-management plan should be comprehensive, with clear leadership, and clear team and individual assignments in the form of roles and responsibilities. It should be upgraded frequently, supported by training and rehearsals, and also co-ordinated and controlled across all levels and units of an organisation. A crisis-management plan also needs to be flexible so that it can adapt to the ways the events unfold. It should be tested at regular intervals to ensure that it works under adverse conditions. Figure 4 shows how YTSE could develop a crisis-management plan.

Time Frame	Activities
Pre-crisis	▪ Anticipate crisis situations ▪ Shape events before they happen ▪ Develop a crisis-management culture ▪ Avert crisis
Crisis	▪ Support crisis-management team ▪ Help allocate and manage limited resources ▪ Monitor events ▪ Assess and decide action
Post-crisis	▪ Evaluate crisis-management performance This includes assessing whether the following crisis-management objectives have been achieved: – to improve morale – to improve efficiency – to create allies from neutrals, neutralise enemies and strengthen and unify existing allies – to inform and educate – to redirect interests – to build credibility and image – to establish a sympathetic audience – to reduce uncertainty ▪ Revise crisis-management processes ▪ Determine damages and costs

Figure 4   Crisis-management Plan

The case of YTSE shows that the leaders of an organisation play a critical role in crisis management. Yu, for example, made himself visible to his front-line staff when undertaking the SARS project in Wanchai. He held an emergency meeting with his staff and communicated important facts to them. He and the managers also controlled and oversaw all aspects of the execution of the project. Once the crisis was resolved, he initiated the evaluation process regarding changes in work procedures and the risk evaluation of projects to make sure that the right lessons had been learned from the experience of the crisis. He was also responsible for setting the strategic objectives for the future crisis-management plan.

Successful leaders are in general:

- Good listeners and available to employees
- Able to communicate effectively and motivate team-building activities
- Capable of overcoming psychological hurdles and able to perceive risk realistically
- Able to express passion and guide employees through challenges
- Able to use internal assessment and environmental scanning to define events that could trigger future crises
- Able to integrate crisis-management preparedness with strategic planning

---

[1] Based on the limited information available, the case writer and the supervisors were not in a position to comment on pending labour disputes or possible litigation facing the company.

[2] Dengue fever is an acute viral disease transmitted through mosquito bites. Symptoms include high fever for three to five days, severe headache, muscle and joint pain, eye pain, nausea, vomiting and skin rash. Minor bleeding, such as gum and nose bleeding, could occur at any time during the febrile phase. Japanese B encephalitis is transmitted by the bites of mosquitoes infected with the Japanese encephalitis virus, and not directly transmitted from person to person. It was a rare disease in Hong Kong, with usually no more than two cases reported each year. The incubation period of Japanese B encephalitis was about 5–15 days. Mild infections could occur without apparent symptoms other than fever with headache. More severe infection was marked by quick onset of headache, high fever, neck stiffness, impaired mental state, coma, tremors, occasional convulsions (especially in infants) and paralysis.

[3] Risk Management Society Publishing Inc. (2004), "The duality of risk", *Risk Management*, 51(1):20, January.

[4] Risk Management Society Publishing, Inc. (2002), "Stepping out of bounds: Phil Grewar has taken risk management out of bounds in British Columbia", *Risk Management*, 49(12):34, December.

[5] Euromoney Institutional Investor PLC (2002), "Getting to grips with risk in your business: risk management preoccupies corporates like never before", *Corporate Finance*: 34, November.

[6] Crain Communications Inc. (2003), "Risk management, return linked at public companies; Study cites importance of risk quality", *Business Insurance*, 37 (39): 21, 29 September. More information on this study can be found at www.fmglobal.com and www.oxfordmetrica.com

[7] Pearson, C. and Clair, J. A., (1998), "Reframing crisis management", *Academy of Management Review*, 23 (1), 59–76.

[8] Nathan, M. (2000), "The Paradoxical Nature of Crisis", *Review of Business*, 21 (3): 12, Fall, St. John's University.

20

Eurasia International
Total Quality Management in the Shipping Industry

ALI FARHOOMAND AND AMIR HOOSAIN

PART I: BACKGROUND AND ISSUES

Introduction

In the 1990s, Hong Kong-based Eurasia International Ltd. ("Eurasia") aimed to set itself apart from other ship managers by implementing Total Quality Management (TQM) principles. The company's president and group managing director, Rajaish Bajpaee — a 30-year veteran of the shipping industry, had been instrumental in establishing the International Ship Managers' Association (ISMA) and assumed its presidency in 2003. In his dual role, Bajpaee believed that a comprehensive approach was needed to address some of the challenges facing his profession.

After a series of high-profile accidents during the shipping crisis of the 1980s, ship managers found themselves dealing with complex and evolving systems of regulation imposed by national and international maritime administrations. The shipping business was suffering from a fundamental image problem, and Bajpaee felt it was losing out to other industries in attracting the best and brightest people. Bajpaee believed that a system of continuous improvement was required to enhance his company's competitiveness, develop its human capital and establish a reputation for quality. For the industry at large, a culture of voluntary compliance could promote safety and forestall a state of over-regulation.

The Rise of Third-Party Ship Managers

> When you go and fill up your car with gas, you never think about how the gas came there in the gas station. Some ship brought it. The coal which is used in the power plant in Lamma — who brings the coal? — The ships. So the contribution of shipping to Hong Kong's economy is not appreciated.
>
> – Rajaish Bajpaee, President & Group Managing Director, Eurasia International

Shipping is one of the world's oldest industries and perhaps the first of a truly global nature. In olden times, a ship's captain was typically also its owner and oversaw the purchase and sale of cargo, the recruitment of crew members and the daily ins and outs of seafaring operations. These ship-owners were renowned for their strong personalities and usually put their own capital at risk.

The form and structure of the shipping industry has been transformed with the tides of history. As the monopolistic mercantile companies of the great European powers went into decline, market forces gradually took over. The industry has become specialised in every area — individual cargoes have given way to bulk pools, container pools and tanker pools; the financing of vessels has become extremely sophisticated, and technological advancement has forever changed shipping operations. Through all this, the individual ship-owner has become a rarity, but the ship manager's role has grown prominent.

It has been estimated that over 90% of the world's commerce involves movements by sea; transported goods include fuel, raw materials, food, furniture, apparel and other finished goods.[1] The fortunes of the industry are directly affected by greater trends in world trade. In the 1980s, the maritime industries suffered from the downturn in world trade, which was further exacerbated by problems of excess capacity, rising costs and falling freight rates.[2] Too many ships were competing for too little cargo, and freight rates were often so low that they barely covered operating costs.

During this period of crisis, banks were often compelled to repossess ships that they lacked the expertise to operate. In the recessionary 1980s, enthusiasm for outsourcing was running high. Ship-management companies offered ship-owners the option of separating shipping operations from the asset management, sales and marketing aspects of their business. This freed the owners to focus on the revenue-generation (i.e., marketing cargo space).

Eurasia Group

Eurasia was founded as a joint venture in Hong Kong in 1981 by three partner companies, with the aim of establishing a technical ship management capability in Asia. Hong Kong had one of the busiest container ports in the world and was chosen for Eurasia's headquarters because it met all five basic criteria that governed the choice of location: a sophisticated telecommunications infrastructure, an extensive air transportation system, an advanced banking infrastructure, a low tax regime and a productive workforce.[3] Each company brought five ships into the partnership, and Eurasia continued to manage its own fleet until 1987, when one of the partners, The Bernhard Schulte Group, bought out the remaining two partners and established Eurasia as a wholly owned subsidiary with a mandate to operate as a competitive third-party ship manager.[4] Eurasia initially relied on Asian ship-owners, particularly from Japan, to build its client base. In the early years, a typical Japanese-owned ship would take raw materials into Japan and carry finished goods out. Over time, however, manufacturing shifted to other countries and by the mid-1990s, the merchant ships that Eurasia serviced were largely engaged in cross-trade.

Eurasia's president and group managing director, Rajaish Bajpaee, had received an education in the sciences and gone on to study at a marine engineering college before spending eight years at sea, where he worked his way up to chief engineer. He left to pursue an MBA and began a shore-based career, initially as a ship superintendent and later rose to management positions, where he gained exposure to the accounting, finance, human resources and marketing sides of the business.

At Eurasia's helm, Bajpaee saw the need to expand beyond an Asian base and to configure the group's business accordingly. He developed a five-year plan to expand Eurasia's customer base and develop operations to cover the three major world regions: Asia Pacific; Europe and the Americas, and the Middle-East and Africa. Disruptions due to the Asian financial crisis of 1997 delayed implementation of this plan by two years. In due course however, Eurasia established regional headquarters in Hong Kong, Bombay and Hamburg, and a number of regional offices, extending its coverage to offer year-round, worldwide services. After starting with a fleet of just a few ships in the 1980s, the company had expanded to a total of 90 ships under management by 2004. Eurasia positioned itself as an Asian company with global operations.

Eurasia's Services

By 2004, Eurasia was offering a suite of services that spanned the entire life-cycle of a ship from construction to demolition. Fifty-six percent of its managed fleet belonged to Asian owners (approximately 80% Japanese) and a growing European element was observed within the remaining component. As a manager of its customers' assets, the group offered services in three categories: ship-management services (by far the biggest category), marine consultancy services and shipping services:

- *Ship Management:* Technical Ship Management, Crew Management, Commercial Ship Management
- *Marine Consultancy:* Newbuilding and Design Consultancy, Quality Assurance Consultancy, Risk Management Consultancy
- *Shipping Services:* Port Agency, Procurement and Logistics, SeaChef Maritime Catering

While some of its competitors employed niche marketing strategies — claiming distinctive competencies in managing certain classes of vessel or as technical, financial management, risk management or liability experts — Eurasia's service offerings were not product-centric. A client could pick and choose among the various services and a service package would be assembled accordingly. To meet customer requirements, Eurasia was able to offer dedicated seafarers qualified for any size or type of tanker, bulk carrier or container ship. It also deployed advanced database-management and computerised information systems that gave users access to timely and accurate information.

Changes in the Shipping Industry

At the turn of the century, there were approximately 50,000 merchant ships in the world, of which approximately 5,000 (10%) were managed by third-party ship managers.[5] The top ten international ship managers could collectively lay claim to about half the market, with the remainder comprising of managers controlling anywhere from one to several ships.

In a bid to enlist lower-cost crews, the shipping industry underwent major restructuring that saw significant growth in the number of open-registry ships operating under offshore management.[6] Ships under open registry accounted for 5% of world shipping tonnage in 1950, 25% in 1980, and 45% in 1995.[7] The industry had become more dispersed and observers were noting a change in the balance of power in world shipping.[8] The shipping business was taking on a very different form from that of earlier times, when shipbuilders, ship-owners, agents and port service providers were concentrated around traditional port cities. At the turn of the century, South Korea, Japan and China were the world's largest producers of ships; Greece and Japan were the largest owners of merchant ships; the Philippines was the largest source of seafarers and Panama had the largest registry.[9]

The 1980s had seen a number of high-profile shipping accidents, culminating in the highly publicised *Exxon Valdez tragedy* of 1989. Ship operators found themselves in the limelight following such incidents, and in the position of having to guard their industry against perceived deficiencies. During this period, third-party ship managers received the lion's share of the blame for allegedly bringing down standards and providing inadequately trained crews. In the ensuing years, safety and environmental standards received more attention as the industry recognised the need for greater environmental awareness. As the industry grappled with such issues, an increasing amount of regulation was being imposed upon it by national governments and international bodies. Ship managers were operating in a climate of increasing complexity.

The Ship Manager's Role

A ship is like a floating factory. A typical ship carries 2,500 boxes … it has the horsepower of a power plant … an engine of about 30,000 horsepower. It has 20 to 30 people on board. It goes at 20 knots, which is about 30 miles per hour, and it manufactures the service of carrying the cargo from A to B safely, cost-effectively, without damaging the cargo … without damaging the ship … without injury to the people … without threatening the environment. This is the essence of what this factory manufactures. And this factory is moving, it is not stationary in Guangzhou or Shenzhen, it is mobile. And it operates in an environment where if there is a fire, you can't call the fire brigade. If there is somebody injured, you can't call an ambulance. You have to take care of it in the middle of the ocean. You are not in a static environment because you are confronted with the fury of the sea.

– Rajaish Bajpaee

A ship manager's primary customer was the ship's owner, but in practice the ship manager's role was also to serve as an intermediary with secondary customers — the ship financiers and cargo owners. Ship-owners typically sought three core competencies in selecting a ship manager:

- *Cost efficiency:* the ability to control the daily running costs of a ship.
- *Earning period:* owners were eager for the revenue-earning potential of their vessels to be fully realised; if a ship was docked or under repair, it would not be generating revenue.

- *Asset preservation:* ship-owners had a vested interest to see that their vessels were well maintained and able to earn revenue for a normal useful life of 25–30 years.

The key to success for a ship manager was to offer cost-effective solutions by outsourcing functions to low-cost areas and by establishing practices based on the latest know-how and technology. Ultimately, to attract and retain customers, it was necessary to offer high service-quality levels, while at the same time offering cost levels that could compete with what an owner could achieve with internal operations. In recent years, this had become more challenging because ship-owners could operate their vessels internally at very low cost by using different flag states and alternative crewing arrangements.

Being the Best, Not Necessarily the Biggest

There had only been a minor increase in the size of the world fleet from 1999 onwards, and consequently third-party ship managers were competing in the same limited marketplace. Some ship managers merged to form larger units, aiming to benefit from economies of scale.[10] Eurasia bucked this trend — its strategy was not geared towards size. As a member of the Schulte group of companies, it could generate economies of scale by pooling resources with the four other management groups under the parent company.

In total, the Schulte Group managers operated some 400 ships; expense items such as training, human resources administration and insurance could be managed as a common pool. Eight thousand diversely experienced seafarers of various nationalities were available to take on contract assignments through the Schulte Group's eight international manning and training centres. Eurasia thus escaped pressures to acquire or merge with other companies to remain cost-competitive. By staying relatively small within the structure of the Schulte Group, the company was able to offer far more personalised services and to maintain a somewhat unique business model. As Rajaish Bajpaee saw it, ship-owners did not care whether a ship manager operated 50 ships or 500 ships; they were only concerned that the vessel they owned was under professional management.

Thus, Eurasia could offer both cost competitiveness and product differentiation as advantages over its rivals. Rajaish Bajpaee believed this two-pronged approach was needed to resolve two seemingly conflicting customer requirements — low costs and personalised service. Bajpaee coined the strategy statement "Being the Best, Not Necessarily the Biggest" as his company's objective — not to strive for significant growth in a given market, but to provide the highest-quality service while satisfying customers, shareholders and staff.

Growing Regulation and the ISMA

From the early 1990s, ship managers found themselves dealing with an increasing regulatory burden as international trade bodies and regional regulators introduced a jumble of rules and security measures. As a result, it was necessary to employ highly skilled support, training and supervisory staff — yet at the same time, ship managers faced constant pressure to maintain or even reduce management fees in the lows of shipping cycles.

As exponents of cost-cutting, ship managers also found themselves being made scapegoats for a perceived decline in shipping standards. Recognising the need to counter these perceptions and to forestall unilaterally mandated legislation, an informal association of leading ship managers founded the International Ship Managers' Association (ISMA) in 1991 to pursue a quality ideal for the industry. The ISMA code of ship management was issued in 1998, stipulating audit-based compliance as a condition for membership.[11]

The ISMA code was a minimum quality benchmark for the industry, assessed impartially and independently by classification societies. Rajaish Bajpaee had served on the executive board of ISMA since its foundation and was a driving force in urging industry colleagues to embrace voluntary standards and to take on a proactive role in shaping the evolution of their industry. Bajpaee assumed the ISMA presidency in 2003 with a mandate to continue the group's pursuit of the highest standards in ship management.

Eurasia's Quality Journey

Having reflected upon the changes taking place in the industry and through his involvement with ISMA, Rajaish Bajpaee believed that the most important determinant of a ship management company's success was its ability to balance the expectations of key constituencies and continuously add value through best practices. With limited resources at hand, the challenge of ship management was to satisfy and balance the expectations of shareholders (who wanted greater dividends), customers (who demanded personalised service at low prices) and staff (who wanted job security, better compensation and good working conditions). Bajpaee saw total quality management (TQM) as a useful model that could place his organisation in a favourable position.

TQM was a system of organisational management based on a framework of continuous improvement. As such, it had both cultural and technical dimensions, and called for proactive leadership and firm commitment on the part of management. Bajpaee joined the global quality council of The Conference Board in 1994 and became its co-chairman for the Asia Pacific region.[12] Through this position, he was able to study processes at companies such as 3M and Xerox that had implemented TQM early on. The TQM approach could be viewed in terms of four components:[13]

- A definition of quality in terms of the customer's requirements
- An organisation-wide quality performance standard
- A work system that included planning, budgeting, reward-recognition and other systems to consistently produce quality
- A meaningful way to monitor and measure the results of the system

With the re-engineering of business processes and establishment of best-in-class benchmarks, TQM was formally implemented at Eurasia in 1995. Within the company's organisational context, Bajpaee saw the umbrella of TQM as one that could efficiently transform Eurasia's key resources — its people, processes and technology — into deliverable outputs.

Crew Recruitment and Training

A ship manager's challenge was first and foremost to have the right people, at the right place and at the right time to operate the vessels under its management. In Bajpaee's opinion, it was necessary to start by acknowledging that constant improvement of the crew was essential to success. In this regard, there were two primary challenges: one was to attract the best people, and the other was to train them into leadership positions. With competing shore-based jobs offering stable work hours and established career paths, Eurasia attempted to create more congenial conditions for shipboard staff — for instance by allowing up to five family members to accompany certain seafarers during their shipboard employment.[14]

Although Eurasia was Hong Kong-based, there were no training or education institutes in Hong Kong geared towards developing maritime professionals. Eurasia recruited seafarers internationally and assembled multinational crews. A ship's captain could be likened to the managing director of a factory — responsible for the ship's mission, for allocating resources and for ensuring the safety of the vessel, its crew and cargo. The chief engineer could be likened to a general manager, and the staff of marine engineers was responsible for all technical aspects of ship maintenance and operations, including communications technology. Vessel crew-members could advance their careers either through education and the accumulation of experience, or by acquiring special skills in the course of their employment. Both seafarers and shore-based staff were formally appraised on a regular periodic basis.

Eurasia's Management Structure

On average, each ship had an annual consumption budget of US$1 million. Shore-based fleet management groups were responsible for fleets of up to 20 vessels and were comprised of a diverse staff including technical superintendents, purchasers and accountants.

The crew for a ship had to be recruited, trained and developed according to the specific type of vessel under management, the particular type of cargo or the voyage in question.[15] It was the role of the shore-based team to provide them with a system of safety, guidelines, policies and procedures so that they would be equipped with the tools and knowledge necessary for any foreseeable eventuality. This had to be backed up with well established daily, weekly and monthly reporting systems; quarterly inspections; pre-embarkment and post-disembarkment debriefings and ongoing satellite-based monitoring to ascertain whether the vessel was making the right progress and consuming resources efficiently.

To ensure that the vessels were operated safely and optimally, Eurasia instituted a management structure that comprised self-check, cross-check and external-check components, corresponding to the company's shipboard, fleet management and support teams:

- The self-check component was conducted by teams on board Eurasia's vessels.
- The cross-check component was conducted by Eurasia's shore-based fleet-management professionals who monitored and reviewed shipboard performance against established policies and guidelines.
- The external check component was conducted by teams of cross-functional support staff who acted as referees in resolving problematic situations.

When any defects or deficiencies were identified, they would be analysed by a "reliability team" to determine whether the root cause was due to failure on the part of the crew, a failure in the system, a failure of equipment or some combination of the three. The appropriate remedy would then be arranged; if the cause of failure was people-related, then the situation was further analysed to determine whether the issue involved crew members' skills, knowledge or attitudes. If necessary, a training module would be established to address the specific problem. If the failure was due to equipment malfunction, then adjustments were made to the maintenance regimen. If it was deemed a failure of the system, then the relevant policies and procedures were modified. Fleet-wide circulars were sent out regularly to disseminate any lessons learned. Total employee training at Eurasia reached its highest level in 2002, while in the same year, employee turnover was at its lowest level ever.

Organisational Performance

The business processes instituted at Eurasia provided the foundation for continuous improvement throughout the organisation. So that management could gauge performance at all functional levels, Eurasia devoted significant resources to maintaining performance measurement systems. In devising a framework for performance measurement, Eurasia's senior management organised individual business targets around a leadership model comprised of four core values: customer value, human value, shareholder value and leadership/intellectual value.

Key performance indicators (KPIs) were established, for which corresponding objectives and responsibilities were set. All sea-based and shore-based groups within the company had performance targets — at the business unit, team and individual levels. This measurement framework allowed senior management to observe how all parameters were working on a virtually real-time basis. To supplement this information, key data from external market and financial information providers were collected and analysed regularly. Various forms of analysis were employed, including financial analysis, root cause analysis, trend analysis and regression analysis; the findings and results were transmitted to the relevant parties for further action.

Eurasia in 2004

I make it a point to mention that in business, profit is like oxygen, and just like your blood flow, you need cashflow. But your purpose of existence is beyond breathing and having a pulse. Similarly, the purpose of a business' existence is beyond profit and cashflow. The purpose is to create value for people. Three constituencies of people: shareholders, customers, and human resources.

– Rajaish Bajpaee

By early 2004, Eurasia's commitment to quality management appeared to be paying off. The company obtained good financial results over a period of economic slowdown and maintained high levels of customer retention and employee satisfaction. Eurasia was awarded the "Best Ship Manager" designation by *Lloyd's Maritime Asia* for the second year running in September 2002, and the Hong Kong Management Association's Quality Award the following year.

After 30 years in shipping and having been at Eurasia's helm throughout its formative period, Rajaish Bajpaee believed the challenges of shipping were fundamentally unchanged. The biggest challenge was to attract, nurture and retain a talented crew. A ship manager had to maintain the necessary HR focus while controlling the ship's cost structure, staying in tune with customer requirements and anticipating the competition. To achieve excellence in these respects, Bajpaee believed a voluntary culture of self-regulation was essential.

From the late twentieth century, certain parties within the shipping industry were developing prototypes of unmanned ships and were anticipating an age when ships could be operated with nobody aboard them at all. Technically, there was no reason why this couldn't be accomplished in an age of advanced satellite communications, when unmanned probes could be sent to Mars. Labour had always been a major issue in the shipping industry, where substantial resources were needed to train and develop an efficient crew. Ship-owners in high-cost countries faced shrinking domestic labour forces and rising costs, high attrition rates within the industry and occasional union problems. All this could be avoided by moving towards automation; the shipyards' R&D functions also stood to gain from such a change. However, Rajaish Bajpaee was sceptical that a state of complete automation would come to pass and felt that, aside from the humanistic arguments, highly-trained and experienced seafarers would always be able to anticipate and respond to trouble in ways that machinery could not.

In the coming decades, ship-owners and managers could anticipate additional changes in the shipping industry. Further global reshuffling of industry players was ongoing, new ships would travel faster and cargo values would probably rise significantly. All this would mean continuing pressure on ship managers to adapt. Managing a diverse fleet in such a climate would challenge even the best of managers, but Bajpaee felt confident that the total quality culture and systems of continuous improvement put into practice would enable Eurasia to navigate rough seas and continue to offer services superior to those of both its competitors and clients.

PART II: LESSONS LEARNED

This case gives an account of how a ship management company was able to set itself apart from competitors and from its clients' own in-house technical and crew-management capabilities by embracing a culture of continuous improvement and by implementing Total Quality Management systems. The shipping industry was not alone in having regulation imposed upon it, but its distinctly international nature made ship managers, as cost-cutting practitioners, particularly open to criticism. A ship management company's very existence hinged upon its ability to convince ship-owners that it would preserve their valuable assets and maximise revenue-earning potential — demonstrating that its collective skills were superior and more cost-effective. As a result, an effective quality assurance system that continuously improved the organisation's human and business systems could enhance efficiency and also have a significant marketing impact.

Key Questions

What were the ship-owners' motivations for outsourcing vessel and crew management to third-party ship managers?

With the rise in outsourcing arrangements, management structures have become more explicit. In the highly competitive international shipping industry, ship-owners were continually seeking ways to keep their costs down and their business performance ahead of the competition. As a result, ship-owners were taking a serious look at the option of outsourcing crew and technical management functions as a way of lowering costs and keeping pace with industry best practices. By concentrating on the sales and marketing function, ship-owners could hive off operations activities to more suitable providers who were knowledgeable about the regulatory climate and on the cutting edge of ship management (in terms of infrastructure, expertise and organisational capabilities).

How was Eurasia able to differentiate itself from the competition?

Eurasia can be said to have taken a boutique approach within its industry, and to have upheld a relentless commitment to serving its customers' interests. Since it was inclined to remain a boutique, Eurasia was cautious about pursuing growth but was still willing to take risks in its company philosophy and business model. As a member of the Schulte Group of companies, it was able to offer the advantages of economies of scale, yet was also able to customise its service delivery to suit different customers' needs. By contrast, many of its larger competitors had gone through mergers and acquisitions to remain economically viable, and thus risked losing their personal touch with the customer. To offer even closer proximity to its clients, Eurasia embarked on a five-year plan to expand its operations, and established a network of regional offices that could operate in the same region and time zone as the customer.

What is total quality management (TQM), and why was it an appropriate organisational change mechanism for Eurasia?

The term TQM was widely used to describe a focus on the pursuit of quality within an organisation. Early discussions of TQM hinged around the Deming Management Method and statistical process control techniques, particularly in connection with manufacturing environments.[16] The works of later TQM experts such as Philip Crosby have been less statistically and technically oriented and more people-oriented. Regardless, TQM is built on core mandates to continually improve systems and processes, and to focus the people and resources of the organisation to delivering customer value — as ultimately, value exists only in the eyes of the customer.

Broadly speaking, the TQM philosophy is founded on several conceptual principles:[17]

- A definition of "quality" in terms of meeting the customer's requirements. Anyone producing work output may be considered a supplier, while any party receiving work inputs constitutes a customer. The customer relationship is held in esteem and a supplier's responsibility is to understand and meet the customer's requirements.
- Quality is achieved by undertaking the right action the first and every time.
- The organisation requires a proactive approach to ensure that quality is achieved, thus a system of prevention must be coupled with a reactive system of inspection.
- Quality must be continually measured; a measurement framework can determine whether organisational resources are being deployed optimally.

Eurasia's president, Rajaish Bajpaee, recognised that a changing regulatory climate, the global dispersal of his industry and intensifying competition among ship managers meant a robust quality assurance system was needed to keep his organisation focused on customer value. With complicating factors on so many fronts — the global distribution of labour, variety in the types of vessels under management, maritime regulations, procurement and logistics, risk and liability — encouraging cross-functional collaboration would increase the flow of information, improve problem-solving capabilities and enhance customer focus. The very process of developing such a framework could offer invaluable insights into the organisation's strengths, weaknesses and position within the industry.

Moreover, an efficient quality assurance system could be the ship manager's best defence against criticism, forced compliance and over-regulation. Most new regulation came about as a reaction to perceived deficiencies; by taking a proactive stance, ship managers could endorse appropriate regulations rather than waiting for legislation to be mandated.

How was management's commitment crucial to the success of Eurasia's TQM effort?

This is a tremendous human resource challenge to ensure that people have a certain set of values, because it is the values which mould perceptions and perceptions mould attitudes. Attitudes mould behaviour; behaviour moulds actions and actions mould results. So if we want consistency … a predictable result, then we have to start from the bottom of the chain — that is the values, and if we can get the values right in each one of our floating factory's staff, then we can expect a predictable result.

– Rajaish Bajpaee

A lack of management involvement is often cited as one of the leading reasons why TQM efforts fail. Management must do more than simply instruct the rest of the organisation to implement quality control mechanisms. The amount of time a senior manager dedicates to quality issues is readily observed by employees, and reflects the organisation's actual priorities.

As Eurasia's president, Rajaish Bajpaee was tasked with the responsibility of adding value to key constituencies, and he held the firm belief that customers ultimately determined the organisation's fate. In leading Eurasia's TQM effort, Bajpaee was intimately involved in defining the need for change and developing new visions and the frameworks needed to mobilise commitment. Leadership entails the ability to articulate those visions and oversee the process of evolution through which the organisation learns new ways and methods.

1 Ng, Wendy (2004), "Shipping firm calls talent to come aboard," *South China Morning Post*, 7 February.

2 In the 1970s, various governments around the world offered cheap ship-construction loans to aid struggling ship-owners. As a result new vessel orders were placed in anticipation of an upturn in world trade.

3 The port of Hong Kong was served by about 80 international shipping lines providing over 400 container liner services per week connecting to over 500 international destinations (Hong Kong Port Development Council). Other major international ship management centres included Singapore, Cyprus and Glasgow. Ship managers served a global market and faced global competition.

4 The Bernhard Schulte Group was a German family-owned company that had been in the shipping business for over 120 years.

5 Interview with Rajaish Bajpaee, ISMA President.

6 Ship-owners from countries such as the UK and the US were required to use crews from the country in which their ships had been registered; work practices and salaries were generally established by union agreements. However, using a so-called "flag of convenience", a ship under open registry in a country such as Panama or Liberia could benefit from substantially lower manning expenses; the state offering the flag of convenience was compensated according to the ship's tonnage.

7 US Maritime Administration Statistics, 2003.

8 Armadillo Marine Consultants.

9 *Lloyd's Register Fairplay* and US Maritime Administration Statistics, 2003.

10 For example, Hong Kong-based Anglo Eastern Group took over Denholm Ship Management in 2001. There had also been talk of possible mergers involving ship managers Wallem and Thome ("Ship Management — Anglo Eastern says goodbye to ISMA", *Lloyd's List*, 9 January 2003).

11 ISMA members are audited twice a year. ISMA membership hit a peak of 32 ship managers in the mid-1990s, but this number has since declined to 10 members due to duplication with the International Maritime Organization's International Management Code for the Safe Operation of Ships and for Pollution Prevention (ISM Code), which was instituted in 2002.

12 The Conference Board is a US-based not-for-profit organisation that functioned as an independent membership organisation, conducting research, convening conferences and publishing information and analysis on leading-edge business practices.

13 Crosby, Philip B. (1984), *Quality without Tears: The Art of Hassle-free Management*, New York: McGraw-Hill.

14 Ng.

15 Training took place at Eurasia's in-house training centres, on training ships, on-the-job or at specialised institutes or colleges.

16 Deming, W. Edwards (1986), *Out of the Crisis: Quality, Productivity and Competitive Position*, Cambridge: Cambridge University Press.

17 Crouch, J. Michael (1997), "What You Can Do To Improve Quality", *Quality Digest*, July.

21

DispatchPro System
Leveraging Government-initiated IT Infrastructure

ALI FARHOOMAND, PAULINE NG AND VINCENT MAK

PART I: BACKGROUND AND ISSUES

Introduction

In early 2000, Info Mapping (Hong Kong) Limited, a Hong Kong-based technology SME with an interest in developing logistics applications for local businesses, spotted a growing demand among Hong Kong companies for an efficient job allocation and job-status reporting system for their outdoor workers. It proceeded to design and develop an innovative software application whereby employers could schedule jobs to employees, and employees could remotely access such work schedules on a real-time basis. However, Info Mapping needed an IT infrastructure that covered the major areas of Hong Kong to leverage the full benefits of the application. The company simply did not have the resources to build such a vast and complicated infrastructure itself. How could it solve this problem and tap the potential market ahead of other companies?

Info Mapping (Hong Kong) Limited

Info Mapping (www.ezmapping.com) was founded by a team of geographical information system (GIS) professionals.[1] Hong Kong Science Park Company Limited ("Science Park") was one of its shareholders, and Info Mapping was one of the Science Park's incubation projects.[2] Info Mapping also received funding from the Hong Kong Government's Innovation & Technology Fund.

The company focused on developing software applications and optimisation engines that could re-engineer traditional workflow and business processes. By integrating intelligent software modules into business applications, the company sought to help organisations enhance their business processes by improving their cost-efficiency. Info Mapping's products included intelligent logistics operation systems, intelligence-based job-scheduling systems, a full range of GIS applications and solutions, GIS data content and mapping, and mobile computing solutions. It had also developed knowledge-based software applications and information products, such as software tools for census data and customer analysis. The company provided clients with professional services and training for the implementation of its solutions. Its team consisted of more than 30 technical-oriented employees. It had alliances with many major IT vendors and consulting companies, including Chinese companies, and had established a client base of major corporations and governmental users.

Identifying the Demand for an Outdoor Worker Management System

By early 2000, there was a growing demand among Hong Kong businesses for outdoor manpower resources and job-fulfilment systems. Such outdoor working teams were usually field engineers for equipment or network maintenance, sales people who needed to visit clients or couriers. However, traditional business systems provided very limited support to these outdoor workers. They were required to report to their back offices in person at least once, if not several times, a day, to get job lists and status reports, pick up delivery notes, access the corporate database and so on. Although distances in Hong Kong were not great by international standards, traffic often posed serious hindrances. So an effective system for outdoor worker management that did not require the workers to return to the back office in person would be very welcome by local SMEs as a means to enhance productivity, reduce operational costs and increase customer satisfaction. But SMEs could not afford the time and cost of installing and maintaining expensive, sophisticated communication systems for their staff. Info Mapping therefore noticed an untapped market opportunity for a cost-effective, intelligent job-scheduling and communication network.

DispatchPro

Info Mapping then set out to design and develop an IT system for managing outdoor workers called DispatchPro. DispatchPro allowed client companies to perform job assignment and scheduling; it also enabled outdoor workers to retrieve job schedules and related information effectively and efficiently through remote access channels. Staff at the back office of the user company could oversee the whole assignment and scheduling of field jobs. They could import/export job order files from external systems, perform order scheduling by system or user mode, visualise job orders on digital maps and browse job order information and status.

Field workers could access their company's DispatchPro system through security login (requiring account name plus password) at the remote access channels. After login, they could check job details, and report and update the completion status of jobs assigned to them. After reporting the completion of an assignment through DispatchPro, the system would automatically set the worker's next assignment. Hence, workers would not need to go back to the office many times a day to check their duties. To ensure security, encrypted data passed directly between the company's back office and the remote access channels.

According to Info Mapping, DispatchPro had the following strengths: flexible job assignment, reduced operation costs and working hours, convenient network, accurate and secure data transmission, enhancement of outdoor workers' productivity and corporate image, improvement in customer service and user-friendliness.

However, DispatchPro as a software application was only half of the solution. For DispatchPro to be useful to SMEs, it needed a practical telecommunications network to run on. It needed remote access channels that would not require costly infrastructure investment upfront. What could Info Mapping do to bridge this last gap in its new business plan?

Looking for the Right Delivery Channel for DispatchPro

First of all, Info Mapping could not build a brand new infrastructure covering Hong Kong. As an SME that concentrated on software applications, it did not have the resources or expertise to build such a vast and complex infrastructure. Therefore, the company would have to rely on an existing infrastructure that would not be too expensive to use. Among the alternatives that Info Mapping could consider in 2000 were:

1. *Mobile phones:* Certain mobile phone service providers in Hong Kong at the time offered WAP wireless Internet connections. Outdoor workers of a DispatchPro user company could access DispatchPro through mobile Internet. At the minimum level, outdoor workers could receive the details of new job orders and send back job completion reports using wireless e-mails or a short messaging service.
2. *Personal Digital Assistants (PDAs):* PDAs could be linked up with mobile phones and could also be connected to the wireless Internet by themselves.
3. *Building an information kiosk network:* Info Mapping could lease phone-booth-sized spaces from shopping malls, housing estates or public transport hubs (underground railway stations, bus terminals, etc.) and set up kiosks linked to the Internet through existing networks. Workers of DispatchPro user companies could then access DispatchPro through these kiosks.
4. *Using existing information kiosk networks:* For example, some large shopping malls in Hong Kong already had information booths equipped with keyboards and monitors that were connected to some networks. Universities also had such kiosks, as did the MTR (Mass Transit Railway) underground railway stations. The information kiosks that linked up the MTR stations were called ESDkiosks.

PART II: LESSONS LEARNED

What Eventually Happened?

The infrastructure that Info Mapping eventually chose to deliver DispatchPro was the sprawling network of easy-to-use IT kiosks established by ESD Services Limited (also called ESDlife) under the auspices of the Hong Kong Government.

ESD Services Limited was a joint venture between the Hong Kong-based international business group Hutchison Whampoa Limited, and US-based IT giant Hewlett-Packard Company. It was contracted by the Hong Kong Government in November 1999 to develop and operate the Electronic Service Delivery (ESD) Scheme (www.esd.gov.hk or www.esdlife.

com). The Scheme was a key initiative under the "Digital 21 Information Technology Strategy" of the Hong Kong Government. The main aims of the Scheme were:

- to deliver high-quality public services to the community in an innovative manner;
- to improve the efficiency and reduce the cost of delivery of public services; and
- to foster the development of electronic commerce in Hong Kong.

On 19 January 2001, ESD formally launched a portal known as ESDlife. It was the world's premier Chinese/English bilingual portal conceived and designed with the objectives of delivering governmental and commercial services via a highly secured and convenient single on-line electronic platform. The ESD Scheme allowed the public to transact business with the government round-the-clock through a diversity of access devices, easily and securely. Services under the ESD Scheme were provided based on a citizen-oriented approach. By late 2002, the public could obtain more than 138 types of online government services from 44 government departments/public organisations participating in the ESD Scheme.

Under the ESD scheme, the one-stop-shop electronic services could be accessed conveniently through various delivery channels, including personal and public computers with Internet connection, through 97 ESDkiosks installed in MTR and KCR (Kowloon-Canton Railway) stations, shopping malls, supermarkets, government offices and cultural and exhibition centres. Each ESDkiosk was equipped with a keyboard, a touch-sensitive screen, smart card/magnetic card reader, Octopus card reader, telephone handset, speakers, a scanner, a ticket printer and a thermal printer.[3] The kiosks accepted a wide range of electronic payment methods, and advanced technologies were used to secure payment.[4] The ESD network was originally designed primarily to give citizens more convenient access to government information and services. However, ESD was, by 2002, quite willing to explore business-to-business applications for its kiosks.

Collaborating with ESD, a kiosk-based DispatchPro Outdoor Worker Management System was launched on 27 November 2002. Figure 1 shows a company's job allocations schedule that could be viewed by outdoor workers after security login at any ESDkiosk located around Hong Kong. Workers could print out the schedule using the kiosk printer.

About 10 Hong Kong companies, including logistics, outdoor equipment maintenance and engineering firms, conducted trials with DispatchPro when it was launched. Each client company was charged a monthly fee of HK$300 to HK$1,000 per user; the exact rate depended on each client's frequency of use and print service requirements. Potential users of DispatchPro were naturally those that had outdoor staff such as couriers, sales people and field survey workers. For example, Innovator System Limited, one of DispatchPro's first users, adopted the system to co-ordinate its team of field engineers responsible for customer software, equipment and network maintenance, so that the engineers could respond efficiently to the frequent customer call-outs that were received at the company's call centre. Removal companies were potential clients as well — the removals teams could obtain details of their next job through ESDkiosks using DispatchPro. In fact, any company that needed to perform timely delivery of products and services every day was likely to find DispatchPro useful.

Figure 1   A Typical List of Job Details for Outworkers*

* The line of Chinese at the top means "DispatchPro System"; the line immediately above the table grid reads: job number/ type/ name of Client/ delivery address/ scheduled delivery time/ status.

Were ESDkiosks the Right Choice for Delivering DispatchPro?

Wireless data transmission in 2000 was limited by speed, and people used it mostly for sending and receiving e-mails and short messages. But efficient communication with a system like DispatchPro required more than just sending short messages. Before a low-cost and efficient wireless Internet network, such as a commercially successful 3G network, appeared, a commericially viable DispatchPro service could only be delivered through fixed-line information networks. But building a kiosk network, although less expensive and complicated than building a brand new communications infrastructure with cables and transmission centres, would still involve a great deal of capital investment for Info Mapping. Moreover, such a project would take time, and it was possible some other companies would start providing a similar service to DispatchPro before Info Mapping finished setting up its kiosks.

Therefore, the ESDkiosk network seemed to be the optimal choice for delivering DispatchPro. Although the network did not cover all of Hong Kong, and in some urban areas in the New Territories the kiosks were rather sparsely located, at least it covered all the major commercial areas. Moreover, the network was maintained by ESD Services, and Info Mapping was just a partner using the network to deliver its services. So Info Mapping would not need to worry a great deal about the technical details or maintenance of the kiosk network. Moreover, the pricing of the DispatchPro service under this arrangement would probably be more affordable to SMEs. Finally, as DispatchPro was itself a new system, Info Mapping definitely needed an inexpensive means of testing it in practice, so that it could improve the system according to customer feedback. Further investment in upgrading the system could come later. Even at its launch stage, the system was already capable of expansion. Applications such as customer relationship management (CRM) and enterprise resource planning (ERP) could be introduced to the back office, and the system could be modified so that it was accessible through mobile phones or PDAs, provided there was an appropriate mobile Internet network.

Conclusion

This case can serve as a best-practice example of an SME managing and furthering business growth through leveraging government-initiated IT infrastructure. The moral of the story is that SMEs such as Info Mapping can capture opportunities provided by the government in terms of funding and infrastructure to identify new business opportunities. Seen from another perspective, it also shows how the Government can promote IT development in practice.

DispatchPro could not have become a practicable service without three vital elements: a) a company, namely Info Mapping, that identified the market need and created an IT system to provide the local business community with a cost-effective means of communication between back-office staff and field workers; b) an existing IT infrastructure, namely ESDkiosks, that provided a practical network for delivering DispatchPro; and c) government financial backing. Government backing came in two forms. First, Info Mapping was itself an incubation project with funding from Hong Kong Science Park and the Innovation & Technology Fund, both of which were government-initiated causes aimed at helping to promote the local development of new technology. Second, the ESD network was also government-initiated and contracted out by the Hong Kong Government to ESD Services Limited, a private company. DispatchPro was the result of synergy between this company and Info Mapping. Info Mapping thus managed to fuel its business growth by leveraging an existing, government-initiated IT infrastructure.

---

[1]   A GIS is a computer system for capturing, storing, checking, integrating, manipulating, analysing and displaying data related to positions on the Earth's surface. Uses included town planning, public utility management, environmental use, resource management, engineering, business, marketing and distribution. Source: www.dictionary.com.

[2]   Among its many functions, the Hong Kong Science Park Co. Ltd. was set up by the Hong Kong Government to help companies commercialise innovative ideas.

[3]   The Octopus card was a very widely used smart card in Hong Kong that could be used to pay a variety of public transport fares and for payment at certain vending machines and chains of convenient stores.

[4]   For example, the scheme accepted payment by debit cards, credit cards and PPS (Payment by Phone Service). Advanced technologies such as SSL (secure socket layer) and SET (secure electronic transactions) were used to provide secure electronic payment.

22

LECCOTECH
The "Whole Product" Concept in Export Marketing

ALI FARHOOMAND AND PAULINE NG

PART I: BACKGROUND AND ISSUES

Introduction

> The marketing of high tech products is dependent on industry recognition, meaning that people within the industry acknowledge the value of your product. This is the primary requirement. The secondary requirement is that when you approach your customer, your product has to be perceived and regarded as a "whole product".
>
> – Kin Chan, CEO, LECCO Technology Ltd.

LECCO Technology Ltd. (LECCOTECH), a Hong Kong-based company, was the pioneer of a Structured Query Language (SQL) optimisation technology. Founded in 1995, the company developed a unique technology that could potentially revolutionise the management and efficiency of corporate databases in all industry sectors. However, the local market was small compared to the US and Japan in terms of IT spending, and the company had to find a way to capture the untapped market.[1] How could a small Hong Kong start-up with very limited funds convince the industry to take notice of its innovation and win over corporate users? How could it compete with the likes of BMC Software, Computer Associates and Precise, much better established software and database management solutions vendors whose presence in the overseas markets was an inspiration to LECCOTECH?

Company Background

In 1989, Richard To, an alumnus of the City University of New York with a particular interest in artificial intelligence, conceived the idea of developing a database optimisation solution. At the time the idea was far-fetched: how could a software programme replace the complicated processes of identifying flaws in SQL statements and provide alternative SQL statements that would enable computer systems to manage databases and operate them more efficiently? He continued to toy with this idea as a pastime while holding a full-time job involving database management in Hong Kong. It wasn't until he shared this idea with Kin Chan in 1995 that the two began to seriously consider the potential for this innovation. At that time, Chan was working as an IT professional in an investment bank in Hong Kong, and was a frequent user of database systems.

The idea resulted in a technology innovation that LECCOTECH called the "Feedback-searching engine". LECCOTECH launched a product called SQL Expert for Oracle in 1998, the first successful commercialisation of the technology. With this, the company set its vision to deliver the ultimate database optimisation solutions to customers worldwide. Its value proposition was to enable its customers to maximise and realise the return on their most important asset-data. Given the proliferation of computer usage, database management was an important issue for companies. Equally important was the issue of maximising the performance of their systems, applications and databases to ensure maximum operational efficiency. This was the integral element of what was commonly known as Enterprise Data Management and Business Technology Optimisation.

The Unique Technology

An analyst report showed that 60 percent of application and database performance problems were caused by SQL statements. While SQL was the only means of accessing data from a relational database, its complexity and ease of use meant that there were a number of ways to construct a statement to arrive at the same result. However, the speed of SQL statements determined the system's efficiency. Some statements were clumsy. It was rare to find slick SQL statements in a programme. Furthermore, since computer systems and applications grew as a business grew, the data processed and stored on them became more and more complex. The sheer quantity of SQL statements in an enterprise application presented a big problem in the process of optimising application performance, let alone finding the best alternatives for each statement. SQL statements that were the most efficient and fast one day were likely to become less efficient over time as a database was a dynamic creature and data volume fluctuated. Given that between 60 and 90 percent of operational time was used to process SQL statements, inefficiencies could significantly slow databases down.

The "Feedback-searching engine" was one of the core technologies of LECCOTECH. Using techniques in artificial intelligence, an SQL scanner would scan SQL statements (i.e., source codes and other database-related objects) on computer applications and databases to identify any problematic SQL statements within minutes. The results were captured by the Feedback- searching engine, which would then generate new SQL statements to provide alternative statements with different execution paths. A benchmark test then compared the time required for processing the alternative SQL statements. Replacing the old SQL statements with new ones was also simple. The impacts of the changes were immediately noticeable to users.

This simple scan procedure in itself often provided sufficient compelling evidence to potential customers for systems efficiency improvements. Whereas companies would previously take a reactive (and manual) approach to finding the SQL statements that were slowing down the system, LECCOTECH's solution was proactive and speedy. Indeed, many companies were not even aware that their systems could be more efficient. Users, regardless of technical aptitude, could run the scanner whenever and as frequently as they liked. Programme developers could use the scanner to identify the many variations to a SQL statement they had just written.

LECCOTECH became the pioneer and an industry leader in database optimisation solutions. While competitors could offer software that helped to identify application performance shortfalls and bottlenecks, LECCOTECH was the only company to offer solutions and benchmarking. The company came to be regarded in the industry as the missing puzzle (solution) in the life-cycle of application performance assurance and business technology optimisation.

Commercialising the Technology

> The point is that our technology is not something we consider is good and unique, but the technology gains the respect of our clients.
>
> – Leo Leung, Vice President — Sales, Asia Pacific

SQL Expert, which ran on the Oracle platform, was the first product launched by LECCOTECH, in 1998. Very soon after, the product was extended to other database platforms, including Sybase and IBM DB2.

Although innovative, the product received only lukewarm acceptance in Hong Kong and Asia. The fundamental problem that LECCOTECH identified in the Asian market was the inability of companies to connect systems efficiency (i.e., the technology) with corporate performance. Overseas, say in the US, companies recognised that IT was a major asset (and often a major investment) of their business, and so systems efficiency was seen to have a direct impact on corporate performance. Because of this mismatch in Asian markets, the initial demand for SQL Expert was low. Leo Leung, Vice President of Sales for Asia Pacific, spent much of his time educating the local market:

> You cannot talk about improving corporate performance without optimising systems performance. There is a chain reaction. If your databases are not efficient, it will affect the whole operation of the company.

Partly as a consequence of this, another limitation for LECCOTECH was the relatively low corporate IT expenditure in Asia compared to Western nations and Japan. Since LECCOTECH's unique technology could be useful to companies in all industries, with any application and database, its market potential went far beyond Asia.

Realising the "Whole Product" Concept in Export Marketing

In 2000, LECCOTECH aggressively attacked the worldwide market and set up regional offices in the US, Canada and England. The motivation was symbolic: LECCOTECH wanted to let its potential customers know that "we are going to be here in the long run". This was particularly important for IT companies. US companies were unlikely to buy from an overseas company that did not have a US presence. Product functionality alone could not win the day. Conversely, it mattered less that a company's product could not perform a certain function, because upgrades and enhancements were anticipated, as long as the company could convince customers that it was here to stay.

In 2002, the company signed a global OEM arrangement with Sybase, a prominent database software company. LECCOTECH became the first home-grown IT software company in Hong Kong or even Asia to sign such an agreement with a major worldwide software vendor. Sybase saw the value in providing its customers with the tools to enhance their database performance. SQL Expert was an add-on feature that Sybase used to sell its software. Since Sybase had a substantial and well-established customer base, the agreement drew in significant revenue for LECCOTECH. The big break landed LECCOTECH on the global stage.

Chan was adamant that in order to succeed in the global market, the company needed to sell a whole product. Recognising that SQL transformation and database optimisation were only a sub-set within the application development and database administration market segments, the company's strategy was to partner with other technology companies to deliver a whole product solution to the two target market segments. In other words, products and services needed to be packaged to present the whole product offerings. Having a unique technology was just one part, albeit a unique selling point, for LECCOTECH's products. However, the market did not see these products as "complete products", although they clearly had distinctive functions. As Richard To explained:

> In the beginning, you have to decide which area you are going to develop first to build up your product. We chose to invest in developing something that man cannot do. It's like building a car: which do you choose to develop first — the engine or the seats? For us, we decided to develop the world's best engine first. But the engine has no value in itself. It's the whole product — the car — that provides the value.

The partnership with Sybase clearly demonstrated to the company the importance of the "whole product" concept. Sybase took LECCOTECH's product to complete its product portfolio. In this way, Sybase had a whole product to sell. Furthermore, the whole product needed to be tightly integrated and targeted for a specific market segment. Hence, DB Expert was packaged for the database administration market segment and SQL Expert was packaged for the systems and applications development market segment.

LECCOTECH in 2003

By 2003, the company had issued more than 4,400 user licences in 46 countries. Among its 1,300 corporate customers were renowned institutions (including Fortune 500 companies) such as Manulife Financial, American International Insurance (AIA), HSBC Asset Management and JP Morgan Chase. It had offices in the UK, Canada and the US, with the overseas staff managing local sales and customer support. There were 45 employees worldwide, with the majority of the R&D staff based in Hong Kong and Zhuhai, China. In Japan, the company sold through a partner, Itochu, which was also a shareholder of LECCOTECH. The Japan market was significant for LECCOTECH because it was the second-largest database market in the world.

The company's annual revenue had grown healthily at a rate of 25 percent in the four years up to 2003. Maintenance renewals as a recurring income doubled every two years and in 2003 represented 25 percent of the company's total revenue. Customer loyalty and retention was an important aspect of the business. Seventy percent of revenue was generated through direct sales, while 30 percent was through channel distribution. Revenue contribution by region was as follows: US — 60 percent, Asia Pacific — 20 percent, Europe — 18 percent. The agreement with Sybase contributed 20 percent of the company's revenue in 2002.

In recognition of its achievements as a technology leader and its success in export marketing, the company was awarded a series of accolades. LECCOTECH was arguably the only company in China and Hong Kong to have developed a pure software technology and successfully commercialised it into products that were deployed globally and used extensively in Global 500 companies.

In spite of its success, LECCOTECH was only touching the tip of the iceberg. The potential for the company was huge, but it had to find innovative means to further exploit the "whole product" concept.[2]

PART II: LESSONS LEARNED

The LECCOTECH case demonstrates the importance of technology management in a firm. The ability to commercialise a new technology or to turn a technology into an innovation is where many companies have failed. This points to the significance of taking a cohesive approach to managing the three integral aspects of research, development and marketing. The absence of any one of these often leads to the downfall of a company. In our discussion of the lessons learned from this case, we will cover all three aspects of technology management and identify:

- The inter-relationship between business strategy, technology and innovation.
- The development of innovations based on the intended geographic reach of the product.
- The way in which technological competencies and capabilities can deliver unique value propositions to users.
- The collaborative approach to marketing innovations.

Key Questions

How are technology, innovation and strategy related?

Technological innovations are the outcome of product, process and market development activities.[3] This argument suggests that a new technology becomes a successful technological innovation in three ways: (1) by being a product that creates value added for the user; (2) through an iterative and concurrent process of refinement of the innovation (as opposed to a sequential process), and (3) by understanding the needs of the market.

Taking this argument further, Burgelman et al. maintain that a company's products or services are an expression of its strategy. It follows that a strategy without any supporting capabilities will lack momentum. Similarly, capabilities without strategy are aimless.

"Strategy thus articulates the ways in which the opportunities that are created by the firm's capabilities can be exploited."[4]

When applying these concepts to LECCOTECH, we gain a better understanding of how strategic management is integrally related to technology and innovation. Technology companies such as LECCOTECH need to develop and manage their technological capabilities in such a way that these create and sustain competitive advantage. Competitive advantage usually arises from the unique aspects of the technology strategy rather than the common characteristics that are shared with others. Successful companies develop technological competencies and capabilities that are distinctive and not easily replicable. This is what LECCOTECH refers to as its unique selling point. However, a good technology strategy also needs to be concerned with what Teece calls the "control of specialised assets".[5] As a first mover in the specialised area of SQL transformation, LECCOTECH needs access to complementary specialised assets that are owned by others. Alliances between start-ups (e.g., LECCOTECH) and established firms (e.g., Sybase) illustrate the importance of complementary assets. Often, understanding the ability to command strong positions in terms of complementary assets determines a company's capacity to exploit potential first-mover advantages.

Why is it important to develop "international" products as opposed to "domestic" products for success in export marketing?

A company may choose whether to develop products for domestic or international users. Kleinschmidt and Cooper (1988) concluded from their research that a strategy of "design for the home market and seek exports in the future" was inappropriate for achieving export success.[6] Instead, the objective should be to design a "world product" in order to succeed in both the domestic and overseas markets. This was what LECCOTECH aimed to achieve from the outset. The nature of its product innovation — SQL optimisation solutions — appealed to the international marketplace. Database administration and development environments, such as Oracle, Sybase and DB2, commanded an international customer/ user base. It was, therefore, logical that if LECCOTECH's core technology/expertise provided a true value proposition to the existing user base, it would have international appeal.

The company identified a market niche within the database administration and development market segments. With a clear understanding of the user needs within these segments, the company set out to win not just on the basis of functionality of the products, but also on providing a solution to customers that would impact their overall business performance.

For SMEs wanting to establish a foothold in the international marketplace, it is important to have an international focus when engaging in product design and development. In assessing the impact of an international orientation on new product performance, Kleinschmidt and Cooper also found that products designed and developed to meet foreign requirements were the top performers in terms of achieving foreign market share. Not only did these products do better in foreign markets, but they also did better at home.

What is the value proposition of LECCOTECH's product offerings?

Using the analogy of building a car, as described by Richard To, LECCOTECH's technical expertise was channelled and focused into producing "the world's best engine". LECCOTECH recognised that to produce just another engine was inadequate for competing against the likes of BMC Software, Computer Associates and Precise. But by leveraging its expertise in artificial intelligence, LECCOTECH was able to produce an engine that was far superior to those offered by its competitors. LECCOTECH's products not only helped users to identify the poorly constructed SQL statements that slowed down their applications and databases; they also provided the definitive solution, namely, the exclusive alternatives, in a timely and cost-effective manner. Without the best SQL transformation technology, the company would not have been able to compete and there would have been no unique selling point.

The unique selling point brought out the value proposition of LECCOTECH's products for its customers. On a practical level, the SQL optimisation solution delivered the following benefits:

- It saved considerable time (and therefore, cost) in finding the SQL statements that were causing system-processing delays/problems and provided solutions for them.
- It enabled a proactive approach to identifying systems problems. Previously, there had been no means to pre-empt potential problems with applications and databases. Developers were also left to their own devices to make sure that an application worked according to requirements, without any accountability for the quality of their work and the efficiency of the applications they wrote. LECCOTECH's products proved invaluable to developers as well as database administrators. Productivity was improved.

On a corporate level, the practical benefits translated into bottom-line cost savings:

- The staff time involved in problem-solving was saved, thus freeing up the staff to engage in more pressing tasks and delivering more value to the business.
- LECCOTECH provided the tool for companies to benchmark their systems performance. The real benefits of being able to compute the time saved in using alternative SQL statements translated into better service quality for end customers.

In describing the product management process as an opportunity to differentiate, Turner identifies several principles of the process:[7]

1. Products should be perceived as solutions to client business problems and should be designed and managed accordingly. Thus, successful products will be those that act as problem-solving, business-enhancing tools for the client.
2. Products should be designed by following a process that depends on understanding the business needs of major account users.
3. Products should be marketed as enhanced solutions derived from a core base.

Our study of LECCOTECH lends support to Turner's principles.

What is the significance of the "whole product" concept for LECCOTECH?

> Customers are not interested in products or services themselves. They are only interested in what products and services will actually do for them and the problems that they will solve.
>
> – Ford et al., *The Business Marketing Cause: Managing in Complex Networks*[8]

In Richard To's analogy of the car, he maintains that the engine on its own is of limited value, even though it might be the world's best engine. Its value must be seen in the context of the whole car. A marketer needs to understand that if he is to solve a customer's problems, he needs to provide a complete offering or a "whole product". A whole product may consist of physical products, services, advice, adaptations, logistics and the costs. The combination of these elements may be different for each customer or target customer group according to their needs. Although the elements of the offering may be fundamentally the same as those offered by competitors, the successful marketer should be able to differentiate some or all of the elements of his offering in order to better solve the customer's problems.

Understanding this "whole product" concept at an early stage meant that LECCOTECH saved a lot of time and resources in pursuing international markets. The whole product was to be developed, produced and delivered to the customer by a combination of companies in the network. LECCOTECH recognised the need to use the resources of other companies and combine them with its own skills and expertise to produce an offering. Ford et al state that for many companies, 70–80 percent of the costs of their offerings are actually accounted for by what they buy from others.

The successful global OEM arrangement with Sybase made it clear to LECCOTECH that its SQL optimisation solution should not be marketed in isolation, but within the context of the whole product offering to its two target market segments: database administration and development. Its expertise became a unique selling point – an element of differentiation — for Sybase.

What is the role of global strategic partnerships for SMEs like LECCOTECH?

LECCOTECH's experience reinforces Porter's theory of the value system in that linkages between companies can be used for the mutual benefit of all within the value chain to create a competitive advantage for them. The win-win-win strategy applies to LECCOTECH, Sybase and the end customers. All parties gain from the partnership.

Global strategic partnerships, as discussed by Keegan,[9] are the quickest and cheapest ways to develop a global strategy. They are attractive because:
1. Partners may have already contributed to high product development costs.
2. Partners may have the skills, capital and know-how that you lack.
3. Partnerships may help to secure access to markets that would otherwise be difficult to reach.
4. Partnerships can provide important learning opportunities.

SMEs should consider forming global strategic partnerships to leverage the assets, knowledge and infrastructures already in place. This was one of the factors that led to LECCOTECH's success in export marketing.

Another factor in the equation, and arguably a prerequisite that an SME will need in order to establish Keegan's view of global partnerships, is a value proposition. SMEs need to ask themselves: "What (new or unique) value am I bringing to the table that will deliver benefits to my company, to my partners and to the end customers?" Invariably, this discussion revolves around product or service innovation. For LECCOTECH, its major selling point is its unique technology that has been commercialised. While technology on its own has little value in itself, it is the ability to turn the technology innovation into a value-adding asset that makes it successful. Issues related to the Four Ps of marketing, branding and sustaining competitive advantage follow on from there.

[1] Eighty percent of worldwide IT expenditure was in the US.

[2] As a company that has been funded by The Applied Research Fund (ARF), LECCOTECH has received not only financial support but also valuable assistance from the ARF, ranging from industry contacts to specialised expertise from its fund managers.

The ARF is a government-owned venture capital fund valued at $750 million, set up in 1993 to provide funding support to technology ventures and research and development projects that have commercial potential. The ARF is controlled and administered by the Applied Research Council (ARC), a company wholly owned by the Government and formed specifically for this role. From November 1998, private-sector venture capital firms were engaged to manage the ARF. The fund managers assess the technical and commercial viability of proposed technology ventures. On behalf of the ARF, venture capital firm Walden International is responsible for overseeing LECCOTECH.

3 Burgelman, R. A., Maidique, M. A. and Wheelwright, S. C. (2001), *Strategic Management of Technology and Innovation*, McGraw-Hill Higher Education, International Edition.

4 Burgelman, Maidique and Wheelwright, p. 6.

5 Teece, D. I. (1986), "Profiting from Technological Innovation: Implications for Integration, Collaboration, Licensing and Public Policy", *Research Policy*, Vol. 15, pp. 285–305.

6 Kleinschmidt, E. J. and Cooper, R. G. (1988), "The Performance Impact of an International Orientation on Product Innovation", *European Journal of Marketing*, Vol. 22, No.10.

7 Turner, P. (1989), "Product Management for Major Accounts — An Opportunity to Differentiate", *European Journal of Marketing*, Vol. 24, No.5.

8 Ford, D. et al (2002), *The Business Marketing Course: Managing in Complex Networks*, John Wiley & Sons Ltd.

9 Keegan, Warren J. (2002), *Global Marketing Management*, seventh edition, Prentice Hall.

23

OneCard
Building a Savings and Benefits Platform

THOMAS M. HOUT AND AMIR HOOSAIN

PART I: BACKGROUND AND ISSUES

Introduction

Customer focus strategies in the restaurant and retail sectors were almost unheard of during Hong Kong's boom years, but weakness in the post-handover economy led to a surge in cross-marketing trends and greater acceptance of the concept of rewarding customers for their business. With the community facing tough economic times, customers were looking for better deals and higher service standards. In response, and in an effort to drive sales, tactical initiatives and loyalty programmes abounded in the retail sector. In addition to merchant-initiated programmes, a number of third-party continuity providers developed merchant networks and offered discounts and benefits by subscription. Khalid Gibran, a veteran of the loyalty membership industry, had already established two successful dining membership programmes in the mere two years since his arrival in Hong Kong. OneCard, his latest and most ambitious venture, was launched in January 2003, but shortly afterwards Hong Kong was hit by the mysterious SARS virus. Retail sales took a nosedive and residents avoided eating out. While many business owners braced for more uncertainty and worried about their survival, Khalid Gibran saw a marketing opportunity amid the many challenges and a chance to grow his merchant and subscriber bases.

Hong Kong's Beleaguered Retail Sector

Before the Asian financial crisis of 1997, Hong Kong's retailers enjoyed a relatively comfortable operating environment, with a robust local consumer base and a booming tourism industry. When economic crisis hit the territory, more than five years of adverse conditions eroded personal wealth and pushed unemployment figures up. As an export-oriented economy, Hong Kong was negatively affected by the slowdown in the US economy; while at home, falling property prices, a slumping equity market and fragile market sentiment all contributed to weakened consumer confidence. To compound these problems, Hong Kong retailers were also losing out to cross-border shopping alternatives. Figures released by the Hong Kong Retail Management Association showed that total retail sales declined by 25 percent between 1997 and 1998 — much of this could be attributed to the phenomenon of weekend shopping sprees to nearby Shenzhen. Figures at the time showed that over 200,000 Hong Kong residents travelled through the Lo Wu border to southern China every weekend, while a further 40,000 travelled to other Southeast Asian destinations to take advantage of favourable exchange rates. Substantially lower prices were the major attraction for shoppers going on such excursions, as high operating costs meant that Hong Kong retailers simply could not compete with their Mainland counterparts.

With the retail sector slumping over a number of years, one consolation was that tourism had remained one of the fastest growing sectors of the economy. In 2002, the local tourism industry saw a 20.7 percent growth in visitor arrivals to 16.6 million, and an estimated 16 percent increase in tourism receipts to over HK$75 billion.[1] Due to an easing in visa requirements, visitors from Mainland China had grown to make up more than half of Hong Kong's total incoming visitors. Tourist spending accounted for about 22 percent of retail sales and the industry was forecast to grow by more than eight percent in 2003.[2]

The Severe Acute Respiratory Syndrome (SARS) outbreak in mid-March 2003 dealt an immediate blow to tourism and, by extension, to Hong Kong's retail establishments. The number of inbound visitors dropped by 10 percent in the second half of March (over the previous year), followed by a 65 percent drop in April. By contrast, the months of January and February combined had seen a 29 percent rise over the same period a year earlier.[3] Hong Kong's international reputation took a battering and earlier hopes for an economic turnaround in 2003 quickly faded.

Customer Loyalty Programmes

In dire economic times, retailers were often under pressure to slash prices in order to maintain volume — a tactic that could initiate aggressive price competition and wipe out profits. Faced with just such pressures, many retailers in Hong Kong tried their hand at customer retention tools in a bid to influence shopping behaviour. In overseas markets such as the US and the UK, some form of customer continuity scheme could be found in virtually every sector of the market. By contrast, in Hong Kong, retention tools such as loyalty cards were initially the domain of airline frequent flyer clubs and the petroleum market. For a number of years, the major gas station vendors such as Shell, Mobil and Caltex had issued magnetic-strip cards that offered patrons the opportunity to accumulate points towards the redemption of household goods. Similar schemes began to be offered by the territory's financial institutions, with the emergence of point-collection programmes linked to credit card purchases. By contrast, the grocery sector favoured shorter-term, tactical initiatives. The territory's two major supermarket chains, Park'N Shop and Wellcome, had been successful in building sales with periodic programmes that rewarded loyal shoppers with bonus certificates redeemable for bargain-priced household products.

Loyalty programmes were becoming an increasingly common part of retailers' marketing strategies. Eventually, it was not uncommon for any business with an interest in a loyalty proposition to make an attempt at establishing its own variation. Following the Asian financial crisis, hundreds of stores ranging from corner shops to large department stores were forced to close their doors. But successful loyalty marketing allowed some companies to thrive and even expand. The Pacific Coffee chain is an especially noteworthy example of a company that successfully launched a stamp-card club to encourage repeat business.[4] Since launching its club in 1992, Pacific Coffee went on to develop a customer database to yield insights into regular customers' demographics and consumption habits. In exchange for the valuable information it gathered, Pacific Coffee issued quarterly newsletters and e-mail updates to its members with details of special events and discounts. Along similar lines, City'super food courts and the international music retailer HMV began offering their own versions of stamp-card clubs and reported success at keeping sales steady despite the depressed market.[5]

As merchant loyalty offerings began appearing in unprecedented numbers, loyalty programmes associated with just one retailer were no longer the rule. As was typical during an economic recession, consumption patterns had changed and consumers were becoming more frugal and discretionary in their spending. Major loyalty programme issuers knew that customers were demanding increased flexibility and a wider variety of rewards. The Countdown discount card — part of an international network including shopping, dining, entertainment and hotel establishments — was launched in Hong Kong as early as 1991, but from the late 1990s a crop of home-grown loyalty programmes were also becoming broader in scope. In a bid to survive, many businesses experimented with cross-marketing: it was not uncommon to find ceramic ornaments offered through a hair salon loyalty card, or discounted health tests redeemable through a video rental chain's membership programme.[6] For many companies, the cross-marketing of services was especially appealing as it removed the hassle of holding inventory for merchandise giveaways.

However, not all experiences with loyalty memberships had been positive. In 1998, the now-defunct KPS video rental chain generated bad publicity when, due to financial difficulties, it terminated its highly popular prepaid discount coupon packages and imposed a forfeiture date on unused coupons. In 2001, up to 2,000 customers were left thousands of dollars out of pocket by a promotions company that offered a "one card, one world" scheme at HK$1,600 per person, promising significant meal discounts and a complimentary night's stay in selected local hotels. Several hotels had agreed to provide the discounts on the understanding that they would be reimbursed, but payments from the company eventually ceased and the discounts were terminated.[7]

Identifying Opportunities in the Local Market

Khalid Gibran had spent over eight years developing and implementing loyalty membership programmes for the hospitality industry in positions that took him to India, the Middle East, Europe and the United States. In 2000, he was convinced by two former colleagues to go to Hong Kong and join them in an effort to launch a dining card venture. Initially based in a hotel room, the trio set to work fervently developing their business proposal and seeking investors. Eventually they gained the backing of a seasoned financier who was able to offer an extensive network of contacts and a team of support staff. From the beginning, they sought to distinguish their service by offering variety, namely by focusing on Hong Kong's dining preferences rather than any particular establishment. In so doing, they identified two prevailing preferences — buffets and premium Chinese restaurant dining.

The company they formed, OnCard (www.oncard.com), billed itself as a provider of "the next generation dining cards". OnCard's flagship service was The Buffet Club dining membership plan in which an annual fee of HK$1,288 entitled members to 30 vouchers for two-for-one buffet dining at over 30 participating buffets in Hong Kong, mainland China and elsewhere in the region. In addition, members were entitled to year-round 20 percent savings on food and beverage purchases at participating restaurants, and received invitations to monthly member events. For its partners, OnCard offered special event marketing services and regular tracking of cardholder activity. OnCard also partnered with Online Credit Card Ltd. to incorporate its dining membership products into a MasterCard product. OnCard's Mun Hon Club offered a similar package of benefits for premium Chinese restaurant dining. Between 3 January and 3 December 2002, 26,000 dining preference cards were sold.

Encouraged by this early success, Gibran saw an opportunity to develop a savings and benefits platform beyond the realm of OnCard's premium dining focus. In late 2002, Gibran left the management of OnCard to his partners and focused his efforts on building a new business: *OneCard*. There was an abundance of single-merchant loyalty cards in Hong Kong and Gibran believed that a platform that consolidated savings and benefits for a broad range of retail, dining, lifestyle and entertainment outlets would appeal to the local market. The international Countdown discount card, based on a similar concept, had been launched in Hong Kong in the early 1990s by Malaysia Borneo Finance Holdings (MBF).[8] In Gibran's view, however, Countdown had been pursued largely as a side-business and offered a confusing and inconsistent discounting structure.

OneCard International

Having established a solid network in building OnCard, Gibran was able to streamline the process of establishing OneCard International (www.onecard.com.hk) with an infusion of personal funds and the investor contacts he had acquired while launching his previous company. OneCard International was launched on 6 January 2003.

From the outset, Gibran saw that his main challenge would be establishing credibility for an unknown brand. Without such credibility, few consumers would be willing to subscribe to a fee-based discount programme, and merchant acquisitions would prove difficult. Gibran saw a possible solution to this hurdle in a common distribution platform that was already entrenched in Hong Kong daily life: the Octopus Card. The Octopus Card was a smart card that allowed users to pay for fares through most of Hong Kong's transportation system, for meals at certain fast-food restaurants and for items purchased at most convenience stores and supermarkets. Over 9.5 million Octopus cards had been issued and it was estimated that about 6.3 million people carried the card on a regular basis. Gibran approached Octopus Cards Ltd. with a proposal to license the Octopus function for his OneCard-branded product.[9]

After a period of due diligence, the OneCard with Octopus function was given approval. For every OneCard issued with the Octopus function, a fee would be paid to Octopus Cards Ltd. After purchasing the OneCard, cardholders could transfer value from their existing Octopus card at one of many outlets and return the old card for a refund of its deposit. The Octopus function was costly, but Gibran felt it was worth the expense for the name recognition of Octopus in the local market.

With a co-branding strategy in place, Gibran set about building his merchant base. A team of four people — one carrying over from his previous organisation and all under the age of 25 — was recruited as the OneCard merchant acquisition team. The team called on merchants and sought perpetual contracts stipulating a requirement of three months' notice should the merchant later opt out of the OneCard network. The major selling point was the prospect of repeat business through participation in the network. As opposed to sales and coupon offers, which typically led to one-time business only, the OneCard promise was to bring return customers in exchange for year-round store discounts.

All categories of merchants were targeted by the acquisition team, with the exception of hotel-based restaurants, since this was the domain of OnCard's dining loyalty programmes. Every merchant participating in the OneCard programme agreed to offer a discount ranging from 5 percent to 60 percent (most discounts were in the 10–20 percent range). The exact amount was clearly displayed in a window decal bearing the OneCard logo.[10] A targeted merchant base of 350 establishments was set before the venture would move on to actual card sales.

Due largely to the high cost of maintaining an in-house sales team, a decision was made to outsource all card sales channels. Arrangements were made with outdoor sales agents, telemarketing companies and other distribution channels, including Daily Stop stores, Bookazine outlets and the HongKong.com Website. All channels were engaged on a commission basis, with outdoor sales set at the highest commission rate, followed by telemarketing and lastly the retail outlets, due to the passive nature of the channels.

In the first four weeks, it was a process of trial and error with the outsourced sales agents. Starting with 22 individuals, Gibran and his team observed their sales activities with regular on-the-spot checks and ultimately settled on the five most professional agents. Early in the sales effort, Gibran observed that about 70 percent of his sales were coming from outdoor sales, 20 percent from telemarketing and the remaining 10 percent from the other distribution channels. The OneCard with Octopus functionality was sold to end-consumers at a price of HK$488. Almost one third of this amount was to cover the cost of the Octopus function. Gibran felt from experience that anything priced above HK$500 would be a much harder sell. The OneCard was largely an impulse purchase and consumers were attracted by a package of merchant coupons to offset the subscription fee.

With the sales function outsourced, OneCard operated with 10 in-house staff divided into three departments: merchant acquisitions, finance and administration, and sales. In hiring employees, Gibran placed more emphasis on drive and ambition than on education or experience. Since the company was a start-up with limited resources, basic salaries were fixed at market rate, with the bulk of an employee's compensation based on commissions. As a trade-off for the lower guaranteed income, employees were promised the opportunity of growth with the company and ownership of their functional responsibilities. His team, while young and relatively inexperienced, was given substantial decision-making authority and the opportunity to participate in setting the course for their respective departments. For Gibran, the shortcomings of managing less experienced staff were far outweighed by the benefits he received, and he was happy to lend greater assistance when the need arose.

Reporting and Oversight

OneCard was a lean organisation with a strong sales orientation, so Gibran sought to maintain effective oversight over ongoing efforts while minimising the burden of reporting for his staff. Each staff member was effectively managed through one sheet of paper that was submitted daily, with key sales figures broken down according to the various sales channels. Brief daily meetings were held to brainstorm, discuss significant variances and settle other matters. Gibran himself compiled weekly reports based on these submissions and developed a monthly sales report to be presented to his board. Gibran further spent at least a week preparing each quarterly forecast and adhered tightly to plans.

OneCard's merchant database and CRM (customer relationship marketing) capability, called "OneTech", was developed in-house by an IT professional who served both OneCard and OnCard. Gibran himself collaborated in specifying the details and information he wanted captured; each department was also involved in laying out the functionality they wanted from the system. OneTech was seen as a core asset for the business and Gibran aimed to develop it to the point where, as a manager, he could track progress across the spectrum of his business at the push of a button.

Comeback Hong Kong

> When the market's down, you need to build on your assets, not try and improve your weakness. So then I thought "I've got 400 odd merchants, and they're hurting ... I need to do something."
>
> – Khalid Gibran

In mid-March 2003, about three months after OneCard began operations, the SARS virus broke out in Hong Kong and sent the retail industry into crisis. Hong Kong was placed under a World Health Organization (WHO) travel advisory and many members of the public limited unnecessary shopping, dining and other excursions. Gibran and his team had acquired about 400 merchants and were suddenly faced with an almost surreal impediment. At a time when retailers in Hong Kong were suffering, Gibran saw an opportunity to turn things in his favour, so he adjusted his strategy almost overnight and launched a "Comeback Hong Kong" initiative.

The OneCard merchant acquisition team stepped up its efforts and enlisted additional merchants at an accelerated rate. Working extended hours, every day of the week, the team persuaded ailing retail establishments to join the network, and many jumped at the chance, eager for a means to boost customer traffic. In the period from January to March 2003, the merchant acquisition team had signed up 450 merchants; in just three weeks from late-March, a further 550 merchants were enlisted. Seeing OneCard as a marketing arm for his merchants, Gibran put together a package of coupons worth a total of HK$14,500 and distributed these with every OneCard sold. The team of outdoor sales agents could be seen at work at prime spots around Hong Kong and sold 2,500 cards in four weeks under the "Comeback Hong Kong" banner, encouraging cardholders to spend and re-energise the local economy. Because the campaign was launched at a time of serious concern over the economic fallout of SARS, OneCard was able to garner substantial press coverage for its campaign.

Primary Challenges

I had 12 months worth of growth in four weeks. I sold 2,500 cards in four weeks. So it was a perfect opportunity, and what I did was, I put my company and the resources to the max. I mean I drove that machine. It's like a Morris Minor, but I drove it like a Ferrari and it started shaking. And in the process, I managed to define certain things. Things like expenses and revenue streams, plus I identified the most suitable sales channels, the most suitable advertising vehicle, the most conducive commission structure for sales agents. So all these things came out of that campaign, it was all done in four weeks. So now, in Q2, my objective is to actually drive these things harder and see if they are long-term revenue streams or not.

– Khalid Gibran

After an eventful beginning, Khalid Gibran had grown his business much faster than anticipated, but was also facing several challenges that required his attention. A major concern in terms of maintaining an expansive merchant network and a growing card-holder base was ensuring that discounts were issued as intended and that all parties remained satisfied. With over 1,000 merchants on the OneCard network, it was not feasible to monitor each one and to track all card-holder interactions. Instead, a "mystery shopper" concept was devised whereby OneCard staff would visit 10 merchants anonymously each week and monitor the shopping process against a checklist of the merchant's commitments to OneCard. In the event of any irregularity (e.g., a store clerk was unaware of the OneCard discount), the team would then follow-up with the proprietor or manager and clarify any issues. In the event of customer complaints over discounts that had not been granted, OneCard staff would examine the individual case and seek to redress the grievance by offering a discount voucher, or in special cases, offering a direct reimbursement of the disputed amount.

A large number of merchants had signed up with the OneCard network during "Comeback Hong Kong," when the general outlook was dire. As a result, there was concern that some merchants might have been after a "quick fix" and that their commitment to the programme beyond the near-term was in question. Gibran felt the best way to handle this issue was to address it openly with his merchants. Emphasis was placed on OneCard's ability to offer both near-term tactical promotions in the form of coupon distribution and promotions, and the longer-term benefit of repeat business and customer loyalty as a result of their involvement. At the time of writing, OneCard did not offer a tracking capability for merchants to monitor their establishment's OneCard activity. Any tracking had to be performed by the merchant internally, however such a capability was identified as something to be pursued during later stages of growth.

In the drive to develop a merchant base, the OneCard team had targeted all classes of merchants, with the aim of building both breadth and depth. While competing loyalty programmes offered discounts and benefits at a limited selection of establishments (often centred on a particular theme), Gibran employed a strategy of targeting any merchant who could be sold on the platform. He did not expect problems to result from overlapping merchants within a category and did not set bounds on the number of establishments that could be included. Gibran saw OneCard as a provider of targeted marketing for his merchants, somewhat analogous to a magazine or newspaper. Any merchant could benefit from the services available through his platform, regardless of whether competing establishments were doing the same. He was only willing to consider the possibility of offering exclusivity in certain categories dominated by a single vendor — for instance if HMV were to express interest in becoming an exclusive music retailer under OneCard.

Although OneCard's merchant acquisitions team had successfully signed a large number of local merchants in a short span of time, acquiring top-tier establishments had proven somewhat more challenging. The process of courting larger establishments and franchises required greater efforts in fact-finding, customising proposals, following up with sales calls and making formal presentations. Even so, the OneCard team made some headway with top-tier merchants following the "Comeback Hong Kong" campaign and had signed contracts with organisations including Kodak Express, the Angel Beauty chain of cosmetic stores, the 97 Group of restaurants and the Harilela Group.

Future Directions — Not Just a Loyalty Card

While the better part of OneCard's first six months of operations had been devoted to launching OneCard in the local market, the actual OneCard card with Octopus functionality was just an initial step in Gibran's greater plans for the platform. The company's core asset was the OneCard logo itself, which could be co-branded with any other card. Gibran's ultimate aim was to develop co-branding arrangements with bank-issued cards, charity organisations, international direct dial (IDD) cards and a host of other organisations. He aimed to market OneCard as a low-cost, high-value proposition for organisations eager to offer something extra to card-holding members. Gibran envisioned that the actual OneCard card would eventually constitute only 5 percent of his total revenues — the remaining 95 percent would come from logo placements.

One of the co-branding areas Gibran was most enthusiastic about was the possibility of logo placements on employee staff-access cards. As many local employers were going through a period of belt-tightening, Gibran felt that offering savings through the OneCard network would be a low-cost means of enhancing employee morale, while in turn generating exposure for the employer. In conjunction with staff-access-card logo placements, customised discount-voucher packages for merchants in the vicinity of a company's office could be ordered for distribution to employees. In preparation for marketing his OneCard-for-staff concept ("OneStaff"), Gibran held a follow-up "Thank You Hong Kong" campaign in Summer 2003, in which he issued complimentary OneCards to members of Hong Kong's nursing community — both as a means of expressing gratitude for their efforts during the SARS crisis and as a way of publicising his proposition to Hong Kong's employers.[11]

As OneCard progressed as a start-up, Gibran envisaged that his staff would gradually fill more of an account-servicing role rather than a pure merchant-acquisition role. Following the Comeback Hong Kong campaign, OneCard began experimenting with outsourcing the merchant-acquisitions function, and focused internal manpower on fostering merchant relations and targeting top-tier businesses. Gibran planned to create a "merchant specialist" position that would focus on research, profiling and maintaining service standards. In the third quarter, Gibran also planned to hire a marketing manager.

To reach a target of 3,000 merchants, Gibran estimated that the company would need 150,000 logos in circulation. To keep the merchants satisfied, OneCard would need to be pro-active on the promotions front, and in maintaining ongoing communications. In the second quarter of 2003, OneCard initiated a weekly merchant communiqué that was distributed by e-mail to inform merchants of the latest OneCard news and happenings. Gibran was confident that, once the merchant specialist position was established, this communications strategy could be fine-tuned; customised marketing events and promotions could be developed by profiling merchant and card-holder data in the OneTech database. Additionally, Gibran planned to launch an annual shopping festival involving OneCard merchants and to develop members-only dining events and product launches.

In line with his entrepreneurial disposition, Gibran was already setting his sights beyond Hong Kong. He had lined up a General Manager to take over managerial duties for local operations and was planning by the end of 2003 to focus his own energies on developing joint ventures in other regional markets. Gibran was close to signing a deal with a publishing company in Singapore that catered to the retail and restaurant trades. This would give OneCard access to existing marketing channels and an expedient entry strategy. The Shenzhen and Guangzhou markets were also targeted due to their geographic proximity to Hong Kong. Moreover, it was hoped that the presence of local smartcard-based travel ticketing systems would allow a replication of the entry strategy that had worked in Hong Kong. Further down the line, Gibran was exploring possible angles for entering Shanghai, as well as Japan, Taiwan and South Korea. The ultimate aim was to develop the pre-eminent savings and benefits platform in the region — with extensive logo placements on one hand and a wide network of merchants on the other.

PART II: LESSONS LEARNED

This case gives an account of how an entrepreneur was able to seize an opportunity to start a new business and to manage a low-cost but effective sales operation. Khalid Gibran exhibited the hallmarks of entrepreneurial style — he viewed rules as guidelines only and was willing to promptly adjust his organisation's priorities to make the most of changing (and challenging) circumstances. In less than three years, he spearheaded two organisations, but in so doing he had to make a number of important trade-offs.

Key Questions

What were the benefits and drawbacks of the management style employed at OneCard?

The entrepreneurial path is marked by long hours, hard work and high levels of stress until the business is established. The decision to follow this path is often born out of a desire for autonomy, a passion for the business and the opportunity to reap unlimited profits. Khalid Gibran was able to seek out investors and staff through a personal network, developed over the course of his career in the loyalty membership business. While an extensive marketing research process might have been prudent for a newcomer to the business, Gibran was able to act on experience and mobilise resources rapidly, thus capitalising on the recent success of his dining card venture. Clearly, the level of discretion Gibran possessed was key to his ability to launch OneCard in such a short timeframe, to adapt strategy and to innovate in the event of unforeseen developments.

One of the enabling factors behind OneCard's relatively rapid launch and subsequent growth was Gibran's decision to draw on expertise from his personal network. Gibran was operating a relatively small organisation, and his ability to rely upon the capabilities of his information technology, administrative support and media planning staff allowed him to devote greater energies to setting a course for growth and to managing the less experienced merchant-acquisition team and his outsourced sales channels. In this sense, it can be said that Gibran was most "hands-on" with those aspects of his business directly tied to revenue growth. This was all completely understandable due to his investors' requirements and his desire to build on momentum.

Given the limited resources of Gibran's start-up business and the broad penetration he was after, it was inevitable that the development and refinement of certain aspects of OneCard's operations would have to be prioritised over others. For instance, the information technology infrastructure and customer service capabilities of OneCard were relatively underdeveloped during the early phases of the business – a fully developed Website featuring an interactive merchant directory and promotional details was not established until some time after the initial card launch. Tracking and reporting capabilities for merchants were not initially on offer, and six months after the launch, OneCard did not yet have a dedicated customer service position.

Did OneCard employ a prudent product launch strategy in tying the OneCard brand with the name recognition of the Octopus network?

Khalid Gibran entered into a costly arrangement with Octopus Cards Ltd. The cost of each OneCard had to be raised to cover this expense, and presumably the resulting price would have been prohibitive to a substantial segment of potential customers. The advantage of the arrangement was that it offered OneCard a certain degree of instant credibility by association with the widely used Octopus network. In addition, the typical Hong Kong commuter used the Octopus card on a daily basis; with Octopus smart card functionality embedded in the OneCard, there was an increased likelihood that consumers would carry the card with them at all times. This meant a higher perceived value would result among subscribers, and increased usage could lead to a demonstrated benefit to the merchants in the network.

In the longer term, Gibran saw the OneCard logo (and the prospect of logo placements) as his company's core asset. Future offerings such as the OneStaff programme could be developed without the Octopus association; yet the initial OneCard with Octopus functionality was the first piece of the puzzle that enabled Gibran and his team to proceed with merchant acquisitions and card sales in building a credible platform. With a merchant base of a certain size and a significant number of paid subscribers, OneCard would not be as dependent on Octopus in drawing subscribers and pursuing new partnerships. The OneCard platform could possibly have been developed without involvement in the Octopus network, but the marketing challenge would have been far greater and the company's growth would probably have proceeded at a slower pace.

What are the key issues and bottlenecks that are likely to arise as OneCard aims for continued growth?

The company has experienced substantial growth over a short period, so a number of pressing issues might pose a challenge for OneCard. On the subscriber side, there is the impending question of annual membership renewals — after indulging in a largely impulse purchase, what proportion of cardholders will opt to renew their memberships at the end of the first year? What renewal fee will maximise retention? Essentially, OneCard has a window of opportunity to demonstrate the value of membership to its subscribers and to develop its other revenue streams (e.g., through the "OneStaff" offering) so that it is not entirely dependent on cardholder renewals.

With the OneCard merchant base, a number of merchants signed up at the height of the SARS crisis when the retail climate was generally bleak. A possible concern might be that the enthusiasm of some merchants for participating in the OneCard network would wane with a recovery in the retail sector. Although a three-month-notice clause existed in the event that a merchant opted out of the network, a merchant could breach the clause by declining to honour discounts or by removing the OneCard decal from their establishment; the mechanism for enforcing compliance was limited. At the time of writing, Gibran was experimenting with outsourcing the merchant-acquisition function and shifting his in-house staff to a predominantly merchant-servicing function. Devoting more resources to servicing the merchant base might go some way towards pre-empting merchant dropouts. The new hires Gibran had in mind for the remainder of 2003 would also be involved in developing more targeted marketing services for merchants.

Pursuing top-tier merchants was another challenging area of OneCard's growth plans. The process of targeting a leading merchant or a prospective organisation for the OneStaff plan involved a substantial time commitment and often the direct involvement of Gibran himself (or in future, the marketing and general managers that were to come on board). If this were to become the major focus of OneCard's acquisition efforts, it would require a different approach from the one that had led OneCard through its period of rapid growth.

Should OneCard expand into other markets at this stage?

Given that not even a year had passed since OneCard's inception, was it appropriate for Gibran to pursue expansion into other regional markets? Since the launch of OneCard, Gibran had attempted to establish a functioning organisation through direct oversight of acquisition efforts and by experimenting with outsourced sales channels. At the same time, he was preparing for his own succession with plans for the eventual hiring of additional management-level staff to oversee the Hong Kong operations. Gibran planned to devote his own efforts to regional expansion and developing joint ventures. As for the Shenzhen and Guangzhou markets, he felt it was important to establish his business as the first-mover by replicating the Octopus card strategy. As OneCard's own success demonstrated, it does not take long for a start-up with limited resources, but capable management and an effective strategy, to establish itself in a market.

---

[1] "The Changing Face of Tourism in Hong Kong" (2003), *Hang Seng Economic Monthly*, January 29. (Hong Kong's currency was pegged at HK $ 7.80 to the US Dollar in 1983 and was permitted to float in a narrow band around that level.)

[2] Interview with Michael Wu, Chairman, Hong Kong Association of Travel Agents, 16 May 2003.

[3] Interview with Michael Wu, 16 May 2003.

[4] Members simply filled out a card that entitled them to a free coffee after a number of purchases.

[5] Wu, Amy (1999), "In Bid to Survive, Hong Kong Retailers Try Customer Loyalty Clubs", *The New York Times*, 31 January.

[6] Tilton, Sarah (1998), "Medicine for Recession: Loyalty cards are springing up across Hong Kong and Asia, as companies look for ways to hang on to their best customers", *The Asian Wall Street Journal*, 31 August.

[7] Bowman, Jo (2001), "Hundreds fleeced in 'discount' scheme", *South China Morning Post*, 25 March.

[8] In April 2000, MBF Holdings entered into an agreement to sell its stake in MBF Discount Card (HK) Ltd to Online Credit Ltd. for 440,000 Ringgit (approximately HK$900,000).

[9] Octopus Cards Ltd. was 57 percent owned by Hong Kong's Mass Transit Railway (MTR).

[10] By contrast, the Countdown discount card decals did not display the discount or benefit. It was up to the consumer to find out through the catalogue, or by enquiring with the merchant.

[11] Specifically, Gibran aimed to target companies with more than 500 employees.

24

PGL

The Entrepreneur in China's Logistics Industry

BENJAMIN YEN AND PHOEBE HO

PART I: BACKGROUND AND ISSUES

Introduction

If the United States can ship their oranges and pears to everywhere in the world, why can't China do the same? China has a long history of fruit cultivation and a good quality of fruits. We can export our fruits worldwide. What will this depend on? It depends on an advanced logistics infrastructure and an advanced logistics management system in China.

– Liu Wu, President of PG Logistics Group Co., Ltd.

Liu Wu recalled a piece of recent news when he looked down from his third-floor office in the PG Logistics (PGL) Building on the bustling crowd and the criss-cross of traffic in downtown Guangzhou. In May 2004, the industrial and commercial sectors of South Korea established the Korea-China Retail and Logistics Committee under the auspices of the Korean Chamber of Industry and Commerce, for the purpose of promoting the development of the logistics industry between Korea and China. The committee comprised 42 members from the industrial, commercial and academic sectors. Liu considered that foreign companies would play a proactive role in the development of China's logistics industry. He sensed that there would soon be consolidation and fierce competition in China's logistics market.

On Liu's desk was a construction proposal for the company's logistics base. The company was planning to build large logistics bases in 15 developed cities in China over the following five years. The company had already constructed two logistics bases: one in Suzhou in the Yangtze River Delta and the other in Guangzhou in the Pearl River Delta. Given that the logistics industry was due to be opened up to foreign investors in 2005, Liu wondered whether the company, at its current pace of development, would be able to compete with foreign enterprises. PGL was a privately owned business, and he was concerned that it might be at a disadvantage in terms of management and capital resources when compared with multinational corporations. Even when compared with the traditional State-owned enterprises, the asset value of the company was small. What should PGL do in its next stage of development in the face of the imminent fierce competition? Should it develop on its own or join hands with State-owned enterprises or co-operate with foreign enterprises? What were PGL's strengths and weaknesses compared with its competitors?

The Logistics Industry in China

> China's logistics industry is in its fledgling stage. We lag behind the developed countries in our management by 10 to 20 years. However, I am confident about the development prospects of China's logistics industry, especially the development of privately owned logistics companies. State-owned enterprises have yet to change their mindset completely, and foreign logistics enterprises have to undergo an adaptation period after setting foot in the Chinese market. Meanwhile PGL can always meet the needs of customers and take the lead in the development of the Chinese logistics industry.
>
> – Liu Wu, President of PGL

The Chinese term *wu liu*, meaning "flowing of goods", or the English concept "logistics", was first introduced into China from Japan in the early 1980s. After 20 years of research and development, "logistics" had become a key component of the Chinese economy. The total value of goods transported in China surged from RMB3,000 billion in 1991 to RMB23,300 billion in 2002, an increase of 6.7 times and an average year-on-year increase of 20.4 percent, significantly higher than the 15.4 percent year-on-year rate of economic growth recorded during the same period. In 2003, the value of goods transported had reached RMB29,600 billion. Of the goods transported, industrial products occupied the largest share and recorded the biggest growth. In 2003, they accounted for 84.6 percent of the total value of transported goods.[1] PRC freight mileage rose from 76 billion tonnes/km in 1952 to 4,381 billion tonnes/km in 2000. From 1982 to 2000, freight volume increased by 3.8 times.[2]

Following the opening up and development of the Chinese economy in recent years, there was now a drastic increase in the demand for professional or third-party logistics. As a result, a multitude of third-party logistics companies had mushroomed in the market, including: a) the long-standing PRC State-owned enterprises such as COSCO, SinoTrans, China Post and China Rail Express; b) multinational forwarders such as UPS, TNT and Maersk; and c) domestic companies in China such as PGL and Haier (see Exhibit 1).

The Development of PGL

The Predecessor

"PGL's growth is attributable to the penetration of foreign-funded enterprises," said Li Hengdi, Vice-President of PGL. In 1988, Procter & Gamble (P&G), the US consumer-products giant, set foot in the Chinese market with the establishment of a major production base in Guangdong. As a new entrant, P&G realised that its ability to grab a share in the China market hinged on its ability to deliver its fast-moving consumer goods (FMCG) everywhere in China in a prompt and timely manner.

At that time, still a foreigner to the "logistics" concept, Liu Wu contracted a freight-forwarding station in Guangzhou. Logistics at the time was limited to the dual functions of warehousing and transportation, which were handled by different business entities, meaning that a customer had to entrust its goods with different parties for warehousing and transport services. This was time-consuming, and cargoes could easily be left unattended and exposed to damage. Meanwhile, Liu's forwarding station provided its customers with 24-hour, one-stop services by arranging both cargo storage and transport services. This was how P&G came to PGL.

P&G's first order was to transport four containers from Guangzhou to Shanghai by train. P&G reaffirmed their standards and requirements clearly and repeatedly, while PGL carried out the assignment as meticulously as possible. The company had to go through its operational procedures again and again, even though everyone was already very familiar with them. As freight trains did not operate according to a fixed schedule, PGL had to independently estimate the time needed for transportation. They worked out the arrival time of the goods based on the average running speed of the train, tracked the train's movement one day in advance of their estimated time, and proceeded with loading and unloading accordingly. To ensure the timely arrival of P&G's goods, Liu even flew to Shanghai to carry out checking and supervision personally. Although the first order did not generate any profit for his forwarding station, it was meant to be a test by P&G. PGL passed the test and secured P&G as its first multinational customer. P&G was now assured that their products were in good hands throughout the whole process. In 1994, the PGL Guangzhou Warehousing and Transportation Company was established. From then on, P&G gradually increased its volume of transactions with PGL, and for a time, even relied on PGL for all of its rail transport needs.

Internal Management Structure

At the beginning, we had to conduct our internal management in strict compliance with P&G's requirements This explains why our branches were established before the head office. To meet P&G's requirements, we set up four branches in Chengdu, Beijing, Shanghai and Guangzhou at that time.

– Liu Wu

PGL was a small set-up on inception, and it had to rent its fleet of trucks and warehouses. Under the auspices of P&G, and with its assistance, PGL began to build up its own logistics services regulatory system. In 1996, using the Good Manufactory Practice (GMP, a quality management system promulgated by the US Food and Drug Administration) as a blueprint, and adhering to the 14 key requirements of GMP (see Exhibit 2), PGL formulated its own serialised quality management system and incorporated the specific standards and the permitted time for each key requirement into a "Quality Control Manual" for full implementation. At PGL's head office, a quality control department was set up to implement the Quality Control Manual. Each and every operational procedure was subject to quality control and tracking from the very first step to ensure stability, consistency and reliability.[3] For example, the moment an order was placed, there were specific rules for each staff member to follow: each staff member was required to document his work in writing for inspection by supervisors, and there were also clear-cut provisions on warehousing, transportation time and average damage rate.

At first, PGL was unable to meet P&G's requirements all the time. P&G had to provide comprehensive training for PGL so as to raise its service standards. As a result, PGL formulated its Key Program Indicators (KPI) for the tracking and objective management of its service categories. Thanks to the GMP and KPI for ongoing service enhancement, PGL enjoyed an expanding customer base and a surge in orders. The number of its employees rose from 12 when it was first established to 498 in 1999 (see Exhibit 3). Initially, PGL managed its branch companies mainly by telephone and facsimile. All orders and invoices from customers had to be confirmed by telephone or fax. Not only was this time-consuming, it was also difficult to ensure that information was communicated accurately between branch companies.

Over time, P&G became more demanding of PGL's services. P&G wanted to know the exact status of its goods, such as the present location, how many items were delivered to customers, the damage rate and so on. PGL had previously managed to meet all of P&G's demands, but now the information it fed to P&G was either inaccurate or not timely enough. As a result, P&G switched part of its orders to other companies, and the exclusive distribution contract for nationwide rail transport was about to expire. It was not until then that PGL realised the importance of an effective information management system.

Information Management System

> The application of information technology is a major factor for PGL to move on to what it is today.
>
> – Li Hengdi, Vice-President of PGL

> We adopt a two-pronged approach to developing our information system, through development on our own and purchase from external sources. Every step of our development aims to satisfy the demands of our customers and the needs of the enterprise instead of running after the fashionable.
>
> – Richard Gu, Assistant to the Information Controller of PGL

As P&G increased its requirements from punctual, accurate and reliable delivery to the provision of dynamic, accurate and timely information about the status of goods, inventory levels and damage rate, PGL realised that it was facing problems of low efficiency, high costs and inaccurate information. These problems were difficult to solve with manpower alone, and PGL started to invest in its information network technology.

Generally speaking, a company had three options when introducing an IT system: first, it could outsource to a professional IT company for the development of a tailor-made system; second, it could develop its own system with the enterprise's in-house IT capacity; and third, it could purchase an off-the-shelf product to meet its IT needs. At that time, PGL was small in scale and limited in funds and IT expertise, so the second and third options were out of the question.

As a first step, PGL connected all its branch companies with Internet/Intranet to improve internal communication. Even the establishment of a simple Intranet was a substantial investment for PGL then. To computerise its entire operational procedures, the company made a total investment of RMB100,000 in hardware and RMB100,000 in software. The hardware was installed internally while the software was contracted out. Thus PGL's IT system was finally launched, with both office automation and business flow computerisation in the head office, in all branches and over 40 operation points. Online real-time tracking of key logistics information about warehousing and transport were also made available. Despite the successful establishment of the IT system, many staff members were emotionally resistant to the system because of they were unfamiliar with it. They still clung to their manual approach. Liu saw the problem and arranged a training seminar for his staff. At the seminar, he related his own experience: "I used to know little about computers, but now I log in every day to check out new knowledge and information. It is up to you whether you should learn something new."

Gradually the staff became familiar with the system and even offered many suggestions for improvement. One of the suggestions was that they wanted the system to produce automated reports for their work functions. As the existing system required multiple steps to achieve the desired result, PGL developed its own system for generating automatic reports. After PGL's information system started operations in May 1998, PGL's business turnover increased by 40 percent, its operation points doubled, the number of customers increased four times and the level of customer satisfaction increased. The use of IT became one of PGL's strong selling points. After P&G, Philips became another of PGL's major customers thanks to the company's use of computer-aided methods such as database and network transmission to verify, categorise and collate information.

In 1999, PGL Warehousing and Transportation Company was renamed the PGL Logistics Group. At the next stage, the company's strategy aimed at strengthening its marketing efforts to attract more customers and increasing the compatibility with customers' IT systems in order to raise its service standard. In 2000, PGL established a VPN-based eXchange Data Interface (XDI) and adopted XML technology to further enhance electronic data interchange with customers. This was designed to enable a seamless exchange and connection with customer data and, in turn, provide tailor-made logistics information for individual customers.

After 2002, PGL aimed to transform itself from a mere third-party logistics company into a one-stop solution provider and executor of supply chain and logistics services. In 2003, PGL started developing the Total Order Management (TOM) system on its own to support the entire order flow, and to attain an order-based, highly efficient and close-ended management system. In the same year, PGL collaborated with IBM to introduce the Warehouse Management System (WMS).

The implementation of PGL's IT system was not entirely smooth sailing. As Richard Gu pointed out:

In fact, PGL attempted to install a system like TQM in 1999. However, the system eventually failed because none of the departments needed this and there was also a problem with technology selection. In selecting a supplier for the WMS system, we picked the one who offered the most reasonable price but eventually found that the supplier could not live up to our expectation in system implementation. We went down not a few crooked roads.

The goal of PGL's information management system was to implement the ERP system across the company from 2004 to 2006 onwards. To cope with this project implementation, PGL's IT department had also grown from four members in 2000 to 17 in 2004. By 2004 they were responsible not only for performing in-house system development and maintenance, but also for helping customers that were relatively weak in IT capability to build up their own information systems. Despite the heavy workload, Richard Gu admitted that a team of 17 was already sizeable and that further expansion would probably pose management difficulties.

Customer Service Orientation

We provide door-to-door services for our customers. All our branch companies do the same to ensure the prompt delivery and proper receipt of the goods. We assess the performance of our branches on the basis of the KPI. In 2003, our inventory accuracy rate was 100 percent, our customer satisfaction rate 96 percent, and our damage rate as low as 0.012 percent.

– Li Hengdi, Vice-President of PGL

The professional services rendered by PGL, especially its low damage rate, have contributed greatly to the Chinese companies' efforts in cutting the overall costs of logistics. Damage rate was a particularly important factor in the logistics industry. In respect to fast-moving consumer goods, the average damage rate in China was 5 percent, but in developed countries it was "far below 1 percent".[4]

With regards to systems integration, PGL was able to offer a variety of solutions as the company's IT department continued to gain valuable experience in the ongoing development and perfection of its information system. For customers that were weak in IT, PGL would be asked to help them set up their own information systems. For customers with strong IT capabilities, PGL would develop a set of tailor-made software for data exchange. In other instances, customers would grant PGL limited access to their terminal systems, in which case PGL would function as a systems operator.

Currently, PGL had more than 80 customers, most of which were multinational companies. Few domestic companies, on the other hand, had realised the importance of logistics, as indicated by a survey by China Storage Association, showing that about 50 percent of the Chinese companies considered that the influence of logistics on their operation was limited.[5] Meanwhile, the majority of the companies surveyed had their own transport and warehousing departments. According to an investigation carried out by the China Storage Association in 2001, third-party logistics companies dealt with just 18 percent of the incoming goods for transportation. As to outgoing goods for transportation, 59.8 percent was jointly dealt with by third-party logistics companies, while only 16.1 percent was dealt with by a single third party on its own.[6]

The Future of PGL

> Regarding our future development, we will continue to enlarge our logistics base, integrate both the upstream and downstream resources, and establish a platform for sharing these resources.
>
> – Liu Wu, President of PGL

Following the commercial operation of the Suzhou international logistics base (serving the Shanghai Municipality and neighbouring provinces, including Anhui, Jiangsu and Zhejiang) in 2002, PGL's integrated logistics base at Huangpu District in Guangzhou (serving Guangzhou and nearby cities, including Shenzhen) was also put into use in June 2003, upon completion of Phase 1 of its construction. PGL planned to set up as many as 15 logistics bases in 15 developed cities around the country. The company started its business in rail transport, and by early 2004, after years of development, 90 percent of its business came from road transport, while rail and sea transport accounted for 8 percent and 2 percent respectively.[7] In terms of the composition of its fleet, PGL owned over 40 trucks for regional delivery in South China, and chartered trucks for thoroughfare transport and distribution in other parts of the country.

Meanwhile, the Chinese government had attached great importance to the development of logistics. In its Tenth Five-Year plan, the Government stated that China would "develop a service sector that meets the needs of the production industry and introduce new business models and technologies, by promoting chain operation, logistics distribution, agency system and multi-modal transportation that aim at reforming and upgrading the traditional circulation industry, transport industry and postal services."[8]

The logistics industry in China was at a fledgling stage, with a highly fragmented market. It was reported that third-party logistics in China accounted for only 2 percent of the total goods transported in China in 2001, much lower than the US (8 percent) and Europe (10 percent).[9] As competition intensified and the logistics industry underwent consolidation, more and more Chinese companies began to meet the service standards set by multinational companies. Now PGL was facing an increasing number of competitors in various regions. Domestically, initiating price wars was a favourite tactic employed by most Chinese companies, and it was likely that this would hamper PGL's profitability in the long run (see Exhibit 1). In addition to competition from State-owned enterprises with abundant assets and extensive networks, and from local privately owned companies with flexible operations, PGL also had to compete with the well-managed, cash-rich international conglomerates. Given such keen competition, how could the company attract and retain its customers without compromising the profitability it needed to fuel its ongoing development? PGL's growth was attributed to the businesses from multinational companies. As the global logistics partners of these multinational customers set foot in the China market, how could PGL retain these foreign customers and simultaneously recruit more domestic customers? Now that the company had put in place an advanced information management system and a comprehensive logistics infrastructure for future development, what should its next sensible move be?

PART II: LESSONS LEARNED

Key Questions

In terms of the life cycle of an enterprise, describe the progression of PGL from its inception to the current stage. Discuss the significant issues PGL faced in this progression, and explain how these are relevant to managing entrepreneurial growth.

The traditional life cycle of an enterprise can be depicted in five stages. These stages include new-venture development, start-up activities, growth, stabilisation, and innovation or decline.[10]

New Venture Development: 1988–1994

PGL entered the New Venture Development stage when Liu Wu established the first freight-forwarding station in Guangzhou in 1988. Liu saw an opportunity to provide one-stop storage and transport services for the US consumer product giant P&G as it sought to set foot in the China market. Creativity, assessment and networking were the crucial factors for the initial strategy formation at this stage. Liu demonstrated his entrepreneurial leadership in setting the vision, philosophy, scope and direction of the company at this stage. His personal inspection, supervision and tracking of P&G's first order from Guangzhou to Shanghai was significant in defining the tone and service standard of the company in the years to come.

Start-up Activities: 1994–1999

This was the period during which PGL carried out the foundation work required for executing and realising the entrepreneurial vision initially set by Liu. Strategic and operational planning steps were designed to identify the firm's competitive advantage, while marketing and financial considerations were paramount during this stage. Based on the standard and requirements of its first major customer, P&G, the company institutionalised its internal management structure, established its first information management system, and built a customer service orientation into its modus operandi. Securing the P&G account and using it as an anchor customer was a milestone achievement for the company at this stage, as it launched its venture and prepare itself for further growth.

Venture Growth: 1999–2004

The year 1999 marked the beginning of the venture growth stage of the company, as PGL Warehousing and Transportation Company was renamed PGL Logistics Group to indicate the expansion of both its business strategy and its scope. This stage had called for a reformulation of strategies as the industry opened up and competition intensified. PGL first realised the administrative and competitive challenges it faced when P&G, its anchor customer, switched part of its orders to other companies. With high business growth, newer and more dominant problems had surfaced, requiring the company to develop a different set of skills to cope with the managerial aspects of the business while maintaining its entrepreneurial perspective.

Business Stabilisation: 2004–2009

In 2004, PGL is entering the Business Stabilisation stage as it plans to execute its five-year plan to build a comprehensive logistics base in 15 developed cities in China. This stage is characterised by a rapidly maturing industry (e.g., the Chinese government's initiative to reform and upgrade the traditional circulation, transport and postal services), increased competition (e.g., potential price wars with other domestic players), commoditisation of product/service offerings (e.g., companies copying PGL's business models), market saturation and proliferation of market entrants (e.g., state-owned enterprises and multinational conglomerates). As sales begin to stabilise, the company needs to identify its growth strategy for the next few years. This is a crucial stage, as the company will either head towards greater profitability or decline to failure, and ongoing innovation is critical to future success.

Using PGL as an example, discuss the decision-making process of an enterprise emerging from the growth stage towards business stabilisation. What major decisions does PGL face at this transition, and how can it restructure itself to achieve long term profitability?

PGL can be classified as a high-growth enterprise, having grown from a single-owner-driven company with 12 employees in 1994 to 1,105 employees in 2004 — it can be called a "gazelle".[11] The current transition from Venture Growth to Business Stabilisation is a dramatic one as the company faces decisions from a number of perspectives. Table 1 summarises the decision-making characteristics in the various stages of the enterprise's life cycle, showing the transition an enterprise has to go through to successfully navigate its growth journey.

Table 1   Decision-Making Characteristics and Stage of Growth[12]

	Early Stage(s)	Growth Stage	Later Stage(s)
Primary Focus	• Product business definition • Acquisition of resources • Development of market position	• Volume production • Market share • Viability	• Cost control • Profitability • Future growth opportunity
Decision-Making Characteristics	• Informal • Centralised • Non-specialised • Short time horizon	• Transitional	• Formal • Decentralised • Specialised • Long and short time horizon

During PGL's early development stages, the primary business focus was to define its service offering to P&G, its first major multinational customer, and acquiring the resources to deliver the services required. Decision-making was informal and centralised, as Liu was the mastermind behind all the logistics planning, train schedule calculation and cargo inspection and delivery. It was a one-off operation as the goal of the endeavour was to satisfactorily fulfil the first order from P&G and pave the way for future business. At these initial stages, the company was unable to define the tasks regarding technology or market development due to the uncertainty levels in the external business environment. Its first investment in an IT system was a conservative one, given the urgent need for a systematic information management and order tracking system. There was little structure in terms of job specialisation, rules or formality. Liu, the business owner, was the central decision-maker, plan-executor and communicator as he conducted user-training seminars himself in the implementation of the IT system.

In 2004, with over 1,000 employees, 8 branch offices and 32 operation points all over China, the company needed to establish a management structure with formality, decentralised decision-making, specialisation in roles and responsibilities, and a long term planning horizon to effectively and efficiently manage its growth and profitability. This transition is particularly crucial at the tail end of its growth stage as the company faces increased challenges from both internal fronts (staff orientation, quality control, delegation of responsibilities, etc) and external fronts (intense competition, government initiatives, etc).

To address the many challenges of rapid growth, some methodologies exist for handling decision-making during the transition. One method focuses on the use of external resources through networking.[13] The aim is to gain additional decision-making capabilities and resource availabilities beyond those under the enterprise's direct control. The collaboration with IBM in developing the Warehouse Management System (WMS) is an example of employing networking to build extra-organisational capabilities. Starting in 1997, Liu had the idea of forming an alliance for collaboration with other logistics service providers, developing a platform for sharing information and integrating upstream and downstream resources in the industry value chain. This concept, however, has proven to be difficult to implement in the traditional Chinese culture. Going forward, the company may also consider using outside consulting assistance to help with administrative and planning matters.

Another method to deal with decisions in an enterprise's growth stage is responsibility charting.[14] This is a group decision-making process involving three major components: decisions, roles and types of participation. These components are combined to form a matrix so that each responsibility can be charted and analysed to identify the best response in each specific decision. The method is effective in clarifying roles and responsibilities, particularly with the influx of new management in times of rapid growth.

Considering the rapid changes in the logistics industry in China, how should PGL conduct an industry analysis as a basis to formulate its future business strategy?

Evaluation of the industry environment is a crucial step in the overall strategy formation of a new venture. One common tool for such evaluation is the SWOT analysis, a critical assessment of the firm's strengths, weaknesses, opportunities and threats. The input into the analysis consists of both macro-environment factors (demographic, economic, technological, political-legal and social-cultural) and micro-environment factors (customers, competitors, distributors, suppliers and stakeholders), with both sets of factors contributing to the profitability of the firm. A sample SWOT analysis for PGL in its current business transition is shown in Table 2.

Conclusion

Business ventures experience the most drastic transition as they emerge from the venture growth stage to achieve business stabilisation. PGL, considered a high-growth enterprise in China's fledging logistics industry, has gained a significant first-mover advantage after

Table 2 SWOT Analysis of PGL in 2004

Strengths	Weaknesses
- Strong, visionary leader committed to the industry and company growth - Entrepreneurial mind-set and an organisation with readiness for innovation and change - First-mover advantage in securing customers and scale in the fledging stage of the industry (ahead of the SOEs in terms of service quality and management modernisation, and ahead of foreign players in local customer and physical network)	- A family business, so limited funding and management experience to compete with giant State-owned and multinational enterprises - Limited capital and network compared with State-owned enterprises (e.g., China Rail Express and China Merchants, which have extensive assets and network coverage in sea, road and rail transport) - Management/technology infrastructure is too immature to accommodate the rapid organisational growth
Opportunities	Threats
- High industry growth as the Government has made the industry the focal point of its Tenth Five-Year Plan - WTO entry, increased international trade, and SOE privatisation will drive increased logistics outsourcing to third-party service providers - Opportunity to drive industry consolidation by alliances with foreign conglomerates/small local players in the current fragmented industry, thus establishing and reinforcing its leadership role	- Potential price wars with local privately owned players in competition for market share - Aggressive international conglomerates entering the market, with skills and experience in modern logistics and global network - Increased foreign/local joint-venture competitors with complementary skill sets and capabilities - Pressure to IPO and/or joint-venture partnership with foreign players; risk of losing entrepreneurial management and control

securing a stable customer base and operational scale. The company is poised to gain further leadership as the industry is expected to undergo exponential growth in the next few years. However, the transition from a single-owner-driven venture to an established organisation is a demanding undertaking, as the company faces unprecedented challenges in multiple areas. Liu and his management team need to balance the trade-offs as they face such imminent decisions as:

- Should the company go public to expand its capital and management resources? If so, what are the implications in terms of management, control and the company's ability to stay innovative and entrepreneurial? If not, how can it maintain its competitiveness against the resource-rich State-owned firms, multinational firms and various forms of joint ventures?
- Should the company form joint-venture partnerships with multinational or local firms for further business expansion? Who would be the most compatible partners in light of the company's market positioning and growth aspirations?

– How can the company transform from a one-person, centrally managed firm to one run by a functionally organised and professionally managed team? How can its entrepreneurship characteristics be retained while adapting to an overarching administrative culture?

PGL is a success story showing how a business venture started up and blossomed under the strong and committed leadership of a visionary. With creativity, accurate market assessment and selective networking, the company has successful navigated through the initial stages of its enterprise life cycle. Whether the company can remain a significant player in China's much coveted logistics industry will depend on its ability to deal with the managerial change associated with its entrepreneurship growth.

1   Xinhua News, http://news3.xinhuanet.com/fortune/2004-07/06/content_1578314.htm/, accessed 28 July 2004.
2   Luo, Y. and Findlay, C. (2002), *Logistics in China: Implications of Accession to the WTO*, http://siteresources.worldbank.org/INTRANETTRADE/Resources/WBI-Training/logisticsLuoFindlayCN.pdf/.
3   http://www.156net.com/Carry3/eg07.htm/, accessed 28 July 2004.
4   EIU.com (December 1999), *China Hand*, http://www.eiu.com/, accessed 28 July 2004.
5   The China Storage Association (2001), "Report on China's Industry Development C Logistics Report 2003", Investigation Report 2001, http://gov.finance.sina.com.cn/zsyz/2004-06-28/13136.html/, accessed 28 July 2004.
6   Luo and Findley.
7   Of the road transport, highway transport accounted for 32 percent, regional distribution 47 percent and municipal distribution 32 percent.
8   *Junmin liangyong iishu yu chanpin* [Military and Civil Technology and Products Website] (2001), http://www.space.cetin.net.cn/docs/mp0102/mp010217.htm/, accessed 28 July 2004.
9   Ho, H. and Lim, C. (2001), "China Logistics", *Morgan Stanley Equity Research Asia Pacific*, 5 October 2001.
10 Kuratko, D. and Hodgetts, R. (1998), *Entrepreneurship — A Contemporary Approach*, Fourth Edition, Fort Worth: Dryden Press, pp. 493.
11 Moreno, A. and Casillas, J. (2003), "High-Growth Enterprises (Gazelles): A Conceptual Framework", http://www.sses.com/public/events/euram/complete_tracks/strategies_change_innovation/moreno_casillas.pdf/, accessed September 2004.
12 Gilmore, T. and Kazanjian, R. (1989), "Clarifying Decision Making in High Growth Ventures: The Use of Responsibility Charting", *Journal of Business Venturing* (January), p. 71.
13 Jarillo, J. (1989), "Enterpreneurship and Growth: The Strategic Use of External Resources", *Journal of Business Venturing* (March), pp. 133–177.
14 Gilmore and Kazanjian, pp. 69–83.

Exhibit 1   Major Logistics Companies in China

Names		Summary
State-owned enterprises	China Rail Express	1. Mainly providing passenger and cargo transport by train; also providing nationwide, network-based and door-to-door courier delivery service; branch organisations in 200 cities and 1,000 vehicles; taking up 1/6 of the market share in domestic postal and package delivery 2. Rail transport; express courier service 3. Principal location of business: China
	China Merchants	1. Substantial assets, including three major ports in the western harbour district of Shenzhen, 41 ships and 300 vehicles; over 30 subsidiaries and branches. 2. Sea and road transport 3. Principal location of business: International
	China Post	1. Strong network built on its post offices throughout the country; operating in 2,000 cities; accounting for 50 percent of the domestic courier service sector; 2. Mainly via road transport; express postal service 3. Principal location of business: China
	COSCO	1. A multinational corporation with 600 modernised merchant ships of around 3000 deadweight tonnes, which annual volume of over 200 million tonnes. As a global corporation focusing on shipping and logistics, COSCO employs about 70,000 staff members in nearly 1,000 member companies all over the world 2. Mainly via sea transport; ship agency; containers 3. Principal location of business: International
International companies	UPS	1. UPS operates 6 cargo flights per week between Shanghai and the US. On this basis, the company plans to increase the number of cargo flights to 12, and plans to set up a transhipment centre in Shanghai in 2007. Its PRC export volume posted a 60 percent surge in the first quarter of 2004, and 70 percent in the second quarter compared with the same period in 2003. 2. Air freight; express delivery
	Fedex	1. Fedex plans to expand its PRC coverage by 100 cities and establish an operations centre in China. China is the fastest growing market in Fedex's global courier business. In the second quarter 2004, Fedex's China business recorded 50 percent growth in volume and a 47% growth in net profit compared with the same period in 2003. 2. Air freight; express delivery
	APL	1. 39 branches and offices in China, with over 40 percent of its annual turnover from the Greater China Region (mainland China, Taiwan and Hong Kong) 2. Shipping; container
	DHL	1. Over 4,700 staff members in 225 offices throughout China, along with four port operation centres, 1,100 operation vehicles and service coverage in 318 cities. In China, DHL is about to set up its third Express Logistics Centre (ELC) and sixth Strategic Parts Centre (SPC). DHL has almost 40 percent of the market share in China's express delivery 2. Shipping, land transport, air freight; express delivery
	TNT	1. Service coverage exceeding 2,000 locations in more than 200 cities in China 2. Land transport, air freight 3. Express delivery

New entrants in China	Haier	1. Built on Haier's internal logistics structure; 16,000 trucks and 42 large regional distribution centres 2. Motor transport

Sources: http://www.cre.cn; http://www.ems.com.cn; http://www.cosco.com.cn; http://www.chinamerchants-logistics.com; http://www.haier.com; http://www.cn.dhl.com; http://www.tnt.com (accessed 28 July 2004).

Exhibit 2   PGL: GMP Management Elements

Key Elements	Description
KE1	Leadership
KE2	Training
KE3	Design, Construction & Installation
KE4	Formula cards, Specifications & Standards
KE5	Written Procedures
KE6	Validity Authentication
KE7	Hygiene, Pest control, Sterilisation & Maintenance
KE8	Storage & Management of Finished Products
KE9	Distribution & Control of Semi- & Finished Goods
KE10	Recording
KE11	Self-improvement System
KE12	Complaints
KE13	Tracking & Enhancement of Quality System Outcome
KE14	Obligations of Contactors

Source: PGL.

25

Jewellworld.com
Leading Web-based IT Development in the Jewellery Industry

BENNETT YIM AND ANDREW LEE

PART I: BACKGROUND AND ISSUES

Introduction

In mid-2004, Jewellworld.com was one of the few surviving jewellery portals, if not the only such portal, in Hong Kong. It provided both business-to-business (B2B) and business-to-consumer (B2C) services through its Website www.jewellworld.com. Being a company in its own right, Jewellworld.com was managed and operated with only four staff in Hong Kong and seven in mainland China. Yet, its service offerings expanded continually in both its B2B and B2C portals. It turned profitable in April 2003, and this small subsidiary of Luk Fook seemed relentless in its quest to meet its customers' needs.

The Founding of Jewellworld.com

Jewellworld.com was established by William Wong in April 2000, chairman and chief executive of Luk Fook Jewellery. Wong was a passionate, self-taught IT professional. As a youngster working at his family's own small jewellery store, he and his brother developed their own point-of-sale (POS) system using BASIC in the DOS environment. When the POS system proved to work very well for their family shop, they decided to market it to other jewellery shops, and they landed quite a few customers. When Wong started Luk Fook Jewellery, some of those customers became his partners. And an improved version of the original POS system had been in use at Luk Fook ever since.

> Luk Fook launches B2B and B2C Web site.
>
> – Jewellery News Asia[1]

When Wong launched the www.jewellworld.com Website, the goal was to take advantage of the potential business opportunity presented by the Internet. Jewellworld.com was a non-wholly owned subsidiary of Luk Fook Holdings (International) Limited, based at the headquarters of Luk Fook. From its inception, the Website, available in both traditional and simplified Chinese, consisted of both the business-to-business (B2B) and the business-to-consumers (B2C) trading platforms. The B2B platform was designed to bring buyers and sellers together, allowing sellers to show their jewellery and buyers to search for their desired products online. The B2C platform allowed consumers to view Jewellworld.com's online selection and to place orders online.

The Development of the B2B Platform

The original vision of Jewellworld.com's B2B platform was for it to be a virtual trade show on the Internet, encompassing all the functions of a jewellery exhibition, i.e., meeting potential business partners, gathering business contacts, viewing products and placing orders. It also provided additional Web-based functions such as a chat room, a message board, Web-mail and even recruitment news.

The Basic Service

Jewellworld.com's B2B services were provided on a membership basis. When it was launched in July 2001, it had an initial membership of about 30. Most of these members were related to Luk Fook in some way, and could be broadly classified into three groups: retailers, wholesalers, and manufacturers. Perhaps the most important function of Jewellworld.com was the shopping basket, which enabled sellers to show their products online for buyers to sample, and buyers to contact sellers through the information provided on the Website or even to place their orders online if they so chose.

According to Joseph Lee, marketing manager of Jewellworld.com, for products that were fairly standard and mature, it was possible for buyers to make the purchase decision online without having to see the actual product. "Items of jewellery such as traditional Chinese style gold bracelets, gold or platinum rings, and gold ornaments, are so mature that they can be selected based on a good quality digital picture and supporting product information," said Lee.

Service Evolution

> The jewellery industry in Hong Kong is very traditional. During the initial phase, less than half of the B2B members were active users. Some had never had a computer until they joined Jewellworld.com. Even when they have one, some don't want to touch it. For others, they want basic functions. So, we need to proactively find ways to help them make use of the technology, while at the same time look for more revenue streams for Jewellworld.com.
>
> – Derek Ling, Project Manager, Jewellworld.com

From its early days, it was apparent that many of the B2B members were not computer-literate. Indeed, only about half of the initial members were avid users of the B2B platform. Some had never owned a computer before. They did not want to touch one and did not even want to learn how to use one. In order for Jewellworld.com to become profitable, it had to find ways to help its customer base and to grow it. It needed to look for additional revenue streams.

First, as a value-added service, Jewellworld.com advised its members about computer and electronic hardware and software purchases, and also provided technical support. At the same time, it assisted some members to take digital pictures of their jewellery items and upload the pictures onto their shopping baskets.

For other members, the shopping basket function was too complicated, and they simply wanted to upload digital pictures of their products onto the Web easily, for other branches or potential buyers to view. In response, Jewellworld.com developed a service called "Photo Courier". As Derek Ling, project manager of Jewellworld.com, put it, "It is a simple three-step process."

1. Put the digital pictures onto the computer.
2. Log on to the B2B portal.
3. Select and post the pictures to a bulletin board.

The system would then generate a number for each picture. The member then simply needed to inform the interested party — perhaps a potential buyer or another retail branch — of the Web address and the picture number, and the interested party could view the product on the Internet. Ling commented, "It was a very basic function, but the take up rate was very good. We also advise them on the digital camera and provide them with a light box so that they can take digital pictures of reasonable quality." Jewellworld.com would police the bulletin board regularly to ensure that only relevant pictures were posted, and would purge the board every few days.

However, this was still not good enough for some members, because they believed that design was the only competitive advantage they had, given the keen competition in the industry, and they did not want their designs to be copied too quickly by others. Even though, in their respective shopping baskets, they could restrict access to selected company or companies, they still did not feel secure. To cater to this need, Jewellworld.com provided an appropriate Web-conferencing tool, so that members could conduct Web-conferencing with a known party via the Internet, and show digital pictures of their designs real-time. (Typical Web-conferencing solutions with Web-cam would not work, because the resolution of the Web-cam was too granular.) To further assist its members, additional functionalities such as basic catalogue-printing or a digital record-keeping were also provided.

Since they could do Web-conferencing, some members then wondered whether they could use similar technology to monitor their facilities/stores? Jewellworld.com therefore came up with another service — a Web-based security surveillance system. From camera selection, to camera location and system set-up, Jewellworld.com offered to guide its customers every step of the way. Unlike CCTV (closed-circuit TV) or other surveillance systems where the video was viewed real time or recorded on tapes, this system stored the video digitally onto a server and allowed customers to view it anywhere, any time, so long as they had access to the Internet.

In 2002, Luk Fook wanted to streamline and standardise the procurement process of all its branches in Hong Kong. Jewellworld.com was selected as the platform to perform the procurement functions for, first, gold jewellery, and then, diamonds. At a later stage, the B2B portal also acted as a diamond inventory system for all Luk Fook jewellery branches in Hong Kong. For Luk Fook's licensees in mainland China, Jewellworld.com's B2B services were bundled as part of the total package.

B2B Services in 2004

By April 2003, Jewellworld.com broke even, and by 2004, it had evolved from a mere B2B portal into an Internet-technology consultancy specialising in the jewellery industry. Its membership grew to 250, consisting of retailers, wholesalers and manufacturers from the jewellery industry, as well as Luk Fook's licensees in mainland China and providers of peripheral services, such as security and renovation services. Its services ranged from the B2B trading portal to Web-based training, Web-based security surveillance systems, official Websites for jewellery expos and so on.

The Development of the B2C Platform

In the early phase of Jewellworld.com, its B2C platform served two major functions: first, it showcased jewellery under the Luk Fook brand, and second, it provided a platform for other retailers to sell directly to consumers.[2] As Wong put it, since selling jewellery online reduced overhead costs significantly, prices could come down accordingly.[3] While the need for the second function eventually subsided, it was felt that the proposition of selling directly online was still plausible.

The B2C portal was re-launched in December 2002. The key focus was on selling discounted jewellery online. After browsing through the online selection, consumers could place their orders online. Jewellworld.com staff would then call the consumer to confirm the order, finalise the payment method and arrange for pick-up or delivery. Local delivery or pickup was guaranteed within three days of order confirmation. Customers could also choose to visit the Jewellworld.com office, if they preferred to see the jewellery.

The target market of the B2C portal mainly consisted of the younger generation, who had access to the Internet and had some disposable income. Hence, Jewellworld.com's jewellery selection was mostly within the price range of HK$1,500 to $3,000, but tended to be trendy and fashionable. Promotional campaigns with credit-card companies or university organisations, and advertisements in local magazines and popular Websites were among the channels employed to reach out to potential customers.

Initially, sales were only recorded when there were active advertising campaigns running. At other times, sales could be lacklustre. Later, however, sales were recorded even when there were no active advertising campaigns running, and total sales had been increasing gradually. While most of the sales were generated from new customers, about 10% to 20% came from repeat customers. Another phenomenon was purchases by overseas Chinese, which accounted for about 20% to 30% of total sales. "They place their orders overseas, and want them delivered either in Hong Kong or overseas," said Ling, adding that "this is certainly a potential market that we should look at exploring."

The Discount Model

According to Ling, the model that Jewellworld.com operated was different from that of the US online jewellery retailers in a number of ways. First, Jewellworld.com operated on a discount model with a limited selection, ie, fewer than 1,000 items. Nonetheless, Ling was confident that it would be extremely difficult for any retail shop on the street to match the discount they offered. On the other hand, online retailers in the US did not necessarily compete on price. Instead, they differentiated themselves by providing customisation. For example, consumers could design their own engagement rings online by selecting from a wide variety of diamonds and other gem stones, and from a wide variety of settings.

Second, unlike its US counterparts, Jewellworld.com did not accept payment online. Ling reckoned that consumers in Hong Kong were not comfortable with disclosing their credit card details online, but felt safer doing so over the phone. From Jewellworld.com's perspective, order confirmation also allowed them to verify the identity of the customer and the delivery address, and this procedure substantially reduced the risk of fraud.

Third, online retailers in the US typically offered a 30-day money-back-guarantee. However, it was not feasible for Jewellworld.com to do so at that point. For one thing, the profit margin for discounted jewellery was already very low. With a small sales volume, the risk exposure for Jewellworld.com was too high. For another, to offer a money-back-guarantee, additional manpower would be required to inspect the returned jewellery, and this was not something that Jewellworld.com could afford.

The B2C Portal in 2004

By 2004, the B2C portal had had over 3,500 customers.[4] Its selection revolved mainly around 18K pendants, necklaces and rings, mostly within the price range of HK$1,500 to HK$4,000. In addition to selling jewellery, flowers were also added to the product bundle. In early 2004, Jewellworld.com ran a special Valentine's Day promotion, bundling jewellery with flowers. And the response was extremely positive. Such flexibility was regarded by Ling as a key competitive advantage of Jewellworld.com.

Leading Web-based IT Development in the Jewellery Industry

> Jewellworld.com aims to be the leading provider of software system, managed network and Interactive e-commerce solutions for jewellery enterprises that need to transform into full-fledged e-business organisations in the PRC.
>
> – Mission of Jewellworld.com

By 2004, Jewellworld.com was no longer just a portal that spanned both the B2B and B2C arenas. It had evolved into an Internet-technology consultancy specialising in the jewellery industry, providing services ranging from a B2B trading portal to eTraining, security surveillance systems, and to diamond inventory management systems, etc. Meanwhile, its B2C business had been improving as well. With its focus on Web expertise and the jewellery industry, Jewellworld.com was ready to take on more opportunities for further development and expansion.

PART II: LESSONS LEARNED

Key Questions

What is the concept behind Jewellworld.com's B2B services? How would you characterise Jewellworld.com's new service development process? What are the key success factors of Jewellworld.com's B2B services?

When Jewellworld.com first launched its B2B services, it had a vision: to make the B2B portal a virtual trade show on the Web where both jewellery suppliers and business buyers anywhere in the world could be linked together using Web technology. Customers could meet potential business partners, gather business contacts, view products and place orders anywhere, anytime, on the Internet. The portal also provided additional Web-based functions such as a chat room, a message board, Web mail, recruitment news, etc.

The new service development process of Jewellworld.com can be characterised as adaptive and evolutionary. Because jewellery industry players in Hong Kong tended to be traditional and not computer-literate, less than 50% of Jewellworld.com's early members were avid users of the services. Jewellworld.com recognised the importance of getting members to use the technology rather than simply selling memberships. First, the company provided assistance to help some members take digital pictures of their jewellery and upload them onto their shopping baskets. But some members wanted a simpler way to show pictures of their designs to potential buyers. So, Jewellworld.com came up with "Photo Courier", a simple three-step process for posting pictures to a bulletin board. Jewellworld. com also continued to respond to changing and ever-demanding customer needs, and developed new services such as Web-conferencing, which allowed known buyers to see new jewellery designs real-time, and Web-based security surveillance systems for monitoring facility/stores real time, etc.

The success of Jewellworld.com can be attributed to a few factors. First, it has a clear vision and customer focus. It is determined to leverage the Internet technology to cater for the specific requirements of the jewellery industry where its expertise lies. Second, it offers unique services that are valued by its target customers: advice on computers and electronic hardware, advice on software purchases, technical support, "Photo Courier," Web-conferencing, Web-based surveillance, procurement, and inventory systems. Third, Jewellworld.com knows that customer participation in service usage is critical, so customer education takes on added importance. This is a common lesson for tech-delivered services where customers are being asked to change their usual behaviour. Finally, Jewellworld.com has been extremely customer-oriented. Most of Jewellworld.com's services are not developed a priori and pushed hard to customers. Instead, they have been developed to respond to customers' needs. Every time a need arises, Jewellworld.com is there to meet it with a solution. So far, Jewellworld.com's value proposition to the traditional jewellery industry has been unparalleled.

What is the business model adopted by Jewellworld.com for its B2C services (i.e., target market, value proposition, competitive advantage, etc.)? What did Jewellworld.com do to meet and overcome the challenges of selling jewellery online?

Jewellworld.com's B2C portal is essentially an online retail business. Its target customer base is limited to those who understand and have access to the Internet, i.e., the younger generation. Generally speaking, this group tends to be fashionable and trendy. They are likely to have some disposal income (though not too much) and are willing to spend it. In order to provide a sound value proposition vis-à-vis competition, Jewellworld.com has made some conscious choices and decisions. First, knowing that its target customers are primarily confined to the younger generation that has a limited disposable income, Jewellworld.com carries jewellery priced mainly between HK$1,500 and HK$4,000 (with most items priced below HK$3,000). It also stresses the much better value for money that it offers in comparison with traditional brick-and-mortar jewellery stores. In terms of designs, it focuses on jewellery that is fashionable and trendy.

Jewellworld.com faces keen competition in the jewellery retail business in Hong Kong because jewellery stores are ubiquitous in Hong Kong. These stores range from small family operations to large chain stores. They typically carry both traditional and fashionable designs, and have a broader product selection than Jewellworld.com. The price range of their goods is much greater and their product assortments have a lot more expensive items than those offered by Jewellworld.com. However, Jewellworld.com has a competitive advantage in that its discounts would be extremely difficult to match by traditional competitors. Its ability to adapt its product range quickly to changing customer needs is also unmatched by the competition.

Selling anything online is not easy — selling jewellery online is especially difficult because jewellery is a relatively big-ticket item, and customers usually prefer to touch and try on items during the purchase process. Jewellworld.com has adopted a set of unique strategies and tactics to meet and overcome some of the challenges of selling jewellery online. First of all, multiple ordering modes are available to consumers — they could place their orders online after browsing through the online product selection. Alternatively, they could choose to visit the Jewellworld.com office, should they prefer to have a look at the jewellery personally. Second, the company has opted not to accept payments online. The reasons are two-fold. Firstly, people in Hong Kong are still not comfortable with disclosing their credit-card information online. Secondly, given Jewellworld.com's small operation and the discount model, the exposure to fraud of accepting online payment is too high. Thirdly, Jewellworld.com focuses its promotional efforts on working with credit-card companies or university organisations, and other offline and online channels that reach out to the younger and Internet-savvy generation. Finally, it even offers package deals that bundle jewellery with flowers for special occasions such as birthday and Valentine's Day; which traditional jewellery stores would not do.

Although it is unclear how viable the B2C portal is as a standalone business, it is clear that Jewellworld.com is well positioned to serve its target customers. The gradual growth in sales is perhaps proof of this. In addition, Jewellworld.com also faces a largely untapped market segment — the overseas Chinese. Nevertheless, tapping into this market segment will require a different marketing strategy, different logistics, and perhaps online payment option and some form of money-back guarantee.

Conclusion

B2B and B2C are undoubtedly two distinct streams of business for Jewellworld.com. For the B2B stream, Jewellworld.com has leveraged its relationship with Luk Fook and has been able to secure a group of captive members, including Luk Fook's branches, its licensees in mainland China, with which Luk Fook has a business relationship. But Jewellworld.com has not rested on its laurels. It continues to attempt to meet customers' needs by leveraging its knowledge and expertise in Web technology and the jewellery industry. This case shows how valuable technology, and in this instance Web technology, can be used positively to change the way business is conducted, even for a traditional industry that is computer-averse. Jewellworld.com's B2C stream represents a completely different set of challenges — sales are irregular, the target customer base is relatively small, and there is strong competition from stores on the streets and in shopping malls. Nevertheless, Jewellworld.com has made a conscious decision to better serve its target segment by selling discounted but fashionable jewellery items, focusing on a specific price range, and minimising exposure to frauds. As the company takes on new challenges, such as the overseas Chinese market, it will have to make more and more choices and decisions. So long as the choices and decisions are based on a sound business rationale and solid business principles, success should be in sight.

---

1   Jewellery News Asia (2001), "Luk Fook Launches B2B and B2C Web site" in *Jewellery New Asia*, February.
2   Jewellery News Asia, "Luk Fook Launches B2B and B2C Web site".
3   *Ming Pao* (2001), "Hi-Tech Weekly", 23 January 2001.
4   *The Economic Daily* (2004) "Luk Fook's Online Jewellery Shop: Online Promotion, Offline Trading", in *IT Week*, 4 February.

26

Hong Kong's Trading Industry
Challenges from Mainland China

MICHAEL J. ENRIGHT AND VINCENT MAK

PART I: BACKGROUND AND ISSUES

Introduction

The import-export trading industry had long been one of the leading industries in Hong Kong. The sector, with about 500,000 people working for 100,000 companies (see Exhibit 1), accounted for roughly 20 percent of Hong Kong's employment and GDP in 2002. However, in the early 2000s, the industry was challenged as there were signs that the Pearl River Delta and Yangtze River Delta regions of mainland China might eventually threaten Hong Kong's position as a major trading centre. Could Hong Kong's multitude of small trading companies continue to thrive? What were their major competitive advantages? And how substantial would these advantages be?

Hong Kong's Trade History in Brief[1]

Hong Kong rapidly developed into a trading port after the Chinese Ching Empire ceded Hong Kong Island to Britain in 1842 as a result of the Opium War. In the early twentieth century, Hong Kong was used mainly as an entrepot in the "triangular trade" between China, India and Britain.

Hong Kong principally relied on the China trade until the Japanese occupation during World War II. After World War II, the establishment of a new communist government in China and the outbreak of the Korean War meant that Hong Kong's dependence on entrepot trade diminished rapidly. The 1951 UN trade embargo on China further slashed trade in Hong Kong's port, forcing the colony to shift its economic focus towards export-oriented manufacturing. Refugees from mainland China provided cheap labour, capital and technical expertise, leading to an era of industrialisation that focused on garments and labour-intensive light manufactured goods.

Export-oriented development continued to dominate in the 1960s, during which time the Hong Kong Trade Development Council was established to support local industries and expand trade. Textile industries thrived, while technology- and capital-intensive industries were also developed. Hong Kong became a leading exporter of electronics, optical goods, clocks and watches. In the 1970s, the development of other export-oriented Asian countries heightened competition in the markets of labour-intensive products as Hong Kong's success drove up its wage rates and costs. Hong Kong imported more cheap goods, food and water from China. Home industries diversified by producing higher-quality electronics and other goods. In addition to legal trade, Hong Kong also became a centre of smuggling traffic because of its thriving free port.

In 1979, economic reform in China began. Special Economic Zones (SEZs) were established, the most notable being Shenzhen, just north of Hong Kong across the border. Hong Kong's traders and manufacturers soon captured the opportunity for new sources of supply provided by the Chinese mainland's vast and inexpensive labour pool. Hong Kong firms began to invest in manufacturing facilities in Guangdong Province — the southern mainland Chinese province that bordered Hong Kong — in droves. As labour-intensive production activities moved to Guangdong in the 1980s, Hong Kong shifted from the manufacturing activities associated with light industrial production to the service activities associated with those same industries. Hong Kong also emerged as an international financial centre and a management centre for foreign multinational firms. Meanwhile, the trend of Hong Kong manufacturers moving their production lines northwards accelerated, and in the ensuing decade Hong Kong investment continued to flow into new industrial zones in mainland China that produced goods for export. Hong Kong businesses contributed the largest portion of foreign investment in southern China's fast-growing Pearl River Delta region (see Exhibit 2), and were pivotal in making the region one of the major engines that drove mainland China's phenomenal economic growth (see Exhibit 3). By the mid-1990s, Hong Kong was the busiest container port in the world and one of the world's largest exporters, although most of its exports were classified as re-exports from mainland China. Hong Kong also remained one of the financial capitals of the world.

After sovereignty passed back to China in 1997, Hong Kong became the Hong Kong Special Administrative Region (HKSAR) and kept its status as a free port and tariff-free zone under the "one country, two systems" arrangement. The Asian financial crisis from 1997 to 1998 was a blow to Hong Kong's economy. Its major trading partners at that time were mainland China and the United States followed by Japan, Taiwan, South Korea and Singapore. The latter regions were victims of the crisis to various degrees, and reduced import demand from them led to a downturn in Hong Kong's exports and re-exports. The economy gradually recovered from 1999 to 2000, only to encounter another slowdown in 2001 brought on by economic problems of the United States and Japan, two of Hong Kong's key trading partners. This dampening in demand was further aggravated by the terrorist attacks on the United States on September 11, 2001, so that weak exports continued into early 2003 (see Exhibit 1). The accession of China to the World Trade Organisation (WTO) in late 2001 was expected to have both positive and negative consequences for Hong Kong.

Despite the economic downturn, by 2003, Hong Kong was the world's tenth-largest trading economy and one the most trade-dependent, with total merchandise trade amounting to US$409 billion — equivalent to 251 percent of GDP — in 2002.

Hong Kong continued to benefit from its position as a gateway between China and the rest of the world. By 2002, mainland China was one of Hong Kong's most important trading partners (see Exhibit 4). China produced one third of the world's suitcases, one quarter of the world's toys, and one eighth of the world's footwear and clothing. Although those products accounted for only about three percent of the products consumed in global markets, China was considered to be on its way to becoming "the world's factory".[2] Hong Kong was an important entrepot for the products from this factory. Nearly 40 percent of mainland China's foreign trade was handled via Hong Kong, and 98 percent of Hong Kong's total re-exports either originated from or were destined for mainland China in 2002.

Given Hong Kong's strategic location, advanced physical infrastrucutre, expertise in conducting international trade and well established legal framework, trading through Hong Kong always provided convenience and certainty. Hong Kong was the world's busiest container port and airport for international airfreight, and was a trading centre performing packaging and integrating functions across a wide spectrum of industries on a regional and global basis.

State of the Trading Industry by 2003

General[3]

By the early 2000s, Hong Kong was a leading sourcing centre in the Asia-Pacific region. More than one in five employed persons in Hong Kong were engaged in import and export trade. The trading sector produced a net output of HK$244.1 billion, or 20 percent of GDP, in 2001. Hong Kong's import and export trading firms were typically small, employing around five people on average (see Exhibit 1). Of the 100,000 firms in the industry, only about 270 had more than 100 employees, so SMEs overwhelmingly dominated the sector. Import-export trade firms accounted for about 35 percent of all SMEs in Hong Kong.[4]

Hong Kong's import and export trading firms were active in sourcing garments, toys, electronic products and other manufactured goods. They carried out three main types of sourcing activities: i) sourcing goods produced in Hong Kong; ii) sourcing goods from around the region for re-exports; and iii) sourcing goods from one country to be shipped directly to a third country without touching Hong Kong ground. The import business of Hong Kong trading firms was generated mainly by the firms' distributing capabilities under the identity of agents or dealers. They usually specialised in one area or products and represented one or more foreign brands. The boundary of their trading map usually included Hong Kong, mainland China (or certain parts of it) or other countries in Asia. The major items being distributed were industrial products such as medical equipment, building materials, machinery, pharmaceuticals, etc.

In most cases, trading firms offered shipping services to their customers, although some customers chose to ship using their own freight forwarders and shippers. Despite the need for speedy shipment of most products, many trading companies had warehousing facilities. For some exporters, especially of durable goods, this allowed them to offer a service to the customer, with the guarantee of certain stock being readily available for shipment. For garment shipment, the general picture was one of temporary storage, for example for faulty products, with the emphasis being on rapid despatch for shipping.

Some trading firms still operated in their traditional activity of matching buyers with sellers. However, such firms were increasingly facing squeezed margins, and there was a trend towards direct dealing between customers and manufacturers. They were thus forced to pare costs to a minimum to survive. Other firms took ownership of the traded goods, assumed the associated risks in finding buyers and arranged for trade finance and freight forwarding. Trading firms also increasingly added value to the services they provided to their customers, including product design and the manufacturing of samples and moulds. In the areas of quality control and production engineering, there was a clear trend towards greater trading company involvement, even though the actual production was still usually sub-contracted.

Trading firms in Hong Kong by 2003 could be divided into three categories:

- Left hand-right hand traders: trading firms that matched sellers and buyers without adding any significant value to the process still dominated the industry in terms of the number of businesses. Those firms were characterised by the conduct of a straight-forward sourcing operation, usually identifying goods produced in the Chinese mainland or Hong Kong, and shipping these generally to Western markets. These firms survived by using the low costs of their suppliers as the source of their competitive advantage as well as their specialist knowledge of the sources of products in the region.
- Traders with some value-added services: many firms had begun to source raw materials for their suppliers and provided finance for these materials. They often used letters of credit from their customers as a guarantee for raising finance for their purchase orders. Other firms developed a sub-contractor relationship with a number of factories, in which they exerted significant control over the management of production, including quality control.
- Traders with sophisticated value-added services: in certain cases, exporting firms added value to their traditional activity to such an extent that it was difficult to maintain the label of exporter. For example, some firms became designers and manufacturers of components for their supplier factories to produce finished goods, which the firms subsequently exported. These firms added value mostly from their design team, and their competitive edge came from their ability to design products that sold well in the target markets.

Export trading firms headquartered in Hong Kong often had sourcing and/or manufacturing operations in low-cost locations on the Chinese mainland, other parts of Asia or beyond. Although there were numerous Japanese, US and European trading companies in Hong Kong, the sector was dominated by indigenous firms. Most of them were family-run businesses and employed traditional ways of doing business.[5] Much trading activity was conducted via postal mail, fax, telephone and personal interaction.

The operations of small and large trading firms were quite different. Both types of firms participated in exporting goods to international destinations, while smaller firms were, in addition, especially strong in selling foreign products into China. In the latter case, they often specialised in one area, say medical equipment, and represented some foreign brands as agents or distributors. Although smaller firms had lower overhead costs than larger companies, they had to do more because of a relative lack of cash reserves. Bigger trading firms were usually strong in sourcing products from the region. They usually had regional or even global sourcing networks and did not specialise in a particular type of product. Important large trading firms in Hong Kong included Li & Fung — the industry leader — and Jebsen & Co.

Hong Kong's Offshore Trade[6]

By the late 1990s, the growth of Hong Kong's re-export trade had slowed down, while offshore trade developed dramatically. Offshore trade, in the context of the present discussion, was a type of international trade in which part of the operation and administration were conducted in Hong Kong, but the goods were either transhipped via Hong Kong or shipped directly without touching Hong Kong ground. The major distinction between Hong Kong's offshore trade and re-export was that for the former, the goods went directly from the suppliers to the destination without going through the customs office of Hong Kong.

The total value of Hong Kong's offshore trades in 1997 was HK$1 trillion, comprising 84.5 percent of the total value of re-exports (see Exhibit 5). In 2000, the value of offshore trade amounted to HK$1.4 trillion, exceeding that of re-exports for the first time. Between 1997 and 2000, offshore trade grew at 10.6 percent per annum, well above the re-export growth rate.

Mainland China, in particular the Pearl River Delta region, was the source of most of this offshore trading, given Hong Kong's proximity and the relocation of Hong Kong's manufacturing bases to the Chinese mainland, especially the Pearl River Delta region.[7] Overall, the expansion of production capability in the manufacturing sector and the availability of related supporting services in the Chinese mainland led to the rapid growth in offshore trade. In particular, the increasing growth of the manufacturing sector and foreign trade in the ex-Guangdong area, especially in the Yangtze River Delta, and the rapid growth in trade supporting services in the Pearl River Delta, contributed largely to the growth in offshore trade. Most trade was conducted offshore in order to reduce transportation costs and to meet customers' preference for direct shipping from the Chinese mainland. As production processes in the Chinese mainland had become more sophisticated and on-site inspection was available, many products no longer required further processing, including final assembly, packaging and quality control procedures, in Hong Kong. The choice between direct shipments and transhipments depended largely on the availability of cost-effective and reliable transport services. The liberalisation of the freight forwarding business, port development and improvements in cargo-handling facilities had enabled more cargo to be shipped directly from the Chinese mainland. Most of Hong Kong's offshore trade was related to low value-added products, while most of the high value-added products, such as jewellery and watches, were still either made in Hong Kong and had some of their final production and packaging processes done in the territory, or were at least re-exported from Hong Kong.

Competition Within the Industry[8]

This was charcterised by long-term, exclusive customer relationships with market-mediated outcomes. Firms tended to focus on different customers or segments, and there was limited direct competition to win customers away from each other. Although it was relatively easy to enter the industry, given the small size of most of the participants, it was often difficult for new entrants to build up the supplier and information network, packaging skills and proven track record required to service a large foreign retailer or importer. Many of the smaller export traders were destined to be niche fillers, holding onto customer relationships for as long as possible. Even among the larger firms, switching costs were high. Only a few export traders could handle very large customers, and a single firm could not deal with large, competing customers easily due to capacity constraints and potential conflicts of interest.

Backward Integration of Retailers and Importers[9]

From the 1990s onwards, some large retailers and importers had set up their own internal sourcing operations, creating a source of external competitive pressure for Hong Kong's export traders.

Cluster Relationships[10]

A notable feature of Hong Kong trading firms was their close involvement in manufacturing activities, even though the actual production was still usually sub-contracted. This development reflected the need for these firms to meet tighter deadlines imposed by shortening production cycles (especially for clothing) and the increasing trend towards smaller batches of more product lines. Trading firms were able to meet these exacting deadlines by transferring production techniques and know-how to their supplier factories, and by becoming involved in solving production bottlenecks.

In fact, Hong Kong's export traders were an integral part of a larger light manufacturing and trading cluster firmly rooted in Hong Kong. These businesses together provided a critical mass of strategic knowledge, manufacturing expertise and information networks for Hong Kong's export traders. They also demanded many of the same support services as the export traders, generating a critical mass of high-quality services in every area needed by this sector (for example trade finance, transportation, communications, insurance services, trade documentation services, advertising, market research, research and development, laboratory testing and product certification, product design and exhibition facilities). There was a positive, two-way dynamic at work. The supporting services generated advantages for local export traders while the latter provided strong and sophisticated demand that drove the service providers forward.

Challenges from the Chinese Mainland

The Pearl River Delta[11]

The Pearl River Delta, a region of Guangdong Province that included Shenzhen, Guangzhou and geographically also Hong Kong and Macau, was one of the major manufacturing regions of China. In the early 1990s, the Chinese mainland part of it (which "Pearl River Delta" is taken to mean in the following discussion) was only a cluster of budding cities, heavily reliant on the investments, technologies and other capital-intensive resources from nearby economies, such as Hong Kong, Taiwan and Japan, where labour and land cost much more than within the Pearl River Delta. By the early 2000s, there were signs that not only would the relocation of production lines to the region continue, but the headquarters of a number of SMEs would also move to there, because of the region's cheap labour, rapidly developing port facilities and vast markets with exploding purchasing power. By 2001, the region boasted a manufacturing industry that was 10 times as large as that of Hong Kong 10 years previously, and a booming tourist industry with a record of 50 million visitors in 2001 alone. It was the major contributor to Guangdong's trade and economy by 2001 (see Exhibit 3), and by that time did not rely on Hong Kong for imports as much as in the mid-1990s (see Exhibit 6).

Exhibit 7 presents a snapshot of the Pearl River Delta region's economy in 2001. The mainland Chinese population of the region by that time was 40 million, 28 million of whom were permanent residents. In addition, many of Hong Kong's seven million people were expected to travel frequently to the region. The restlessly urbanising region was therefore desperately in need of better port-and-airport networks and other associated transportation infrastructure to cater for the needs of some 50 million people, and the escalating import-export trading activities. From 1999 to 2002, the annual growth of total imports and exports in Guangdong Province was 10.8 percent.

An indication of the region's rising competitiveness could be seen in the increasing prominence of its seaports. It used to be that more than 90 percent of Pearl River Delta's export were made through Hong Kong's terminals. However, as a number of seaports around the Shenzhen and Guangzhou areas, such as Yantian, Shekou, Chiwan and Guangzhou's own port, continued to grow, more than 20 percent of the export activities were carried out directly through ports in the region by 2001. Shenzhen and Guangzhou handled four million and two million TEUs per annum respectively by 2001, far behind Hong Kong's 18.1 million, but they were certainly catching up.[12] Although an increase in shipping volume did not necessarily correspond to an increase in trading volume handled by companies based at the port (trading activities at a port could well be handled by companies based outside it), a rapid increase in container traffic indicated a favourable background for the indigenous trading industry to thrive. On the other hand, labour costs and processing fees associated with exporting through Hong Kong were consistently much higher than in the Pearl River Delta. Therefore, it had been predicted that, by 2010, only 30 to 50 percent of the import and export trading activities in the region would be made through Hong Kong, compared to 80 percent in the early 2000s.

The Yangtze River Delta[13]

It was not only the Pearl River Delta that posed a threat to Hong Kong. Shanghai and the Yangtze River Delta, which were fostering manufacturing and trading activities, were also a threat. The region benefited from a large, and by mainland Chinese standards affluent, population. It was the home of some of China's leading universities; was geographically close to South Korea, Japan and Taiwan, and had good connections to other Chinese cities and other countries through its most important city, Shanghai. Shanghai had received both political and financial support from the Central Government of China, and was designated by the Central Government to be the main financial centre for mainland China. Shanghai's seaport handled five million TEUs of container volume per annum by 2001, which was 28 percent of the volume handled by Hong Kong, and was growing rapidly.

Exhibit 7 shows how fast the Yangtze River Delta region was growing economically, and also the size of its industrial output and consumer goods market. From 1999 to 2002, the annual growth of total imports and exports in Guangdong Province was 10.8 percent, while that of mainland China excluding Guangdong was 19.7 percent, and that of the Yangtze River Delta was 26 percent. Therefore, it was likely that the centre of light manufacturing and/or import/export trade would shift northwards to the rapidly developing Pearl River Delta or even the Yangtze River Delta.

Potential Threats to Hong Kong's Position as a Trading Centre[14]

Many people feared that Hong Kong trading companies would face increased competition from foreign firms that were also able to access the China market directly, or Mainland firms that dealt directly with foreign buyers. With the improvements in mainland China's port facilities, more goods were expected to be shipped directly to and from China's other markets without going through Hong Kong. The growth in offshore trade demonstrated that this trend was real; the question was: How far it would go?

In short, competition from the Chinese mainland led to the possibility of two new scenarios:
1. The movement of trading functions to the Pearl River Delta region; and
2. The movement of light manufacturing and trading to the Yangtze River Delta region.

It was possible that manufacturers in the Pearl River Delta region and their buyers would also deal directly with each other in the future, rendering Hong Kong's trading agents unnecessary. By 2002, some of the world's major distribution chains, such as Levi's and Wal-Mart, had relocated their buying operations for South China into the Pearl River Delta region, and this type of relocation could have gained momentum. These very large firms were perceived as having sufficient clout with officials in mainland China to strike favourable deals. They could also have enjoyed sufficiently high-quality professional service support to navigate the operating environment in the Pearl River Delta region without relying on Hong Kong's soft infrastructure and professional service clusters. They increasingly had the financial clout to subcontract the establishment of dedicated consolidation centres convenient to the maritime port facilities in Shenzhen, which in turn were sufficiently developed to accommodate their shipping requirements.

Taiwan–China Trade

By 2000, indirect trade between Taiwan and mainland China accounted for about six percent of Hong Kong's trade.[15] A lot of that trade was between Taiwan and Southern China, particularly the Pearl River Delta region, while a lot of the trade between Taiwan and northern China was by then carried out through ports in South Korea or Japan. There was no direct trade between Taiwan and mainland China, because the latter considered the former a renegade province. If the political tension between mainland China and Taiwan eased up, direct trade might begin to take place across the Taiwan Strait, which might worsen Hong Kong's trading position. After both mainland China and Taiwan entered the WTO in 2001, there was fear in some quarters that direct cross-Strait trade was more likely to occur.

PART II: LESSONS LEARNED

Advantages of Hong Kong's Trading Industry[16]

The other side of the argument was that Hong Kong still possessed many advantages in its role as the "gateway to China" for trade and manufacturing coordination and as the "nerve centre" of the Pearl River Delta region's economy. For instance, Hong Kong offered a free flow of information, transparent regulation, low taxation and a British-based legal system of commercial laws and the enforceability of contracts, but the Pearl River Delta lagged behind in developing such mechanisms. For example, the concept of payment in fair consideration of value delivered was a fundamental precept of British common law, and Hong Kong inherited it. The notion of fair payment in exchange for value delivered was relatively weak in mainland China. "Pearl River Delta firms would often undertake to meet higher quality standards in exchange for a higher price, and then substituted lower-quality inputs in an effort to boost their profit margin without understanding that the substitution went to the 'heart' of the contract," as the authors of the study "Hong Kong & the Pearl River Delta: the Economic Interaction" pointed out.[17] More generally, they asserted that:[18]

> Hong Kong's business standards have been enriched by contributions by major Hong Kong firms as well as Hong Kong's large and well-established community of international firms. These business standards have been developed and enforced for decades by the courts and a community of service providers operating at international standard.

Mainland China could not assimilate such standards overnight — one example was that the collection of payment was notoriously difficult, not only for Hong Kong firms within the Chinese mainland but also for multinationals of every nationality. Against this background, Hong Kong's leadership in overseas markets with respect to business values and business standards was likely to endure. It should play an important role in preserving Hong Kong's "foreign market access" function into the foreseeable future.

Hong Kong was also the place where many multinationals had their regional headquarters, where businessmen could respond flexibly to shifting patterns of production, and where people were used to forward-looking strategic thinking. These were further complemented by the strong clustering support of financial, transport, logistics, garments and toys industries in Hong Kong (the latter two in the form of headquarters based in Hong Kong). Hong Kong had the telecommunications, logistics and other infrastructure needed to help international companies design, source, package, finance and market using e-commerce and ship using supply chain management. The local trading community had powerful ongoing customer relations with international customers, and there was limited direct competition for customers among them. Their strong integration expertise, interpretive creativity and cross-cultural communication skills could have offset much of the disadvantage of Hong Kong's relatively costly labour and real estate.

Moreover, China's entry into the WTO in late 2001, and the subsequent easing of import quotas, especially those on apparel and textile imports, could have led to substantial growth in Hong Kong's trading industry. China's WTO accession also meant that Hong

Kong trading companies (including exporters of Mainland products and import agents of foreign goods) would be allowed to operate on the Chinese mainland and extend Mainland sourcing and distribution services to their overseas clients.

As for the backward integration of "giant" multinational buyers, Hong Kong importers and producers continued to play value-adding roles in their strategies despite their physical relocation into the Pearl River Delta region. In a variety of light-manufactured goods, these buyers continued to buy almost exclusively from Hong Kong-owned firms with production capacity inside the Pearl River Delta region, rather than from Mainland-owned firms. The Hong Kong-owned factories continued to dominate by virtue of their ability to deliver on time and to high specification within acceptable product defect parameters. The large buyers also continued to rely on Hong Kong-based traders to design products and mastermind their outsourcing within the Pearl River Delta region. It might not be so straightforward for the large buyers to internalise the "packaging and integrating" function still performed by Hong Kong-based traders, except perhaps in very basic commodity-type goods.

Even if there was a trend for trading activities to move to the Pearl River Delta, they could still be controlled by Hong Kong businessmen. This was reflected in the fact that offshore trading had been rising in the early 2000s, and most of it was attributable to the Pearl River Delta. The value of Hong Kong's offshore trading in 2000 (see Exhibit 5), which was equivalent to US$183 billion (US$1 = HK$7.8 approximately), compared favourably with the total trade of the Pearl River Delta in 2001, which was US$168 billion (see Exhibit 7). This suggests that, even if not as much trading would be carried out within Hong Kong as in the old days, Pearl River Delta trade might just be controlled by Hong Kong businessmen with all their international networks, expertise, business standards and good reputations.

A similar development could also have happened if trading moved to the Yangtze River Delta — Hong Kong trading firms could have simply set up offices there and occupied a significant market share. As for the possibility of direct Taiwan-mainland China trade, most of Taiwan-Mainland trade that went through Hong Kong by 2002 was for the Pearl River Delta — a trading route that would not be seriously affected by the appearance of direct cross-Strait trade.

By the early 2000s, it seemed that Hong Kong's trading industry was in the middle of great changes. However, it was probable that for some years at least, the territory would still retain the advantages delineated above — advantages in everything from the legal system to the international connections that had been built up over decades. Hong Kong was likely to see the range of activities it performed narrowed to many of the highest-value-added management, co-ordination, financial and information activities, and the numbers of firms and types of firms performing such activities were likely to expand significantly. Meanwhile, the Pearl River and Yangtze River Deltas were likely to develop deeper and broader economies, with a faster growth of service industries.

How were SME Trading Firms Responding to the Challenges?

The numerous trading firms in Hong Kong were responding to such changes with a range of approaches. Some of them followed the example of large industry leaders, which had become full supply chain management firms, and expanded their logistics operations to cover some portions of the supply chain. Some sharpened their business foci, intending to become expert middlemen for buyers and suppliers in individual niche markets, from home shopping to corporate gifts. Some even developed their own brand as trading firms. Some set up branch offices in the Pearl River Delta and Yangtze River Delta, regions that were sure to rise in prominence. In general, there was also a move towards providing more valued-added services, such as design, production planning and providing real-time information to buyers and suppliers. With a strong business tradition, infrastructure and cluster of supporting industries to fall back on, coupled with its significant flexibility and adaptability, Hong Kong's trading industry was likely to remain dominant in the region for a long time to come.

1   PBS, "Commanding Heights: Hong Kong Trade Policy", www.pbs.org/wgbh/commandingheights/lo/countries/hk/hk_trade.html/; Tdctrade.com, "Profiles of Hong Kong Major Service Industries: Import and Export Trade", www.tdctrade.com/main/si/spimex.htm/.

2   Markus, L., Banerjee, P. and Ma, L., (2002), "Electronic Marketplaces in Hong Kong's Trading Industry", Proceedings of the 35th Hawaii International Conference on System Sciences. http://www.computer.org/proceedings/hicss/1435/volume7/14350182abs.htm/.

3   Tdctrade.com, "Profiles of Hong Kong Major Service Industries: Import and Export Trade".

4   "SME Profile: Hong Kong", ACTETSME website, www.actetsme.org/hong/hong98.htm/.

5   Markus, Banerjee and Ma.

6   Tdctrade.com, "Profiles of Hong Kong Major Service Industries: Import and Export Trade"; Wong Chun Xin (2002), "The Characteristics and Prospects of Hong Kong's Trade Transformation", 1 November, http://www.tdctrade.com/econforum/boc/boc021101.htm.

7   A survey conducted by the Hong Kong Trade Development Council in early 2001 showed that, among those respondents who dealt with Chinese exports, 86.9 percent said their products were either completely or partly manufactured in Guangdong province. This suggests that most of Hong Kong's offshore trade was related to the Pearl River Delta region. See Tdc.com, "Hong Kong's Trade and trade Supporting Services: New Developments and Prospects", http://www.tdctrade.com/econforum/tdc/tdc020102.htm, accessed 24 January 2002.

8   Enright, M., Scott, E. and Dodwell, D. (1997), The Hong Kong Advantage, Hong Kong, China: Oxford University Press (China), pp. 141–142.

9   Enright, Scott and Dodwell, p. 142.

10 Enright, Scott and Dodwell, p. 142.

11 Cheng, T. C., (2001), "Pearl River Delta Region Development", talk at Urban Development in China: A Journey to Guangzhou 2001, organised by the Centre of Urban Planning & Environmental Management, the University of Hong Kong, www.hku.hk/cupem/2002/guangzhoutrip2001/prd.htm.

12 TEU — twenty-foot equivalent unit — is a measure of container box volume. One TEU is the size of a standardised container measuring 20ft x 8ft x 8ft.

13 Cheng; Enright, M., Chang, K. M., Scott, E. and Zhu, W. H., (2003), "Hong Kong & the Pearl River Delta: the Economic Interaction", www.2022foundation.com, p. 192.

14 Tdctrade.com, "Profiles of Hong Kong Major Service Industries: Import and Export Trade"; Enright, Scott and Dodwell, pp. 142–144; Enright, Chang, Scott and Zhu, pp. 56, 174–176; Wong Chun Xin.

15 Kwok, K. C. (2000), "Impact on Hong Kong of direct Taiwan-China trade", tdctrade.com, http://www.tdctrade.com/econforum/sc/sc001004.htm.

16 Enright, Scott and Dodwell, pp. 144; Enright, Chang, Scott and Zhu, pp. 174–175.

17 Enright, Chang, Scott and Zhu, p. 175.

18 Enright, Chang, Scott and Zhu, p. 174.

Exhibit 1   Basic Industry Data

Import and Export Trade	December 2002 Figures
Number of Establishments	103,383
Employment	499,735

Value in HK$ billion	1997	1998	1999	2000	2001
Export of Trade-related Services	77.9	84.0	81.5	97.6	106.4
Contribution to Services Exports	26.1%	30.0%	29.2%	30.7%	32.7%

Value in HK$ billion	1980	1985	1990	1995	2000	2001
Exports	19.10	30.15	82.04	172.32	201.63	189.87
Total Trade	40.80	59.82	164.41	363.49	414.19	390.92

(US$1 = HK$7.8 approximately)

Value in HK$ million	2002	2003 Jan-Jun	% Change	
			02/01	03/02 Jan-Jun
– Domestic Exports	130,926	54,505	-15	-11
– Re-exports	1,429,590	747,483	8	17
– Imports	1,619,419	835,402	3	13
Total Trade	3,179,936	1,637,389	4	14
Balance	-58,903	-33,414	-32	-10

Major Export Markets of Trade-related Services (HK$ million):

	1999	Share (%)	2000	Share (%)	2001	Share (%)
China	24,640	30.2	28,952	29.7	32,271	30.3
US	22,507	27.6	26,251	26.9	29,908	28.1
Japan	4,364	5.4	6,963	7.1	6,527	6.1
Germany	4,510	5.5	3,677	3.8	3,628	3.4

Source: Tdctrade.com, (2003), "Profiles of Hong Kong Major Service Industries: Import and Export Trade", http://www.tdctrade.com/main/si/spimex.htm; "Hong Kong's External Trade Performance — Statistical Highlight", http://stat.tdctrade.com/monthly/light.htm/, accessed 18 August 2003.

Exhibit 2   Funds from Hong Kong and Macao Used in the Pearl River Delta Region

	Amount (US$ million)	As % of Total Foreign Funds
1985	671.14	90.82
1985-1999	56,941.10	70.76
1986-1990	4,514.79	73.61
1991-1995	21,932.37	74.46
1996-1999	29,822.80	67.55

Source: Enright, M., Chang, K. M., Scott, E. and Zhu, W. H. (2003), "Hong Kong & the Pearl River Delta: the Economic Interaction", www.2022foundation.com, p. 51.

Exhibit 3   Relative Importance of the Pearl River Delta Region (PRD) in Guangdong Province (GD) and Mainland China, 1980–2000

Year	PRD Proportion of GD Total (%)			PRD Proportion of Mainland Total (%)		
	GDP	Exports	Realised Foreign Capital	GDP	Exports	Realised Foreign Capital
1980	47.7	28.4	47.2	2.6	3.4	3.3
1985	52.6	55.2	70.4	3.4	6.0	16.5
1990	55.9	76.7	76.0	4.7	13.0	14.9
1995	68.0	81.5	70.9	6.7	31.0	17.8
2000	76.4	92.2	86.0	8.2	34.0	21.1
2001	78.6	95.2	90.1	8.7	34.1	28.6

Source: Enright, M., Chang, K. M., Scott, E. and Zhu, W. H. (2003), "Hong Kong & the Pearl River Delta: the Economic Interaction", www.2022foundation.com, p. 54.

Exhibit 4   Hong Kong's Major Trading Partners in 2002

Rank	Total Trade			Domestic Exports			Re-exports			Imports		
	Region	Value	%	Region	Value	%	Region	Value	%	Region	Value	%
1	M. China	1,330,317	41.8	USA	41,908	32.0	M. China	571,870	40.0	M. China	717,074	44.3
2	USA	424,429	13.3	M. China	41,374	31.6	USA	291,043	20.4	Japan	182,569	11.3
3	Japan	266,281	8.4	UK	7,588	5.8	Japan	80,743	5.6	Taiwan	115,906	7.2
4	Taiwan	150,487	4.7	Taiwan	4,388	3.4	UK	46,644	3.3	USA	91,478	5.6
5	Singapore	107,325	3.4	Germany	4,273	3.3	Germany	44,567	3.1	South Korea	75,955	4.7
6	South Korea	106,351	3.3	Netherlands	3,470	2.7	Taiwan	30,193	2.1	Singapore	75,740	4.7
7	Germany	81,836	2.6	Japan	2,969	2.3	Singapore	29,424	2.1	Malaysia	39,729	2.5
8	UK	80,313	2.5	Malaysia	2,637	2.0	South Korea	29,264	2.0	Germany	32,997	2.0
9	Malaysia	55,182	1.7	Canada	2,411	1.8	Netherlands	22,775	1.6	Thailand	29,556	1.8
10	Thailand	46,336	1.5	Singapore	2,161	1.7	Canada	21,109	1.5	UK	26,082	1.6
11	Philippines	39,107	1.2	Philippines	1,717	1.3	France	19,243	1.3	Switzerland	22,695	1.4
12	Italy	37,210	1.2	France	1,264	1.0	Australia	17,962	1.3	Philippines	21,135	1.3
13	Netherlands	36,970	1.2	South Korea	1,132	0.9	Philippines	16,255	1.1	Italy	20,998	1.3
14	France	35,666	1.1	Mexico	1,076	0.8	Thailand	15,802	1.1	India	19,452	1.2
15	Canada	31,706	1.0	Thailand	978	0.7	Italy	15,548	1.1	France	15,160	0.9
16	Australia	31,290	1.0	Spain	866	0.7	Malaysia	12,816	0.9	Australia	12,503	0.8
17	India	30,691	1.0	Australia	825	0.6	Mexico	11,814	0.8	Indonesia	11,617	0.7
18	Switzerland	30,177	0.9	Vietnam	716	0.5	India	10,829	0.8	Bel-Lux	11,426	0.7
19	Bel-Lux	21,559	0.7	Sweden	692	0.5	UA Emirates	10,039	0.7	Netherlands	10,726	0.7
20	Indonesia	18,343	0.6	Italy	664	0.5	Spain	9,806	0.7	Canada	8,185	0.5
	World Total	3,179,936	100.0	World Total	130,926	100.0	World Total	1,429,590	100.0	World Total	1,619,419	100.0
	EU	345,934	10.9	EU	20,356	15.5	EU	186,380	13.0	EU	139,198	8.6
	APEC	2,643,258	83.1	APEC	105,177	80.3	APEC	1,146,654	80.2	APEC	1,391,427	85.9
	ASEAN	278,186	8.7	ASEAN	9,218	7.0	ASEAN	88,906	6.2	ASEAN	180,062	11.1

Value in HK$ million. M. China — Mainland China, Bel-Lux — Belgium-Luxembourg.

Source: Trade and Industry Department, HKSAR, (2003), http://www.tid.gov.hk/english/trade_relations/mainland/trade.html.

Exhibit 5   Hong Kong's Offshore Trade

Value in HK$ billion	Offshore Trade by Hong Kong Companies				
	1988	1991	1994	1997	2000
Total exports	493	766	1,170	1,456	1,573
- Domestic exports	218	231	222	211	181
- Re-exports	275	535	948	1,245	1,392
Offshore trade	140	270	655	1,052	1,425
Ratio of offshore trade to re-exports	50.9%	50.5%	69.1%	84.5%	102.4%

Source: Tdctrade.com, (2003), "The Evolution and Contribution of Hong Kong's Manufacturing and Trading Sectors", www.tdctrade.com/econforum/tdc/tdc030704.htm.

Exhibit 6   Guangdong-Hong Kong Trade in 1995–2000

Year	Total Value of Guangdong Exports	Exports to Hong Kong		Total Value of Guangdong Imports	Imports from Hong Kong	
		Value	%		Value	%
1995	56,592	22,255	39.3	47,380	6,055	12.8
1999	77,705	26,891	34.6	62,663	4,139	6.6
2000	91,919	32,105	34.9	78,187	5,335	6.8

Value in US$ million, US$1 = HK$7.8 approximately.
Source: Enright, M., Chang, K. M., Scott, E. and Zhu, W. H. (2003), "Hong Kong & the Pearl River Delta: the Economic Interaction", www.2022foundation.com, p. 54.

Exhibit 7   Main Indicators of the Pearl River Delta Region (PRD) and the Yangtze River Region (YRD), 2001

	PRD	YRD	Mainland China
Land area (square kilometres)	41,698	100,113	9,597,000
Population (million)			
- Registered, 2001	23.37	74.94	1,276.27
- Census, 2000	40.77	82.28	1,265.83
Total GDP in 2001 (RMB billion)	834.39	1,698.10	9,593.30
Annual average GDP growth			
- 1980-1990 current prices	22.0%	13.0%	15.2%
- 1990-2000 current prices	23.8%	15.5%	9.3%
- 1980-1990 constant prices	14.0%	9.3%	10.15%
- 1990-2000 constant prices	17.5%	15.5%	9.6%
Retail sales of consumer goods (RMB billion)	312.01	560.98	3,759.52
Gross industrial output, of enterprises with above RMB 5 million in sales (RMB billion)	1,150*	2,323.0	9,544.9
Value added % of gross industrial output, 2001	26.29%	29.92%	29.68%
Total trade, 2001 (US$ billion)	167.75*	137.15	509.80
- Exports (US$ billion)	90.43*	73.60	266.20
- Imports (US$ billion)	77.33*	63.54	243.60
Utilised foreign capital, 2001 (US$ billion)	13.93*	16.06	46.8

*Approximate average from two sources.
US$1 = RMB 8.28 approximately.
Source: Enright, M., Chang, K. M., Scott, E. and Zhu, W. H. (2003), "Hong Kong & the Pearl River Delta: the Economic Interaction", www.2022foundation.com, p. 200.

27

Mainland China's Travel Liberalisation and Hong Kong's SMEs in Late 2003

MICHAEL J. ENRIGHT AND VINCENT MAK

PART I: BACKGROUND AND ISSUES

From March to May 2003, Hong Kong's tourism industry underwent a serious downturn upon the outbreak of the Severe Acute Respiratory Syndrome (SARS) in the territory, which caused 1,755 cases in Hong Kong before July. Inbound tourism practically ground to a halt between 2 April and 23 May, during which the World Health Organization (WHO) advised the public to consider postponing all but essential travel to Hong Kong.

Then, in a dramatic twist, the industry received a significant boost in late July, when residents of four nearby mainland Chinese cities were allowed to apply to visit Hong Kong on an individual basis as part of the Mainland and Hong Kong Closer Economic Partnership Arrangement (CEPA). Formerly, mainland Chinese tourists could only visit Hong Kong with tour groups. By September, tourists from the major cities of Beijing, Shanghai, Guangzhou and Shenzhen could also visit Hong Kong on an individual basis. Mainland tourists began to flood in as a result, bringing up total visitor arrival figures to a level that even surpassed pre-SARS statistics. Even more easing of travel restrictions was expected in the first half of 2004. How could Hong Kong's SMEs, much battered by the economic woes in recent years that were capped by the SARS attack, capitalise on the new opportunities offered by the liberalisation of Mainland travel?

The International Tourism Industry

Definition and Brief History [1]

> Tourism comprises the activities of persons travelling to and staying in places outside their usual environment for not more than one consecutive year for leisure, business or other purposes not related to the exercise of an activity remunerated from within the place visited.

The above definition of tourism was adopted by the Madrid-based World Tourism Organization (WTO), an affiliate of the United Nations.[2] The WTO classified tourism into several forms: domestic, inbound, outbound, internal and national.[3] Tourism was considered a service industry; the services that a tourist "bought" might include an airline seat, hotel room, meals and the opportunity to relax on a sunny beach. More generally speaking, tourists were buying the temporary use of a strange environment, incorporating novel geographical features — old-world towns, tropical landscapes, famous architecture snow-capped peaks, etc. — plus the culture and heritage of the region and other intangible benefits such as atmosphere and hospitality.

Tourism already existed in ancient civilisations: some early tourists took to vandalising buildings with graffiti to record their visit, and Egyptian graffiti of this nature dating back to 2000 BC had been discovered. Tourism for pleasure or for business had never stopped since then, but in the West, it developed especially rapidly in the nineteenth century, partly because of the expansion of the colonial empires, but also due to development of steam engine railways and steamships. In the early twentieth century, tourism continued to expand, as the post-Victorian European population had acquired more wealth and had become more curious and outgoing, while travelling had become safer and faster. The disastrous First World War proved to be only a temporary setback to this development. The popularisation of motor cars and the emergence of air travel gradually decreased people's reliance on railways and steamships.

Tourism grew again at a rocketing pace in the several decades after World War II, exceeding 10 percent per annum from 1950 to 1960 (see Exhibit 1A). This growth reflected the pent-up demand that the war years, and the economic recovery in the years that immediately followed them, had constrained. The war promoted the growth of aircraft technology, which led to the establishment of a viable commercial aviation industry in the post-war years: the number of passengers crossing the Atlantic by air exceeded those by sea for the first time in 1957. The liners gradually gave up their traditional regular routes; some turned to cruising and some to ferry services that were welcomed by private motorists taking their cars on their trips. Tourism grew especially rapidly in both sides of the North Atlantic, where most of the affluent nations were located; tourists from those nations often chose southern, sunny regions for their destinations, such as the Mediterranean and Caribbean islands and North Africa. In 1970, the first wide-bodied jets (Boeing 747s), with a passenger capacity reaching 400, appeared in service, further consolidating mass-market tourism across nations. Meanwhile, the ability of tour operators to charter flights in order to drive down costs led to the development of package tours as a major form of tourism. In the Pacific, the growth of post-war tourism originating from Japan was noteworthy, bringing much revenue to destinations ranging from Australia to Europe and beyond. At the same time, business tourism attained a growing importance worldwide, in the form of individual as well as conference and incentive business travel.

The strong growth in the 1950s and 1960s was not sustained into the 1970s and 1980s, but annual growth between 1970 and 1998 still averaged 4.9 percent, and remained above four percent in the early 1990s, when there was a global recession. Sometimes, however, the industry had to bear with a high short-term volatility in demand. Wars, terrorist attacks, epidemics, economic recession, new government policies and many other factors could create sudden and rather unforeseeable fluctuations in the tourism industry of a region.

The Late 1990s and Early 2000s

> For years, we didn't focus on tourism as an economic-development tool, but we have found out that it can be a good source of growth, infrastructure development and poverty alleviation. ... Every hotel room creates two jobs. That's the rule of thumb.
>
> – Iain Christie, consultant at World Bank[4]

In the late 1990s, a strong global economy propelled an international tourist boom. Travel and tourism had probably become the most important industry in the world by then, accounting for more than six percent of the world's gross domestic product (GDP) and employing some 127 million people around the world — one job in every 15. Some 663 million international trips were taken in 1999, with worldwide tourism receipts (excluding the costs of international fares) reaching US$456 billion. Moreover, these statistics do not include the vast number of people taking trips within their own countries.

Europe was the most popular destination, followed by the Americas. International tourism was generated for the most part from Europe, North America and Japan, as a result of frequent flights, large and wealthy populations and the availability of low-price travel. Japan, in particular, became a leading tourist-generating country, despite a recession throughout the 1990s, because the population was still wealthy and willing to take trips. These trends persisted into the early 2000s (see Exhibits 1B to 1G).

By the early 2000s, foreign visitors spent close to US$500 billion a year on travel, hotels, meals and attractions in other countries, roughly 10 percent of all international trade and five percent of total global economic output. International tourism, as an export of services from the country visited, was nearly four times as large as global steel exports, 50 percent bigger than global exports of clothes and textiles, and roughly equal to global exports of cars. In popular tourist centres, tourism's importance was very significant. The industry contributed to about six percent of the total economy in Thailand and France, seven percent in Malaysia, 11 percent in Spain, 50 percent in Bali in Indonesia and more than 60 percent in the Bahamas.

A series of events from 2001 to 2003 created a momentary downturn in international tourism. The terrorist attacks on New York's World Trade Centre on 11 September 2001, brought diplomatic tensions and wars in the two years that followed. Notable events included the US military campaign against the Taliban regime in Afghanistan that was believed to provide shelter for Osama bin Laden, the suspected mastermind behind the World Trade Centre disaster. The military campaign brought down the Taliban regime in December 2001, but soured Western-Middle Eastern relationships. Then the US government turned to pressure Saddam Hussein's regime in Iraq on the issue of weapons of mass destruction. Months of international diplomatic tension followed that led to "American tourists shunning Europe, and European tourists shunning the United States".[5] In March 2003, the United States led an invasion into Iraq with a group of allied countries. The campaign came to an end by May 2003, with Saddam Hussein going into hiding and the whole country being taken over temporarily by the United States and its allies. Meanwhile, the world had been under terrorist attacks that were carried out to retaliate against Western countries for the Afghan and Iraqi wars. One of the most serious among such attacks were the bombings at two clubs on the Indonesian island of Bali in October

2002, which killed more than 200 people, mostly foreign tourists. Bali suffered a severe downturn in its tourism industry after those attacks.

To add to all these woes, a new infectious disease called Severe Acute Respiratory Syndrome (SARS), the earliest cases of which appeared in Guangdong Province in southern mainland China in November 2002, became recognised as a global health threat by mid-March 2003. Areas particularly affected included Toronto in Canada, Vietnam, Taiwan, Singapore, Beijing, Guangdong Province and Hong Kong. Between March and July, tourism in the seriously affected areas suffered huge blows, especially in places such as Toronto, Beijing and Hong Kong. The World Health Organization (WHO) had advised people to postpone all but essential travel to such places (all WHO travel advisories had been lifted by July 2003). In early July 2003, the WHO reported that the last human chain of transmission of SARS had been broken. But it was feared that the disease would return in late 2003 or early 2004. By October 2003, doctors had found neither a vaccine for SARS nor a treatment that would work with a 100 percent success rate. Between November 2002 and August 2003, the disease had claimed 916 deaths out of 8,422 cases reported from 32 countries and regions.

By 2003, the tourism industry involved a network of buyers, suppliers and support services. Basically, the industry could be understood as a distribution chain of products (mostly in the form of services) with a host of support services from both public and private sectors. Transport, accommodation and attraction providers formed the producers in the industry. Tour operators were the wholesalers; travel agents were the retailers and tourists were the consumers. However, the producers often sold directly to the tourists without passing through the tour operators and travel agents, and the tour operators often sold directly to the tourists.

The Hong Kong Tourism Industry by 2003

Hong Kong was made up of three distinct geographical areas: Hong Kong Island, Kowloon Peninsula, and the New Territories and outlying islands. The famous Victoria Harbour was flanked by Hong Kong Island and the Kowloon Peninsula, while the New Territories bordered mainland China to the north and Kowloon to the south. The city was located near China's Pearl River estuary, and as such, was seen as a southern gateway to China. It also lay at the centre of East Asia and, by 2001, had around 70 airlines connecting it to more than 120 cities around the world.[6] The city prospered and become a bustling metropolis as a colony of the United Kingdom from the mid-nineteenth century until 1997, when it became a Special Administrative Region (SAR) of China after an official handover ceremony on 1 July 1997.

Hong Kong continued to develop as an Asian business centre after 1997, and had attracted organisations, visitors and relocated professionals from all over the world. The opening of the new US$20 billion international airport in July 1998 helped with this development. By the early 2000s it was the most visited city destination in Asia,[7] and remained one of the top tourist destinations in the Asia-Pacific and in the world (see Exhibits 1E, 1H, 1I). Hong Kong had become attractive as a destination for conferences, exhibitions and incentive packages as well. Visitors from most countries — numbering more than 170 by 2002 — did not require visas for periods ranging from one week to six months. The Hong Kong currency was pegged to the US dollar at about US$1 = HK$7.8.

With a distinctive blend of Eastern and Western heritage and culture, Hong Kong offered many sights to tourists, from monasteries, temples, baronial houses, colonial architecture and dense clusters of modern skyscrapers along the harbour, to beaches, hills and parks. A wide range of cuisines was available at its numerous restaurants. Hong Kong also had a wide variety of festivals, including the Chinese New Year festival with its colourful parades and fireworks over the harbour. The Star Ferry that crossed the harbour from Hong Kong Island to Kowloon had itself become a sight, as had the Hong Kong Tramways double-decker trams that still slowly paced along the Island every day. Shopping in Hong Kong had long been known for the huge variety of consumer goods available.

In the 1990s, the booming Asian (and global) economy coupled with the imminence of Hong Kong's handover to Chinese rule brought about a surge in the tourism industry. A widely expected culmination of this trend in 1997 turned out to be an anticlimax: tourist arrivals and tourism receipts both fell in that year from the previous year's high levels (see Exhibit 2A). The reasons for this included the loss of the "handover factor" after July, fear of political repression after the handover, extortionate hikes in room prices by greedy hoteliers,[8] reports of Hong Kong overtaking Tokyo as the world's most expensive city[9] and most importantly, an Asian economic recession that began in the latter half of 1997. Most of Hong Kong's tourists originated from within Asia — it had been reported that, in 1993, 63 percent of the tourists in Asia were intra-regional travellers.[10] Exhibit 2B also indicates that the bulk of Hong Kong's visitor arrivals in the late 1990s were from within Asia. Tourism figures dropped further in 1998 and were only a little better in 1999 (during which tourism receipts fell slightly while visitors arrival went up 10 percent). But as Asia gradually recovered from its economic crisis, tourism figures of Hong Kong also recovered, and were record-breaking in 2000 (see Exhibit 2A). The annual key statistics kept going up in 2001 and 2002; arrival figures had significantly surpassed the 1996 level, but tourism receipts still lagged behind.

In 2002, tourism remained one of the major economic pillars of Hong Kong, despite the continuous global economic downturn and threats of terrorism. Tourism contributed to about six percent of Hong Kong's GDP that year. Occupancy in the 98 hotels (38,949 rooms) and 397 tourist guest houses (4,675 rooms) was over 80 percent (see Exhibit 2C).[11] Tourism spending per capita was about HK$4,500 (see Exhibit 2D). The industries that most benefited from tourism included hotels, catering and retail.

The inbound travel agency business of Hong Kong was not regulated at all before 2001.[12] There were, in fact, reports from time to time about tourists being ripped off by unscrupulous tour operators. In 2001, the Hong Kong Government began to channel resources into organising this lucrative sector. In the same year, the Hong Kong Inbound Travel Association (HKITA) was established, with Paul Leung Yiu-lam as its founding chairman (he was still the chairman in 2003). Leung, himself the chairman of a small travel agency, said in 2003 about the previous state of affairs:

> Business went up and down but nobody controlled inbound agents in the past and nobody cared ... There was no system at all. ... Anyone could set up an agency and organise tours of overseas travellers coming to Hong Kong.

In November 2002, the Hong Kong Government finally passed a law that implemented a licensing policy for all inbound agencies. About 650 agents handled inbound travel in Hong Kong by 2003, according to the Travel Industry Council of Hong Kong. Travel agents (inbound or outbound) were supposed to become members of the Council before applying for a licence. However, the HKITA had only 138 members.[13]

Mainland China had been the largest market for Hong Kong tourism since 1994, after the Hong Kong Government simplified entry formalities for mainland Chinese travellers in 1993.[14] The number of Mainland travellers had been increasing steadily from 1.7 million (19 percent of total visitor arrivals) in 1993 to 2.6 million in 1998, when they made up 27.1 percent of the total visitor arrivals. By the late 1990s, Hong Kong had become the number-one destination for mainland Chinese people travelling abroad. Mainland Chinese tourists spent HK$13.48 billion in Hong Kong in 1999, about one-fourth of the total tourism receipts in that year.[15] Tourists from mainland China still made up the largest share of tourists in the early 2000s (see Exhibit 2B). The Hong Kong Tourism Board stated that in 2001, each Mainland tourist spent on average HK$5,169 and stayed for 3.46 nights during their stay in Hong Kong.[16]

Hong Kong had two advantages in capturing the Mainland market: its geographical and cultural proximity to the Mainland, and family ties between many Hong Kong and mainland Chinese people. Mainland tourists did not need to take a plane to come to Hong Kong; they could just take a train or a bus, as Hong Kong was geographically connected to the Mainland. Although Hong Kong used traditional Chinese characters (mainland China used simplified Chinese characters) and Hong Kong Chinese commonly spoke the Cantonese dialect (Mainlanders spoke Putonghua), at least both regions were using the Chinese language and were mostly populated by Chinese. The Chinese government's open-door policies and the loosening of travel restrictions on Mainland visitors after the handover both led to the increase in the number of Mainland tourists in the late 1990s. From the beginning of 2002, the daily quota limits on tour-group travel to Hong Kong — Mainland tourists could only visit Hong Kong in tour groups — were completely abolished by the Mainland government. At the same time, the number of mainland Chinese agents authorised to offer Hong Kong tours was allowed by the authority to rise sharply from four before early 2002 to more than 500 in late 2002, leading to increased competition in the pricing and packaging of tour products.[17] The rising living standards in the Mainland also meant that Mainlanders had more money for travelling and were more interested in shopping in Hong Kong, which often provided a larger variety of all types of consumer goods than in many Mainland cities. The three "Golden Weeks" — Chinese New Year, Labour Day (1 May) and National Day (1 October) holidays — were usually peak periods for the influx of Mainland tourists.

The Impact of SARS

Although September 11 and the ensuing wars had affected Hong Kong's tourism industry, their impact was nothing compared to that of SARS. According to the WHO, the onset of the first probable SARS case in Hong Kong took place on 15 February 2003. The disease first spread within a hospital but was soon transmitted in the community, culminating in the appearance of more than 300 almost simultaneous new cases in late March, all being traced to a housing estate. On 2 April, the WHO advised the public to consider postponing all but essential travel to Hong Kong and Guangdong Province. The WHO recommendation was not removed until 23 May. The onset of the last probable case, as of early August 2003, was dated 31 May. Hong Kong was declared SARS-free by the WHO on 23 June. By early August, WHO statistics showed that 1,755 SARS cases, 300 of which ended in death, had occurred in Hong Kong.

Of all the industries in Hong Kong, the tourism industry was battered the worst by SARS. Even before the WHO issued its travel advisory, daily total arrivals and departures at Hong Kong's international airport fell from 61,400 on 14 March 2003, to 32,500 on 2 April 2003.[18] Total arrivals plunged from a 19.1 percent year-on-year growth in the first 15 days of March (before the outbreak) to a 9.9 percent drop in the last 16 days of the same month. After the travel advisory was issued, the city's inbound tourism industry practically came to a halt. In April, visitor arrivals underwent a dramatic 64.8 percent drop compared with April 2002, recording the lowest monthly arrival figure since February 1991, at the height of the 1991 Gulf War. Arrivals from mainland China, however, numbering 493,666, fell by a more modest 38.7 percent that month, according to the Hong Kong Tourism Board. Average hotel occupancy was 22 percent in that month, compared with 87 percent in April 2002. Hong Kong's tourism industry as a whole (inbound and outbound) was estimated to have suffered a monthly loss of HK$6 billion.

In May, the disaster became even worse, with the year-on-year drop in visitor arrivals reaching 67.9 percent. Arrivals from mainland China, numbering 311,821, fell the least among the major markets, by "only" 42.7 percent. It was originally estimated that about 400,000 Mainland visitors would come to Hong Kong during the week-long Labour Day holiday starting on 1 May, but the impact of SARS and the Mainland government's decision to cut short the holidays (effectively by two days) reduced the figure significantly.[19] Hotel occupancy was a meagre 18 percent in May (for more statistics see Exhibits 2E to 2G). Hotels in the top-tariff category were the most severely affected during the SARS outbreak. Shops, streets and restaurants that had previously been crowded with locals and tourists alike were empty. Retail sales dropped 15 percent year-on-year in April and 11 percent in May.[20]

At least 40 percent of the 20,000 employees working in Hong Kong's travel industry had already been affected by May, from accepting salary reductions to unpaid leave to being laid off.[21] In a desperate attempt, Hong Kong's tour operators began to turn to the domestic market, offering Hong Kong people one-day domestic tour packages, with content such as sightseeing Hong Kong attractions plus packed lunch and transport at bargain prices that went as low as HK$38 per head.[22] After all, Hong Kong people were not allowed to travel or would not be welcomed in foreign countries, so they could only join local tours to experience a semblance of travelling. As a result, weekend visitors to the remote outlying islands of Po Toi surged several times during the SARS period compared with pre-SARS times. As Leung said in May 2003:[23]

> We don't see any signs of the revival of Hong Kong's tourism industry anytime soon. That's why we have decided to organise tours for Hong Kong people to help our companies survive the crisis ... For small travel agencies like us, the only way we can compete with the big operators is by offering low-price tours ... The revenue we get from

these tours is only enough to hire drivers and pay for gasoline …We have to come up with self-rescuing measures as the Government cannot help us.

Hong Kong's tourism industry showed signs of recovery after the WHO lifted its travel advisory concerning Hong Kong in late May (see Exhibits 2E and 2F). But the figures were still weak in June and July. Spending on shopping, a part of which was by tourists, fell 2.5 percent year-on-year in July; it had been recording negative growth since January.[24]

Mainland Travel Liberalisation

Before July 2003, all Mainland tourists could only visit Hong Kong with tour groups, and the availability of the tour groups — although the daily quota for them was abolished in early 2002 — put a cap on the fast growth in the number of Mainland tourists visiting Hong Kong.

In the aftermath of SARS, the Mainland and Hong Kong governments began tying up the final loose ends in the Closer Economic Partnership Arrangement (CEPA), a kind of free-trade agreement between the HKSAR and mainland China.[25] Then it was announced that from 28 July 2003, onwards, as part of the implementation of CEPA, residents from four Guangdong cities — Dongguan, Jiangmen, Zhongshan and Foshan — would be allowed to visit Hong Kong on an individual basis.[26] Guangdong residents with permanent household registration in the four cities could apply for an exit endorsement from the Mainland government for about HK$20; they only needed to provide residential cards and identification cards when applying for the passes to Hong Kong. Residents of Guangzhou, Shenzhen, Zhuhai and Huizhou in Guangdong were also allowed to enjoy these new rules starting from 20 August. On 1 September, the new arrangement began to apply to Beijing and Shanghai residents as well.[27] These changes were also applicable for travel to Macau. It was expected that the individual visit scheme would be extended to the whole of Guangdong province by May 2004.[28]

The effects of the new rules were nothing short of dramatic. The number of monthly visitor arrivals in August 2003 surpassed the August 2002 level — the first instance of a year-on-year increase in monthly figures since the SARS outbreak (see Exhibits 2E and 2F; visitor arrivals from all other markets than mainland China were still dropping year-on-year in August). Within the first eight months of 2003, only the cumulative number visitor arrivals from mainland China had increased year-on-year (see Exhibit 2G). Hotel room occupancy was also up two percentage points in August compared with August 2002, with middle-brow hotels benefiting the most (see Exhibit 2H).[29]

Spending on shopping rose by 1.2 percent in August compared with the previous year, and part of this recovery was attributed to a greater influx of individual tourists from mainland China.[30] Individual Mainland tourists had been estimated at that time to spend about HK$8,000 on average per trip.[31] While many Mainlanders came with a tight budget, there were reports of Mainlanders going on extravagant shopping sprees in Hong Kong, swooping up designer clothes, trendy handbags, consumer electronics goods, jewels, precious foodstuffs (such as swallows' nests) and the like with grand gestures. Some even bought flats — sometimes even flats at the very top end of the market — and purchases by Mainland tourists made up two to three percent of the total home sales in Hong Kong in August.[32] By late October, more than 200,000 mainland Chinese people had visited Hong Kong on an individual basis.[33] During the National Day "Golden Week" holiday, which lasted from 28 September to 5 October that year, 287,000 mainland Chinese people visited Hong Kong, a rise of 21 percent compared to the same week in 2002. Among them, about 80,000 to 90,000 came as individual tourists.

PART II: LESSONS LEARNED

How should Hong Kong's SMEs capitalise on the easing of travel restrictions on Mainland tourists into Hong Kong?

For the accommodation sector, the main benefits of the travel liberalisation will go to the low- to medium-tariff hotels and guesthouses, as Exhibit 2H indicates. The reason for this is that although some Mainland tourists spend an astounding amount on shopping in Hong Kong, most are on a tight budget. In fact, Exhibit 2H suggests that many visitors do not want to spend more than HK$300 per night per room for accommodation. Hotels therefore should not, as has been reported, raise their prices because of a perceived increase in demand — Mainland tourists will simply turn to their friends in Hong Kong or will find cheaper accommodation. But it does not seem that there will be severe pricing competition either, since there are so many tourists flooding in. The best strategy could be to maintain a moderately competitive pricing policy while improving services, such as the Putonghua proficiency of hotel staff members, a Renminbi-Hong Kong dollar currency exchange service, the provision of Chinese cuisine (especially breakfast, which many tourists have at their hotels as part of a package), Mainland newspapers, and Mainland TV channels on hotel room televisions. Hotels should also improve their transport connections. While many hotels are already located near a railway station, it would even be better if they provided a free shuttle-bus service to the main railway station (at Hung Hom in Kowloon) for trains to mainland China.

For inbound tour operators and travel agents in Hong Kong, the travel liberalisation means finally being able to break the monopoly of Mainland tour operators when it comes to arranging Mainlanders' Hong Kong tours. While Mainland tour operators previously contracted Hong Kong tour operators for some parts of Hong Kong tours, the latter would be at the mercy of the former with regards to pricing. Moreover, the Hong Kong operators would earn less revenue from the sub-contracting arrangements than if they did it on their own with individual Mainland travellers under the new rules. Given that there were about 650 inbound travel agents in Hong Kong while individual Mainland tourists come in tens of thousands every month, the market is simply too huge to lead to vicious pricing competition. Meanwhile, the inbound travel agents should think of capturing niche markets through alternative packages that offer more than just seeing the main city sights, such as taking interested tourists to archaeological sites, historical monuments or scenic countryside locations. Tour guides should further improve their Putonghua proficiency, their understanding of Mainland customers' tastes, culture and customs, and also their ability to provide useful information about the sights to tourists. That is, they should do more than just taking tourists to have shopping sprees — since shopping is a staple tourist activity, it does not provide much competitive edge for a tour operator. Hong Kong inbound travel agencies should also start setting up direct contact with the Mainland market by forming joint ventures with Mainland agencies, under conditions set out by CEPA.

Some sectors of retailers automatically benefit from the liberalisation. Vendors of high-quality consumer goods such as consumer electronics, designer apparel and precious foodstuffs are especially welcome. Since tourists do not stay very long in Hong Kong, and since many of them are not very well informed about prices or do not have much time for seeking out the best bargains in town, there will only be price competition between vendors who are located near each other. And even that kind of competition will not be severe because there are just too many tourists. The important thing for the retailers to do is to work with the Hong Kong Tourism Board as well as inbound travel agencies to promote their neighbourhood, so as to make sure that tourists will know about them and visit them. They should also maintain a good reputation. Salespersons at shops should hone their Putonghua skills and improve their service. Retailers should also consider accepting payment in Renminbi, and should put up signs and posters in simplified Chinese characters. They could also provide discount coupons that could be distributed widely to travel agents and tourist centres. Placing advertisements in tourist maps and brochures would also be a useful move. The points mentioned here are also applicable to eateries; in addition, it would help if restaurants provided menus in simplified Chinese characters and fine-tuned the flavour of some of their dishes to make them more appealing to Mainland customers.

[1]   Major source: Holloway, J. Christopher (2002), *The Business of Tourism* (Sixth Edition), Essex, UK: Pearson Education Limited, Chapters 1–4.

[2]   This definition appeared on the webpage www.world-tourism.org/statistics/tsa_project/ TSA_in_depth/chapters/ch3-1.htm.

[3]   This case is focused on inbound tourism into Hong Kong; the WTO formal definition for "inbound tourism" was the tourism of non-resident visitors within the economic territory of the country or region of reference.

[4]   Neuman, Scott, Mitchell-Ford, Constance and Lederman, Erika (2003), "A Global Journal Report: SARS Hurts Tourism, but Tech Firms Persevere — Disease Follows Terrorism and War in Cutting Travel", *Asian Wall Street Journal*, 8 April.

[5]   Neuman, Mitchell-Ford and Lederman.

[6]   Swarbrooke, John and Horner, Susan (2001), *Business Travel and Tourism*, Oxford, UK: Butterworth-Heinemann, Chapter 27.

[7]   Wong, Kevin and Kwan, Cindy (2001), "An analysis of the competitive strategies of hotels and travel agents in Hong Kong and Singapore", *International Journal of Contemporary Hospitality Management*, Vol. 13, Issue 6.

[8]   *South China Morning Post* (1998), "Tourism reels as visitors turn backs on SAR", 12 January.

[9]   Leiper, Neil and Hing, Nerilee (1998), "Trends in Asia-Pacific tourism in 1997–98: from optimism to uncertainty", *International Journal of Contemporary Hospitality Management*, Vol. 10, Issue 7.

[10] Wong, Kevin and Kwan, Cindy (2001), *International Journal of Contemporary Hospitality Management*, Vol. 13, Issue 6.

[11] Statistics of number of hotels and guesthouses and their rooms are as of December 2002.

[12] Lui, Prudence (2003), "Job with a Challenge", *TTG Asia*, 14–20 March.

[13] Lui.

[14] Heung, Vincent (2000), "Satisfaction levels of mainland Chinese travellers with Hong Kong hotel services", *International Journal of Contemporary Hospitality Management*, Vol. 12, Issue 5.

[15] *Asian Wall Street Journal* (2000), "Tourist Spending in Hong Kong Falls 4.1%", 14 February. However tourists from South and Central Americas, Northern Europe and the Middle East were the biggest spenders at the level of HK$6,000 to HK$7,000 per capita.

[16] Hong Kong Tourism Board, Annual Report 2001/2002.

[17] Hong Kong Tourism Board, Annual Report 2001/2002.

[18] Project SARS Rebound Webpage, "Tourism Industry", Centre for Asian Business Cases, the University of Hong Kong, www.cabc.org.hk/sars/industry.asp?doc=tourism.

[19] Project SARS Rebound Webpage; Li, Sandy (2003), "Tourism industry plans huge comeback", *South China Morning Post*, 24 April.

[20] *BBC News* (2003), "Tourists return to HK shops", 7 October.

[21] Project SARS Rebound Webpages.

[22] Li, Sandy (2003), "Travel agencies offer local tours for $38", *South China Morning Post*, 25 May.

[23] Li (2003), 25 May.

[24] *BBC News*, 7 October 2003.

[25] Talks on a free trade agreement between Hong Kong and mainland China had been going on since shortly after China joined the World Trade Organisation in November 2001; the agreement was renamed CEPA in January 2002. Hong Kong companies hoped to gain preferential access to the Mainland market through CEPA.

[26] CEPA also included the commitment that there would be no geographic restriction on Hong Kong travel agencies forming joint venture travel agencies in the Mainland where the Mainland agencies had majority shareholding.

[27] Xin, Dingding (2003), "New rules on Macao, HK travel prove popular", *China Daily*, 7 October.

[28] DBS Macroeconomic Outlook: Hong Kong, Q4 2003 Market Outlook & Strategy, "HK: China Came to Rescue".

[29] There were reports of Hong Kong hotels charging high prices by September 2003, so much so that some Mainland tourists preferred to stay with local relatives, e.g. Chan, Alfons (2003), "300,000 individual travellers expected", *China Daily HK Edition*, 27 September.

[30] *BBC News* (2003), 7 October.

[31] Chan.

Mainland tourists were limited by the Chinese government to carry only RMB6,000 (about HK$5,600) renminbi cash with them, but they could also carry foreign currencies equivalent to US$5,000. Mainlanders who had businesses in Hong Kong might be able to get extra funding from banks for tourist purchases, or they could get help from Hong Kong relatives.

[32] Sito, Peggy (2003), "Surge in buyers from the Mainland to boost sales of flats by 20pc, says agent", *South China Morning Post*, 26 August.

[33] Cheung, Gary and Chan, Carrie (2003), "Hong Kong is boosted by record number of visitors in first week of October", *South China Morning Post*, 22 October.

Exhibit 1 International and Asia-Pacific Tourism Statistics

A. The Growth of International Tourism from 1950 to 2000

Year	Arrivals (million)	Receipts (US$ billion)
1950	25.3	2.1
1960	69.3	6.9
1970	159.7	17.9
1980	184.8	102.4
1990	455.9	264.1
1995	550.4	403.0
2000	687.3	473.4
2001	684.1	459.5
2002	702.6	474.2

B. International Tourist Arrivals
(million)

	1990	1995	2000	2001	2002
World	455.9	550.4	687.3	684.1	702.6
Africa	15.0	20.0	27.4	28.3	29.1
Americas	93.0	108.8	128.0	120.2	114.9
Asia and the Pacific	57.7	85.6	115.3	121.1	131.3
Europe	280.6	322.3	392.7	390.8	399.8
Middle East	9.7	13.6	24.0	23.6	27.6

C. International Tourism Receipts by Region

	Total Receipts 2002 (US$ billion)	Change (%)* 01/20	Change (%)* 02/01	Receipts per Arrival 2002 (US$)
World	474.2	-1.0	0.3	675
Africa	11.8	14.8	2.0	405
Americas	114.3	-9.9	-4.8	995
Asia and the Pacific	94.7	5.1	5.1	720
Europe	240.5	-1.1	-1.8	600
Middle East	13.0	-1.6	13.3	470

* Local currencies, constant prices

D.   Leading Destinations by International Tourist Arrivals

Rank	Region	2002 Arrivals (million)	Change (%) 2002/2001
	World	702.6	2.7
1	France	77.0	2.4
2	Spain	51.7	3.3
3	United States	41.9	-6.7
4	Italy	39.8	0.6
5	Mainland China	36.8	11.0
6	United Kingdom	24.2	5.9
7	Canada	20.1	1.9
8	Mexico	19.7	-0.7
9	Austria	18.6	2.4
10	Germany	18.0	0.6

E.   Leading Destinations by International Tourism Receipts

Rank	Region	2002 Receipts (million)	Change (%) 2002/2001
	World	474.2	3.2
1	United States	66.5	-7.4
2	Spain	33.6	2.2
3	France	32.3	7.8
4	Italy	26.9	4.3
5	Mainland China	20.4	14.6
6	Germany	19.2	4.0
7	United Kingdom	17.8	9.5
8	Austria	11.2	11.1
9	Hong Kong	10.1	22.2
10	Greece	9.7	3.1

F.   International Tourist Arrivals by Origin

(million)

	1990	1995	2000	2001	2002
World	455.9	550.4	687.3	684.1	702.6
Africa	9.9	12.8	16.1	16.3	16.8
Americas	99.2	107.9	130.5	123.7	120.2
Asia and the Pacific	60.2	89.8	118.9	121.6	131.2
Europe	263.9	317.6	394.8	394.3	404.9
Middle East	8.0	9.5	14.2	14.6	16.0
Origin Unspecified	14.7	12.9	12.9	13.7	13.5
Same region	361.4	437.9	538.8	543.2	561.9
Other regions	79.8	99.6	135.6	127.2	127.2

G. Leading Origins of Tourists by Tourism Expenditure

Rank	Region	2002 International Tourism Expenditure (US$ billion)	Change (%) 2002/2001
	World	474.2	3.2
1	United States	58.0	-3.6
2	Germany	53.2	2.4
3	United Kingdom	40.4	10.8
4	Japan	26.7	0.6
5	France	19.5	9.8
6	Italy	16.9	14.4
7	Mainland China	15.4	10.7
8	The Netherlands	12.9	7.5
9	Hong Kong	12.4	0.8
10	Russia	12.0	20.5

H. Asia and the Pacific: International Tourist Arrivals

Major Destinations	T2002 Arrivals (in thousands)	Change (%)*	
		01/00	02/01
Asia and the Pacific	131,295	5.1	8.4
Australia	4,841	-1.5	-0.3
Mainland China	36,803	6.2	11.0
Hong Kong	16,566	5.1	20.7
India	2,370	-4.2	-6.6
Indonesia	5,033	1.8	-2.3
Japan	5,239	0.3	9.8
South Korea	5,347	-3.3	3.9
Macau	6,565	12.4	12.4
Malaysia	13,292	25.0	4.0
New Zealand	2,045	6.9	7.1
The Philippines	1,933	-9.8	7.6
Singapore	6,996	-2.8	4.0
Taiwan	2,726	-0.3	4.2
Thailand	10,873	5.8	7.3

I.   Asia and the Pacific: International Tourism Receipts

Major Destinations	2002 Receipts (US$ million)	Change (%)*	
		01/00	02/01
Asia and the Pacific	94,697	1.2	7.7
Australia	8,087	-9.8	6.1
Mainland China	20,385	9.7	14.6
Hong Kong	10,117	5.0	22.2
India	2,923	-4.0	-3.9
Indonesia	—	-5.9	—
Japan	3,499	-2.1	6.0
South Korea	5,277	-6.4	-17.2
Macau	4,415	16.8	17.9
Malaysia	6,785	39.7	6.4
New Zealand	2,918	4.2	25.0
The Philippines	1,741	-19.3	1.0
Singapore	4,932	-15.6	-2.9
Taiwan	4,197	6.7	5.2
Thailand	7,902	-5.5	11.7

Source: World Tourism Organisation, Tourism Highlights, Edition 2003. Table A is supplemented with information from: Holloway, J. Christopher (2002), *The Business of Tourism* (Sixth Edition), Essex, UK: Pearson Education Limited, p. 47.

Exhibit 2   Hong Kong Tourism Statistics

A.   Annual Visitor Arrivals and Tourism Receipts, 1996-2002

Year	Visitor Arrivals (million)	Tourism Receipts (HK$ billion)
1996	13.0	84.5
1997	11.3	72.1
1998	9.6	55.3
1999	10.7	53.0
2000	13.1	61.5
2001	13.7	64.3
2002	16.6	78.9

B. Visitor Arrivals by Country/Territory of Residence: 1997, 2001, 2002

Country/Territory of Residence	1997	2001	2002
Total	11,273	13,725	16,566
Mainland China	2,364	4,449	6,825
Taiwan	1,920	2,419	2,429
South East Asia	1,459	1,493	1,593
Japan	1,624	1,337	1,395
Europe	1,170	1,020	1,084
U.S.	861	936	1,001
Australia & New Zealand	374	382	405
Canada	192	250	265
Others	1,309	1,441	1,569

(All figures in thousands)

C. Hotel Room Occupancy Rates

	2002 (%)	2003 (%)
January–December	84	—
January–August	82	61

D. Breakdown of Tourism Receipts
(HK$ million)

	2000	2001
Total Tourism Receipts	61,514.06	64,282.12
Visitors	59,283.12	62,209.61
Servicemen	134.09	987.36
Aircrew Members	952.32	963.80
Transit/Transfer Passengers	1,144.53	1,010.35
Per Capita Spending (HK$)	4,539	4,532

E.   Visitor Arrivals and Average Hotel Occupancy Rate, March 2002–August 2003

Month	Visitor Arrivals	Average Hotel Occupancy
03/2003	1,297,219	86%
04/2002	1,403,041	87%
05/2002	1,332,248	83%
06/2002	1,174,202	79%
07/2002	1,368,693	82%
08/2002	1,501,078	86%
09/2002	1,370,279	82%
10/2002	1,584,563	85%
11/2002	1,570,192	92%
12/2002	1,668,474	89%
01/2003	1,545,978	82%
02/2003	1,408,139	81%
03/2003	1,347,386	79%
04/2003	493,666	22%
05/2003	427,254	18%
06/2003	725,236	34%
07/2003	1,291,828	71%
08/2003	1,644,878	88%

F.   Number of Visitors in Four Months in 2002 and 2003

Major Market Areas	06/2002	08/2002	06/2003	08/2003
Total	1,174,202	1,501,078	725,236	1,644,878
Americas	109,958	100,560	29,222	87,893
Europe, Africa & the Middle East	85,175	94,371	31,670	74,714
Australia, New Zealand & South Pacific	32,523	28,569	11,693	23,364
North Asia	139,278	167,362	35,937	119,161
South & Southeast Asia	156,796	151,518	49,005	127,335
Taiwan	181,972	232,388	64,576	204,828
Macau	44,737	66,584	32,571	61,461
Mainland China	423,763	659,726	470,562	946,122

G.   Cumulative Number of Visitors in the Period January to August 2002 and 2003

Major Market Areas	01–08/2002	01–08/2003	Growth (%)
Total	10,372,874	8,884,365	-14.4
Americas	871,411	510,697	-41.4
Europe, Africa & the Middle East	783,607	496,504	-36.6
Australia, New Zealand & South Pacific	259,801	168,380	-35.2
North Asia	1,197,456	730,273	-39.0
South & Southeast Asia	1,170,376	697,103	-40.4
Taiwan	1,616,569	1,123,858	-30.5
Mainland China	4,110,047	4,874,490	+18.6

H.   Hotel Room Occupancy in August 2002 and 2003 by Category

	08/2002 (%)	08/2003 (%)	Average Room Rate in 08/2003 (HK$)
All Categories	86	88	471
High Tariff A Hotels	78	78	969
High Tariff B Hotels	89	89	428
Medium Tariff Hotels	89	94	271
Tourist Guesthouses	81	83	216

Note: High tariff A hotels have the highest room rates; tourist guesthouses the lowest.
Source: Hong Kong Tourism Board Partner Net, http://partnernet.hktourismboard.com; Census and Statistics Department, the HKSAR Government; press archives.

28

Hong Kong's Container Truckers
The Mid-stream Fee Dispute

MICHAEL J. ENRIGHT AND VINCENT MAK

PART I: BACKGROUND AND ISSUES

Introduction

> At present, container transportation is not profit-making. This $50 [mid-stream] fee, if it remains, will simply be adding salt to the wounds for the entire transportation trade.
> – Ricky Wong Kay, China-Hong Kong Transportation Joint Conference, commenting in November 2000[1]

In November 2000, the eight-member Hong Kong Mid-stream Operators Association (HKMOA), which controlled 90 percent of the mid-stream container handling business in Hong Kong, announced that they would charge shippers an extra fee. When the shippers refused to pay that fee, the container truck drivers, who delivered the containers to the mid-stream depots, were asked to pay it for the shippers first and then claim it back from the shippers. The truckers promptly refused. A series of industrial actions ensued, and the Government, shippers and liners were involved in subsequent negotiations. The rounds of tussles between the HKMOA and the truckers lasted into June 2001. Eventually, the HKMOA won, the truckers had to pay the mid-stream fee, and in many cases could not recoup it from the shippers. Why did the truckers become the victims of the HKMOA? Why could the mid-stream operators win? What could public policy-makers do to prevent similar disputes from happening again? What[2] could the truck drivers, who in many cases were self-employed, do to protect themselves from more new charges in the future?

The Hong Kong Container Trucking Industry

As a mode of freight transport, trucks were used for carrying relatively small-volume cargoes over short distances. They were especially useful in harsh natural environments or areas with poor infrastructure. They also had the advantage that they could provide a door-to-door service. Hence, transportation between customers and any sea, railway or air cargo terminals relied on trucks.

The container trucking industry in Hong Kong was made up of a large number of companies. A large container trucking company might have more than 100 trucks, but many companies were small, with only one truck. As such, the industry had rather low entry barriers. Some companies provided both domestic haulage and cross-border haulage between Hong Kong and mainland China — in particular the Pearl River Delta region just north of Hong Kong — while others provided only one of these two services. Every company had its big and important customers, which might include port terminals, freight forwarders and large multinational manufacturers. Apart from these, trucking companies also accepted orders from smaller customers such as small shippers (shippers being exporters who took care of all shipping-related issues of the cargo, such as documents and logistics, and who, in the case of Hong Kong, were mostly SMEs plus a limited number of large players). On an average day, there could be several hundred orders for a large container trucking company, and customers could place orders at almost any time. If there was a shortage of trucks on a peak day, the trucking company would outsource some orders to subcontractors.

Container trucking companies in Hong Kong carried out four types of orders:

1. Container yard order: picked up a container at a container yard, brought it to the customer's location, such as a warehouse, for loading or unloading, and returned the container to a drop-off point (a container terminal or outside depot).

2. Shuttling order: pure delivery of a container without loading or unloading during the whole trip of the truck.

3. Pick-and-drop order: the truck changed its chassis when carrying out this type of order. During a "relay order" for Hong Kong-mainland China cross-border haulage, tractors that had licences to operate only in Hong Kong or mainland China exchanged their chassis at the border, so that the containers that they carried could be delivered across the border. Changing of chassis could also happen during a "batch pick-and-drop order" at a large warehouse or distribution centre. In such case, since the loading or unloading of a container could take two to three hours, a truck might leave its chassis and container at the warehouse and work on another order by taking up another chassis, so as not to waste time. The original chassis and container would be taken up by another truck later.

4. Container rental order: a rarer type of order, in which a trucking company leased a truck with a container to a customer to serve as a moving medium for the customer's cargo. The container was not to be dropped off at the end of the trip, but would return with the truck to the trucker.

The tariffs the customers needed to pay for container haulage were calculated according to the length (which measured the size) of containers, the types of orders, the geographical locations of the pick-up point, the customer's location, and the drop-off point. The customer also needed to pay a surcharge if the vanning (loading) or devanning (unloading) time was too long. The operator of a fleet faced six major costs: wages, subcontractors, maintenance, fuel, insurance and surcharges (such as tunnel fees and parking fees). Of these, wages comprised the largest part, as trucking was a labour-intensive industry.

Industry Statistics

Delivery between Hong Kong and mainland China was important to the Hong Kong container trucking business. By 2002, about two-thirds of Hong Kong's South China cargo was transported to/from the port by truck. There were approximately 2,800 container haulage companies with about 14,000 trucks providing cross-border services.[3]

Exhibit 1 shows Hong Kong-mainland China cross-border container truck traffic from 1998 to first half of 2003, indicating the growing trend of this traffic. By May 2002, some 15,000 container trucks crossed the border every day, with roughly half of them travelling northward to the mainland and the other half heading south towards Hong Kong.[4] Of the 7,500 trucks heading northward, approximately 2,000 were laden and 5,500 were empty; of those heading in the other direction, 2,000 were empty and 5,500 were laden. An average cross-border delivery trip cost the shipper $3,000. The three highway border-crossing points between Hong Kong and Shenzhen accounted for the transit of some 360,000 TEUs of cargo each month by 2002.[5] The busiest crossing point for truck traffic was at Lok Ma Chau, which handled 75 percent of the overland cargo flows into Hong Kong.[6]

Container Trade In and Near Hong Kong

Around 80 percent of the cargo handled by Hong Kong by 2002 was processed through its port; most of it was container cargo.[7] In 2002, the port of Hong Kong handled 19.2 million TEUs of container goods, an increase of 7.4 percent over the previous year. This enabled the city to maintain its status the busiest container port in the world. Containers were either handled by the container terminals, or loaded and unloaded between barges and vessels that anchored inside the harbour without docking. The latter case was called mid-stream operation. In the former case, containerised sea freight was handled at the container terminals at Kwai Chung. Sea trade along Pearl River ports (which lay just to the west of Hong Kong along the Pearl River estuary) that used small vessels for shallow channels was handled at a variety of waterfront locations. In terms of throughput, about 64 percent of the container cargo was handled by the container terminals, 17 percent by mid-stream operators, and the remaining 19 percent by river trade operators.[8]

The Kwai Chung Container Port

The Hong Kong Government provided the back-up land, navigation channels, infrastructure and utilities for the Kwai Chung terminals, but the terminals themselves were owned and managed by four private operators.

By the early 2000s, Hong Kong handled a large portion of mainland China's trade cargo, mostly originating from the thriving manufacturing region of the Pearl River Delta. By 2002, Hong Kong's eight container terminals consisted of a total of 18 berths at Kwai Chung and the nearby Stonecutters Island. Total capacity was estimated to be around 25 million TEUs. The container throughput of Hong Kong was 17.83 million TEUs by 2001, 11.3 million TEUs of which were handled at Kwai Chung and the rest by ocean and river vessels. Hong Kong's container terminals were unique in the world in that they were fully funded, owned and managed by the private sector with no Government involvement. By 2002, the biggest of Hong Kong's four container terminal operators was Hongkong International Terminals (HIT), a subsidiary of the Hutchison Whampoa Group. It operated 10 berths on its own. HIT and China Ocean Shipping Company (COSCO) operated two additional berths under a joint venture. The second-largest operator was Modern Terminals Limited (MTL), which operated five berths and was owned by Swire Pacific, Wharf, China Merchants and Jebsen & Co. The smallest operator was CSX World Terminals, which operated the remaining one berth.[9]

Meanwhile, the city of Shenzhen, the immediate northern neighbour of Hong Kong, was developing its own container ports. In the 1980s, the Shenzhen authorities decided to develop its own ports in Yantian, Shekou, and Chiwan. Starting from 1990, the throughput volume handled by Shenzhen grew rapidly; it reached 5.1 million TEUs by the end of 2001, 4.1 million TEUs of which were containerised, making Shenzhen the eighth-busiest container port in the world. Certain major Hong Kong container terminal operators had shareholder or business interests in the Shenzhen ports. Swire Pacific, China Merchants and COSCO had interests in Chiwan and Shekou, and MTL held the management contract for Shekou. Yantian, the largest of the three, was 48 percent owned by Hutchison Whampoa. Yantian was seen as the pacesetter among Shenzhen terminals in terms of pricing; its throughput was 2.7 million TEUs in 2001, 0.5 million above its rated capacity.

Cargo volumes brought across the Hong Kong-mainland Chinese border by trucks had been falling in the mid-1990s as some businesses had moved to mainland Chinese ports. Bargers or feeder vessels were also carrying a larger share of the cargo. Hong Kong container truckers who had previously carried containers from the Pearl River Delta factories in the Chinese mainland to Hong Kong's container ports faced competition from Mainland truckers who carried goods to Shenzhen ports. The cost of trucking from Pearl River Delta factories to the Shenzhen ports was only half that of trucking to Hong Kong, while Terminal Handling Charges (THCs) — which shippers, the truckers' customers, had to bear — in Shenzhen could be 21 to 49 percent lower than in Kwai Chung (see Exhibit 2).[10] Trucking cargo into Hong Kong via the border with Shenzhen was also considered a major inconvenience: the average waiting time for goods vehicles at the border control points was between two and four hours, but could be much longer at peak time. Even after 24-hour border-crossing for cargo became available in late 2002, most drivers preferred to wait until the morning to cross through, because only one kiosk was open late at night, leading to long queues.[11]

River Trade and Mid-stream Operations

Three rivers flowed into the Pearl River Delta, creating more than 5,000km of navigable waters — a natural transport system for shipping and trade.[12] River trade in the Delta involved both containerised and non-containerised cargoes (bulk and others). At the end of 1990, well over a third of total container movement between mainland China and Hong Kong was by river, and it was roughly equal in weight to the amount of containerised freight. Overall, a higher tonnage of freight moving across the border was moved by river (48 million tonnes in 2001) than by road (38 million tonnes in 2001). The movement of shipping containers by river between mainland China and Hong Kong had almost tripled over the period 1995 to 2001, from 1.6 million TEUs to about 4.7 million TEUs per annum. River trade had become the fastest-growing mode of transporting cargo and containerised goods between Hong Kong and the Pearl River Delta by that time. Growth in river trade of containers comprised the largest part of the growth in container traffic handled by Hong Kong's port in early 2000s. Barge operators provided 320 daily feeder services linking six river ports and terminals in the Pearl River Delta and Hong Kong.

There were more than 20 large and small mid-stream operators and numerous companies dealing with river trade in Hong Kong by the early 2000s.[13] Mid-stream operation throughput had been hovering around three million TEUs since 1996, about 20 percent of the total container throughput in Hong Kong.[14] Mid-stream operators provided a low-quality, cheap service, especially for operators of mid-size vessels who did not want to bear the expensive fees (about 60 percent higher than that of mid-stream depots) for using the large container terminals.[15]

There were several types of waterfront locations at which river trade or mid-stream connectors could load and unload.[16] They included private waterfronts, such as berths in container terminals assigned for barges, which could usually only be used by vessels belonging to the waterfront operators or their customers. The short-term tenancy waterfronts were owned by the Government but leased to private operators, and again were used usually by the operators or their customers. The public cargo working areas (PCWAs) were open to the public on a charged basis. Since PCWAs served mostly river trade with ports along the Pearl River Delta waters, they were located on the western side of Hong Kong. By 2002, over 160 river-trade operators were operating 185 berths using eight PCWAs (which provided 300,000 square metres of storage space and 7,200 metres of quay frontage), three feeder berths at Kwai Chung container terminals, and a River Trade Terminal (RTT) in Tuen Mun. The RTT's shareholders were Hutchison, COSCO, Sung Hung Kai Properties, and Jardine Matheson. The PCWAs handled 40.5 percent of river trade cargo in 2001; the Kwai Chung terminals handled 24 percent, the RTT handled 15 percent, and the remainder was handled by small berths and wharfs, and also mooring buoys.

The RTT Dispute[17]

The RTT was completed at the end of 1999, but operation had already started in October 1998. In January 1999, the RTT began charging a $50 registration and parking fee per entry to all container truckers using the terminal. The truckers protested, saying that the charge would cause their costs to rise by 10 percent, and would lead to unemployment in the long term. The RTT defended its position by stating that its fee was 25 percent below that of the PCWAs (which charged $66 per container vehicle per hour), and was charged per entry without any time limit. Negotiations dragged on for one month. On 1 February, about 100 container trucks took part in a protest drive from Kwai Chung Container Terminal to the RTT. The drivers threatened to raise the level of their protest, such as blocking the RTT, if the terminal operator insisted on charging the fees from drivers. Two days later, the dispute was settled, with the RTT agreeing not to charge the truckers.

The Mid-stream Fee Dispute[18]

The eight-member Hong Kong Mid-stream Operators Association (HKMOA), which controlled container depots in Tsing Yi, Cheung Sha Wan, Stoncutters Island and Tuen Mun, handled about 90 percent of mid-stream business in Hong Kong. They had planned to charge truckers an extra "documentation fee" in 1995 and 1998, but had to scrap the plans in both cases because of strong opposition from the truck drivers.

In early November 2000, HKMOA members started requesting a HK$50 "documentation fee" from shippers. The Hong Kong Shippers' Council refused to pay it, saying it was unreasonable. The HKMOA insisted, and turned instead to pressuring the truckers who used the association's facilities to pay the HK$50 for the shippers. Although the HKMOA argued that the Shippers' Council did not represent the opinions of all shippers, there was of course a great deal of doubt as to whether the truckers could recoup the fee from reluctant shippers. The China-Hong Kong Transportation Joint Conference (CHKTJC), formed out of six transport groups, announced that it was against the truckers paying the fee, and urged the drivers of the 5,000-odd trucks that used HKMOA depots to refuse to pay it. The HKMOA meanwhile insisted that the imposition of the new fee was a purely commercial decision, and that if the truckers (and shippers) did not want to pay it, they were free to patronise non-HKMOA depots. The association also claimed that its members were independent companies that did not operate as an oligopoly. Some commentators pointed out that the HKMOA members included subsidiaries of powerful conglomerates, such as Hutchison, Swire and Jardine, which also controlled some of the Kwai Chung container terminals.

Officials from the Hong Kong Government were involved in the ensuing emergency negotiations, which failed, and the truckers promptly took action. On 6 November, about 300 trucks blockaded the Kwai Chung container terminal and seven other container depots operated by HKMOA members. The entrance to each depot was blocked by at least one container truck, and the remaining trucks parked around or queued up in one lane of the road to the depot to show support. The protest disrupted container-handling operations and road traffic, particularly at Kwai Chung. Ricky Wong Kay, spokesman of the CHKTJC, said the truckers were determined to carry on the protest even if it meant each truck driver would lose up to HK$2,000 a day. On the other hand, it was estimated that the protest led to the loss of some HK$400,000 a day in terms of container-handling business. After one more day of protest and Government mediation, the HKMOA backed down and stopped asking truckers to pay the fee.

From December 2000 to January 2001, the HKMOA, the Hong Kong Shippers' Council, and the Hong Kong Liner Shipping Association — which represented the interests of liners, including Orient Overseas Container Line, the family business of Hong Kong Chief Executive Tung Chee-hwa — held a series of talks in the hope of settling on a new fee and the payment method. But when it seemed that the talks were not getting anywhere, the HKMOA called them off, and announced in early February that it would go ahead with a HK$40 surcharge to help improve its services and staffing. Again, the HKMOA said it was only targeting the shippers to pay the charge, but the payment process would mean that the truckers would have to pay for the shippers at HKMOA depots. The truckers protested again, and the CHKTJC, now consisting of seven groups and 16,000 truckers, mobilised more than 1,000 trucks to blockade the Kwai Chung container terminal, not only stopping mid-stream business but also disrupting ordinary container handling there. At the height of the protest, truckers occupied two lanes of the road to the terminal, and drove slowly in the fast lane. They claimed that the new fee would eat up one third of their HK$15,000 monthly income. The HKMOA retaliated by seeking a court injunction to stop the blockade and filing suits against some drivers and transport companies for damages.

The action lasted from 9 February to 13 February. The loss to the industry was estimated by one source at HK$200 million per day, but others thought that the damage was not that high; for example, loading and unloading could take place in the evening, after the truckers finished their daily protest. On 13 February, following the involvement of the Government, shippers, and shipping lines — the latter two of which supported the truckers — the HKMOA announced that it would delay implementing the fee and promised that the truckers would not be charged directly. The truckers' protest ended that same evening.

Talks went on between the parties afterwards. The Shippers' Council called for greater transparency in how the HKMOA arrived at the fee, while the HKMOA hoped to implement a system whereby shippers would pay the new charge using pre-paid coupons purchased at various outlets. In March, the HKMOA began to implement the mid-stream fee (MSF) coupon system under which truck drivers presenting such coupons could enjoy priority in the delivery and collection of containers. The shippers' representatives, however, denied that they had ever agreed on paying the new charge. They stated that they had no contractual relationship with the mid-stream operators, and that what the shippers paid to the shipping lines as THC was supposed to cover all the necessary charges already. On top of that, the shippers said they were already paying an exorbitant THC.

The truck drivers then complained that the delivery and collection of their containers were delayed by mid-stream operators because they could not present the coupons. The truckers held a slow-drive protest in early March to show their dissatisfaction, paralysing traffic near Kwai Chung. After talks between truckers and the HKMOA, the latter agreed on a three-month grace period.

In June, the HKMOA re-instated the coupon system. The Hong Kong Shippers' Council reiterated its refusal to pay the fee, saying that it was against traditional business practices and was calculated without a transparent mechanism. The issue was far from resolved, and truckers were still virtually forced to prepay the MSF for shippers — with little chance that they could claim it back from the shippers. By then, the fee was described by the HKMOA as payment for a "value-added service". Truckers without coupons not only had to wait in long queues, there were also reports that two mid-stream operators would not even permit truckers without coupons to enter their container yards to pick up or drop off cargo. Smaller-scale slow-drive protests were held from Kwai Chung to Central in June, but this time to no avail for the truckers. In November, the CHKTJC again asked the Government to intervene, and asked for meeting between truckers, shippers, shipping lines, and the HKMOA. The CHKTJC said that 4,000 to 5,000 truckers were paying the fee by then — the HKMOA later claimed that about 95 percent of its customers had been paying it since June — and about half of them could not recoup it from shippers. Moreover, some truckers who were not willing to pay the fee had been taken to court by mid-stream operators.

The mid-stream fee was discussed several times by the Panel on Economic Services of the Hong Kong Legislative Council in 2001. At a meeting on 18 December, 2001, the HKMOA claimed that its fee was for value-added service, so that a trucker without coupons could still enter HKMOA depots, but needed to wait one to two hours before his containers could be handled — about twice as much time as a trucker with a coupon. But the CHKTJC representative said that, without a coupon, a trucker would have to wait two to three hours. The minutes of the meeting included this entry:[19]

> The [Panel] Chairman [James Tien] commented that comparing with the situation in the past, no value was in fact added to the service mentioned by mid-stream operators at all, for in the past, free service was provided to users without waiting for a long time. He remarked that taking into account the long queuing time for trucks, the value of the paid service delivered by the mid-stream operators had in fact been diminished.

By 2003, the dispute had not been officially settled, while the truckers were still grudgingly paying the fee. In an interview published in early 2003, Cliff Sun, Chairman of the Hong Kong Exporters' Association, summarised the issue and the shippers' standpoint as follows:[20]

> The truckers have been very reasonable, in their charges and services. We pay the trucker a fee for carrying our goods from the point of dispatch to the dock. What we find unreasonable is the non-transparent fees that follow the shipment — mainly the terminal handling charge and the mid-stream operators' fee. The mid-stream operators are basically also composed of companies that are under the same major group as the terminal operators.
>
> We shippers have no business dealing with mid-stream operators who are charging truckers ... The truckers are instructed to bring our cargo from our point of dispatch to the terminal. The terminal operator then loads it on the ship. The business contract is between the truckers and the shippers; and, on the other hand, between the mid-stream operator and the shipping line. ... Exporters have an agreement with the shipping line — we ... pay a fee which includes the terminal handling charge, to have our cargo taken from the point of discharge by the trucker and put on the boat. ... The shipping line pays the terminal operator to bring the cargo from the truck to the vessel. That is the contract between the carrier and the mid-stream operator. Now, the mid-stream operator, instead of raising the costs of the contract with the liners, have instead turned to the trucker and asked them to pay and to claim it [the MSF] back from the shipper. It is totally unreasonable; as a shipper I have no business dealing with the mid-stream operator as my contract is only with the shipping line!

An industry veteran was quoted as saying:[21]

> The mid-stream operation has for long been a thorn in the side of the major terminal operator [Hutchison Whampoa's HIT], with much lower charges than ondock operations ... [Hutchison] is gradually buying them up through indirect holdings and can now start to increase charges. It's still less controlled than the ondock duopoly [of HIT and MTL, which together handled about 85 percent traffic at Kwai Chung], hence the idea of hitting more or less captive truckers after unsuccessful pursuit of shippers and lines.

Perhaps the following comment by an industry executive was the most biting:[22]

[The mid-stream fee is] like making the pizza man pay you a fee for bringing the pizza through your door. Not everyone was comfortable with it.

PART II: LESSONS LEARNED

This case serves as an overview of the container trucking industry in Hong Kong, and, in narrating the mid-stream fee dispute, illustrates some of the pricing problems that small and medium enterprises in Hong Kong may face because of the actions of powerful buyers and/or suppliers.

What Would You Do from a Public Policy Standpoint to Prevent Similar Disputes from Occurring Again?

Public policy makers first need to identify why the dispute flared up. It seems that the market of mid-stream operators is dominated by a small group of conglomerates that are willing to act together on pricing under the guise of the HKMOA. In fact, not only mid-stream operation but also the RTT, the Kwai Chung and Shenzhen container terminals, as well as the shipping lines, are all controlled by small groups. All these sectors look dangerously like an oligopoly. Moreover, some of the conglomerates that dominate mid-stream operation, such as Hutchison Whampoa, also control the Kwai Chung container terminals. Hence, price cartels are likely to form across the whole container-handling industry in Hong Kong. However, given a choice, the cartel would rather pressure small companies than large ones to pay high prices for its services, simply because small companies usually have less negotiating power and less influence in the political sphere (note that one of the major shipping lines is run by the family of Hong Kong's Chief Executive). Therefore, the truckers become the easy target of new fees.

A fair competition law could solve part of the problem. The truckers could then file a suit if they feel that they have to pay an unfair fee that is forced on them by a cartel. If such a law has an anti-trust element, the Government might be able to break up the oligopoly and potential pricing cartels in Hong Kong's mid-stream and container terminal operation. However, the enactment of such a law is bound to meet huge resistance from powerful conglomerates, and from politicians who have strong ties with the conglomerates. Even if it could be enacted, court proceedings on such matters would take a long time and would cost a lot of taxpayers' money.

In the short run, policy-makers cannot really do much except to minimise the immediate damage caused by truck drivers' public protests, such as re-arranging traffic flows during protests and mediating negotiations between the parties involved.

What Would You Do from the Truckers' Standpoint to Prevent Similar Disputes from Occurring Again?

Without fair competition laws, the only way the truckers can fight back is by industrial action, such as protests and blockades, but these actions are destructive to both sides, and could even result in a poor public image for the truckers because of the traffic jams and economic losses that would follow. The truckers, moreover, are liable to be brought to court by the operators. Nevertheless, persistent, large-scale industrial actions can bring down powerful conglomerates, since such actions could seriously disrupt the social and economic well-being of society. In fact, transport workers' strikes are usually more powerful than workers' strikes in many other industries, because strikes by transport workers cause more serious damage to society. The HKMOA was indeed compromised more than a few times before mid-2001, and the truckers also won the battle against the RTT in 1999. The industrial actions that were carried out during the mid-stream fee dispute, even though they ultimately proved futile, did arouse some public sympathy and Government concern, and helped bring the different parties — truckers, shippers, mid-stream operators and shipping lines — back to the negotiating table.

Industrial action, therefore, can be very powerful. It can greatly enhance the truckers' bargaining power to counterbalance the raw market power of the mid-stream operators. But to fight new fees in the future, the truckers need to organise themselves effectively, consolidate their organisation further, and maintain good relationships with politicians as well as shippers — who are in very similar situations as the truckers in the THC dispute.

---

[1] Chan, Felix (2000), "Trucks block cargo depot in protest", *South China Morning Post*, 7 November.

[2] Wan, Yat-wah, Lecture Notes for Course IEEM 141 "Logistics and Freight Transportation Operations", available at: http:// iesu5.ieem.ust.hk/dfaculty/wan/ieem141.html, Notes for Week 11.

[3] CLSA Emerging Markets (2002), *Hong Kong Strategy — Market Outlook*, October, p. 21.

[4] Tradelink-eBiz (2002), "Supply-chain Collaboration Across the Border", www.tradelink-ebiz. com/english/331n08or3m9a51l/newscast/ie_0203b.html, March.

[5] TEU means twenty-foot equivalent unit, which is a measure of container box volume. One TEU is the size of a standardised container measuring 20ft x 8ft x 8ft.

[6] Enright, Michael, Chang, Ka-mun, Scott, Edith and Zhu, Wen-hui (2003), "Hong Kong & the Pearl River Delta: the Economic Interaction", January, available at: www.2022foundation.com, p. 60.

[7] Economic Services Bureau of the Hong Kong Government (2001), "Legislative Council Economic Services Panel Paper: Mid-stream Fees", http://www.edlb.gov.hk/edb/eng/papers/panel/122001b. htm, December.

[8] Economic Services Bureau.

[9] CSX was a joint venture between US container shipping line Sea-Land Services, Hong Kong-based Orient Trucking, and ATL Logistics Hong Kong. ATL was a joint venture between CSX World Terminals, Hongkong Land, New World, and Sun Hung Kai Properties.

10 Sources: CLSA Emerging Markets, pp. 21–24; Hong Kong Consumer Council (2002), "Assessment of complaints against members of shipping line agreements", July; Hong Kong Shippers' Council Website, www.hkshippers.org.hk.

11 Enright, Chang, Scott and Zhu, p. 91.

12 CLSA Emerging Markets, pp. 20–21.

13 Hong Kong Shippers' Council, "Hong Kong Port", www.hkshippers.org.hk/p2b.html.

14 CLSA Emerging Markets, p. 21.

15 Wan, Notes for Week 8.

16 Wan, Notes for Week 8.

17 Source: media reports.

18 Source: media reports.

19 Accessible at: www.legco.gov.hk/yr01-02/english/panels/es/minutes/es011218.pdf.

20 "Successful transition of Hong Kong exports", *Shippers Today*, Vol. 26#2, March/April 2003, accessible at: www.tdctrade.com/shippers/vol26_2/vol26_2_trade01.htm.

21 Bangsberg, P. T. (2001), "HK port blockade seen ending", *Phoenix Intl-News-Industry News*, http://www.phoenixintl.com/news/news_02_14_01.asp, 13 February.

22 Wong, Jesse (2001), "Hong Kong Truckers Win Fight", *Asian Wall Street Journal*, 14 February.

Exhibit 1   Hong Kong-Mainland China Cross-Border Container Truck Traffic

(Number of trucks)

Year	To Hong Kong	To Mainland
1998	1,974,556	1,973,364
1999	2,135,573	2,137,046
2000	2,320,393	2,322,609
2001	2,202,178	2,207,149
2002	2,379,687	2,388,000
2003 (first 6 months)	1,095,902	1,101,823

Source: Transport Department, the Government of Hong Kong.

Exhibit 2   Terminal Handling Charges (THCs) in Selected Major Ports

(in HK$)	USA 20'	USA 40'	Europe 20'	Europe 40'	Asia 20'	Asia 40'
Hong Kong	2,140	2,855	2,060	2,750	1,800	2,650
Shenzhen	1,096	2,087	1,100	2,100	1,096	2,087
Taiwan	1,271	1,589	1,150	1,450	1,096	NA
Singapore	788	1,170	720	1,020	788	1,170
Japan	749	936	1,870	2,680	686	1,030
Indonesia	1,012	1,557	NA	NA	1,051	1,557
South Korea	657	891	620	840	657	891
Malaysia	590	880	480	710	590	880
Thailand	478	718	480	710	478	718
Shanghai	510	680	120	180	113	175
The Philippines	85	113	270	340	507	669
Germany	NA	NA	1,110	1,110	NA	NA
The Netherlands	NA	NA	790	790	NA	NA

THCs for Europe are as of March 2001. All other THCs are as of August 2002.

Note: 20' is a standard unit for container volume. It is equivalent to the volume of a container measuring 20ft x 8ft x 8ft. 40' is similarly equivalent to the volume of a container measuring 40ft x 8ft x 8ft.

Source: CLSA Emerging Markets, *Hong Kong Strategy — Market Outlook*, October 2002, p. 23.